Children's Literature

BLACKWELL GUIDES TO LITERATURE
Series editor: *Jonathan Wordsworth*

This new series offers the student thorough and lively introductions to literary periods, movements, and, in some instances, authors (Shakespeare) and genres (the novel), from Anglo-Saxon to the Postmodern. Each volume is written by a leading specialist to be invitingly accessible and informative. Chapters are devoted to the coverage of cultural context, the provision of brief but detailed biographical essays on the authors concerned, critical coverage of key works, and surveys of themes and topics, together with bibliographies of selected further reading. In the case of Shakespeare space otherwise afforded to authors will be devoted to documenting the theatre of the day. Students new to a period of study (for example, the English Renaissance, or the Romantic period) or to a period genre (the nineteenth-century novel, Victorian poetry) will discover all they need to know, to orientate and ground themselves in their studies, in volumes that are as stimulating to read as they are convenient to use.

Middle English	HEATHER O'DONOGHUE
The English Renaissance	ANDREW HADFIELD
Shakespeare	DAVID SCOTT KASTAN
The Seventeenth Century	MARSHALL GROSSMAN
The Eighteenth Century	ROBERT DEMARIA, JR
The Romantic Period	JONATHAN WORDSWORTH
Victorian Poetry and Poetics	VALENTINE CUNNINGHAM
Modern Irish Literature	STEPHEN REGAN
Children's Literature	PETER HUNT
Gothic	DAVID PUNTER and GLENNIS BYRON
Twentieth-Century American Poetry	CHRISTOPHER MacGOWAN

Children's Literature

Peter Hunt

Blackwell
Publishing

© 2001 by Peter Hunt

350 Main Street, Malden, MA 02148-5020, USA
108 Cowley Road, Oxford OX4 1JF, UK
550 Swanston Street, Carlton, Victoria 3053, Australia

First published 2001 by Blackwell Publishing Ltd
Reprinted 2003, 2004

Library of Congress Cataloging-in-Publication Data

Hunt, Peter, 1945–
    Children's literature / Peter Hunt.
      p. cm. — (Blackwell guides to literature)
    Includes bibliographical references (p.) and index.
    ISBN 0–631–21140–3 (acid-free paper) — ISBN 0–631–21141–1 (pbk. : acid-free
paper)
      1. Children's literature, English—Handbooks, manuals, etc. 2. Children's
literature, American—Handbooks, manuals, etc. 3. Children's literature,
English—Bio-bibliography—Dictionaries. 4. Children's literature,
American—Bio-bibliography—Dictionaries. I. Title. II. Series.

PR990 .H85 2001
820.9′9282—dc21   00-042930

A catalogue record for this title is available from the British Library.

Set in 10 on 13 pt Galliard
by Graphicraft Ltd, Hong Kong
Printed and bound in the United Kingdom
by Athenaeum Press Ltd, Gateshead, Tyne & Wear

For further information on
Blackwell Publishing, visit our website:
http://www.blackwellpublishing.com

Contents

Key Texts

Topics

Acknowledgements

Having absorbed myself in this subject for some years, and as this is a work of synthesis, I would like to acknowledge all those writers whose work (if not words) echoes throughout this book. There are so many, that to single out a few names seems invidious: I shall take the risk, though, and say that I am particularly indebted for inspiration to the remarkable scholarly and critical work in this field of Perry Nodelman, Lissa Paul, Roberta Trites and, of course, Brian Alderson; for specific help to the equally inspiring Rod McGillis, Kim Reynolds, David Rudd, Lynne Vallone and Christine Wilkie-Stibbs; and for friendship and encouragement above and beyond the call of duty, Geoff Fox, Chip Sullivan and Tony Watkins. And all my other good friends in the children's literature business.

However, my real debt is to my daughters, Chloë, Abigail, Amy and Felicity, who have not only read almost every book mentioned here, but who continually remind me that they are (temporarily) children, and it is their judgement that actually counts.

How to Use This Book

As the primary purpose of this book is to provide information about materials for study, rather than the reasons for or methods of study, readers may wish to go directly to the key texts or authors. Almost all the books and authors have been selected not only for their individual importance, but also because they are exemplars of genres, modes, types, and so on. Rosemary Sutcliff, for example, is central to a discussion of the historical novel; Anne Fine is central to the radical changes in British children's literature; Judy Blume is central to American attitudes to childhood; *Little Women* is central to the development of the family story in the nineteenth century; Patricia Wrightson is central to the development of Australian children's literature and folklore.

For those who wish to construct a history, or to understand related developments, the Chronology is designed to interpret movements and suggest interrelationships (and can be mined to produce an integrated sequence).

Publication dates for works of fiction are generally those for the first appearance of texts in book form in their country of origin (details of periodical publication are noted where necessary). Authors' dates have been included only where they are useful to inform or clarify the discussion.

Children's literature has, as we shall see, distinctive virtues and difficulties, genres and modes. Some of these are explored in the Topics section.

The study of children's literature has moved over the last hundred years from prescription, to description, to criticism. As it has been associated with education and academic literary studies it has become preoccupied with how texts mean generally, rather than with the interaction of storyteller and hearer, with the single, irreproducible event of story being transmitted in an individual situation. (The pendulum may now, very challengingly, be swinging back.) At the same time, the involvement of disciplines as apparently disparate as critical theory, or providing for people with disabilities has meant that no single approach to the subject dominates.

Throughout this book I have been deliberately eclectic, adopting the critical approach which seemed to me to be most appropriate and rewarding for each subject. The experience of children's literature for its primary readership is (or can be, or should be) one of revelation, expansion and exploration – of pushing back limits. For us, the secondary, critical readers, I think that it is the same: we should approach this subject (however we choose to construct it) in a spirit of adventure. Perry Nodelman has suggested that

> we adults must do everything we possibly can to make children aware of the 'obviousnesses' that texts work to impose upon them and to give them the means to weigh and consider the implications of the subject positions that texts offer. . . . We must teach them to be divided subjects in their reading and in their lives – to be involved as both implied readers of texts and critical observers of what texts demand of them in that process. (Perry Nodelman, 'Fear in Children's Literature', in Beckett, 1997: 12)

This book is based on the assumption that 'we adults' can do this for ourselves in the context of children's literature. But, above all, children's literature is, as it were, present laughter. In all our historical or professional investigations, it is the joy of the subject that should guide us.

Note on the Bibliographies

Each entry in this book is followed by an integrated bibliography of books and articles and additional reading relevant to that topic. To avoid repetition of citations, books which are referred to several times throughout this volume are listed in the General Bibliography and Guide to Further Reading.

At a conservative estimate, over the last decade books and articles on or closely related to English-language children's literature have appeared at the rate of around 500 a year. While there is, naturally enough, a fair amount of what Brian Alderson has wryly called 'assistant professorial' writing, and a good many 'minimum publishable units', I have tried to select samples from the challenging and intellectually alert majority. The journals most often cited are as follows:

CCL   *Canadian Children's Literature–Litterature Canadienne pour la Jeunesse. A Journal of Criticism and Review.* Guelph: Canadian Children's Press and the Canadian Children's Literature Association.

CL   *Children's Literature. Annual of the Modern Language Association Division on Children's Literature and the Children's Literature Association.* New Haven, CT: Yale University Press.

CLE   *Children's Literature in Education.* New York: Human Sciences Press.

ChLAQ   *Children's Literature Association Quarterly.* Battle Creek, MI: Children's Literature Association.

IRCLL   *International Review of Children's Literature and Librarianship.* London: Taylor Graham.

LU   *The Lion and the Unicorn.* Baltimore, MD: Johns Hopkins
            University Press.
Papers   *Papers: Explorations into Children's Literature.* Burwood,
            Victoria: Deakin University.
Signal   *Signal: Approaches to Children's Books.* South Woodchester,
            Glos.: Thimble Press.

Chronology

Year-by-year lists of books and events, fascinating as they look, often require an expert eye to decode them and make links that provide a coherent picture.

The chronologies that follow are based on the most common interpretations of history and would ideally be read as parallel columns. The historian's urge to construct history in manageable, meaningful chunks is, of course, frustrated by both the complexity of facts and the crudeness of classifications; so, for instance, as genres, periods and groupings overlap, some books should appear on more than one list. Equally, of course, it should be possible to construct a quite different history from these materials, or to include other, quite different materials. In terms of research, the subject is still in its infancy, so any claim for 'earliest' or 'first' in the annotations should be taken as provisional.

Early History: Pre-eighteenth Century

Contenders for the earliest children's literature:

1391	Chaucer, *Tretis of the Astrolabe* (written for his son)
1659	Comenius, *Orbis Sensualium Pictus* (arguably the first illustrated text for children)

Religious and Evangelical Writers

This tradition was fundamental to the development of children's books and was gradually absorbed into the mainstream towards the mid-nineteenth century.

1686	John Bunyan, *A Book for Boys and Girls*
1692	James Janeway, *A Token for Children*
1715	Isaac Watts, *Divine Songs*
1778/1794/1803	Mrs Barbauld, *Lessons for Children*
1786	Mrs Trimmer, *Fabulous Histories*
1788	Mary Wollstonecraft, *Original Stories from Real Life*
1801	Maria Edgeworth, *Early Lessons*
1818/1842/1847	Mrs Sherwood, *The History of the Fairchild Family*
1858	Frederick Farrar, *Eric, or Little by Little* (the evangelical school story)
1867	'Hesba Stretton', *Jessica's First Prayer* (an example of 'ragged children' books)
1879–1967	*Boy's Own Paper* (published by the Religious Tract Society to combat 'penny dreadfuls')

Early Australian, Canadian and New Zealand Landmarks

1841 (A)	Charlotte Barton, *A Mother's Offering to her Children: by a Lady, Long Resident in New South Wales*
1852 (C)	Catherine Parr [Strickland] Traill, *Canadian Crusoes, A Tale of Rice Lake Plains*
1864 (A)	William [Still] Stitt Jenkins, *The Lost Children*
1874 (NZ)	Mary Anne, Lady Barker, *Boys*
1874 (A)	J[ohn] H[oward] Clark, *Bertie and the Bullfrogs: an Australian Story for Big and Little Children*
1890 (C)	J[ames] Macdonald Oxley, *Up Among the Ice Floes*
1894 (C)	[Margaret] Marshall Saunders, *Beautiful Joe, The Autobiography of a Dog*
1894 (A)	Ethel S[ybil] Turner, *Seven Little Australians*
1898 (C)	Ernest [Evan] Thompson Seton, *Wild Animals I Have Known*
1899 (A)	Ethel Pedley, *Dot and the Kangaroo*
1903 (C)	Kate Douglas Wiggin, *Rebecca of Sunnybrook Farm*
1908 (C)	Lucy M. Montgomery, *Anne of Green Gables*
1910 (A)	Mary Grant Bruce, *A Little Bush Maid*
1918 (A)	Norman Lindsay, *The Magic Pudding*

USA Landmarks

All of these books were highly influential in the UK; indeed, they were, increasingly, international bestsellers. From the 1960s both popular and mainstream American books became a major part of children's books in the UK; only fairly rarely was this traffic reversed.

1823	Clement Clarke Moore, *A Visit from St Nicholas*
1827	'Peter Parley', *Tales of Peter Parley About America* (first of a huge number of educational texts)
1850	'Elizabeth Wetherell', *The Wide, Wide, World* (bestselling romance, arguably not a children's book)
1868	Louisa M. Alcott, *Little Women*
1868	Horatio Alger Jr, *Ragged Dick*
1871	'Susan Coolidge', *What Katy Did*
1873	Mary Mapes Dodge (ed.), *St Nicholas* (–1940)
1876	'Mark Twain', *The Adventures of Tom Sawyer*
1886	Frances Hodgson Burnett, *Little Lord Fauntleroy*
1900	L. Frank Baum, *The Wizard of Oz*
1904	Laura Lee Hope, *The Bobbsey Twins*
1905	Frances Hodgson Burnett, *A Little Princess*
1911	Frances Hodgson Burnett, *The Secret Garden*
1912	Howard Garis, *Uncle Wiggly's Adventures*
1913	Eleanor H. Porter, *Pollyanna*
1916	Dorothy Canfield, *Understood Betsy*
1922	Carl Sandberg, *The Rootabaga Stories*
1927	'Franklin W. Dixon', *The Tower Treasure* (the first Hardy Boys book)
1930	'Carolyn Keene', *The Hidden Staircase* (the first Nancy Drew book)
1932	Laura Ingalls Wilder, *Little House in the Big Woods*
1935	Carol Rylie Brink, *Caddie Woodlawn*
1937	'Dr Seuss', *And to Think that I saw It on Mulberry Street*
1938	Marjorie Kinnan Rawlings, *The Yearling*
1938	Robert L. May, *Rudolph the Red-nosed Reindeer*
1938	Elizabeth Enright, *The Thimble Summer*
1940	Maud Hart Lovelace, *Betsy-Tacy*
1941	Eleanor Estes, *The Moffats*
1943	Esther Forbes, *Johnny Tremain*

Fairy-tales and Folk-tales in English

These are from collections and translations of original books, which were absorbed into the mainstream towards the end of the nineteenth century.

1699, 1707	Countess D'Aulnoy, *Diverting Works*
1729	Charles Perrault, *Histories, or Tales of Past Times. Told by Mother Goose*
1823	Jacob and Wilhelm Grimm, *German Popular Stories*
1846	Hans Andersen, four volumes of tales
1846	F. E. Paget, *The Hope of the Katzekopfs* (original fairy-tale)
1851	John Ruskin, *King of the Golden River* (original folk-tale)
1854	George Cruikshank, *Fairy Library* (teetotaller versions)
1855	W. M. Thackeray, *The Rose and the Ring* (satirical pastiche of tales)
1868	Charles Dickens, *A Holiday Romance*
1869	Jean Ingelow, *Mopsa the Fairy*
1871	George Macdonald, *The Princess and the Goblin*
1889	Andrew Lang (ed.), *The Blue Fairy Book* (the first of a highly influential collection)
1890	Joseph Jacobs, *English Fairy Tales*

Key Translations

1814	Johann Wyss, *The Family Robinson Crusoe*
1848	Heinrich Hoffman, *The English Struwwelpeter* (satires on evangelical poems)
1883	'Carlo Collodi', *Pinocchio*
1884	Johanna Spyri, *Heidi*
1928	Felix Salten, *Bambi*
1931	Eric Kästner, *Emil and the Detectives*
1934	Jean de Brunhoff, *The Story of Babar*
1965	Anne Holm, *I Am David*

Commercial Publishing for Children

1744	Mary Cooper, *Tommy Thumb's Song Book*
1744	John Newbery, *A Little Pretty Pocket Book*
1749	Sarah Fielding, *The Governess*

1801   Maria Edgeworth, *Early Lessons*
1804   Jane and Ann Taylor, *Original Poems for Infant Minds*
1807   Charles and Mary Lamb, *Tales from Shakespeare*
1839   Catherine Sinclair, *Holiday House*
1846   Edward Lear, *A Book of Nonsense*

Commercial Publishing for Boys

1841   Harriet Martineau, *The Crofton Boys* (early school story)
1841   Captain Marryat, *Masterman Ready* (early sea story written as a riposte to *Swiss Family Robinson*)
1855   Charles Kingsley, *Westward Ho!*
1856   R. M. Ballantyne, *The Young Fur Traders*
1857   Thomas Hughes, *Tom Brown's Schooldays*
1858   Frederick Farrar, *Eric, or Little by Little*
1866–1906   *Boys of England*
1871   G. A. Henty, *Out on the Pampas*
1879–1967   *The Boy's Own Paper* (published by the Religious Tract Society to combat 'penny dreadfuls')

Commercial Publishing for Girls

1855   Mrs Molesworth, *The Carved Lions*
1856   Charlotte Yonge, *The Daisy Chain*
1867   'Hesba Stretton', *Jessica's First Prayer*
1868   Louisa M. Alcott, *Little Women*
1880–1965   *The Girl's Own Paper*
1906   Angela Brazil, *The Fortunes of Philippa*
1920   Elsie J. Oxenham, *The Abbey Girls*
1925   Elinor M. Brent-Dyer, *The School at the Chalet*

The First 'Golden Age'

1863   Charles Kingsley, *The Water Babies*
1864   Lewis Carroll, *Alice's Adventures in Wonderland*
1870   Kate Greenaway, *Under the Window*
1871   Lewis Carroll, *Through the Looking Glass*
1871   'Susan Coolidge', *What Katy Did*
1871   George Macdonald, *The Princess and the Goblin*

1873–	Mary Mapes Dodge (ed.), *St Nicholas*
1876	'Mark Twain', *The Adventures of Tom Sawyer*
1877	Anna Sewell, *Black Beauty*
1882	Richard Jefferies, *Bevis*
1883	Robert Louis Stevenson, *Treasure Island*
1885	Robert Louis Stevenson, *A Child's Garden of Verses*
1886	Frances Hodgson Burnett, *Little Lord Fauntleroy*
1894	Rudyard Kipling, *The Jungle Book*
1894	Ethel S[ybil] Turner, *Seven Little Australians*
1898	J. Meade Faulkner, *Moonfleet*
1898	Ernest [Evan] Thompson Seton, *Wild Animals I Have Known*
1899	Helen Bannerman, *The Story of Little Black Sambo*
1899	Rudyard Kipling, *Stalky and Co*
1899	E. Nesbit, *The Story of the Treasure Seekers*
1899	Ethel Pedley, *Dot and the Kangaroo*
1900	L. Frank Baum, *The Wizard of Oz*
1902	Rudyard Kipling, *Just So Stories*
1902	E. Nesbit, *Five Children and It*
1902	Beatrix Potter, *The Tale of Peter Rabbit*
1903	Kate Douglas Wiggin, *Rebecca of Sunnybrook Farm*
1905	Frances Hodgson Burnett, *A Little Princess*
1906	Rudyard Kipling, *Puck of Pook's Hill*
1908	Kenneth Grahame, *The Wind in the Willows*
1908	Lucy M. Montgomery, *Anne of Green Gables*
1910	Mary Grant Bruce, *A Little Bush Maid*
1911	Frances Hodgson Burnett, *The Secret Garden*
1913	Eleanor H. Porter, *Pollyanna*

Between the World Wars

This period marks the consolidation of children's literature and the dominance of fantasy, possibly in reaction to the First World War.

1920	Hugh Lofting, *The Story of Dr Dolittle*
1922	Richmal Crompton, *Just-William*
1924	A. A. Milne, *When We Were Very Young*
1926	A. A. Milne, *Winnie-the-Pooh*
1927	John Masefield, *The Midnight Folk*
1927	A. A. Milne, *Now We Are Six*
1928	A. A. Milne, *The House at Pooh Corner*
1929	Alison Uttley, *The Squirrel, the Hare and the Little Grey Rabbit*
1930	Arthur Ransome, *Swallows and Amazons*

1932   W. E. Johns, *The White Fokker* (first 'Biggles' book)
1934   P. L. Travers, *Mary Poppins*
1934   Geoffrey Trease, *Bows against the Barons*
1936   Joanne Cannan, *A Pony for Jean*
1937   Enid Blyton, *The Story of the Wishing Chair*
1937   J. R. R. Tolkien, *The Hobbit*
1937   Eve Garnett, *The Family from One-End Street*
1940   Eric Knight, *Lassie Come-Home*

The Second Golden Age

1945   Revd W. Awdrey, *The Three Railway Engines*
1950   C. S. Lewis, *The Lion, the Witch and the Wardrobe*
1952   Ben Lucien Burman, *High Water at Catfish Bend*
1952   Mary Norton, *The Borrowers*
1952   E. B. White, *Charlotte's Web*
1954   Lucy M. Boston, *The Children of Green Knowe*
1954   Rosemary Sutcliff, *The Eagle of the Ninth*
1958   Philippa Pearce, *Tom's Midnight Garden*
1964   Lloyd Alexander, *The Book of Three*
1964   Roald Dahl, *Charlie and the Chocolate Factory*
1965   Susan Cooper, *Over Sea, Under Stone*
1967   Alan Garner, *The Owl Service*
1967   Ursula K. Le Guin, *A Wizard of Earthsea*
1967   Russell Hoban, *The Mouse and his Child*
1967   K. M. Peyton, *Flambards*
1967   S. A. Wakefield, *Bottersnikes and Gumbles*
1968   Ted Hughes, *The Iron Man*
1968   Patricia Wrightson, *I Own the Racecourse*
1969   Peter Dickinson, *The Weathermonger*
1969   Penelope Farmer, *Charlotte Sometimes*
1972   Richard Adams, *Watership Down*
1977   Jan Mark, *Thunder and Lightnings*
1977   Catherine Paterson, *Bridge to Terabithia*
1978   Alan Garner, *The Stone Book*

The New Realism

1964   Louise Fitzhugh, *Harriet the Spy*
1969   Paul Zindel, *My Darling, My Hamburger*

1970   Judy Blume, *Are You There, God? It's Me, Margaret*
1972   Norma Klein, *Mom, the Wolfman, and Me*
1974   Robert Cormier, *The Chocolate War*
1975   Judy Blume, *Forever*
1983   Cynthia Voight, *Homecoming*
1990   Gillian Cross, *Wolf*

Key Picture Books and Illustrated Books

1902   Beatrix Potter, *The Tale of Peter Rabbit*
1903   L. Leslie Brooke, *Johnny Crow's Garden*
1928   William Nicholson, *Clever Bill*
1929   Hergé, 'Tintin' books (Belgium)
1933   Marjorie Flack, *The Story about Ping* (USA)
1936   Edward Ardizzone, *Little Tim and the Brave SeaCaptain*
1936   Munro Leaf, *The Story of Ferdinand* (USA)
1937   'Dr Seuss', *And to Think that I saw It on Mulberry Street* (USA)
1939   Virginia Lee Burton, *Mike Mulligan and his Steam Shovel* (USA)
1941   Robert McClosky, *Make Way for Ducklings* (USA)
1941   H. A. Rey, *Curious George* (USA)
1942   Virginia Lee Burton, *The Little House* (USA)
1942   Diana Ross, *The Little Red Engine Gets a Name*
1950   Roger Duvoisin, *Petunia* (USA)
1963   Maurice Sendak, *Where the Wild Things Are* (USA)
1974   Quentin Blake [and Russell Hoban], *How Tom Beat Captain Najork and His Hired Sportsmen*
1977   Anthony Browne, *A Walk in the Park*
1977   John Burningham, *Come Away from the Water, Shirley*
1982   David McKee, *I Hate my Teddy Bear*
1986   Janet and Allan Ahlberg, *The Jolly Postman*

War Books

1940   Kitty Barne, *Visitors from London*
1941   P. L. Travers, *I Go By Sea, I Go By Land*
1941   Mary Treadgold, *We Couldn't Leave Dinah*
1956   Ian Serraillier, *The Silver Sword*
1965   Anne Holm, *I Am David*
1967   Jill Paton Walsh, *The Dolphin Crossing*
1969   Jill Paton Walsh, *Fireweed*

1970   Susan Cooper, *Dawn of Fear*
1971   Judith Kerr, *When Hitler Stole Pink Rabbit*
1973   Nina Bawden, *Carrie's War*
1973   Bette Green, *The Summer of my German Soldier* (USA)
1975   Robert Westall, *The Machine Gunners*

Introduction

About Children's Literature and This Book

One of the delights of children's literature is that it does not fit easily into any cultural or academic category. While we might expect that readers of a guide to, say, Renaissance drama might be a fairly homogeneous group, the readers of this book might well be students of literature interested in exploring a new literary field; but they might equally be librarians or teachers concerned with what children's books can *do*; or historians, or sociologists, interested in how this highly influential body of books impinges on their discipline; or they might be (as well) parents, or non-specialist human beings. Each of these readers will have a different purpose, mindset and method to their reading, and they will also define the *subject matter* of the field differently.

At the extremes, there might be those who would exclude Roald Dahl as being ephemeral rubbish, but who would include a little-read writer such as Sarah Fielding, as being pivotal in the history of children's books. An opposing camp might consider Fielding totally irrelevant to any conceivable contemporary child reader, and Dahl central to the modern child's experience. Similarly, a postcolonialist perspective might suggest, as does the Australian Heather Scutter, that

> Now is the time for a powerful renegotiation of the status of otherness and difference . . . while we re-imagine our field without the secure authority of controlling metanarratives. (Scutter, 1997: 35)

Of course, all of this is complicated by the inclusion (or exclusion) of the child reader in the critical equation. The Canadian critic Perry Nodelman recounts how, when he was first preparing a children's literature course in the 1970s, he was struck by the attitude of the available guides to children's literature:

> They all made judgements of excellence in terms of the effects of books on their audience – and that astonished me, for in the ivory tower of literary study I had hitherto inhabited, one certainly did not judge books by how they affected audiences; in fact, one often judged audiences by the extent to which they were affected by books, so that, for instance, anyone who wasn't overwhelmed by Shakespeare was simply assumed to be an intransigent dummy. (Nodelman, 1985: 4)

The selection of authors, texts and topics presented in this book as 'children's literature' is a negotiation between these – and many other – points of view. It covers a form of literature that has existed in parallel (and interwoven) with other literature since at least the eighteenth century and virtually every literary genre (including one rarely found in other literature); it extends into non-print media; it ranges across the world. In short, we are dealing with a parallel universe to the world of canonical literature, a universe of very large numbers of texts with a massive cultural influence (how did you become interested in literature?) and in many ways more complex, more *difficult* to talk about than other literatures. The main criterion for inclusion has been 'significance', which is naturally relative and related to the wide range of potential readers and users of children's books, and to the wide range of relevant approaches and responses that naturally result. It is this diversity of texts and responses that is one of the great challenges of children's literature. Like most writers of fantasy who try to describe new worlds, I have attempted to be both radical and comprehensible.

Matters of 'Theory' and Definition

One of the most interesting starting points for the study of children's literature is the term itself. Here, I should like to be ruthlessly brief. To some, 'children's literature' might well be a contradiction in terms: the values and qualities which constitute 'literariness' naturally (that is, have come to mean culturally) cannot be sustained either by books designed for an audience of limited experience, knowledge, skill and sophistication, or by the readers. (This is a further stage in Nodelman's suggestion that audiences are judged by their responses to books. Readers get what they deserve – or are assumed to deserve. For further discussion of this issue, see Hunt, 1991; Lesnik-Oberstein, 1994, 1998; Nodelman, 1996, Townsend, 1990.)

The most accurate term for our subject might, instead, be 'texts for children', allowing that the meanings of all three words have to be highly flexible.

Texts can be taken to mean virtually any form of communication. One of the distinguishing features of children's literature has been its lack of generic 'purity': one of the claimants for the most significant (if not the earliest) of children's books, John Newbery's *A Little Pretty Pocket Book* (1744), was sold as (in effect) a multimedia, gendered experience. In the twentieth century and increasingly (it seems safe to say) into the twenty-first, the idea of the book as a 'closed' form will be replaced by the multi-dimensional experience. The book, the film, the video, the retellings, the prequels and sequels, the merchandising, the diaries, the television series with 'new' episodes, the 'making of the television series', the 'back stories', the biographies of the stars who appear in the television series . . . all of these are part of the 'experience' of what, reductively, we call 'the text'. Children's literature, perhaps more obviously than other literary forms, has been a part of this from the outset – adapting, reworking, absorbing – and driven simultaneously by creativity, concern and commercialism. Picture books in the latter half of the twentieth century became the site of some of the most complex, experimental, polyphonic and multi-referential work in the textual world.

The voraciousness of children's literature in subsuming and assuming other forms (either positively, or more commonly by default) has led to some very curious anomalies both in its content as a body of texts and its composition as a subject of study. Children's texts are commonly assumed to be restricted (as well as restrictive) and yet the subject embraces – and is expected to embrace – oral forms, folk-tales, fairy-tales and legends (with, of course, international implications), the illustrated text, the highly illustrated text and the picture book. And because it passes constantly across the borders of high and popular culture, children's literature is now taken to include virtually *anything* produced for the entertainment, exploitation or enculturation of children. In academic terms (that is, in terms of arbitrary, organizational convenience) our texts reside in literature, media studies, graphic art, history, folklore, theatre, dance and so on.

All of these require (or have acquired) specialist critical theories and terminologies, which are only now being developed and refined specifically in relation to children. On the whole, those of us who are involved in the field of children's literature find this range of 'texts' to be an invigorating, if occasionally bewildering source of inspiration.

That texts are *for* children can be declared by the author, assumed by the publisher, or – less manageably for those trying to create a coherent discipline – assumed either by those who give books to children, or (even more confusingly) by the children themselves. None of these categories is reliable, even without the problem (see below) of what a child might actually be said to be. Authors' intentions have been ambivalent (as with Mark Twain and *The Adventures of Tom Sawyer*, Rudyard Kipling with *Rewards and Fairies*, or A. A Milne) and their judgements challenged by critics and readers (Kenneth Grahame, Judy Blume, Robert Westall). Books that make no concessions to inexperienced readers, or whose subject matter might seem at best irrelevant to and at worst undesirable for children, have appeared on children's lists. Famous or infamous examples have included Alan Garner's immensely complex and violent *Red Shift*, presumably because Garner had hitherto been a writer 'obviously' for children, and because the protagonists are teenagers; Raymond Briggs's existentialist and endlessly allusive *Fungus the Bogeyman*, or even more bewilderingly, his apocalyptic *When the Wind Blows*, because they are in cartoon format; and Russell Hoban's *The Mouse and His Child* (complete with its parody of Samuel Beckett), presumably because it is about toys. There is nothing new about this 'misallocation': *Animal Farm* and *The Lord of the Flies* have been staples of the British secondary school curriculum for many years. Roald Dahl's *Boy* and *Going Solo*, one of which might be intended for children, and one of which might not, both appear in editions for children.

All this should demonstrate the difficulties in which writers on children's literature constantly find themselves. Are all those adjectives that I have applied to books as defining 'adult' or excluding 'child' – complex, violent, existentialist, allusive, apocalyptic – features that reflect the childhood that I want to create, define and preserve, or are they what the culture itself sees as defining childhood (or are they what I perceive the culture as seeing)? And if the second of these is true, how can these cases have occurred?

Theorists such as Karín Lesnik-Oberstein are therefore correct when they argue that criticism of children's literature is always clouded by stated or unstated attempts to wrestle with childhood (however locally and 'realistically' defined). Where I think such theorists are incorrect is, first, their assumption that wrestling with the audience is not a feature common to all criticism (however deeply suppressed); and second, that this is not a *positive* feature of children's book criticism. The establishment of a three-way engagement between book, reader and other readers also dispels any ideas of universality or authority, whatever their supposed basis.

The 'forness' is judged differently by different generations and by those with different interests. Hence there is a long tradition of myths, legends, folk- and fairy-tales being marketed for children, in defiance of almost all stated standards for the content of children's books. Such confusion is most obvious in the long (and in many ways distinguished) output of the Walt Disney studios; with very few exceptions the animated feature films (*Snow White*, *Sleeping Beauty*, through to *The Little Mermaid* and *Beauty and the Beast*) are entirely about adult or late-adolescent concerns (exceptions might include *Peter Pan* – as Disneyfied). Only recently, with *Pocahontas* and *The Hunchback of Notre Dame*, does it seem to be tacitly acknowledged that these films are only incidentally for children.

There is also a long – and far from dead – tradition of didacticism, which holds that children's books must be moral and educational; this is perhaps an inevitable consequence of adult dominance, when both the child characters and the child readers are subservient to the adult voice in the book. Whether or not this amounts to a violation of childhood or children in some way, or denies the possibility of a 'pure' concept of children's literature, is still debated (see, for example, Rose, 1984).

As if that were not enough, children's books seem to have been the site of subversion: sometimes with the collusion of adult authors with their readers against the rest of the adult world; sometimes by adults using the form to sublimate or escape from their problems; and sometimes by adults using children, in effect, as weapons. Yet it might be questioned how far children's books could ever be genuinely subversive. It could be argued that they share with much popular culture the disruptive surface which disguises a profound conservatism. Thus books such as Pat Hutchins's *Rosie's Walk* or David McKee's *I Hate My Teddy Bear* which seem to address the 'child' exclusively may well be no more than exceptions that prove the rule.

A good deal has been written about the assumptions that lie behind the use of the word *children* to imply or construct a homogeneous (and thus simple, subservient and marginalized) group. At many levels, such definitions are inherently sinister and are in any case often demeaning to both the oppressors and the oppressed. The relationship between children and childhood and adults and adulthood is extremely complex and is continuously reflected in the books: they are also very often not what they appear to be. Thus childhood can be seen by adults as a desirable area of innocence or retreat, and yet it is constructed as a state that the child wishes to grow out of. Indeed, the very status of 'children's literature' reflects a society of adults anxious to reject or forget about childhood. If this is not the case, why is literary theory concerned with readers so silent about the learning process in childhood? (Thacker, 2000).

Childhood has been conceived by societies as a state that can be manipulated (another reason for its low status), or by romantics as a pure state, or by psychologists as a series of developmental states. In so far as it can be generally defined at all, it might be as a period of life without responsibility, in which case it is likely to be defined not by age, but by class or social circumstances (see, for example, Jenks, 1996).

Specific attitudes to childhood which mould and are moulded by the books provided for children can be endlessly surprising. For example, there is plenty of evidence to suggest that in the nineteenth century, children were constructed as *wanting* to die – to go to God – as a comfort to their parents; what to the twenty-first century seems to amount to a wholesale slaughter of the innocents in fiction is a complex weave of salvation, fear, control and loss (see Hollindale, 1988; and on childhood, see Gittins, 1998; Lesnik-Oberstein, 1998.)

Thus, although it is possible to make some generalizations about how a culture or a society constructs the child – and publishers have made and make (probably self-fulfilling) assumptions – 'the child' is an infinitely varied concept, from house to house and from day to day. In talking about children's books some generalizations have to be made or the language becomes unmanageable, but the fact that the concept of the child is an ever-present problem for children's literature criticism cannot be forgotten.

Consequently, you will not find in this book any of those phrases of shining untruth so beloved of reviewers and students: 'children like . . .', 'all children will love . . .', 'suitable for year/grade x'; nor those more patrician evasions such as 'the reader feels . . .'. All of these assumptions and phrases have contributed to making texts for children what they are, and some commentaries on them what *they* are. There is, of course, an understandable desire to categorize books: 'for five- to seven-year-olds', 'a book to help with divorce/anorexia', '*for* boys or *for* girls'; after all, for many readers, selection and application is the whole point of writing *about* books. On the other hand, there are not many reviews which say 'a book ideal for the 38–43 age group . . .' or 'Joanna Trollope's new novel should be prescribed reading for 50-year-old widows with angst'. The manipulation of childhood is a deeply ingrained habit, be the motives never so pure. (Few writers have the courage of the psychologist Nicholas Tucker (1981) in his descriptive,

Piagetian survey *The Child and the Book* to constantly qualify his categorizations and insist – in the face of huge commercial and cultural pressures – on the necessary individuality of *a child*).

We may, then, take short-cuts for the sake of practicality, but we cannot totally evade the underlying complexity of our subject.

Bibliography

Gittins, Diana 1998: *The Child in Question*. London: Macmillan.

Hollindale, Peter 1988: 'Ideology and Children's Books'. Signal, 55, 3–22.

Jenks, Chris 1996: *Childhood*. London: Routledge.

Nodelman, Perry 1985: 'Introduction: Matthew Arnold, A Teddy Bear, and a List of Touchstones.' In Nodelman 1985: 1–12.

Nodelman, Perry 1997: 'Fear in Children's Literature: What's Left (or Right) After Theory?' In Beckett 1997: 3–14.

Scutter, Heather 1997: 'Hunting for History: Children's Literature Outside, Over There, and Down Under.' *ARIEL: A Review of International English Literature*, 28 (1), 22–36.

Thacker, Deborah 2000: 'Disdain or Ignorance? Literary Theory and the Absence of Children's Literature.' *LU*, 24 (1), 1–17.

Townsend, John Rowe 1990: 'Standards of Criticism for Children's Literature.' In Hunt 1990: 57–70.

Matters of History

Constructing History

All books are ultimately generated and regulated by their audience (even if that audience can be manipulated and to some extent 'created'). With children's literature, this process is more visible and more fundamental to the nature of the books produced. Children's literature is, at least in part, about control, and the primary result of that is that it reflects first of all what society wishes itself to be seen as, and secondly, subconsciously and retrospectively, what it is actually like. The histories we construct reflect these overriding 'truths'.

Similarly, chronology may be less important than an awareness of the relationship between childhood and cultural and historical change. While it is possible to trace the influence of some writers – Lewis Carroll, Edith Nesbit, Richard Jefferies, for example – directly or indirectly, it is possible to argue that children's writers continually re-invent their fictions and forms in response to changing commercial and cultural constructions of childhood. Possibly as a result of the marginal status of the texts, but also because of children's literature's affinity with popular culture, *progress* and *development* are not easy or necessarily relevant concepts. For all our contemporary gestures towards liberalization, there are plenty of rawly didactic books today of which the eighteenth-century puritans would have been proud; while critics who bemoan the degeneration and brutality of contemporary writing for children and look back to an age of innocence, have clearly not read very widely in nineteenth-century children's books.

However, there is an underlying idea of what a children's book should be which does not, perhaps surprisingly, change very much – whether it is the middle-class, 'respectable' text, or the popular-culture bestseller. Even when the wheel is re-invented, it looks much like the traditional one because it has much the same function.

Consequently there is much to be gained by an historicist approach (broadly, placing books in a complex context and trying to understand what they meant in that context); an extreme example might be the evangelical texts of the late eighteenth century. To the post-romantic, let alone the postmodernist reader, these seem to be savage, repressive and manipulative, with sexist and racist overtones; in simple visual and practical terms, they seem to be unreadable. Even the titles of the most successful series, *Cheap Repository Tracts* (1795– 8) by Hannah More, or *Evenings at Home* (1792–6) by Anna Laetitia Barbauld, may not now inspire; but their effect on contemporary children must have been considerable – and in ways which liberal advocates of contemporary children's books would approve. It is also salutary for a twenty-first-century reader such as myself to find that these books are often compulsively readable: there is a verve and pace and inevitability about the writing and the structure which, while (or because) it may appeal to (what may now appear to be) less admirable instincts of power and punishment, is gripping.

In addition, almost certainly as a result of cultural inertia and neglect and the conservatism of publishers, children's books, even in today's publishing climate, have a long shelf-life. It is sometimes hard to remember that Enid Blyton's Famous Five and C. S. Lewis's Narnia books are over fifty years old, and William, Milly-Molly-Mandy, and Superman, over seventy. Incidental features that, over time, incapacitate popular fiction (the Saint's early reliance on telephones in Post Offices, James Bond's now comparatively mild sexual exploits) do not appear to register with (to construct another fiction) the average child reader. This is possibly because inexperienced readers draw the boundaries of fantasy in places different from experienced readers. Enid Blyton's still very popular St Clare's series (dating from the 1940s) is populated with characters with names like Doris, Elsie and Gladys, which are perhaps accepted without comment because they are as outlandish (for the moment) as the scenes and the action. But the reason that these books remain on the shelves (perhaps in much the same way as adult 'classics') is partly because of the lack of discrimination (meant in no derogatory way) of the audience (children can only read what they are allowed to read), but partly because they are 'safe' for adults and for adults' concepts of childhood. The overwhelming dominance in the 1990s of Roald Dahl's books, or the longevity of Blyton's, can be seen as the result of deliberate acts of commercial conservatism.

This said, the history of children's literature resembles its theory, in that it is being reshaped before it has been properly researched. Much of the history of the subject is invisible: it was for a long time rejected as a subject of serious study, along with childhood, although, as C. S. Lewis (1966: 25) tartly put it, 'critics who treat "adult" as a term of approval, instead of a merely descriptive term, cannot be adult themselves'. As with other 'popular' forms, hard historical evidence is not easy to find (although it has, obviously, not been looked for very carefully). A striking example is the fact that the earliest significant collection of nursery rhymes, Mary Cooper's *Tommy Thumb's Song Book*, is only *assumed* to have existed on the evidence of the surviving 'Voll. II', and what is *probably* a reprint produced in America. Children's books were read to destruction, largely because they were genuinely popular, but partly, again, because they were marginalized and regarded as disposable; but thanks to assiduous (and occasionally visionary) collectors such as Iona and Peter Opie in Britain, A. S. W. Rosenbach in the USA, and Ken Pound in Australia (see Smith, 1998; Avery and Briggs, 1989; Hunt, 1999), there are vast amounts of material in libraries around the world awaiting rereading. That rereading will inevitably revise our 'conventional', partial picture. In terms of potential academic study which could change our whole perception of cultural history, the children's book archives must be unrivalled.

In view of this, the value of presenting the 'standard' history, a chronological sequence, is distinctly questionable for three reasons: the first is that it is staggeringly incomplete; the second is that it has largely been shaped by a certain kind of writer (middle class, male, western) with values that might not be appropriate to the subject; and the third is (as we have seen) that the *significance* of chronology is not altogether clear.

The basic, conventional history of English-language children's literature might read (reductively) as follows. Britain was, as it were, the fountainhead; American booksellers imported or pirated British books through the late seventeenth and eighteenth centuries. Since then, American and British developments have been broadly similar, with, from the mid-twentieth century, the USA exporting extensively to the UK. Australia, Canada and New Zealand developed their sometimes highly individualistic children's literatures from the mid-nineteenth century, although there has been a general homogenization over the past forty years. The very broad pattern of development from religion through education to reading for pleasure (plus commercialization) can be found throughout the world. In continental Europe, children's literature is largely a nineteenth-century phenomenon; in the Indian subcontinent and Africa, the reliance on imported texts has clashed with quite different cultural needs. In totalitarian states, children's books have been treated in the same way as any others, that is censored or manufactured (which, of course, reflects their political importance).

Children before the seventeenth century shared narrative, whether oral or through chapbooks, with adults. The first widely distributed texts for children were by puritan writers; in the mid-eighteenth century books began to be produced commercially, usually with an educational slant and/or based on folklore. By the end of the century, evangelical writers were producing hundreds of texts for children, and the nineteenth century saw a continued battle between entertainment and instruction. Boys' books were generally adventure stories, often about empire or school life; girls' stories featured philanthropic middle-class children, or domestic fantasy. There was also a divide between the 'respectable', middle-class texts and the ephemeral mass-produced texts.

As childhood came to be more valued at the end of the nineteenth century, so children's books became more respectful towards the child and imagination, and less directly didactic. Children's books and adults' books, which often overlapped, now went their separate ways. After the First World War, fantasy, possibly as a result of cultural retreatism, dominated, and children's books developed as a respectable part of the publishing industry. This trend was repeated after the Second World War, when children's publishing became a lucrative and distinctive field, with a burst of original, high-quality work. In the last decades of the twentieth century, despite large numbers of titles (over 8,000 in the UK in 1997), publishing has tended towards the bland, mechanistic and conservative (Reynolds and Tucker, 1998), with the possible exception of the picture book, which has maintained something of its experimental strengths. The most striking change since the 1970s has been a shift away from books written in a recognizably 'literary' tradition, to those written in more 'dynamic', less reflective mode. This may also be a reflection of competition from other media, which in turn suggests that internationalism in the form of the internet will modify writing for (and by) children out of all recognition in the foreseeable future.

Traffic between the UK and the USA has been extensive, to the extent that in 1999 a book by the American author Robert Cormier found its way onto the shortlist for the British Carnegie Medal (presented annually by the Library Association for the 'best' children's book). American 'series' books which have flooded the market (Point Horror, Babysitter's Club, Sweet Valley

High, etc.) have generated many British imitations. American books have also tended to take over from British as the major world influence.

Very recently, spectacular international successes such as Philip Pullman's *His Dark Materials* trilogy and J. K. Rowling's Harry Potter books have suggested to journalists that children's books are in a much healthier condition than adults' books. S. F. Said wrote in the British *Daily Telegraph* of Rowling's 'undiscovered treasure trove of original, sometimes disturbing, but always boldly imaginative writing', contrasted with 'the jaded knowingness and compulsion to irony that cripple so much contemporary fiction'. For the children's book specialist, his conclusion is touchingly romantic (and ironic, because it recurs quite frequently): 'children's stories can touch "those parts of us that haven't yet become bored, damaged or embarrassed by existence – and can help those parts that have"' (quoted in Connell, 2000: 3).

This seems to be entirely plausible, even coherent, as a history, but might not, on the whole, be either useful or true. There has, for example, been a significant amount of discussion of medieval (and earlier) children's literature (see Adams, 1998; Wooden, 1986) and there are many elements that it does not take into account.

For example, the relationship between children's literature and the rest of history (and literature) is somewhat eccentric, complicated by the need to control or protect the child. Between the world wars British children's books virtually ignored the General Strike, the Spanish Civil War and the rise of fascism; where, in American children's books, was the Wall Street Crash or the New Deal? An event as momentous as the Second World War only appeared in 'mainstream' texts twenty years after the event. Children's literature's relationship with movements of literature in general is equally tortuous, being on the whole highly conservative and yet showing remarkable peaks of experimentation, as in the novels of Aidan Chambers in the UK and Gary Crew in Australia, and the picture books of Maurice Sendak and Chris van Allsburg in the USA.

Thus it may well be that the most important features of any history are the *attitudes* inherent in the production of texts for children; we might also usefully differentiate, among others, the history of tone and address, the history of content, the history of gender, politics and ideology, and the effect of internationalism. In that way, we may be making useful, usable statements, rather than simply presenting a chronology whose significance is multiple. (The chronology to this book is, accordingly, arranged thematically and generically.)

Tone and Address

In the earliest printed books (for example, *Reynard the Fox* printed by Caxton in 1481), although they were obviously read by children, no distinction seems to have been made between writing for children and for adults (although there is still a good deal of discussion about what distinctions the society made between children and adults). The earliest texts specifically for children (which, one assumes, would also be read by adults) are simple, the tone and mode of address acknowledging a stable relationship between writer and child. As printing and a literate child-public developed, texts were seen (as in Britain in the eighteenth century) as agents of religious propaganda or social engineering. Thus the most famous and (tenuously or tenaciously) enduring texts of what might be called the early period, such as Maria Edgeworth's *The Parent's Assistant* (1796) or Mary Martha Sherwood's *The Fairchild Family* (1818 and sequels), assume that the authorial voice has a natural authority over the child reader, just as the head of the family stood 'in place of God' to the children. They are only the tip of a huge iceberg of many thousands of tracts, novels and stories which make no secret of their manipulative aims, and firmly construct both the reader and the relationship.

Parallel to these texts are those which derive from popular culture – notably from the folk-tale – widely (but far from universally) regarded as trivial or appealing to basic or elemental sides of the readership. Initially, these cheap texts, sold as 'chapbooks' in Britain from the sixteenth century, and transmogrifying into penny dreadfuls and dime novels, were shared by adults and children. However, as attitudes to childhood changed and families became smaller and infant death-rates declined, a tone of voice which accorded more respect for children – which acknowledged a tacit equality – emerged through writers such as Lewis Carroll and Edith Nesbit, Louisa May Alcott and Mark Twain, Ethel Turner and Ernest Thompson Seton. Whereas in the nineteenth century a writer like G. A. Henty, ostensibly, obviously, a writer for boys, would have had a substantial adult readership, in the twentieth century the tone and narrative stance of the children's book separated it from adult texts.

But this is a complex matter, because to describe the characteristics of such a style is complex, and because this is far from a sequential progress. The Australian critic Barbara Wall has suggested that there are three kinds of narrative address that writers for children may use:

First, they may write as Ransome does for a single audience, using single address; their narrators will address child narratees, overt or covert, straightforwardly, showing no consciousness that adults too might read the work. . . . Secondly, they may write for a double audience, using double address, as Barrie does; their narrators will address child narratees overtly and self-consciously, and will also address adults, either overtly, as the implied author's attention shifts away from the implied child reader to a different older audience, or covertly, as the narrator deliberately exploits the ignorance of the implied child reader by making jokes that are funny primarily because children will not understand them. . . . Thirdly, they may write for a dual audience, using dual address . . . either using the same 'tone of seriousness' which would be used to address adult narratees, or confidentially sharing the story in a way that allows adult narrator and child narratee a conjunction of interests. . . . Dual address . . . is rare and difficult, presupposing as it does that a child narratee is addressed and an adult reader simultaneously satisfied. (Wall, 1991: 35–6)

This extremely useful categorization can be seen in all three forms in different parts of A. A. Milne's *Winnie-the-Pooh*: double when he is joking about Pooh bear living 'under the name of Saunders'; dual when Pooh encounters Eeyore; and single when Pooh and Piglet play together. However, I would argue that it is *dual* address that is most characteristic of the twentieth century (rather than single address, as Wall suggests) and of which Ransome is the master, while single address is both practically and theoretically virtually impossible to achieve.

In the last decades of the twentieth century the boundaries fundamentally set by narrative voice have begun to be eroded again: K. M. Peyton's *Flambards*, Anne Fine's *Goggle-Eyes* and Michele Magorian's *Goodnight Mr Tom* have been dramatized for television as general or adult entertainment; Richard Adams's *Watership Down* and J. K. Rowling's *Harry Potter and the Philosopher's Stone* have been issued simultaneously in adult's and children's editions (with identical texts but different prices). Such has been the influence of popular music, and the videos and television that accompany it, that a style – and, more interestingly – a subject matter have emerged that cross old boundaries. The most successful purveyors of this new composite style have been, in fiction, Jacqueline Wilson, and in non-fiction, Terry Deary with jokey but factually accurate texts (such as Horrible Histories) – both of them much imitated. Deary has stated the issue of tone explicitly and targeted an increasingly characteristic twenty-first-century reader, either adult or child:

When I'm writing, I have an imaginary audience. It's someone who is not a particularly fluent reader and doesn't have a large attention span. The vital thing is for me *not* to come over as, 'I'm an adult, I know this and I am going to tell you. Are you listening?' That is absolute death. . . . What I am is an ignorant person saying, 'You'll never believe what I found out. . . . I'm going to share it with you.' (Carter, 1999: 96)

This is about as opposite to the attitude of the average writer for children of 1800 as it is possible to be – except, of course, for the ultimate intent to influence and educate. Whatever the tone or the voice, children's literature cannot cease to be a site of power imbalance. And the matter is further complicated by issues of content (and the associated categorization of books).

Content

The history of the 'content' items of children's literature reflects closely attitudes to children and childhood. It has been assumed, at least recently, that childhood has become less innocent and that, certainly since the 1960s, subjects have been treated in children's literature that were not permissible before. This nostalgic and protective view is not even generally true.

Children's literature is rooted in (and has been deliberately directed towards) stories *not* calculated to protect childhood from horror; or, it might be said, in expanding children's experience at too rapid a rate. Thus folk- and fairy-tales routinely contain examples of murder, dismemberment, death and sexual violence and a good deal more. Chapbooks and their successors featured topical sensational incidents such as executions. Evangelical writers from the seventeenth to the nineteenth centuries dwelt upon savage punishments (burning to death was a favourite) for recalcitrant children, and in the case of Protestant writers, on the atrocities perpetrated by Roman Catholics. Graphic descriptions of poverty, violence and death were endemic in the thousands of books describing charitable children; the heroes of the empire as depicted by Henty and his fellows encountered (and sometimes indulged in) atrocities and massacres described (to the modern eye) with gratuitous relish. As Maria Tatar observed, 'The numbers of children who go up in flames in nineteenth-century story books is nothing short of extraordinary. . . . Even those who survive the conflagrations they have set off must endure months of torment' (Tatar, 1992: 94–5).

And the horrors are not all external. The classic writers of the British 'first golden age of children's books' (from around 1860 to 1914), commonly (if unconsciously) used children's books as a kind of therapy to sublimate their deviant feelings – very often caused by childhood traumas (see, for example, Carpenter, 1985). Thus, it is not difficult to read questionable sub-texts into the work of Carroll, Charles Kingsley, George MacDonald and their successors, notably C. S. Lewis, Enid Blyton and Roald Dahl. (It is commonly assumed that it is only knowing and – by implication – corrupt adults who might see such things, bringing, as it were, their own evil with them into paradise, but that is conveniently to ignore the subconscious perceptions of child readers.) Even those writers who might be thought of as the most psychologically 'normal' (for example, Beatrix Potter) did not flinch from at least some of the more questionable realities of human nature.

As the twentieth century progressed and (middle-class at least) childhood became an increasingly protected area, so it is true that the residually disturbing elements that one finds in the work of Milne (for example) of threat and deprivation are increasingly filtered out, and explicit unpleasantness is rare. Fear is transposed into fantasy (as in Lucy Boston's *The Children of Green Knowe* or Ursula K. Le Guin's Earthsea), where it becomes more abstract. Where there were realistic treatments of problems, they were embedded in complex, literary settings (such as Jill Paton Walsh's *Goldengrove* and *Unleaving* or Penelope Lively's *Astercote*). For fifty years, then, mainstream (middle-class) children's books were (broadly) a reflection of the innocence that adults wished to impute to childhood: Arthur Ransome's idyllic Lake District, or Eleanor Estes's New England, or Maud Hart Lovelace's small-town Minnesota were the unironic ideal. (This is, of course, not true of children's reading in general; in popular culture the most degrading and horrific sides of human behaviour are routinely fed to children.)

And so in the 1970s when mainstream children's books began to register (at last) the vulnerability of childhood by directly addressing unpleasant realities – or, as Terry Pratchett put it, to write 'relevant' books, 'books set firmly in the child's environment, or whatever hell the writer believes to be the child's environment' (Pratchett, 1995: 5) – they were judged against the background of a protective century. The two most outstanding (and controversial) books were Robert Cormier's *The Chocolate War* and Judy Blume's *Forever*. The first gave a brutal and bleak view of school life; the second an explicit and unjudgemental account of teenage sex. The response (which in parts of the USA involved banning the books) generally hinged on the reluctance of adults to acknowledge the way in which childhood and the world were developing.

The 1980s and 1990s saw a vast increase in the number of books dealing with social 'realism', which is not of course the realism (and I may be being very optimistic here) that 90 per cent of the population encounters, but the realism that involves unpleasant sex, violence, poverty, war and drugs. There is, of course, an insidious normalization in one's exposure to such materials, to the extent that now only a few high-profile examples excite comment. The Carnegie Medal is a natural enough target, and Robert Swindell's *Stone Cold* (winner in 1996) about serial killing among the homeless, and Melvin Burgess's *Junk* (winner in 1997) about teenage drug addicts, roused the childhood protectionists to what looks almost like a last stand. Whereas, as Roald Dahl observed, 'in England more censorship pressures are coming from the left than the right' (West, 1988: 73), in the USA (especially) the right wing have been instrumental in harrying writers who portray anything 'deviant' – from men washing up to the theory of evolution. In 1999 Rowling's Harry Potter books were among the 'most challenged', on the grounds that they portrayed witchcraft in a favourable light.

But, as we have seen, things have not changed. The reflection that Kipling's *Stalky and Co* (1900) has similar brutality levels and an equally brutal underlying ideology as *The Chocolate War*, is not usually mentioned (perhaps to perpetuate the myth that civilization has in some way advanced over the century). Similarly, the thing that differentiates *Forever* from thousands of stories for girls is not so much its explicitness, but its *lack* of passion. The twenty-first-century reader of twentieth-century girls' school stories that feature girl chums having passionate affairs (see Cadogan and Craig, 1986), or encounter the perfervid romance of a book like Eleanor Farjeon's *Martin Pippin in the Apple Orchard* (1921), may be led by political correctness to assume that their grandmothers were blissfully innocent or ignorant: the truth of the matter may be rapidly becoming unknowable.

The thesis of past innocence does not hold up if we consider the adult bestsellers of eighty years ago (for example, E. M. Hull's *The Sheikh*, 1921), or the power of the *in*explicit. One aspect of the (potential) subversiveness of children's literature may be that, as with the literature of other downtrodden groups, its subversiveness exists in passing its messages without the knowledge of the ruling elite.

Such is the confusion over this issue that a writer like Roald Dahl is, on the whole, praised for an oeuvre that is as savage as that of any nineteenth-century writer; and series such as the blatantly sexist Sweet Valley High or the blatantly violent Point Horror are sold in their millions, extensively in the UK at school book fairs within schools. All of this may of course

indicate ignorance about the books, or lack of concern, or a tacit endorse-
ment of the attitudes in the books.

In respect of content, then, children's literature (and public perception
of it) is in a state of near-terminal confusion. It is one thing to agree with
Edward Ardizzone's dictum that 'if no hint of the hard world comes into
these books, then I am not sure that we are playing fair' (quoted in Hunt,
1989: 16), but another to establish how fair we should be. Concepts of childhood ebb and flow, and concepts of acceptable realism ebb and flow with
them. For example, after thirty years of fighting for the right to warn their
children through fiction of what is 'out there', American liberals are now
confronted with a right wing that believes that ignorance is the best defence
and that knowledge *per se* corrupts.

Gender, Politics and Ideology

As we have seen, children's literature (like all other literatures) reflects – must
reflect – the culture that surrounds/permeates it. Gender is a central example.
Storytelling, reading, writing, publishing, disseminating and criticizing
children's literature have been primarily a female preserve, and so the her/
history of the form might well be – and probably should be – completely
redrawn.

In respect of gender, the conventional history of children's literature
follows the pattern of adult literary history; the major influences (and the
biggest sellers) who were women, have become invisible (although, as
children's literature criticism tends to short-circuit adult critical procedures,
it may be belatedly learning from them). Just as the many British female
novelists of the eighteenth century have been 'buried' beneath the 'big four'
of Richardson, Fielding, Sterne and Smollett, so the hundreds of female
writers of nineteenth-century children's books have been largely ignored in
favour of Carroll, Kingsley, Macdonald and Kipling. A female history and
a female poetics of the subject would be, rather than revolutionary, a truer
reflection of the situation.

I am probably not the only academic to people a university children's
literature course with the 'great writers' (male) of the nineteenth century,
or the 'great writers' (male) of the twentieth – Grahame, Milne, Ransome,
Garner, William Mayne, and even Dahl – in the knowledge that these writers
may well carry more weight with validating committees than a female roster.
And with the best (male and radical) will in the world, the book you are

reading may well reflect this. Only comparatively recently has criticism turned its attention to eighteenth-century pioneers such as Barbauld, Cooper, Edgeworth, Trimmer and Wollstonecraft, or the prolific nineteenth-century writers such as Alcott, Burnett, Charlesworth, Molesworth, Nesbit and Stretton, and the creators of some of the major series, characters and individual key books of the twentieth century, such as Brazil, Cooper, Garnett, Geras, Le Guin, Norton, Pearce, Rowling, Storr, Travers, Ure, Voight, Wilder and even Blyton. (If the absence of forenames in that list caused any difficulty, then I consider my point well made!)

The whole question of how far gender is inexorably bound up with children's literature is discussed under the appropriate heading, but at this point we might reflect on these two views by John Goldthwaite:

> There are too many women in children's books, and far too many holding down editorial positions. This imbalance of male and female sensibilities might have been accepted in 1919, when Macmillan put together the world's first juvenile department, and, under the delusion that children's books belonged to the ladies, gave it over to one; but there is no excuse for it today.

and

> In this henpecked world, no one speaks the unspeakable: that, with the exception of Beatrix Potter [sic], every great children's novel was written by a man, and nearly all of them by a man with little or no professional interest in children or their literature. (Goldthwaite, 1980: 396, 398)

It takes a writer like Ursula K. Le Guin to approach this kind of attitude, which is of course deeply political: as she says, 'The deepest foundation of the order of oppression is gendering, which names the male normal, dominant, active, and the female other, subject, passive. To begin to imagine freedom, the myths of gender, like the myths of race, have to be exploded and discarded' (Le Guin, 1993: 24).

And gender, of course, is political. Le Guin continues:

> Oh, they say, what a shame, Le Guin has politicized her delightful fantasy world, Earthsea will never be the same.
> I'll say it won't. The politics were there all along, the hidden politics of the hero-tale, the spell you don't know you're living under until you cast it off. (Ibid.: 24)

It should be clear that, far from inhabiting some unworldly, unfallen plane, children's literature is not only *necessarily* infused with and part of the ideological structure of our world, but it is more prone to manipulation than most. This is naturally more obvious in retrospect or at some other kind of remove: the specific social and political ploys of a Mrs Sherwood or a G. A. Henty are clear, the ideological structure which underpins and motivates them relatively easy to deconstruct (from where *I* stand). And assessments change: Eve Garnett's portrait of the worthy working classes, *The Family from One End Street* (1937) and its sequels, was initially seen as a break-through – a documentary that pushed back the borders of children's literature; it has since been condemned as patronizing and untrue – which merely demonstrates that ideology is the air we breathe.

Thus *every* entry in this book is concerned, implicitly, with some ideological standpoint, some matrix of tensions between what the text is saying, assuming and disguising. The matrix includes the concept of childhood and its disappearance (see Postman, 1982), matters of control and freedom (which come into sharp focus with writers like Dahl), and matters of explicit politics, racism, censorship and so on. In 1934 Geoffrey Trease had some difficulty in placing his politically radical *Bows Against the Barons*; now, one might be forgiven for thinking that almost every new book deals with a political issue. Writers with an overtly political agenda include James Watson, whose *Justice of the Dagger* (1998) has the background of the Indonesian occupation of East Timor, and Martin Waddell (as Catherine Sefton), dealing with contemporary Northern Ireland in books such as *Starry Night* (1986).

Internationalism

Children's literature sees itself as international, as if there were an international republic of childhood (another romantic notion). There are flourishing international organizations which emphasize the similarities of childhood and the similar concerns of adults, notably IBBY (International Board on Books for the Young), IRSCL (International Research Society for Children's Literature) and ChLA (Children's Literature Association). Conscious efforts are made to co-operate academically, educationally and commercially: books on English-language children's literature are more likely to include reference to, say, *Emil and the Detectives, The Story of Babar, Madeline, Heidi* and *Bambi* (as live, integrated texts, rather than as 'influences'), than their adult equivalents.

Yet internationalism as a liberal, democratic movement needs to be treated with some caution: translation, notably, has been largely one-way traffic from English. Whereas as many as 70 per cent of books for children produced in France are translations into French, fewer than 1 per cent of English-language books are translations. Historically, of course, translated books have been extremely important, both in general terms with folk- and fairy-tales and with specific titles. Collections such as *Arabian Nights Entertainments* (translated 1706–21) and the fairy-tales of Madame d'Aulnoy (first translated 1699, 1707) and Charles Perrault's *Histories, or Tales of Times Past. Told by Mother Goose* (translated 1729) were gradually adopted by (or absorbed into, or taken over by) British culture and, increasingly, thought of as 'for children'. The same is true of the work of the Grimms, Hans Andersen and others in the nineteenth century.

The question is then, how far is all this an innocent traffic, and how far does it represent invasive colonialism? As Heather Scutter notes,

> How are we to write histories of children's literature now that the world has turned on its axis? The cultural maps we write can no longer assume imperial supremacies by emptying out huge portions of the written world, rendering them alien, irrelevant, invisible, and inscrutable. Is it possible any longer to construct a global history, to survey the parameters of a 'field' of literature in space and time, synchronically and diachronically. . . . Two antipathetic but deeply linked urges seem evident: the one, the need to collect, amass, substantiate a body of evidence to . . . make material available; the other the drive to disturb that very body of evidence, to dismember it. . . . (Scutter, 1997: 22)

To present readers with the field as it exists – to present the corpus for admiration, resuscitation or dismemberment – is, from any genuinely radical point of view, merely to sustain the status quo. On the other hand, to rethink a subject requires a certain critical mass of the knowledgeable and enthusiastic, and this book aims to help in developing that critical mass – even in reaction to its premises. To re-imagine a subject is to re-imagine significances, and every entry in this guide can and should be challenged: they must, however, be challenged for significance, and the question then is, significance to whom? Which brings us back to the problem of audience with which I opened my introduction.

Bibliography

Adams, Gillian 1998: 'Medieval Children's Literature: Its Possibility and Actuality.' *CL*, 26, 1–24.

Connell, Jolyon 2000: Editorial. *The Week*, 247, 3.

Goldthwaite, John 1980: 'Notes on the Children's Book Trade: All is Not Well in Tinsel Town.' In Egoff, Stubbs and Ashley 1980: 389–404.

Hunt, Peter 1989: 'Edward Ardizzone's *Little Tim and the Brave Sea Captain*: An Art of Contrasts.' In Nodelman, Perry (ed.) 1989: 14–21.

Pratchett, Terry 1995: 'Let There Be Dragons.' *Books for Keeps* 83, 6–7. Reprinted in Egoff, Stubbs, Ashley and Sutton 1996: 201–5.

Scutter, Heather 1997: 'Hunting for History: Children's Literature Outside, Over There, and Down Under.' *ARIEL: A Review of International English Literature*, 28 (1), 22–36.

Smith, Louisa (ed.) 1998: 'The Great Collectors.' *LU*, 22 (3), 277–337.

Wooden, Warren W. 1986: *Children's Literature of the English Renaissance*. Lexington: University Press of Kentucky.

Writers

Janet Ahlberg (1944–1997) and Allan Ahlberg (1938–)

The children's picture book, that most underrated of modes, has produced few allusionists to match the Ahlbergs. Their work has exploited inter-textuality in an area which, it might have been assumed, was intended for readers incapable of appreciating it, and has experimented with the relationships between word, illustration and the developing reader.

The process began with *Jeremiah in the Dark Woods* (1977), an illustrated text rather than a picture book, in which Jeremiah, in pursuit of tarts stolen from his mother, encounters characters borrowed from folk- and fairy-tale, including the three bears. This approach was continued in *Each Peach Pear Plum* (1978), where the complex illustration to each rhyme features the next character to be rhymed about: 'Three Bears out hunting / I spy Baby Bunting / Baby Bunting fast asleep / I spy Bo-Peep . . .' This kind of ingenuity culminated in *The Jolly Postman* (1986) and its two sequels. The format of these books – a story punctuated with items of mail (in built-in envelopes) – raises questions about how texts are experienced; several different forms of text, with different narrators and narratees are combined into one, and all the texts themselves assume a wide knowledge of the genres of folk-tale, fairy-tale, nursery rhyme and books in general. In *The Jolly Postman*, for example, the Postman delivers a copy of Princess Cinderella's memoirs (complete with its own ISBN) to the palace. The letters are widely varied: in an envelope addressed to 'B. B. Wolf Esq. c/o Grandma's Cottage, Horner's Corner' and on the letterhead 'Meeny, Miny, Mo & Co., Solicitors. Ally O Buildings, Toe Lane', we find:

Dear Mr Wolf,
We are writing to you on behalf of our client, Miss Riding-Hood, concerning her grandma. Miss Hood tells us that you are presently occupying her grandma's cottage and wearing her grandma's clothes without this lady's permission.

Please understand that if this harassment does not cease, we will call in the Official Woodcutter, and – if necessary – all the King's horses and all the King's men.

On a separate matter, we must inform you that Messrs. Three Little Pigs Ltd. are now firmly resolved to sue for damages . . . and all this huffing and puffing will get you nowhere.

But this sample pales beside some in the later books, as it has merely six (?) different intertextual references. As the books progress through to *The Jolly Pocket Postman* (1995), allusions become more complex and (in reference to period items) perhaps more adult-oriented: *The Jolly Pocket Postman* involves the hero in the worlds of Carroll's Alice and Baum's Dorothy, and contains a tiny book postulating an alternative narrative (*If The Tyre Had Not Been Flat*), which itself contains a pocket – containing a postcard from Alice and Dorothy. The almost relentless intellectual ingenuity is balanced by the whimsicality of the detailed illustrations.

The same is true of *It Was a Dark and Stormy Night* (1993), which could be used on any theoretical course on the nature of narrative, as the hero tells the tale that he is in. *Peepo!* (1981) is an excellent visual guide to social history and popular culture during the Second World War in the UK: life is seen from a baby's point of view, and no specific reference is made to the detailed portrait of a period.

The Baby's Catalogue (1982) and *Starting School* (1988) do much the same for the multi-ethnic, multicultural Britain of the 1980s. Each is as close to a 'single-address' book as it is theoretically possible to be: that is, a book which implies only the 'child' audience (rather than aiming at an adult audience at the same time). *The Baby's Catalogue* was predicated on the observation that the books most popular with pre-verbal children were mail-order catalogues, and although it does, overall, have a sequence (one day), it is designed to be (and is most likely to be) read associatively. *Starting School*, for a rather older implied audience, encompasses a primary-school term and suggests an acceptance of the textual linearity that children of a certain age have learned. Nonetheless, the Ahlbergs' constantly innovative approach provides a text that begins *before* the title page: 'Gavin and Errol and Sophie and Sushma and David and Kate and Robert and Alison are . . . [page break to title page] Starting School.'

Intelligent, richly detailed on several levels, and produced with an unusual awareness of book design and production techniques, the Ahlbergs' books demonstrate what can be achieved in the 'lowly' picture book – and, deceptive as they are, demand an intelligent and detailed response from the critics. They are, as might be expected, becoming the focus for more theoretical academic explorations, as well as remaining consistently popular with British children.

They epitomize a period in the production of picture books in which the claim that the picture book is sometimes the most innovative form was amply justified. The work of Anthony Browne, for example, strongly influenced by surrealism, provides both constant visual jokes and allusions to other artists;

latterly, to his own work. Raymond Briggs has developed the strip-cartoon into an art form of considerable complexity, which has crossed the boundary between children's and adults books with *Fungus the Bogeyman* (1978), *The Man* (1992) and the tragic *When the Wind Blows* (1983). Genuine innovations have come from John Burningham (notably *Come Away From the Water, Shirley*, 1977), Lane Smith (for Jon Scieszka's *The Stinky Cheese Man*, 1992), Chris Van Allsburg (for example, *The Mysteries of Harris Burdick*, 1985), David Weisner (*Tuesday*, 1991) and even the apparently traditionalist Shirley Hughes (*Chips and Jessie*, 1995). This experimentalism has gone side-by-side with the work of highly individual stylists such as Charles Keeping, Maurice Sendak (q.v.), David McKee, Satoshi Kitamura and Michael Foreman.

Allan Ahlberg has also worked with other illustrators, perhaps most notably Colin McNaughton and Fritz Wegner. His most successful books have been two collections of verse centring on school life, *Please, Mrs Butler* (1983) and *Heard it in the Playground* (1989).

Bibliography

Martin, Douglas 1989: *The Telling Line: Essays on Fifteen Contemporary Book Illustrators.* London: Julia MacRae.

Stephens, John 1991: ' "Did I Tell You about the Time I Pushed the Brothers Grimm off Humpty Dumpty's Wall?" Metafictional Strategies for Constituting the Audience as Agent in the Narratives of Janet and Allan Ahlberg.' In Michael Stone (ed.), *Children's Literature and Contemporary Theory.* Wollongong: New Literatures Research Centre, 63–75.

Louisa May Alcott (1832–1888)

The assessment of Louisa May Alcott's career commonly hinges on *Little Women* (1868) (q.v.) and her three other books about the March children, *Good Wives* (also known as, among other things, *Little Women Part 2, Little Women Wedded*, and *Nice Wives*, 1869), *Little Men* (1871) and *Jo's Boys* (1886), but her career as a writer epitomizes the problems and status of a generation of women and women writers. Especially since the discovery of a large number of previously unknown books and stories, her biography, as much as her work, is being reassessed from new feminist and historicist viewpoints.

Her idealistic (although 'self-centred' might seem a more appropriate term to the modern reader) father, Amos Bronson Alcott, reduced his family to poverty through a series of high-minded ventures, from a school run on advanced concepts of the education of the 'whole' child, to a communal farm. While this meant that Louisa and her sisters knew some of the major American thinkers of their day, such as Henry Thoreau and Julia Ward Howe (they were especially close to the Emersons, whose daughter Louisa tutored for a time), it also meant that first her mother and then Louisa had to be the breadwinners of the family. The sympathetic portrayal of Bronson Alcott as Mr March in *Little Women* might therefore seem surprising; in relation to the acceptance of (or suppressed rejection of) patriarchal dominance, it is very suggestive. Louisa's highly productive work-space in (the preserved) Orchard House at Concord, Massachusetts is cramped compared with Bronson's unproductive study, a fact that has not escaped contemporary critics such as Lissa Paul. Paul's conclusion is respect for Louisa's

> ability to have it both ways: to appear to be supporting the patriarchal order of her own time (and so earn money in an act of subversion of that order), and still to communicate her own desire for autonomy, her own creativity, across time and across space. (Paul, 1998: 54)

Louisa tutored and sewed and wrote anonymous dime novels, teaching herself to be ambidextrous in order to maintain her output (of over 270 items). After a period of nursing during the Civil War (1862–3) she published *Hospital Sketches* and *On Picket Duty* (1864). In September 1867 her publisher, Niles, asked her to become the editor of a journal for children, *Merry's Magazine*, and to write a book for girls. Her diary reads: 'Said I'd try. Began work at once on both. Didn't like either.' The contract she was given for 6.66 per cent of purchase price eventually made her fortune when sales accelerated on the publication of *Little Women Part II*, although she continued to write prolifically until her death.

In *Little Women* and its sequels, Alcott took some of the key features of contemporary romance (middle-class benevolence, the virtuous death, the safely iconoclastic female hero) and blended them with quite complex characterizations and some mild (to the modern eye) feminist thinking. The books are, nonetheless, rooted in evangelical thought: Jerry Griswold (1992: 156–66) points out that *Little Women* (especially) is a series of contrivances intended to humble the characters, and that an atmosphere of self-reproach pervades the text.

Alcott's mild radicalism is perhaps best seen in the third book of the series, *Little Men*, which shows Jo March as a successful educationalist and career woman, yet still the dutiful and supportive wife.

However, 'advanced' ideas of education are explored and perhaps satirized in the figure of Dr Alex, Rose Campbell's uncle and guardian in *Eight Cousins* (1875). Alcott's effectually (if not intentionally) shrewd conservatism – shown, for example, in the traditional assumption that the ultimate goal for a woman is marriage – undercuts (again, to the modern eye) the forcefulness of Rose's radical suffragette views in the sequel, *Rose in Bloom* (1876). *An Old-Fashioned Girl* (1870) also explores aspects of female education and criticizes contemporary culture; this was a common theme among evangelical writers, although Alcott suggests that there can be a more liberal motivation for such criticism.

Under the Lilacs (1878) and the fourth 'March' novel, *Jo's Boys*, show considerable diminution of her originality, and the latter signals clearly Alcott's disengagement from her characters.

Alcott is particularly interesting to the historian of children's literature criticism as, since the 1970s, academia has appropriated her as a suitable case for treatment. Her gothic fiction has been rescued and republished; her biography and her feminist credentials have been extensively re-examined. In one sense, this demonstrates the de-academicizing of the academy: the need to take into account widely read but 'uncanonical' texts, but it is also proving to be a remarkable attempt to 'deconstruct' attitudes that have long been irrelevant. To discover the independently minded writer of lurid thrillers behind an icon of American respectability and female submission is, to say the least, refreshing. To see, as Paul (1998: 54) calls her, 'a "foremother" of feminist literature' in a writer so long regarded as a model for conservative values, is radically refreshing.

Bibliography

Keyser, Elizabeth Lennox 1993: *Whispers in the Dark: The Fiction of Louisa May Alcott*. Knoxville: University of Tennessee Press.
MacDonald, Ruth K. 1983: *Louisa May Alcott*. Boston: Twayne.
Stern, Madeline B. 1984: *Critical Essays on Louisa May Alcott*. Boston: G. K. Hall.

Edward Ardizzone (1900–1979)

The period between the two world wars saw the birth of the modern picture book, with an immensely rich and varied output from author/artists such as Wanda Gág (*Millions of Cats*, 1928), Kathleen Hale (*Orlando the*

Marmalade Cat, 1939), 'Hergé' (Tintin from 1921) and Robert Lawson (*Story of Ferdinand*, 1936) – and this is quite apart from the development of the American comic book with Superman and Batman, or the cartoons of Walt Disney.

To pick a representative figure is a fairly arbitrary exercise, but Edward Ardizzone was both of pivotal importance for the British picture book and also pioneering in his manipulation of new production techniques.

There were important predecessors: William Nicholson's *Clever Bill* (1926) is widely regarded as a masterpiece of the early lithographic technique, and Jean de Brunhoff's *L'Histoire de Babar le Petit Éléphant* (1931), which came into English in 1934 in large-format volumes using high-quality photo offset-lithography, demonstrated the picture book's true potential. But it was artists like Ardizzone and the experimental Polish team of Jan Lewitt and George Him (Diana Ross's *The Little Red Engine Gets a Name*, 1942) who genuinely popularized the new styles and technique.

Ardizzone was a prolific book illustrator, whose pictures were particularly effective in evoking nostalgia (often with rural settings). His children's books portray a timeless world, located vaguely around the 1920s in the small seaside towns he knew as a boy, a factor which may account for his success with adults (who, of course, are the primary buyers of books for children).

Ardizzone's first success, *Little Tim and the Brave Sea Captain* (1936), was originally told to his children and printed in the USA. The first edition is something of a curiosity: due to problems with drying the ink, it appeared not as a 'standard' 32-page book, but as a 64-page book printed on one side of the paper only. (It was redrawn in 1953 to match a standard format of alternate pen-and-colour and pen-and-monochrome openings that Ardizzone had developed for *Tim to the Rescue*, 1949.) Critics are unanimous that his melding of text and illustration, his bold, flowing lines and his effective use of 'lighting' effects demonstrated the 'dynamic' possibilities of the picture book. Ardizzone himself looked back to what he called the 'robust splendours' of satirists such as Cruikshank and late nineteenth-century picture-book artists such as Randolph Caldecott.

His plots often hinge on loneliness and loss as much as on adventure and danger: in *Tim All Alone* (1956) Tim returns home to find that his parents have moved away; in *Tim and Charlotte* (1951) Tim and his friend Ginger find Charlotte washed up on a beach and suffering from amnesia. Ardizzone had a robust view of children and their books:

I think we are possibly inclined, in a child's reading, to shelter him too much from the harder facts of life. Sorrow, failure, poverty, and possibly even death, if handled poetically, can surely all be introduced without hurt. After all, books for children are in a sense an introduction to the life that lies ahead of them. If no hint of the hard world comes into these books, then I am not sure that we are playing fair. (Ardizzone, 1969: 293)

He was equally unimpressed when his second book, *Lucy Brown and Mr Grimes* (1937), was a failure, especially in the USA, because Mr Grimes, an ugly old man who haunts the children's playground, is attracted to the little Lucy, and buys her an ice-cream (he later adopts her). Ardizzone dismissed the opinions of 'silly women librarians' as 'absolute nonsense' (Tucker, 1970: 24), but nevertheless, *Lucy* . . . was redrawn and modified before its reissue in 1970.

It seems clear that Ardizzone's influence was wide, especially in terms of the overall design of books. The British artist Helen Oxenbury cites him as one of her favourite artists ('that wonderful seaside atmosphere'), Faith Jaques regards him as the modern link to the great Victorian artists, and he was well-known in the USA. As Maurice Sendak put it:

With easy aplomb, Edward Ardizzone has weathered the storms of fashionable style that have shipwrecked many talented but less sturdily dedicated illustrators. An artist whose work harks back to the great nineteenth-century watercolorists (and to the ingeniously constructed picture books of his countryman William Nicholson), Ardizzone has perpetuated the honorable tradition of English book illustration, adding sharp strokes of humor and insight that make his work unusually fresh and immediate. (Sendak, 1988: 119)

Bibliography

Alderson, Brian 1972: 'Edward Ardizzone: a Preliminary Handlist of His Illustrated Books, 1929–70.' *The Private Library*, Second Series, 5 (1).
Ardizzone, Edward 1969: 'Creation of a Picture Book.' In Egoff, Stubbs and Ashley 1980: 289–98.
Hunt, Peter 1989: 'Edward Ardizzone's *Little Tim and the Brave Sea Captain*: An Art of Contrasts.' In Nodelman 1989: 14–21.
Sendak, Maurice 1988: *Caldecott and Co. Notes on Books and Pictures*. New York: Noonday Press/Farrar, Straus and Giroux.
Tucker, Nicholas 1970: 'Edward Ardizzone.' *CLE*, 1 (3), 21–9.
White, Gabriel 1979/1980: *Edward Ardizzone, Artist and Illustrator*. London: Bodley Head; New York: Schocken.

Quentin Blake (1932–)

In an era of outstanding stylists, Quentin Blake stands out. His style might best be described as apparently casual: he uses pen-and-ink with coloured washes, and his sketchy, wild caricatures are, more often than not, remarkably subtle. (His working methods belie the casualness.) The overall impression of his books is of great integrity and intelligence, and of a benign, and *seriously* playful, uncondescending view of the world. He is also a not-inconsiderable theorist, concentrating on the balance of words and pictures: 'illustrating, as an activity distinct from drawing, demands a sense of what you simply mustn't do' (Moss, 1986: 100). Similarly, the overall design of the books is basic: 'The underlying consideration . . . is . . . that the total effect of a book is of a complete sequence of drawings, not an assortment of individual drawings assembled together' (Beetles, 1996: 6).

He has produced many picture-books with John Yeoman, perhaps the best of which have been the bucolic *Our Village* (1988) and the satirical *The Puffin Book of Improbable Records* (1975); he has also illustrated J. P. Martin's *Uncle* series, Michael Rosen's poems, and Nils-Olof Franzén's 'Agarton Sax' series (and around 200 others).

His most famous collaboration has been with Roald Dahl. This began with *The Enormous Crocodile* in 1978; Blake subsequently illustrated or re-illustrated all of Dahl's children's books. In some ways it is a curious association, the contrast between Dahl's savage and cynical vision and Blake's more gentle and ironic one producing, overall, books that are the more balanced for it.

It could be argued that Blake's collaboration with Russell Hoban produced one of the twentieth century's masterpieces for children, *How Tom Beat Captain Najork and his Hired Sportsmen* (1974), in which Hoban's deadpan prose and Blake's sly images combine to produce a composite text which remains on the child's side. Blake's virtually incomprehensible picture accompanies Hoban's description of the game of 'womble':

> The Captain's side raked first. Tom staked. The hired sportsmen played so hard that they wombled too fast and were shaky with the rakes. Tom fooled around the way he always did, and all his stakes dropped true. When it was his turn to rake, he did not let Captain Najork and the hired sportsmen score a single rung, and at the end of the snetch he had won by six ladders.

Blake uses a similar device – of allowing the reader of the picture superiority over the characters – in *Cockatoos* (1992); as he observes, 'One of the best tools in the picture-book creator's armoury is the difference between the text and the pictures'. The eccentric professor, searching the house for his cockatoos, 'can't find any, but we can see them. . . . The pleasure is not so much in finding the birds, because that's easy, but in feeling that we have an advantage over this rather tiresome adult' (Blake, 2000: 60). This may sound simple, but in Blake's hands the idea of multiple viewpoints is taken to virtuoso lengths.

Increasingly, his own texts have nurtured the gentle and the eccentric, especially in the characters in *Quentin Blake's Nursery Rhyme Book* (1983), and in *Mr Magnolia* (1980), *Mrs Armitage on Wheels* (1987) and *Mrs Armitage and the Big Wave* (1998). While books of great energy and charm, such as *All Join In* (1990) and *Clown* (1995), have brought him major awards, my own favourites lie in his more reflective work. He has produced what are in effect novellas (if the combined pictures-and-word texts are considered) with *The Story of the Dancing Frog* (1984) and *The Green Ship* (1997). In these, it is the relationships between children and adults, and their complex perceptions of past and present that are important. It is, as Blake has said, easy 'to read children's books wrongly – by which I mean quickly, without exploring the possibilities' (Blake, 2000: 62). Blake's surface style positively encourages quick readings, but to read quickly is to misread a master.

Quentin Blake has been Head of the Illustration Department and is now visiting Professor at the Royal College of Art, London. He was appointed the first British 'Children's Laureate' in May 1999.

Bibliography

Beetles, Chris, Ltd 1996: *Quentin Blake*. London: Chris Beetles.

Blake, Quentin 2000: 'The Strange Story of the Unidentical Twins: The Patrick Hardy Lecture.' *Signal*, 91, 52–63.

Martin, Douglas 1989: *The Telling Line: Essays on Fifteen Contemporary Book Illustrators*. London: Julia MacRae.

Moss, Elaine 1986: *Part of the Pattern: A Personal Journey Through the World of Children's Books 1960–1985*. London: Bodley Head.

Judy Blume (1938–)

Charting the critical career of the most famous (or notorious) of American writers for teenagers of the 1970s and 1980s (even, perhaps, of the twentieth century), it is difficult not to conclude that she was ahead of her time.

Her third book, *Are You There God, It's Me, Margaret* (1970), broke some well-entrenched taboos by featuring a central character concerned with (although not, as some critics might have one believe, obsessed by) menstruation and other aspects of adolescent female development. Since then, Blume has become one of the most regularly challenged and censored authors in the USA (a 'challenge' according to the American Library Association Office for Intellectual Freedom, is a formal written complaint to a school or library). In 1999, for example, *Blubber* (1974) was the third most-challenged book (J. K. Rowling's Harry Potter books headed the list), on the grounds of offensive language and unsuitability for the readership age-group.

Blume's books for younger children, such as *Tales of a Fourth Grade Nothing* (1972), mildly sardonic portraits of American 'middle-class' life, have largely escaped the criticisms levelled at her books for teenagers. In these, however, Blume took on subjects that made certain sections of the American public feel very uncomfortable, such as masturbation (*Deenie*, 1973), bullying (*Blubber*), divorce (*It's Not The End of the World*, 1972) and, most notoriously of all, full-frontal sex (*Forever*, 1975). *Tiger Eyes* (1981), on the other hand, which centres on a bloody murder, has met with general approval.

Discussions of Blume's books, as a result, tend to be concerned with what might be called extra-literary matters, and she has become the target of the right-wing 'moral majority' movement in the USA, as well as of local censorship. Blume has proved to be an intelligent and articulate defender of her position (encouraged, no doubt, by her huge sales and remarkable numbers of supportive letters from young readers). She takes the view that 'adults are so uncomfortable about their own sexuality that they can't begin to deal with their children's', and that 'Adults have always been suspicious of books that kids like . . . many adults do not trust children (West, 1988: 10, 11). As a consequence, perhaps, she has had a large and enthusiastic following; her collection *Letters to Judy: What Your Kids Wish They Could Tell You* (1986) demonstrates (possibly) that her books fill a need. They are, in effect, exemplars of the way in which popular culture operates, genuinely subverting received cultural standards.

Forever, with its almost mechanistic description of teenagers learning about sex, was written in deliberate reaction to novels which took a moralizing attitude to sex. Ironically, it was written at a time of relative sexual freedom: it is unlikely that *Forever* would find a publisher today as it is too explicit. The 'moral majority' now appears to take the view that ignorance is the best defence, and it is clear that *Forever* owed at least some of its success to the straightforward technical detail it provides, rather than to any eroticism (which, many adult readers find, it singularly lacks).

Much of the condemnation of the book rests upon the simplistic assumption that writing about something is tantamount to encouraging it; if this were or could be true, criticism of *Forever* seems to be wide of the mark. Overall, the book reaches a conservative conclusion: that emotional involvement is a desirable prerequisite for physical involvement.

More liberal critics have levelled two equally emotive criticisms at Blume. The first is that it is sad that such solipsistic and obsessive behaviour seems now to be endemic, let alone that sex and romance seem to have become disconnected. Such a lament merely demonstrates the gap between the world as it is and the world as a certain kind of critic wishes it to be. As Nicholas Tucker (1994: 180) observed, 'there is . . . a deeper rejection of the whole concept of childhood as a time for intense sexual curiosity. . . . It remains a side . . . of childhood that we do not much want to think about, and children's writers who meet such interests at least half-way have to accept the aggressive critical consequences'. Second, such critics lament the relentless teenage demotic that Blume uses: not only do all the narrators sound much the same, but they fail to distinguish between the trivial and the significant.

These criticisms seem to me also to be wide of the mark. Blume has not been acknowledged as the genuine realist she is; the teenage world can very well be solipsistic; significance is something imposed upon life by the novelist (or the optimistic adult), not distinguished by a fifteen year old. In both her view of the world and how she expresses it, Blume has produced a remarkably accurate portrait of the age, and has written books authentically *of* adolescence. To argue that teenagers are impoverished by hearing their own voices on the page is to argue against most literature!

Thus, when this ageing, middle-class, adult, British male (with three teenage daughters) reads Judy Blume's books with as open a mind as possible, he is struck by how affecting and dramatic they can be, especially *Are You There God* . . . , largely because the voice seems authentic, and the good and the bad, the significant and the insignificant, the exciting and the banal, are all described as equally important. The effect (especially of the apparently inconsequential conversations) is ultimately mesmeric and may well give an excellent and much neglected insight into the teenage reader's mind. Blume, as Tucker noted (as an implied fault), 'does not produce novels that both adults and children can share and treasure' (Tucker, 1994: 81), but that is precisely the point. The uncompromising single-audience focus in effect makes Blume's books for teenagers inaccessible (that is, trivial and boring) and (therefore) dangerous to many adult readers: hence the silence of criticism before them.

Other writers who might be mentioned in the same breath as Blume, as often witty chroniclers of American teenage angst – such as Paul Zindel, Norma Klein, Paula Danziger and Lois Lowry – should not be confused with the hundreds of writers of the 1980s and 1990s who ventured into the 'problem' novel (sometimes unkindly called the 'anorexic' novel). These (predominantly) first-person narratives built stories around medical and social problems, often with deliberate bibliotherapeutic intent. The difficulty with many such books is that while they appear to be dealing with serious problems, they provide resolutions which accord more with wish-fulfilment than probability. The problem is that unlike Blume and her peers, that wish-fulfilment is often adult wish-fulfilment imposed upon a construction of childhood.

Bibliography

Tucker, Nicholas 1994: 'My Affair with Judy.' In Chris Powling (ed.), *The Best of Books for Keeps*. London: Bodley Head, 177–81.

Enid [Mary] Blyton (1897–1968)

Interest in Enid Blyton – beyond regarding her merely as a sociological phenomenon – must hinge on two possibilities. Do we see her books as simple texts which must be read simply and which therefore have no intellectual influence except to inculcate bad literary habits? Or do we regard them as *necessarily* complex, the way they are read as unfathomable, and necessarily highly influential because they are among the most-read books in the history of the world?

I would argue that the writer who is most read by most children (she is commonly rated as one of the top five bestselling authors of all time) is the one whose attitudes and politics are most likely to be stamped (through subconscious osmosis) into the national consciousness. By this calculation Enid Blyton, with her middle-class, middle-English, interwar ideology, her shrewd commercial mind, and her striking personal life, has to be taken seriously.

In so far as she is taken seriously (from the literary point of view as a curiosity of popular culture), interest in her is largely statistical. She was among the most prolific of all authors, producing between 1922 and 1968 something over 600 titles, and taking offence when it was assumed that she was a syndicate. One of the few authors to maintain (and even increase) her output during the Second World War, she was routinely capable of producing a 60,000-word novel in a week, and extremely shrewd in designing and marketing her series (notably the Noddy books). Since her death, her books have been constantly reprinted and revised (according to prevailing political orthodoxies) and augmented by other authors, notably Claude Volier, whose 'The Five' series is translated from the French. In 1996, when the Blyton family sold the rights to her work to the Trocadero group for £17 million, Blyton began to be marketed in the USA, with a heavily revised version of her Noddy series and extensive merchandising. Her sales figures – a median estimate of six million copies a year – show no signs of diminishing and her books have an apparently permanent and dominant place in the retail bookshops of the UK. A recent major research project, *Children's Reading Choices*, demonstrates that she remains the second most popular author after Dahl, and her Famous Five books remain the most popular series of all (Hall and Coles, 1999: 17–55).

Although her reputation for being banned from British libraries is more a matter of legend than fact, her work was frowned upon in the 1950s because she dominated the market, and in the 1960s because she was racist and sexist (which is undeniable). More recently, she has been rehabilitated on the grounds that her books contain 'traditional values' and are less unacceptable than some contemporary writing. (The Enid Blyton Society – for adults – even called itself for a time the Enid Blyton Literary Society.)

Blyton has become a literary byword for cheap, undemanding writing ('Noddy-language') with repetitive language structures and plots, and conservative politics which place males above females, and the English middle classes above everyone else. Blyton also stands accused of reducing any material (myths, legends, the natural world, the Bible, Jean de Brunhoff's *The Story of Babar*) to cosy innocuousness. For example, her fairies are exactly those nineteenth-century 'little buzzflies with butterfly wings, and gauze petticoats, and shiny stars in their hair' that Kipling's Puck attacked so scornfully in 1906 in *Puck of Pook's Hill*.

On the face of it, these accusations are justified, and doubtless Blyton would have seen them as compliments. In 1949, she wrote that her books

> give children a feeling of security as well as pleasure – they know that they
> will never find anything wrong, hideous, horrible, murderous or vulgar in my

books, although there is always plenty of excitement, mystery and fun. . . .
I am not out only to tell stories. . . . I am out to inculcate decent thinking,
loyalty, honesty, kindliness, and all the things that children *should* be taught.
(Stoney, 1992: 212)

This is, of course, a fine piece of writing to deconstruct from our superior
stance some fifty years on, because many adults might read not only petty
snobbishness and demeaning power-plays on the surface of her books, but
disturbingly sadistic and sexually questionable attitudes beneath the surface.
(There is, perhaps, the need to refute the apparently infinitely repeated plaint
that 'children would not see or understand such things.' There are two
simple answers: the first is, how do we know? The second is, if we reject
any possible negative influences, how do we account for the effectiveness of
positive influences?)

In short, Blyton does not and indeed *could* not write 'simple' texts. The
fact that she often *tells* rather than *shows* is sometimes taken as reducing
the amount of imaginative work required of her readers, but it does not
simplify the reader–narrator relationship. Her style is not as 'crude' as might
be assumed. Consider the variation in the way in which this character's
thoughts and perceptions are mediated to the reader – directly, indirectly,
tagged and untagged, and using free indirect discourse in which it is not
clear whether we are reading the character or the narrator:

> He looked up at the tower. A small, forlorn face was looking out of the window
> there. Julian's heart jumped and beat fast. That must be poor old George up
> there. He wondered if she had seen them. He hoped not, because she would
> know that he and Dick had been captured and she would be very upset.
>   Where was Timmy? There seemed no sign of him. But wait a minute – what
> was that lying inside what looked like a summer house on the opposite side
> of the yard? *Was* it Timmy? (*Five Fall into Adventure*, 1950)

She often builds the narrator into the text as an intrusive persona, by turns
'jolly' and insistently moralizing. This has been widely derided, but Blyton
writes uncompromisingly for a single audience, not winking over the children's heads at other adults for approbation: it is the 'transferred storyteller'
who forms the adult part of the contract, not the adult reader.

Taking Blyton seriously – and taking the concept of the series seriously –
quickly demonstrates the complexity of ideas beneath the apparently simple
surface. David Rudd (1995: 194) has argued cogently that the 'laundering'

of Blyton's books, notably to rid them of their sexism, has ignored the tensions in Blyton's work that 'mirrors what is still the gender reality of many children'. A good deal of critical fun has been generated by contemplating the (unconscious?) sexual symbolism of the books – lighthouses, caves, underground rivers, etc. – but that does not remove it. Some of her repetitive symbolism, such as the stress upon positively orgiastic amounts of food, may be put down to sociological impulses; others, such as her idealization of the absent father, may lead into biographical and psychological waters. But what of the masks, the caravans, the wild landscapes and the secure bedrooms? They may be potent symbols mangled by the mill of popular culture, but that does not make them any the less potent.

Accounting for Blyton's success is also a perennial game, usually as fruitless as it is thoughtless and pointless. It may be a public service to short-circuit the process by listing those factors generally adduced: she provides vocabulary, characterization and plotting at a level appropriate to the mechanical reading skills of her audience; she understands attention span; her series books are predictable and thus not disturbing; her characters are egocentric, like her readers, and even her apparently realistic books are fantasies; her narratives are always resolved; they have clear, simple, child-centred morality; adults are simplified or caricatured, and marginalized; there is plenty of food and no sex; settings are stylized; there is a good deal of mild animism; and she seems to have been totally committed and sincere . . . and so on.

The fact that tens of thousands of other authors have had exactly the same attributes – and the same marketing skills – but have not reached Blyton's heights does not seem to trouble formula-spotters. As with many literary 'greats', Blyton was in the right (or wrong) place at the right time. She has been well-served by the snowball effect in publishing and by the chronic conservatism of children's book retailers: good brand names live a long time.

She has naturally been the target of a good deal of witty invective: Noddy has been described (in *Encounter* in 1958) as 'the most egocentric, joyless, snivelling and pious anti-hero in the history of British fiction', her prose so drained of difficulty as to have 'aesthetic anaemia', and her plots have been summed up in Eileen Colwell's famous dictum: 'what hope has a band of desperate men against four small children?' But for all that, Blyton remains both a formidable cultural figure and an enduring challenge to literary and cultural criticism.

Bibliography

Hunt, Peter 1996: 'Enid Blyton.' In Hettinga and Schmidt 1996: 50–71.
Ray, Sheila 1982: *The Blyton Phenomenon* London: Deutsch.
Rudd, David 1995: 'Five Have a Gender-ful Time: Blyton, Sexism, and the Infamous Five.' *CLE*, 26 (3) 185–96.
Rudd, David 2000: *Enid Blyton and the Mystery of Children's Literature*. London: Macmillan.
Smallwood, Imogen 1989: *A Childhood at Green Hedges*. London: Methuen.
Stoney, Barbara 1992: *Enid Blyton: A Biography*. Revised edition. London: Hodder and Stoughton.
Tucker, Nicholas with Reynolds, Kimberley (eds) 1997: *Enid Blyton: A Celebration and Reappraisal*. London: National Centre for Research in Children's Literature.

Mary Grant Bruce (1878–1958)

It took some years for Australian writing to find an individual voice. The first books set in Australia, by writers such as W. H. G. Kingston and G. A. Henty (q.v.), were routine adventure stories, and the setting was more or less arbitrary (Henty at one point confused Aborigine dialect with American Negro stage dialect). 'The first work written in the Colony expressly for Children', as its preface claims, was *A Mother's Offering to her Children: by a Lady, Long Resident in New South Wales* (1841) by Charlotte Barton (1797–1862). Although it followed a very old English model of (didactic) dialogue between mother and daughters, this book contains enough original material, anecdotes and descriptions of natural history to set it apart. The account given of the Aborigines is a fascinating mixture of racial superiority, fear and misunderstanding, demonstrating the sometimes uneasy relationship between the European settlers and their surroundings.

An example of this is William [Still] Stitt Jenkins's *The Lost Children* (1864), a verse account of a true story: the three Duff children, Isaac (9), Jane (7) and Frank (3), were lost in the bush for nine days. This fear of (and respect for) the outback has been explored by many writers, the three most well-known books being Ethel Pedley's *Dot and the Kangaroo* (1899), James Vance Marshall's *Walkabout* (1961) and Ivan Southall's *To the Wild Sky* (1967). (A similar motif appears in Canadian children's literature, for example in a romanticized form in Catherine Parr Traill's *Canadian Crusoes*, 1852.)

With greater urbanization the idea of the outback became increasingly a matter of symbol and theory, and Mary Grant Bruce's books are pivotal. For a generation of Europeans her family saga of 15 books centred upon (in a particularly literal way) the Victorian sheep station, 'Billabong', from *A Little Bush Maid* (1910) to *Billabong Riders* (1942), epitomized Australian life. It was also a celebration and in some senses a creation of a symbolic way of life for Australians themselves.

Billabong is an ideal of family and home which, as Heather Scutter (1993: 18) puts it, 'appears superficially to emblematize a crowded house of all nations, a rattle-bag of voices, and a magic pudding of creature comforts'. The roots of 'Billabong' are Australian codes of independence and 'mateship', and the books also say a great deal about the relationship of Australia and the British Empire.

A map of Billabong in later editions shows the large house with verandas, kitchen wing, dairy and office, and surrounding it, stables, paddocks, a breaking ring and stockyards, orchard, woolshed, tennis court, lagoon and creek, airfield – and an arrow pointing to the goldmine. In an atmosphere of enlightened paternalism, Norah Linton grows up and marries: she is individual rather than independent, enjoying male freedom and yet encapsulating a female civilizing influence. The books are robust and generally unsentimental, celebrating the idea of mateship. Although there are plenty of quintessentially Australian incidents (droughts, bushfires), the Billabong books draw – inevitably, perhaps – on the conventions of the family saga.

It is interesting to observe how the stock (and broadly comic) characters Lee Wing and Black Billy were gradually absorbed into the culture of Billabong, moving from racial (and arguably racist) stereotypes to stalwart and respected (if subordinate) partners. By the end of the series, as Brenda Niall observes, 'Billabong has . . . become a melting pot, a multi-racial community whose founding fathers are Murty O'Toole, Lee Wing and Black Billy, equal partners in a perfect society' (Niall, 1982: 174). Whether this is a genuine multiculturalism, or whether the Billabong books simply reflect the entrenchment of the white hegemony, is still being debated.

Bibliography

Niall, Brenda 1982: *Seven Little Billabongs: The World of Ethel Turner and Mary Grant Bruce*. Ringwood, Victoria: Penguin.
Scutter, Heather 1993: 'Back to *Back to Billabong*.' In Stone 1993: 18–26.

Frances Hodgson Burnett (1849–1924)

If ever the popular power of folk-tale motifs has been demonstrated – and demonstrated as appealing across the age range – then it is in the work of Frances Hodgson Burnett. Her books might almost have been included in the later section on folk-tales: they are often variants on the recurrent themes of loss, restoration, wish-fulfilment, empowerment of the disempowered, and simple and satisfying victories over evil found in those tales.

Burnett was a prolific and very successful commercial writer for much of her life; she was born in Manchester, and emigrated with her family to Tennessee in 1865: her work draws from and is designed for two different cultures.

Her first great success for children (although it was at least as successful with adults) was *Little Lord Fauntleroy* (1886), a much more robust narrative – and central character – than its reputation sometimes allows. Cedric Errol, heir to the Earl of Dorincourt, and his American mother ('Dearest') epitomize goodness and innocence; when they come to England, candour gradually demolishes the Earl's pride and prejudice.

> He leaned back against the cushions and regarded the Earl with rapt interest for a few minutes and in entire silence.
> 'I think you must be the best person in the world,' he burst forth at last. 'You are always doing good, aren't you? . . .'
> His lordship was so dumbfounded to find himself presented in such agreeable colours that he did not know exactly what to say. . . . To see each of his ugly, selfish motives changed into a good and generous one by the simplicity of a child was a singular experience.

This is one of the most potent of folk-tale devices, the power of the powerless, blended with a romantic ideal of the saving innocence of childhood. Not surprisingly, it is to be found in many bestselling children's books, perhaps most notably L. M. Montgomery's *Anne of Green Gables* (1908) (q.v.) and Eleanor Porter's *Pollyanna* (1912) (q.v.).

Beyond this, *Little Lord Fauntleroy* is crafted with great skill in narrative terms, and the character of the Earl of Dorincourt has just enough intelligent irony to shuffle the reader over the plot's increasing implausibility, and the saccharine relationship between Cedric and 'Darling'. It remains a neat fable, and like the best of popular-culture texts it at once challenges and reinforces the status quo, blurring the distinction between life and art: Cedric's long curls and velvet suits became the (frequently resented) fashion for a generation of young boys (such as A. A. Milne).

Burnett's second lasting children's book, *A Little Princess* (1905), has provided an interesting case study for textual scholars, in that it is an expanded version of a long short story, *Sara Crewe, or What Happened at Miss Minchin's* (1887), incorporating material from a stage version. This is Cinderella meets Dickens – or, at least Hesba Stretton and her city-waif novels: it is the fairy-tale crossed with the nineteenth-century social novel and flavoured with melodrama. Burnett carries it off with the aplomb of the skilled, single-focus writer: she is not making a point, she is playing (as did the folktale) on uncomplicated and unashamed emotionalism – wishes with which we can privately indulge ourselves. It is interesting that her sentimental books for adults have gone out of fashion: perhaps such fundamental emotions can only be allowed when readers are in the privileged area of the children's book.

Sara Crewe is a paragon of virtue *despite* being fabulously rich, and when her money is lost, she is turned into a drudge by the 'hard, selfish, worldly' headmistress of her school, Miss Minchin. Here Burnett thoroughly milks the riches-to-rags-to-riches theme, even if she does not go as far as the 1995 Alfonso Cuarón film version, in which Sara not only walks a precarious beam between two houses – in a storm – to escape Miss Minchin, but also has her father restored to her. Burnett, one suspects, would have enjoyed those touches because they are from the same stock of romantic melodrama which reflects (however unsubtly) human desires and fears.

The miraculous transformation by the formidable Indian servant, Ram Dass, of Sara's bare attic into a sumptuous feasting-place, her verbal triumphs over the malignant Miss Minchin (because of her natural superiority), the coincidence that those searching for her take the house next door to the school – all of these effects are professionally handled, although some readers may feel that Burnett is inclined to lay them on with a trowel. Consider the turning point of the book, where Sara, dispossessed, is sent out 'cold and hungry and tired' on errands by the cruel Miss Minchin.

> For several days it had rained continuously; the streets were chilly and sloppy and full of dreary cold mist; there was mud everywhere – sticky London mud – and over everything the pall of drizzle and fog. Of course there were several long and tiresome errands to be done – there always were on days like this – and Sara was sent out again and again, until her shabby clothes were damp through.

She finds a fourpenny-piece in the mud (through which she 'almost had to wade') and, outside the bun shop, a starving girl – 'a little figure more forlorn even than herself'; she buys some buns, and gives all but one to the girl.

> 'She is hungrier than I am,' she said to herself. 'She's starving.' But her hand trembled when she put down the fourth bun. 'I'm not starving,' she said – and she put down the fifth.

Roderick McGillis has suggested that *A Little Princess* may be fruitfully read in terms of 'the debate over women's roles within an imperial context. . . . Its interest in both social and utopian themes fits the fin de siècle concerns with a socialist encouragement of the poor and with its insistence on aesthetic experience as ameliorative' (McGillis, 1996: 15). *A Little Princess* fundamentally deals with self-respect and self-worth and the power of the imagination over cruelty, loss and loneliness. As in her other books, Burnett's ideas operate at symbolic levels rather than allegoric or specifically moral ones. This is demonstrated clearly in *The Secret Garden* (1911) (q.v.), which borrows enthusiastically from the nineteenth-century gothic romance, but blends it with an incipient feminism.

Of her other books, only *The Lost Prince* (1915) is still read, although any tension in the plot is dissipated by page two. The long short story *Editha's Burglar* (1888), about a small girl confronting a burglar ('"Don't be frightened," she said, in a soft voice. "I don't want to hurt you . . ."'), is an object-lesson in how to walk the fine line between whimsical fantasy and dangerous realism. It shows clearly how Burnett could manipulate a fashionable and sentimental view of childhood – that innocence could overcome evil – within a reasonably realistic context.

The questions that Burnett's books leave us with involve many strands of the feminist, popular culture and postcolonial debates. Centrally, are the books tales of empowerment (of the female, of the child, of the colonial worlds) or acknowledgements of the continuing *lack* of power? Does the fact that these books are romances provide hope for their readers, or does it underline the fact that the male, adult, empire hegemony cannot be defeated except by fantasy?

Bibliography

Bixler, Phyllis 1984: *Frances Hodgson Burnett*. Boston: Twayne.
McGillis, Roderick 1996: *A Little Princess: Gender and Empire*. Boston: Twayne.
Thwaite, Anne 1974: *Waiting for the Party: The Life of Frances Hodgson Burnett*. London: Secker and Warburg.

Lewis Carroll (Charles Lutwidge Dodgson) (1832–1898)

As one of Carroll's biographers, Donald Thomas, put it:

> Charles Lutwidge Dodgson is one of those figures, like Sade, who tempts every age to revalue him. The works of the Reverend Dodgson seem particularly hazardous to critics, whether the psychoanalytical school, so piteously hoaxed in the 1930s, or the later schools of sterner critical theory and practice. Such diligent hunters of the seminar room, waddling along with nets and traps in the wake of the Cheshire Cat and its companions, are apt to take a prisoner which uncannily deconstructs itself, leaving only a grin for their contemplation. (Thomas, 1996: xi)

Certainly, Carroll must be the most written about of writers for children, largely because *Alice's Adventures in Wonderland* (1865), *Through the Looking-Glass and What Alice Found There* (1871) and *The Hunting of the Snark* (1876) have been (generally) admitted to the adult canon. In children's book history, they have been credited with being the first works to avoid didacticism – to 'liberate' children's imaginations. The texture of apparent nonsense, however, seems to disguise intricate reflections and robust satires on local and national politics, mathematics and philosophy, and to reward all kinds of psychological readings. To some extent Carroll's playful and formidable intelligence appeals to the postmodern intellectual fashion; equally, his supposed relationship to children has produced considerable tensions in readings of his books.

For much of his life Dodgson/Carroll was an academic at Christ Church, Oxford University. He was an obsessive man who catalogued his own correspondence (around 100,000 items); who had a reputation as a photographer of the famous; a preference for photographing small (and scantily dressed) girls – and a sentimental tendency to fall in love with them; a man with an intense interest in political and social issues both intricately local and broadly national; and a man who was an accomplished logician and mathematician. His biographers (most notably Morton Cohen (1995) and Donald Thomas) place differing emphases on these features, and critics have generally been either divided or ambivalent about Carroll's sexual preoccupations and how they impinge on the books.

Alice's Adventures comes with its own built-in mythology. Carroll, it is generally believed, extemporized a story for the three Liddell sisters, daughters of the Dean of his college, while on a rowing picnic on the Thames at Oxford in 1862. He then wrote a 'fair copy' of the story for Alice Liddell's birthday in 1864 (this was printed in facsimile in 1886 as *Alice's Adventures Underground*). Carroll expanded the text considerably for *Alice's Adventures in Wonderland* and used (Sir) John Tenniel, a celebrated political cartoonist, as illustrator.

The book is highly episodic and consists largely of the insouciant Alice encountering a succession of outlandish and generally violent or aggressive characters. In a somewhat sentimental final chapter (in strong contrast to the rest of the book) the whole story is revealed to be a dream. The sequel, *Through the Looking-Glass*, is also cast as a dream, but is based on a game of chess: Alice's role as a pawn who (except for one brief occasion) cannot see what is happening around her, increases her isolation. The books, packed with death jokes, word games and mathematical puzzles, can be argued to be classic examples of texts that can be read on whatever level the *reader* is capable of.

The most straightforward interpretations of the books see Alice as a representative of repressed Victorian childhood: a 'luxurious captivity' – especially for girls – surrounded by irrational, rule-making and solipsistic adults. Notable are the self-satisfied philosophers, the Cheshire Cat and the hookah-smoking caterpillar, the eccentric inventor, the White Knight, and Humpty Dumpty, the proto-literary critic with his lecture on semantics and his deconstruction of the nonsense poem *Jabberwocky*. Alice has considerable trouble with size and identity, and it is not difficult to find a good deal of sexual symbolism running through the texts. And that is not to dwell on class, or the subversion of authority, or arbitrary brutality.

One level 'down' from all of that is the nihilistic sub-text, exploring anger and frustration and death. As Alice falls down the rabbit hole (towards birth, perhaps?) she muses:

'After such a fall as this, I shall think nothing of tumbling down stairs! . . . Why, I wouldn't say anything about it, even if I fell off the top of the house!' (which was very likely true).

In *Through the Looking-Glass*, Tweedledum and Tweedledee discuss, in effect, Bishop Berkeley's view that all things are ideas in the mind of God, through the threatening image of the Red King, asleep and 'dreaming' Alice: ' "If that there King was to wake," added Tweedledum, "you'd go out – bang! – just like a candle" '. However, as Humphrey Carpenter (1985: 62) observed, 'that the *Alice* books should consist . . . on their deepest level, of an exploration of violence, death and Nothingness is not in itself very surprising. Comedy tends to lead in that direction'.

Carpenter's conclusion, that Carroll created 'something that is specifically a mockery of Christian belief', leads us into a world of interpretation where the books become allegories or coded satires, or *romans-à-clef*. To take but three examples, to stand for many, Jo Elwyn Jones and J. Francis Gladstone (1998) see the books as portraying important figures, among them Walter Pater (the Carpenter), Sir Richard Owen (the Cook), F. D. Maurice (the Dormouse), Sir John Millais and the Royal Academy in 'The Voice of the Lobster', Charles Kingsley (the Mad Hatter) and W. E. Gladstone (the Unicorn). The puppy that Alice encounters in the garden is a beagle which looks very much like Charles Darwin; Alice hides behind a thistle (Thistleton Dyer was a noted biologist). The reason for Carroll's choice of an illustrator who was a nationally known political caricaturist becomes clear. John Goldthwaite (1996: 74–169) sees *Alice's Adventures* as an extended and detailed gloss on Charles Kingsley's *The Water Babies*, while John Docherty (1995) argues that Carroll's books and George MacDonald's books were complex responses and ripostes to each other over forty years. These are, comparatively, uneccentric interpretations, and it is clear that the texts can support them with little strain.

Almost any chapter could be used to demonstrate the Carroll method. In Chapter 8 of *Through the Looking-Glass* Alice, wondering what dream she is in, symbolically comes to the end of childhood, ceasing to be a pawn in the chess game and becoming a queen. She meets the White Knight, perhaps a self-portrait of Carroll (although the picture makes him look rather like Tenniel). The Knight repeatedly falls off his horse in front of Alice, grasping her hair as he does so; he gives her a lecture on logic and language which should be required reading for all young language students, despite the fact that Carroll (for once) makes a logical error himself; and he sings her a sentimental Victorian ballad that emerges as a ruthless parody of Wordsworth's cumbersome homily, *Resolution and Independence*.

> I'll tell you everything I can:
> There's little to relate.
> I saw an aged aged man,
> A-sitting on a gate.
> 'Who are you aged man?' I said.
> 'And how is it you live?'

And his answer trickled through my head,
Like water through a sieve.

This is, of course, only one of many parodies and Carroll places himself firmly on the side of his child-audience in demolishing pious poetry. Among the many victims are the very long-lived 'Against Idleness and Mischief' from Isaac Watts's *Divine Songs* (1715) (q.v.): 'How doth the little busy bee / Improve each shining hour' becomes 'How doth the little crocodile / Improve his shining tail'. The innocent 'Twinkle, twinkle, little star' from Anne and Jane Taylor's *Original Poems for Infant Minds* (two volumes: 1804, 1805), becomes 'Twinkle, twinkle little bat'. Some, such as 'Beautiful soup . . . Soup of the evening, beautiful soup', have quite replaced their originals, in this case James M. Sayles's popular song 'Star of the evening . . .'

Carroll also took the occasional swipe at the children's literature of the time. Alice has just found the bottle labelled 'DRINK ME':

It was all very well to say 'Drink Me', but wise little Alice was not going to do *that* in a hurry. 'No, I'll look first,' she said, 'and see whether it's marked "*poison*" or not': for she had read several nice little stories about children who had got burnt, and eaten up by wild beasts, and other unpleasant things, all because they *would* not remember the simple rules their friends had taught them: such as, that a red-hot poker will burn you if you hold it too long; and that, if you cut your finger *very* deeply with a knife, it usually bleeds; and she had never forgotten that, if you drink much from a bottle marked 'poison', it is almost certain to disagree with you, sooner or later.

Viewed in terms of the development of narrative voice in children's literature, Carroll's approach was complex. He could use a direct address ('If you do not know what a Gryphon is, look at the picture'), but more often he colludes with his audience and his character:

Here one of the guinea-pigs cheered, and was immediately suppressed by the officers of the court. (As that is rather a hard word, I will just explain to you how it was done. They had a large canvas bag, which tied up at the mouth with strings: into this they slipped the guinea-pig, head first, and then sat upon it.)

'I'm glad I've seen that done,' thought Alice. 'I've so often read in the newspapers, at the end of trials, "There was some attempt at applause, which was immediately suppressed by the officers of the court," and I never understood what it meant till now.'

One curious offshoot of the two Alice books was *The Nursery 'Alice'* of 1890. Gone is the savage intellectualism: now the sentimentalism that hovered around the edges of the books has taken over. In the preface 'Addressed to any Mother', Carroll wrote:

> And my ambition *now* (is it a vain one?) to be read by Children aged Nought to Five. To be read? Nay, not so! Say rather to be thumbed, to be cooed over, to be dogs' eared, to be rumpled, to be kissed, by the illiterate, ungrammatical, dimpled Darlings, that fill your Nursery with merry uproar, and your inmost heart of hearts with a restful gladness!

The text is reduced to little more than a commentary on Tenniel's pictures: 'So it really *was* a *little* Puppy, you see. And isn't it a little *pet*?'; '*The Queen has come!* And *isn't* she angry? Oh, my poor little Alice!'; 'Oh dear, oh dear! What *is* it all about? And what's happening to Alice?' Whether all this represents a change of attitude, another side of Carroll's character, or a potentially dark side of the Victorian psyche can be debated.

The kinds of complex interpretations made of the Alice books can also apply to the surreal, nightmare excursion, *The Hunting of the Snark* (1876), which is only dubiously for any audience, let alone children. Carroll's only other substantial books for children, *Sylvie and Bruno* (1889) and *Sylvie and Bruno Concluded* (1893), are mawkishly sentimental in patches and, in contrast to the central texts of the Alice books, highly orthodox in their Victorian politics and religion. They have never been particularly popular and seem only to survive in collected editions of Carroll. Like *The Nursery Alice* they point up just how revolutionary the Alice books were for Carroll himself.

The Alice books have more often been used as devices for parody, rather than being parodied themselves. There have been imitations, most notably *The Wallypug of Why* (1895) and its sequels by G. E. Farrow. The Wallypug books are full of often very ingenious word-play and make use of the 'beautiful child' cult that was developing (and which survived into the 1920s): it is only linguistic accident that makes Farrow's choice of name for his heroine – 'Girlie' – so unfortunate. But they differ from Carroll's books in two major and significant ways: first, Carroll was writing exclusively *of* and *for* childhood, and second, he was making no intellectual compromises in doing so. Recent research on (the invisible) women writers of the century suggests that many of them appropriated Carroll's texts as a means to comment not only on Carroll's 'reading' of femininity, as represented by Alice, and the ideology of femininity that informed his creation of that icon, but to dramatize discursively their own struggles to authorize themselves in the literary marketplace. (Sigler, 1998: 353)

That so much has been written about the Alice books – that there appears to be so *much* to write about them – is partly a function of their status as canonical texts: there is a symbiotic relationship between what a text is and what can be written about it which is, by definition, generally limited in children's literature. Whether the books are now enjoyed by children – or ever were – seems to be irrelevant to theorists, except in a whimsical way. However, it can be argued that Carroll succeeded in writing a quintessential *children's* children's book in the sense that he empathized with the pragmatic frustration and mystification of a child in relation to the adult world. For this reason, the books, although undoubtedly children's books in that sense, might be *too* realistic to be interesting to children.

The description of Carroll as the first writer to liberate children's imaginations is a pardonable exaggeration, and it is often taken to mean that children were released from the didactic. It might be better to say that with *Alice's Adventures in Wonderland* children's literature was liberated from simplicity.

Bibliography

Cohen, Morton 1995: *Lewis Carroll: A Biography*. London: Macmillan.

Docherty, John 1995: *The Literary Products of the Lewis Carroll–George MacDonald Friendship*. Lewiston: Mellen.

Dusinberre, Juliet 1987: *Alice to the Lighthouse: Children's Books and Radical Experiments in Art*. London: Macmillan.

Gardner, Martin (ed.) 1967: *The Annotated Snark*. Harmondsworth: Penguin Books.

Gardner, Martin (ed.) 2000: *The Annotated Alice: The Definitive Edition*. New York: Norton.

Jones, Jo Elwyn and Gladstone, J. Francis 1995: *The Red King's Dream*. London: Cape.

Jones, Jo Elwyn and Gladstone, J. Francis 1998: *The Alice Companion*. London: Macmillan.

Knoepflmacher, U. C. 1986: 'Avenging Alice: Christina Rossetti and Lewis Carroll.' *Nineteenth Century Literature*, 41 (1), 299–328.

Phillips, Robert (ed.) 1974: *Aspects of Alice*. Harmondsworth: Penguin Books.

Sigler, Carolyn (ed.) 1997: *Alternative Alices: Visions and Revisions of Lewis Carroll's Alice Books*. Lexington: University Press of Kentucky.

Sigler, Carolyn 1998: 'Authorizing Alice: Professional Authority, the Literary Marketplace, and Victorian Women's Re-Visions of the *Alice* Books.' *LU*, 22, 351–63.

Thomas, Donald 1996: *Lewis Carroll: A Portrait with Background*. London: John Murray.

Robert Cormier (1925–)

I don't think that having a happy ending should be one of the requirements of a children's book. Kids want their books to reflect reality, and they know that the good guys don't always win. They know that the bully doesn't always get his come-uppance in the end. (West, 1988: 30)

We know life isn't always fair and happy. There are enough books with happy endings. I think there is room for the realistic novel about things that really go on in the world. I try to write a warning about what's waiting out there. (Elkin, et al., 1989: 13)

Thus Robert Cormier in interviews in 1988 and 1989, and it is hardly surprising that such a view of children's books received a fairly dusty reception from critics uneasily intent on preserving some kind of innocence around 'young adulthood' or, failing that, to present a 'balanced' view of life. What *is* perhaps surprising is the tenacity with which the idea of 'innocence' in children's books hangs on in the face of the 'disappearance of childhood'.

Cormier is the most outstanding, the most uncompromising and the most censored of the neo-realist writers in the USA in the 1960s and 1970s. These included the groundbreaking Paul Zindel (*My Darling, My Hamburger*, 1970) and John Donovan (*I'll Get There, It Better Be Worth The Trip*, 1969), who faced the realities of teenage sexuality and unreliable adults. Cormier has produced a group of texts characterized by extremely bleak scenarios combined with subtle, professional writing. 'The almost universal distress about Cormier's work', Sylvia Iskander has written,

springs directly from the power and consistency of his imagined world, *which convinces readers that it bears a recognizable relationship to the 'real world'* and yet appears to leave no room for anything but pessimism about the survival of [his] protagonists. (Iskander, 1987: 7; my italics)

Cormier is probably in the top ten writers who are essential reading for an understanding of the development of children's literature in the twentieth century and for understanding the category of 'young adult' or 'adolescent' novel. *After the First Death* (1979), for example, portrays a hijack and a betrayal, in which the central teenage character is killed in what must be one of the most harrowing accounts of a death in any fiction. *The Bumblebee*

Flies Anyway (1983) deals with dying children and medical research. Cormier's narrative complexity can be seen in the oblique narrative of *I Am the Cheese* (1977) covering the psychological breakdown of a boy whose family has been 'terminated' by a government agency, and *Fade* (1988), a remarkably complex exercise in metafiction, which uses the device of invisibility in a modern context to expose all manner of corruption (and to some critics' minds steps over the borders of pornography.)

Dark books, then, whose characters are often pragmatic and optimistic, but who are overwhelmed by the circumstances of the modern world. If one book is essential reading, it remains Cormier's first novel for non-adults, *The Chocolate War* (1975). This is a study in corruption which is (perhaps incidentally) a corrective to the conventions of the school story genre, almost on the scale of Kipling's *Stalky and Co*. The schoolboy mafia, 'The Vigils', led by the ruthless Archie and abetted by the corrupt Brother Leon, in effect destroy the clean-limbed new boy, Jerry Renault, who tries to stand up to them by refusing on principle to sell chocolates for a fundraising scheme. He is finally beaten in a boxing match and collapses 'like a hunk of meat cut loose from a butcher's hook'. He comes to in the arms of a sympathetic friend, Goober, having found, he thinks, a great truth.

> 'It'll be alright, Jerry.'
> No, it won't. He recognized Goober's voice and it was important to share the discovery with Goober. He had to tell Goober to play ball, to play football, to run, to make the team, to sell the chocolates, to sell whatever they wanted you to sell, to do whatever they wanted you to do. He tried to voice the words but there was something wrong with his mouth, his teeth, his face. . . . Don't disturb the universe, Goober. . . . Just remember what I told you. It's important. Otherwise, they murder you.

Beyond the Chocolate War (1985) brings the events of *The Chocolate War* into a more conventional focus, with a repeated message that 'fighting back against a fighter is yourself becoming what you are fighting' (Nodelman, 1992: 33), but if the apparently innocent are not actually innocent, the corrupt winners have only a corrupt victory.

Cormier's books are concerned with the *nature* of realism, and as Frank Myszor argues (writing on *After the First Death*), Cormier does not merely acknowledge the intelligence of his readers, but demands intellectual involvement from them:

Because the narrator . . . is dramatized as a character in the novel and because of the nature of his character, the reader soon comes to question his reliability. . . . Cormier breaks down the realistic illusion by exposing the inner mechanisms of the novel; the discontinuities of the text, so characteristic of postmodernist writing, put into question not only the individual witnesses but the very ordering of event and perception into text. (Myszor, 1988: 87)

Just as it can be argued that J. D. Salinger's *The Catcher in the Rye* was indirectly responsible for many thousands of novels which exploited its first-person demotic but not its subtleties, so it may be that Cormier's books opened the way for books which portrayed certain kinds of incident without the intellectual subtlety. Thus one may question whether writers of the 1990s in the UK (notably Robert Swindells and Melvin Burgess) whose account of life can be as downbeat as Cormier's are as subtle as he, or given the change in narrative mode in the novel since the 1970s, can be or need to be.

Certainly, for the last few decades of the twentieth century Cormier stood as an icon of where the boundaries of 'children's' literature – in terms of content – could be said to lie. It is striking, however, that his more recent work, such as *In the Middle of the Night* (1995), *Tenderness* (1998) or *Frenchtown Summer* (1999) seems positively mainstream. Nonetheless, Cormier has the distinction that, for many years, he indicated the intellectual possibilities of this field of writing.

Bibliography

Campbell, Patricia J. 1989: *Presenting Robert Cormier*. Revised edition. Boston: Twayne.

Cormier, Robert 1981: 'Forever Pedaling on the Road to Realism.' In Hearne and Kaye 1981: 35–44.

Elkin, Judith, et al. 1989: 'Cormier Talking.' *Books for Keeps*, 54, 12–13.

Head, Patricia 1996: 'Robert Cormier and the Postmodernist Possibilities of Young Adult Fiction.' *ChLAQ*, 21 (1), 28–33.

Iskander, Sylvia Patterson 1987: 'Readers, Realism, and Robert Cormier.' *CL*, 15, 7–18.

Junko, Yoshida 1998: 'The Quest for Masculinity in *The Chocolate War*: Changing Conceptions of Masculinity in the 1970s.' *CL*, 26, 105–22.

Myszor, Frank 1988: 'The See-Saw and the Bridge in *After the First Death*.' *CL*, 16, 77–90.

Nodelman, Perry 1983: 'Robert Cormier Does a Number.' *CLE*, 14 (2), 94–103.

Nodelman, Perry 1992: 'Robert Cormier's *The Chocolate War*: Paranoia and Paradox.' In Butts 1992: 22–36.

Richmal Crompton [Lamburn] (1890–1969)

Anyone interested in exploring the elusive borderland between children's and adult books can do no better than to look at the work of Richmal Crompton. From the 1919 magazine story 'Rice-Mould', until 1970, when the thirty-seventh book of short stories, *William the Lawless*, appeared (*Just William's Luck*, 1948, is a novel), William Brown, the most famous 'bad boy' of British literature, was the scourge of settled middle-class England. For many years the stories, perhaps best described as 'situation comedy', appeared in popular magazines aimed primarily at women (*Home Magazine* 1919–22, *Modern Woman* 1940–6) or 'family' audiences (*Happy Mag* 1922–40); only in the 1940s did Crompton aim them at a child audience.

Of course, by then the adoption of the stories by children was a *fait accompli*; the collections *Just – William* and *More William* were published in book form for children (both 1922); it is interesting to speculate why. There might be an obvious appeal to anarchy: William almost invariably wins a guerrilla war against adults and respectability; he is remorselessly logical, ingenious, and impulsive; he is invariably scruffy, invariably the despair of his family. His gang, the 'Outlaws', have an (almost) unswerving loyalty to him; he has satisfying enemies in the form of the fat boy Hubert Lane and his associates. And he has a robust disdain for females – except for those he falls in love with – and except for the remarkable Violet Elizabeth Bott who, by threatening to 'thcream n' thcream till I'm thick. I can', imposes her six-year-old will on him.

But the point of view adopted by Crompton is not always that of William: the text, very knowingly, operates what Barbara Wall called 'double narrative' (see Matters of History, pp. 13–14); that is, addressing two audiences simultaneously but separately, and the adult audience primarily:

'Now, William,' said his mother anxiously at lunch, 'you'll go to the dancing-class nicely this afternoon, won't you?'

'I'll go the way I gen'rally go to things. I've only got one way of goin' anywhere. I don't know whether it's nice or not.'

This brilliant repartee cheered him considerably, and he felt that a life in which one could display such sarcasm and wit was after all to a certain degree worth living. . . . Mrs Brown was still looking after him anxiously. She had an uneasy suspicion that he meant to play truant from the dancing-class.

When she saw him in his hat and coat after lunch she said again: 'William, you *are* going to the dancing-class, aren't you?'

William walked past her with a short laugh that was wild and reckless and dare-devil and bitter and sardonic. It was, in short, a very good laugh, and he was proud of it. ('William's Birthday', *William's Happy Days*, 1930)

Essentially a satirist, Crompton on the whole pokes gentle fun at affectations and oddities; these are generally very English, and very much of their time. She mocks the fashionable 'Brains Trust' fad of the 1940s, social pretensions (especially in the form of Mr Bott, the *nouveau riche* sauce-maker) and perhaps especially fey artists and quasi-mystic poets – and dancers:

The New School of Greek Dancing was a few miles down the coast from where William and Ginger had originally set forth in the boat. The second afternoon open-air class was in progress. Weedy males and aesthetic-looking females dressed in abbreviated tunics with sandals on their feet and fillets round their hair, mostly wearing horn spectacles, ran and sprang and leapt and gambolled and struck angular attitudes at the shrill command of the instructress and the somewhat unmusical efforts of the (very) amateur flute player. ('An Afternoon with William', *Still – William*, 1925)

Among her more specific targets was Christopher Robin Milne, who appeared as the obnoxious Anthony Martin in the story 'Aunt Arabelle in Charge' (1931) (*William – the Pirate*, 1932). This world-famous brat has a mother who writes poems about him, which are not too far away from Milne's 'Vespers': 'Anthony Martin is doing his sums' and so on. The insouciant William, his physical and literary opposite, has of course never heard of him.

In terms of content, the William books also provide an interesting case study for series writing. In the course of the saga, William remains eleven years old, although he has at least two birthdays and several Christmases. But there are stories that deal with the Nazis (or 'Nasties') in 1934, the ARP (Air Raid Precautions) in 1939, and William encounters air raid shelters, an unexploded bomb, scrap-metal collections during the Second World War. In the 1950s and 1960s he is involved with protest marches and pop singers. The illustrations by Thomas Henry and Henry Ford trace fashions (especially women's) accurately.

In literary–historical terms William is in the tradition (very firmly rooted in America) of the 'bad boy': from Thomas Bailey Aldrich's *The Story of a Bad Boy* (1869), through Mark Twain's *The Adventures of Tom Sawyer* (1876) (q.v.), to G. W. Peck's *Peck's Bad Boy and his Pa* (1883) and Booth

Tarkington's *Penrod* (1913), although Crompton 'had no memory of ever reading Tarkington's stories before producing William' (Cadogan, 1993: 83). It might seem surprising that the William stories have not been published in the USA, but William's family, his village, and the mores he approaches do not seem to be exportable (much as, for example, Maud Hart Lovelace's domestic, mid-western 'Betsy-Tacy' stories of 1940–55 have not been published in the UK).

Films, television series and abridgements of the stories for radio (although in the 1990s these were broadcast in an adult's rather than children's time-slot) have maintained William's popularity, despite or because of the ambivalence of the narrative voice, which seems often to privilege the adult view of childhood while endorsing childhood's victories over the adult.

Richmal Crompton also wrote many novels for adults, none of which have survived; her attempts to produce a younger version of William, Jimmy, are also little known (and in any case Jimmy is scarcely distinguishable from William).

Bibliography

Cadogan, Mary 1993: *The Woman Behind William: A Life of Richmal Crompton*. London: Macmillan.
Cadogan, Mary, with Schute, Richard 1990: *The William Companion*. London: Macmillan.
Stewart, Ralph 1988: 'William Brown's World'. *ChLAQ*, 13 (4), 181–5.

Roald Dahl (1916–1990)

It is extremely difficult to find any serious analysis or discussion of Roald Dahl's books for children, beyond polemic for or against, which demonstrates how deep is the division between literature and popular culture. Dahl is probably the most successful worldwide children's author of the twentieth century, surpassed in sales only by the far more prolific Enid Blyton, and his popularity must say a great deal about and to the culture, yet most comments on him do not rise much above the visceral.

The issue has been clouded (or perhaps enriched) by the fact that Dahl was a highly skilled writer and a resourceful self-publicist. He presented himself as a very self-opinionated and 'difficult' character, and his formidable intelligence was occasionally devoted to outwitting interviewers. A typical comment, given in one of his last interviews, sums up his attitude to children's books – at least, the attitude which he wished to perpetuate:

> I have a great affinity with children. I see their problems. If you want to remember what it's like to live in a child's world, you've got to get down on your hands and knees and live like that for a week. You find you have to look up at all these bloody giants around you who are always telling you what to do and what not to do. . . . So subconsciously in the child's mind these giants become the enemy. . . . When I wrote *Matilda* I based it on this theory. . . . Children absolutely warm to this. They think, 'Well, Christ! He's one of us.' I don't think you find many chaps . . . in their mid-seventies who think like I do and joke and fart around. (Sykes, 1991: 82)

It is hardly surprising, then, that critics are divided between those who espouse his ostensible 'child-centredness' and cheerful anarchy, and those who deplore his vulgarity and blatant manipulations. That his work for children is very uneven and fluctuates between the outrageously original (episodes of *The BFG*, 1982) and the expedient (*The Giraffe, the Pelly and Me*, 1985) seems to be overlooked.

Certainly, anarchy and vulgarity can be seen as natural to childhood and dangerous to adults' authority, and it depends where you are standing whether you find this invigorating or threatening. Dahl's response to those who have accused him of violence, sadism and sexism was that he was writing farce or pantomime and that such accusations were simply irrelevant. The demolition of the Aunts Sponge and Spicer in *James and the Giant Peach* (1961), or the demise of the demented Grandmother (the 'old hag', the 'filthy old woman') in *George's Marvellous Medicine* (1981) are, he might have said, merely cartoon effects. They are intended to be funny, not a demonstration of misogyny. Indeed, although the gruesomely evil witches in *The Witches* (1983) are necessarily female, not only does the narrator go out of his way to disclaim sexism, but the book is provided with a very strong female character in the form of the Grandmother.

But despite this logic, the fact lingers around his children's books that Dahl had a worldwide reputation as a writer of sinister short stories (collected as *Kiss Kiss*, 1960, *Switch Bitch*, 1974, and others) that dealt with very dark corners of human nature, before he became a writer for children. Can such a zestful exploitation of childish instincts for hate and revenge, prejudice and violence, be as innocent as it appears?

Such is the strength of Dahl's popular support that it is hardly surprising that his first children's book, *James and the Giant Peach* (1961), which yields the most subtle and coherent sub-text as an account of the psychological exploration of self, has been most cautiously approached by his admirers. Equally, it is a sad reflection on the standards of criticism of children's books that Dahl's first major success, *Charlie and the Chocolate Factory* (1964) was greeted with delight for its apparent anarchy. It is, in fact, a straightforward moral tale with solid nineteenth-century origins. Those children who are lazy, stupid or spoiled come to suitably sticky ends: the poor and pure child is rewarded, not just with chocolate, but with the chocolate factory. The manic presence of Mr Wonka gives the book its edge: he is the explicit voice for the pet hates that Dahl parades in his other books (fat women, used-car salesmen, tyrannical school teachers) and an essentially unreliable character. *Charlie* certainly contains Dahl's key ideological trick of appearing deeply anarchic in practice ('Veruca Salt, the little brute / Has just gone down the rubbish chute'), while being deeply conservative in principle ('A child can't spoil herself you know').

From *Charlie* onwards, Dahl's *oeuvre* demonstrates a skilled craftsman who has found a goldmine and who worked it efficiently. Some books, notably *Charlie and the Great Glass Elevator* and *The Twits* (1980), have a good deal of the aimlessness and the (somewhat desperate) expediency of the bedtime storyteller. In others, Dahl's argument that he is writing only fantastic farce (that nobody is supposed to sympathize with the Ugly Sisters) runs into difficulties. Such is the forcefulness of his writing that the Ugly Sisters have, as it were, become human: not only has their evil become palpable, but morally they deserve to be treated as humans. Children, Dahl had claimed in effect, enjoyed the simplicity of revenge, and were in no danger of confusing the fantastic with the real; his own writing changed that: his remarkable talent for fierce psychological realism shifts his fantasy onto an uncomfortable plane. The skills of *Kiss Kiss* are now employed in an even more uncomfortable interaction.

There are other areas where readers might feel as much discomfort as delight. Dahl's chutzpah in including the reigning monarch in *The BFG* might just be tempered for some by scepticism:

> The Queen was still staring at Sophie. Gaping at her would be more accurate. Her mouth was slightly open, her eyes were round and wide as two saucers, and the whole of *that famous rather lovely face* was filled with disbelief. [My italics]

Similar oddities are to be found in *Matilda* (1988), published in effect as a work in progress because of a disagreement between Dahl and his editor, Stephen Roxborough. We are able to see, as it were, Dahl in the raw. In this version of the text, Dahl indulges himself: the book begins with a lengthy diatribe on parents and unpleasant children, and provides a long list of books that he clearly regards as essential reading. As with his tirades against (among other things) chewing gum and television in *Charlie and the Chocolate Factory*, readers of liberal persuasion may be caught between approving the principle and deploring the execution. His description of the ways in which Miss Trunchball deals with recalcitrant children might also seem to be excessive: many are pure farce, but the torture-box (the 'chokey') and the extended chocolate cake-eating episode with Bruce Bogtrotter strike some as edging into sadism.

As an illustration of the difficulties Dahl presents, we can consider a scene from *Matilda*, bearing in mind the faith that Dahl clearly had in the influence of literature, especially thoroughly read, *seductive* literature. The slim, delicate Miss Honey (one of the illustrator Quentin Blake's masterworks, if not Dahl's) is taking her protégé, Matilda, to tea. From crude farce-land we are taken into a rural idyll, with two pages of blackberries and old man's beard and hazels, until we reach Miss Honey's gate. Dahl seems to be mesmerized by the symbolism of it all:

> Miss Honey paused with one hand on the gate and said, 'There it is. That's where I live.'
> Matilda saw a narrow dirt-path leading to a tiny red-brick cottage. The cottage was so small it looked more like a doll's house than a human dwelling. The bricks it was built of were old and crumbly and very pale red. It had a gray slate roof, and there were two little windows at the front. Each window was no larger than a sheet of tabloid newspaper. . . . An enormous oak tree stood overshadowing the cottage. Its massive spreading branches seemed to be enfolding and embracing the tiny building, and perhaps hiding it as well from the rest of the world.

Miss Honey, 'in a rather wonderful slow voice', recites part of Dylan Thomas's 'In Country Sleep' in which the poet tells 'my girl riding far and near' not to fear the wolf that 'blithely shall leap . . . / out of a lair in the flocked leaves . . . / To eat your heart out in the rosy wood.' Matilda, 'who had never before heard great romantic poetry spoken aloud, was profoundly moved.' But she is now rather frightened of the cottage:

It was like an illustration in Grimm or Hans Andersen. It was the house where the poor woodcutter lived with Hansel and Gretel and where Red Riding Hood's grandmother lived, and it was also the house of The Seven Dwarfs and The Three Bears and all the rest of them. It was straight out of a fairy tale.

'Come along my dear,' Miss Honey called back, and Matilda followed her up the path.

To say that *Matilda* is a book fractured between the farcical grotesque and the sinisterly realistic (if Miss Trunchball is a caricature of a monstrous sadist, what is Miss Honey up to?) is to describe several of Dahl's books. And as in *Danny, The Champion of the World* (1975) or *The Witches* we can observe what must have been a sharp intelligence coming up against the central problem of children's literature: affect and allusion. Perhaps it is better to resist drawing any conclusion from all this, for which author, faced with a psychological third-degree, should 'scape whipping?

As ever, it is futile to pursue the essence of Dahl's success. After all, his basic ingredients – empowering the child, writing the fantastic as though it were the real, satisfying basic instincts such as revenge by lurid and exaggerated means – and even his shock tactics are shared by many other writers, including of course the quietly provincial Enid Blyton.

But as current surveys and common observation show, with fewer than twenty books Dahl has dominated the children's sections of bookshops (and lists of children's favourite writers) through the 1980s and 1990s in a quite unprecedented way. That from *Charlie* to *Matilda* there was an erratic decline in style and subtlety seems to have become irrelevant; for a popular critical audience, any iconoclasm is daring. Dahl is engaged in a conspiracy not only of child against adult, but of culturally dispossessed adults against culturally powerful adults. That this may have been a psychological confidence-trick is irrelevant.

That Dahl was constantly engaged with a mixture of professional entertainment, the needs of childhood (constructed on his own model) and the relationship between child and adult may have considerable consequences. Dahl's books both reflected and helped bring about a profound change in English-language children's literature.

Bibliography

Sykes, Christopher Simon 1991: 'In the Lair of the BFG.' *Harpers and Queen*, October, 1991, 80–5.

Treglown, Jeremy 1994: *Roald Dahl: A Biography*. London: Faber and Faber.

West, Mark I. 1985: 'Regression and Fragmentation of the Self in *James and the Giant Peach.*' *CLE*, 16 (4), 219–25.
West, Mark I. 1992: *Roald Dahl.* Boston: Twayne.

Dr Seuss (Theodor Seuss Geisel) (1904–1991)

The idea of solemn critical articles being written about the cheerful non-sense of Dr Seuss may either confirm one's worst suspicions about the desperation of academics, or encourage one that at last academics are working on something real and relevant, for with the egregious Dr Seuss we enter a tricky area for critics. What are we to make of the fact that he wrote the bestselling *Green Eggs and Ham* (1960) to win a bet that he could produce a book using only fifty different words? Or that he founded the 'Beginner Book' series in 1957 with deliberately controlled vocabulary? Or, for that matter, that he found his brief academic career at Oxford full of 'astonishing irrelevance' (Wolf, 1995: 162). This is not the stuff of art, even though (or especially because) his individual books, such as *And To Think that I Saw it on Mulberry Street* (1937), and the series continue to sell in their millions, and have become part of world and especially American culture. Criticism may therefore retreat to the popular-culture position of accounting *for.*

More tenacious critics can naturally dismiss the innocent remarks of Clifton Fadiman that 'the extraordinary animals he draws are not symbolic but merely the consequence of his liking to draw extraordinary animals . . . Dr Seuss is a craftsman, not an allegorist, or a satirist in disguise' (Fadiman, 1980: 281, 283). Nor can we accept that nonsense has no meaning: *The 500 Hats of Bartholomew Cubbins* has been read as a 'phallic duel' (and who would doubt the seriousness or even the validity of the interpretation?), while 'possible gender-specific psychosexual implications' can also be seen in the arrangement of the ham and eggs in *Green Eggs and Ham:*

> A sexual symbol here might be seen as Seuss's way of associating the imagination with the child's libidinal drives, not only making us want the imagination to triumph, but causing us to associate the imagination with the will to live and with the deepest roots of personal identity. Perhaps in Seuss, the parent's acceptance of the child, of the child's sexuality, and of the child's imagination becomes indistinguishable. (Wolf, 1995: 162, 163)

Perhaps. After all, *all* texts must necessarily have many meanings and there is no need to make Seuss a test case for eccentricity in criticism. In fact, Seuss's exuberance and eccentricity are such that they seem to be able to subsist productively alongside the necessary intellectual and emotional freight the books carry. *The Cat in the Hat* (1957), for example, is gloriously 'politically incorrect', as the Cat and his friends wreck the house where the children have been left unattended; yet is this a book about lack of communication, or the triumph or taming of the imagination? Taking Seuss seriously is surprisingly easy and it is obvious that he does provide small explicit homilies on tolerance (for example, *Horton Hears a Who!*, 1954), while *The Butter Battle Book* (1984) uses a Swiftean device to take on nationalism and the arms race. *The 500 Hats of Bartholomew Cubbins* (1938) can be read allegorically, and even *And To Think That I Saw it on Mulberry Street* (1937) explores the boundaries of fantasy and realism from within fantasy as it were. Beyond that, the interpretative world is your oyster bed.

Dr Seuss himself took an amused view of all this and proved a splendidly wry match for interviewers. When asked, for example, what the pedigree of his 'fantastic creations' was, he replied that they 'probably come into existence because I actually do not draw very well and have trouble putting together conventional animals'. He was equally unhelpful to educationalists over the idea of controlled vocabularies (*The Cat in the Hat* has 223 different words): 'I have since come to despise controlled vocabularies and ignore them altogether' (Wintle and Fisher, 1974: 118, 122).

The paradox of Dr Seuss (which also surfaces obliquely in Roald Dahl's work) is that here we have apparent anarchy, and yet the purpose of the books is to educate children into the discipline of reading. It is perhaps not such a paradox that once a certain kind of imagination is unleashed into the field of nonsense, a great deal that was not consciously intended and which is not nonsensical is unleashed with it. For myself, I take great comfort in the fact that the Spelling Checker on my computer would like to replace 'Seuss' with 'Zeus'.

Bibliography

Arakelian, Paul G. 1993: 'Minnows into Whales: Integration Across Scales in the Early Styles of Dr Seuss.' *ChLAQ*, 18 (1), 18–22.

Fadiman, Clifton 1980: 'Professionals and Confessionals: Dr Seuss and Kenneth Grahame.' In Egoff, Stubbs and Ashley 1980: 277–83.

Nel, Philip 1999: 'Dada Knows Best: Growing Up "Surreal" With Dr Seuss.' *CL*, 27, 150–84.

Reimer, Mavis 1989: 'Dr Seuss' *The 500 Hats of Bartholomew Cubbins:* Of Hats and Kings.'
  In Nodelman 1989: 132–42.
Wintle, Justin and Fisher, Emma 1974: *The Pied Pipers.* London: Paddington Press.
Wolf, Tim 1995: 'Imagination, Rejection, and Rescue: Recurrent Themes in Dr Seuss.'
  CL, 23, 137–64.

Anne Fine (1947–)

Anne Fine epitomizes the successful contemporary British children's writer. She is deeply committed to social and personal issues, active in schools, responsive to the demands of the marketplace, speaks wittily and effectively at conferences, and has won all of the major UK children's book prizes. (In 1990, she won the Guardian Award, the Smarties Prize, the Carnegie Medal, and a special PEN award.) She is as commercially successful as a children's writer can be who is not Roald Dahl or Joanna Rowling, and she has also built a reputation as an adult novelist with books such as *Taking the Devil's Advice* (1992) and *Telling Liddy* (1998).

Across her career Fine has moved from books reminiscent in their tone and attitude of the 'second golden age' (*c.* 1950–70) of British children's books, to the much more theme-led books of the 1990s. The difference between, for example, *The Summer House Loon* (1978) and *The Book of the Banshee* (1991) is much more than a shift from the bucolic to the sardonic: it is a difference in style which reflects a particular belief in what books should be doing. Both are about relationships, but the second looks for answers in a way that the first doesn't.

By Fine's own account her first novels, *The Summer House Loon* and *The Other, Darker Ned* (1979), were products of depression, of her situation as 'trapped' wife (which some of her later books politicize). They are neat, apparently light comedies in a Wodehousean mould, centring around the benign and eccentric household of the blind Professor Muffet and his daughter Ione. There is an almost elegiac approach to young adulthood, and in this golden world even Ione's age remains indeterminate. In contrast, the household in *The Book of the Banshee* is described in terms of a battleground with the teenage daughter Estelle at the centre: 'I'm not too young. I'm not! You just don't understand how things are these days. *Everyone* in my year is allowed to smoke. *Everyone's* allowed to drink. And *everyone's* allowed to go to the discotheque.'

Fine's early manner shaded into the more serious and – more importantly – specific concerns of *The Stone Menagerie* (1980) and *Round Behind the Ice House* (1981). From *The Granny Project* (1983) onwards, her books are rooted in situation and *issues* rather than the more allusive, character-led and theme-led approach of earlier years. *Goggle-Eyes* (1989) is concerned exclusively with coming to terms with divorce and the remarriage of a parent; *Flour Babies* with a device for dealing with almost-delinquent boys (1992); *The Tulip Touch* (1996) with a seriously disturbed child. One of her most successful books (for younger children), *Bill's New Frock* (1989), has a tough little boy encountering sexism first-hand. The emphasis and the technique have changed. Her books are well-researched, dramatic and sometimes harrowing (as in *Step By Wicked Step*, 1995, which recounts six experiences of step-parenting) and can be distinguished from many others in the same mould by her mordant authorial humour and her astute observation. But they represent almost a new form: the book, in the world, is performing a different function from the books of an earlier generation.

It has taken some time for the critical and reviewing world to come to terms with this. Fine's most famous book thus far, *Madame Doubtfire* (1987; USA: *Alias Madame Doubtfire*, 1988, and filmed as *Mrs Doubtfire*), is best described as a black farce, although it has been marketed as a comedy. It is a bleak account of marital breakup, with scenes like this, in which the parents have been having a screaming row in front of the children, Lydia, Christopher, and Natalie.

There was so much hate between them that each was silenced.

Lydia rose. Her rage lent her an ashen, fierce dignity that neither parent had seen before.

'I hate you *both*,' she informed them in an unsteady voice, and, turning, she walked into her bedroom and shut the door.

Christopher rose too.

'So do I,' he told them. He was in tears. 'You are disgusting and ugly, both of you!'

Instead of going into his own room, he followed his sister into hers.

Natalie was left alone at the top of the stairs. Her little face crumpled.

After the first split second of shock, Miranda leaped towards her, to take her baby in her arms, and comfort her. But just as she came close, Christopher rushed out of Lydia's bedroom and, pushing Miranda roughly aside, snatched Natalie up in his arms.

'Go on with your filthy quarrel!' he screamed. 'Leave poor Natty *alone*!'

He carried her, weeping, through the door, and banged it behind him.

It may come as something of a surprise, then, to find reviews such as these: '*Alias Madame Doubtfire* is sweet and amusing. I can't imagine anyone not enjoying it' (*New York Times*), and 'A comedy about divorce . . . which had us howling with laughter' (*Times Educational Supplement* Books of the Year) (quoted in Hunt, 1999: 16).

Madame Doubtfire focalizes the plot initially through the father, thus presenting him as victim; when he dresses up as a housekeeper and is employed by his ex-wife, the account shifts to the wife as victim. By the end of the book, the children are clearly the victims, and there is no easy resolution, unlike (ironically) the resolved ending of Fine's adult divorce comedy, *Taking the Devil's Advice* (1992). What happened to *Madame Doubtfire* in the course of its adaptation into a film is in itself a case-study of that process: all of the squalor and most of the bitterness was expunged, presumably in the name of transatlantic family acceptability.

But if times have not changed in family cinema, they have in children's books. It is virtually impossible to imagine a writer for children before 1970 expressing the same opinions as Anne Fine – and these are *positive* opinions:

> The one thing I try to do . . . is to give children a sense that, even though these cataclysmic things happen . . . it's not as bad as they think or even if it is as bad as they think they will somehow come to terms with it. (Podmore, 1996: vi)

Fine's modern horrors are largely emotional, with violence largely offstage, but they can be no less effective for that.

At the beginning of *The Book of the Banshee* there is what looks suspiciously like a self-portrait: the writer Alicia Whitley, a shrewd, forceful pragmatist, arrives at a school and describes in great detail the stages of writing a book, through several intricate drafts, to the final product: 'She obviously thought writing books was the most interesting topic in the whole world.' Anne Fine's commitment to the craft of writing is clear, but so is the fact that the craft of writing has changed and that she herself has been one of the writers most instrumental in changing it.

Perhaps the most successful British exponent of the new mode (and one of the rare writers who has reversed the trend of importing children's literature's equivalent of 'street' novels from the USA to the UK) is Jacqueline Wilson. Her first-person narratives, such as *The Suitcase Kind* (1992) and *Double Act* (1995), while presenting themselves as jokey and colloquial, in fact chronicle sad and sometimes tragic displaced children and families, and can be tough-minded about happy resolutions. For all that they seem (comparatively) to be genre fiction, they should not be underestimated: they demonstrate that an apparently simplistic mode can say a great deal, both about the theoretical postmodern condition and practical realities.

Bibliography

Hunt, Peter 1999: 'Anne Fine and the Revolution in Children's Books.' *LU*, 23 (1), 12–21.
Podmore, Bryan 1996: 'The NAWE Interview: Another Little Spanner?' *Writing in Education* 8, insert i–viii.

Alan Garner (1934–)

A good many critics (although not always those most closely involved with children) might regard Alan Garner as a strong candidate for the title of the twentieth century's greatest British writer for children. Garner might be more inclined to describe himself as simply a writer. From the age of twenty-two until his first adults' novel, *Strandloper* in 1996, he has published ostensibly for children, each book being meticulously crafted over a long period and each deeply infused with a sense of scholarship, vocation, high respect for the intelligence and sensibility of his audience, and what might be called radical conservatism. It is precisely these qualities that have made him somewhat problematic as a major figure in a field rather inclined towards the prolific, the ephemeral and the accessible, and one also inclined (the uncharitable might say) to anti-intellectualism. His intellectual individualism, not to say egocentricity, has produced similar problems for his supporters.

Garner has traced his own intellectual development (and its attendant depressions) in his collection of essays and talks, *A Voice that Thunders* (1997). At the considerable risk of reductiveness (and of taking him at his word) this may be summarized thus. A descendant of a long line of craftsmen in metal and stone, deeply rooted in Cheshire (precisely, Alderley Edge), Garner felt himself closely linked to West Mercian culture and dialect (or, as he might prefer to call it, language) and was a classical scholar at the highly academic Manchester Grammar School, but took an individualistic, non-academic route.

This background marks his books, which began with two 'page-turners': *The Weirdstone of Brisingamen* (1960) and *The Moon of Gomrath* (1963).

These are fantasies of the type in which myth intrudes upon the contemporary world; his two central child-characters were deliberately conceived as bland, neutral figures, repositories for the adventures. The rest of the 'realistic' Cheshire landscape was filled with what comes close to being a farrago of mythical figures garnered, as it were, from 'the universal myth-kitty': many in *The Weirdstone* are Scandinavian, whereas *The Moon of Gomrath* draws largely from the Celtic traditions. (The influence of Robert Graves's *The White Goddess* may be seen here, as in the work of other writers in the same vein, such as Susan Cooper and Penelope Lively.) The overall effect can be seen as overkill: as one critic observed, 'Mr Garner's horrors make Cheshire rather an untidy place' (quoted by Philip, 1981: 33). Garner later revised these books and partly repudiated them, although they have many passages of genuinely dynamic narrative (notably the claustrophobic Earldelving sequence in *The Weirdstone*).

Elidor (1965) was a transitional book: laden with scholarship which is so understated as to be easily overlooked, it is a 'parallel-world' fantasy in which the most convincing elements are, ironically, the non-symbolic, 'realistic' scenes. The overall effect is rather slight, for all Garner's (characteristic) claim that he had to 'read extensively textbooks on physics, Celtic symbolism, unicorns, medieval watermarks, megalithic archaeology; study the writings of Jung; brush up my Plato' (Philip, 1981: 63).

The accusation of slightness cannot be levelled at *The Owl Service* (1967), which has become in the UK the kind of classic widely prescribed in schools. It is predicated on the repetition from generation to generation of a passionate triangle, traced ultimately to a story in the Fourth Branch of the Welsh myth-collection, the Mabinogi. The book may have gained a certain credibility from this connection, although it is not clear whether uninformed readers will actually have any access to the supposed 'resonances'. It has incident and intensity enough to stand on its own; it is notable for its oblique narrative and its elisions (for example, the dominant mother-figure never actually appears). There are, however, two problems: the first is that the supernatural manifestations appear crude besides the intricacy of the mythological references; the second is how to make the adolescent love-triangle as significant (or as interesting) as the mythic one that it echoes.

This is true of the minimalist *Red Shift* (1973), which cuts together three violent stories from different times, happening in the same space (Roman soldiers, a civil war massacre, a teenage romance). But the paradox is not that the teenagers and their emotions are too trivial, but that they are too *knowing*. At this stage Garner, with his apparently conservative privileging of the past, seems to be unable to empower his present-day characters through validating the solipsism that he so accurately portrays.

Tom, the central character of *Red Shift*, is a 'word child', representing the intellectual reluctantly encountering the physical. This focus on intellectualism is matched in modern children's books only by the influential critic Aidan Chambers, whose novels (from *Breaktime*, 1978, to the winner of the 2000 Carnegie Medal, *Postcards from No Man's Land*, 1999) have the same unremitting intensity and intellectual complexity, except with far more words. The intensity of the adolescent vision has something to do with the acknowledgement of ego. As Garner said in an interview with Chambers:

> I discover that only when I am being at my most idiosyncratic and obsessively personal do I come anywhere near approaching the universal. And I find this a significant paradox. One that, I think, causes all the heat and no light when people start to write for political means or social means and ends. I think the children as a result are impoverished, because the story will not have many options. (Chambers, 1980: 299)

Red Shift is a difficult book; one reviewer called it 'probably the most difficult book ever to be published on a children's list', while another observed sardonically that 'the meaning of the title is just as obscure as everything else about this book, and the most interesting character in it was the stone-age hand-axe' (Philip, 1981: 87, 86). Part of the difficulty is the spareness of the language (with, for example, very few speech-tags), which reflects the minimal referential help that the reader is given.

Garner turned away from the supernatural to a kind of 'place-mysticism' in *The Stone Book Quartet* (q.v.) (for children) and *Strandloper*. In the latter he almost manages to establish a universality of nature-mysticism, although his social realism (eighteenth-century transportation ships) is highly effective. The book is based on meticulous research into Australian aboriginal thought, although, as Philip admits, 'some readers will feel that the characters are flat and the mysticism portentous. The marks of making are all too clear on *Strandloper*' (Philip, 1997: 28). Garner has been strongly criticized for implicit neo-colonialism, of appropriating another culture for his own ends. Heather Scutter has observed that 'all of us need to be wary of the imperial centrality of the ideological claims in such a work . . . [As] writers, critics and teachers we have not been sufficiently alert to the implications of myth-borrowing, mythologizing and mythicizing' (quoted in Hunt and Sands, 1999: 42).

In some ways Garner is unfashionably conservative and sexist; in others, ambitiously mystic. But like Chambers, and the perhaps more pragmatic Jan Mark (q.v.), Philip Pullman (q.v.) or William Mayne (q.v.), he cleaves to those literary values which are now so often doubted or rejected. As he has said:

> By being an industry, by pandering to those unqualified to differentiate, children's literature loses its creative bite. And, without bite, literature can cope with nothing more substantial than gruel. (Chambers, 1980: 327)

Bibliography

Chambers, Aidan 1980: 'An Interview with Alan Garner.' In Chambers 1980: 276–328.
Garner, Alan 1997: *The Voice that Thunders*. London: Harvill Press.
Hunt, Peter and Sands, Karen 1999: 'The View from the Center: British Empire and Post-Empire Children's Literature.' In Roderick McGillis (ed.) 2000: 39–53.
Philip, Neil 1981: *A Fine Anger: A Critical Introduction to the Work of Alan Garner*. London: Collins.
Philip, Neil 1997: 'England's Dreaming.' *Signal* 82, 14–30.

Virginia [Esther] Hamilton (1936–)

Virginia Hamilton is the first author to win the three major American children's book awards (the Newbery, the *Boston Globe–Horn Book*, and the National Book Award), with the deceptively subtle *M. C. Higgins the Great* (1974). Her work is central to the period of postwar American writing, like that of Patricia MacLachlan (q.v.) and Katherine Paterson, who understood the mythic implications of their stories. Her grandparents escaped from slavery on the 'underground railroad' and she has written that 'everyone who is black who has lived and those now living have something to say to me and have something to do with the person I am' (Hearne, 1989: 423). There is a nebulous quality about Hamilton's work, an acceptance of the mythic in the mundane, perhaps at its most challenging in *Arilla Sun Down* (1976). As Hamilton has said:

> Time and space become almost mythical. I suffer through them as I imagine, historically, others have suffered through them . . . my fictions for young people derive from the progress of Black adults and their children across the

American hopescape. . . . The people are always uneasy because the ideological difference they feel from the majority is directly derived from heritage. (Hamilton, 1987: 8, 10)

This mode of thinking shows in books like *The Planet of Junior Brown* (1971), in which urban children live in a mutually protective sub-world, and in *M. C. Higgins*, the eponymous character lives in strip-mined countryside with a spoil heap threatening his house.

Only a few miles from the Ohio River, they were in country where once – no more than ten years ago – there had been elk and deer. It was still deep country where people liked nothing better than the quiet of staying close to home. Boys M.C.'s age endured school in the steel town of Harenton. Awkward, with twitching hands and no pine-needles to touch or branches to hang from. In class, tongue-tied, they thought themselves stupid. Their teachers thought them slow. They endured it all. Until time to go home, to live again, ingenious in the woods.

M. C. Higgins also demonstrates Hamilton's ability to fuse, by implication, several periods of time simultaneously: 'I'm unable to deal with one time frame . . . I seem not to be able to create a character in one dimension of time' (Apseloff, 1983: 205). M. C.'s story is more than that of saving his house against the ravaged, sliding mountain; it is arguably as much about self-validation and the validation of a whole race.

Hamilton's view that 'Black life is . . . better for some, worse for most' infuses her books with a certain sombreness. But as in *A Little Love* (1984), her portrait of the disadvantaged teenagers, Sheema and Forrest, resists any temptation to sentimentalize or sensationalize.

Given the faint air of other-worldliness even in what passes for contemporary realism, it is not surprising to find Hamilton producing a ghost story, *Sweet Whispers, Brother Rush*, in which the female hero, Tree, is able to extrapolate lessons learned from the ghost of her uncle to her real-life judgement of her mother.

Yet Hamilton's ultimate view seems to be optimistic. In her introduction to her collection of Black folk-tales, *The People Could Fly* (1985), she notes

These tales were created out of sorrow. But the hearts and minds of the black people who formed them, expanded them, and passed them on to us were full of love and hope. We must look on the tales as a celebration of the human spirit. (Hamilton, 1985: xii)

Bibliography

Apseloff, Marilyn 1983: 'A Conversation with Virginia Hamilton.' *CLE*, 14 (4), 204–13.
Hamilton, Virginia 1985: *The People Could Fly: American Black Folktales*. New York: Knopf.
Hamilton, Virginia 1987: 'Ah, Sweet Rememory!' In Harrison and Maguire 1987: 6–12.
Hearne, Betsy 1989: 'Virginia Hamilton.' In Chevalier 1989: 422–4.

G[eorge] A[lfred] Henty (1832–1902)

There is no doubt that the immortal Henty and his host of imitators have made the British nation the most conceited people on this earth. It is the plotless trash of authors who shelter themselves behind the section in the library catalogue entitled 'Books for Boys', which has given the average young Englishman that very excellent opinion of himself which he now enjoys. Putting aside the question of the utter impossibilities of the usual boys' book, it is quite easy to see the harm the authors of these volumes cause by the exaggeration of the deeds and opinions of their *invraisemblables* heroes. After fourteen or fifteen years' perusal of 'piffle' written apparently for his education, the young Englishman leaves home and country with the very firm idea in his head that he, personally, is equal to two or more Frenchmen, about four Germans, an indefinite number of Russians, and any quantity you care to mention of the remaining scum of the earth – R. van Eeghen, *The Captain*, May 1908. (Eldridge, 1996: 68–9)

In the nineteenth century the British adventure story was inextricably bound up with a matrix of cultural ideas and institutions: empire, masculinity, codes of behaviour, sexism and racism, public (that is, private) schools (and their symbiotic literary genre), and class. A writer like G. A. Henty, who represents the height of Victorian imperialism in books primarily for boys, was writing in a powerful, mature genre that both reflected and influenced British attitudes and behaviour in the empire, fuelled by a heady mixture of racial superiority, arrogance, fortitude, a complex system of codes, and a jingoistic appropriation of Christianity. Henty was equally popular in the USA (his books were extensively pirated until the International Copyright Act of 1891), where similar themes were found in the 'dime novels' which followed the success of James Fenimore Cooper's 'Leatherstocking' novels (1823–41). His influence on the teaching of history – his books, like others of the genre, were packed with facts – was also considerable.

The tradition of the adventure story, with its undercurrent of imperial exploitation, goes back to the eighteenth century with writers like Smollett and Defoe, whose *Robinson Crusoe* (1719) – much adapted for children in the eighteenth century – established a genre of its own in the nineteenth century, the Robinsonnade. However, the adventure story does not emerge as a significant form in Britain until the 1840s. Captain Frederick Marryat (1792–1848), whose *Masterman Ready* (1841–2) was written as a correct- ive to the wildly optimistic geography and biology of *The Swiss Family Robinson* – set a fashion for expansive adventure with a modicum of moralizing. The moralizing is less obvious in R. M. Ballantyne (1825–94), whose long career began with *The Young Fur Traders* (1856), which still in parts makes brutal and lurid reading, with murder (notably of a 'half-breed' girl, graphically hacked to death) and massacre interspersed among wholesome adventure and 'useful information'.

Throughout the genre it is (perhaps surprisingly to the modern reader) the chunks of information that are as interesting as the action. Here, for example, is a newcomer to the frozen north in *The Young Fur Traders*, insisting on wearing his accustomed leather boots:

> In a few minutes, the feet begin to lose sensation. First the toes, as far as feeling goes, vanish; then the heels depart, and he feels the extraordinary and peculiar and altogether disagreeable sensation of one who has had his heels and toes amputated, and is walking about on his insteps. Soon, however, these also fade away, and the unhappy youth rushes frantically home on the stumps of his ankle-bones – at least so it appears to him, and so in reality it would turn out to be if he did not speedily rub the benumbed appendages into vitality again.

Probably the most enduring of Ballantyne's books was *The Coral Island* (1858), which again combines the idea of manly men in a colonial paradise with a good deal of gruesome bloodshed (of both natives and pirates). The book resonates through the century and perhaps its most famous successors have been very different orchestrations of its themes: *Treasure Island* (q.v.) (almost a parody), *Peter Pan* (q.v.) (a very uncomfortable attempt to domesticate its horrors) and, facing up to its inherent savagery, William Golding's adult novel about childhood, *The Lord of the Flies* (1954). The fact that this last has become a standard text in secondary schools in the UK says a great deal about attitudes to 'childhood'. *The Coral Island* was of course a Robinsonnade, drawing on and reinforcing the fashion for stories in which man triumphs over nature, with obvious implications for empire and racial superiority.

Ballantyne was a colourful figure, who personally researched his long series of books, such as *Fighting the Flames* (1867) for which he joined the London fire brigade. It was this spirit of adventure that was carried through many other prolific writers, notably Captain Mayne Reid (1818–83) and W. H. G. Kingston (1814–80), who produced stories with resounding titles such as *From Powder Monkey to Admiral: or, the Stirring Days of the British Navy* (1879).

Vast numbers of stories appeared, often in 'penny dreadfuls': cheap, sensationalized and very often unpleasantly brutal texts. As a consequence, in 1879 the Religious Tract Society established *The Boy's Own Paper* (which ran until 1967) to provide more wholesome fare (although it is not always easy to distinguish the wholesome racialist massacre from the unwholesome one). There were many similar magazines, such as Kingston's *Union Jack* (1880–3); not unnaturally, one of the most notorious publishers of penny dreadfuls, Edwin Brett, followed suit with *Boys of England* in 1866. (In the USA several magazines, notably *Demorest's Young America* of 1866–75, provided similar 'healthy' reading.) *The BOP* was not over-militaristic (at least by the standards of its day), but it provided a strong set of codes of behaviour: in 1891, for example, it printed the following reply to a letter (which was *not* printed).

> We are glad you have seen the error of your ways in time. Live well. Take lots of exercise and always have something to employ your mind. Cold bath every morning. Hard mattress. Not much bed clothing. Medicine: simple tonic but not *iron*. (Warner, 1976: 93–4)

As Jeffrey Richards points out, imperialism changed from 'the evangelicalism, the commercial and cultural imperialism' of Ballantyne and Kingston, to the 'aggressive militarism' of Henty and Gordon Staples, 'as the evangelical impulse itself became secularized and fed into full-blown imperialism, which became in many ways a new religion blended of the Protestant work ethic and the public school code' (Richards, 1989: 5).

G. A. Henty was one of the major contributors to *The BOP*, and his formula distilled many elements of the genre. His heroes are young Englishmen: healthy, manly, honest, chivalrous, innately superior to anyone else, modest (and frequently priggish). Henty places them in real historical situations (*With Wolfe in Canada, or, The Winning of a Continent*, 1887; *Held Fast For England. A Tale of the Siege of Gibraltar*, 1892), surrounded them with large chunks of raw history, and let them make good. Producing more than eight books a year by dictation at up to 6,000 words a day may not seem to be the recipe for subtle literature, but there is a singularity of vision and purpose that remains mesmeric, not to mention simple value for money. In the course of just one book, *Winning His Spurs. A Tale of the Crusades* (1882) – also issued as *The Boy Knight; Fighting the Saracens* – the young Cuthbert captures the castle of an evil Baron (who is own brother to Sir Reginald Front-de-Bœuf of Scott's *Ivanhoe*); he joins King Richard's crusade, and on the way across Europe saves the king's betrothed, the Princess Berengaria from kidnap; encounters pirates, and helps to capture Cyprus (the whole campaign takes two pages); reaching Jerusalem he is captured by and escapes from the Saracens, and has more adventures in Switzerland and Germany on his way back to England. There he (plus some Saxon outlaws) rescue Lady Margaret of Evesham from the villainous Sir Rudolph (taking another castle) and then he accompanies the minstrel Blondel to France and Austria to find King Richard. The ending, wherein Cuthbert is married and receives his due lands, is something of an anti-climax.

On almost every page of Henty the complex moral and social codes show themselves. A characteristic touch of militaristic morality is found in Jack Stilwell's adventures during the French invasion of Catalonia. In *The Bravest of the Brave, or, With Peterborough in Spain* (1887), the Count of Cifuentes, retreating, wastes the countryside:

> 'I have also ordered the wells to be poisoned.'
> Jack looked grave. 'I own that I don't like that,' he said.
> 'I do not like it myself,' the Count replied; 'but if an enemy invades your country you must oppose him by all means. . . . But I don't want to kill in this way, and have given strict orders that in every case where poison is used, a placard, with a notice that it has been done, shall be affixed to the wells.'
> 'In that case,' Jack said, 'I quite approve of what you have done, Count; the wells then simply cease to exist as a source of supply.'

The Henty tradition, with such writers as 'Herbert Strang' (George Herbert Ely, 1866–1958 and James L'Estrange, 1867–1947), F. S. Brereton (1872–1957) and Percy F. C. Westerman (1876–1959), dominated adventure-writing and reading well into the 1930s, by which time it was serving a new concept of empire. Jeffrey Richards has pointed out that

> it was no longer to be equated with militarism or expansion but seen as a bulwark of peace, geared to the maintenance of the rule of law and the

enlightened and equitable administration of colonies and protectorates. It is this ethos which forms the framework for such inter-war imperial adventures as W. E. Johns's Biggles stories. (Richards, 1989: 5–6)

The whole ethos might be summed up in the famous poem 'Play Up and Play the Game' by W. Cecil Laming, MA, published in *The BOP*, which makes the same parallel between school and empire found throughout the century from Mrs Ewing's *Jackanapes* (1879) to Kipling's *Stalky and Co* (1899) and far beyond:

> When the match is going against you, that you've striven hard to win,
> When the forwards rush the scrimmage, and the halves keep romping in,
> When the score's three goals to one
> With ten minutes more to run,
> And victory seems hopeless, and you're very tired and lame,
>   Remember, schoolboy pluck
>   Will often turn the luck:
> Play up! Play up! Play up! Play up and play the game!
>
> When the foes are closing round you, and the bullets whistle past,
> And it's hard to keep your courage, with your comrades falling fast,
> When fighting hand to hand
> You make one desperate stand,
> And home is distant, death is near, and glory seems a name,
>   Remember, British pluck
>   Has often turned the luck:
> Play up! Play up! Play up! Play up and play the game!
>
> (Warner, 1976: 140)

All of which was sufficiently powerful an attitude (totally blind to the circumstances under which the fight might have been provoked, of course) that it still needed to be demolished in the bitter words of the Polish officer in Robert Westall's *The Machine Gunners* (1975), who mocks the concept of fair play in the face of grim realities. 'Ah, the English gentleman – always so bloody fair. Perhaps if your homes had been burnt to the ground you would not be so concerned to be bloody fair.'

Bibliography

Arnold, Guy 1980: *Held Fast For England: G. A. Henty Imperialist Boy's Writer*. London: Hamish Hamilton.

Bristow, Joseph 1991: *Empire Boys: Adventures in a Man's World*. London: HarperCollins.

Butts, Dennis 1992: 'The Adventure Story.' In Butts 1992: 65–83.

Dawson, Graham 1994: *Soldier Heroes: British Adventure, Empire and the Imagining of Masculinities*. London: Routledge.

Eldridge, C. C. 1996: *The Imperial Experience: From Carlyle to Forster*. London: Macmillan.

Green, Martin 1980: *Dreams of Adventure, Deeds of Empire*. London: Routledge and Kegan Paul.

Warner, Philip (ed.) 1976: *The Best of British Pluck: The Boy's Own Paper*. London: Macdonald and Janes.

Russell [Conwell] Hoban (1925–)

If it takes a particular form of genius to be unclassifiable, then Russell Hoban has it. He has produced maverick bestsellers for adults, such as *The Lion of Boaz-Jachim and Jachim-Boaz* (1973), and books that fit uneasily between classifications, such as *Riddley Walker* (1980), a sustained linguistic experiment depicting post-apocalyptic degeneration of language. Straddling the adult–child divide, *The Mouse and His Child* (1967) has been taken to be a children's book, but its existentialist gloom, its taciturn heroes, and its manic villain, Manny Rat, seem to belong to the darker reaches of adult allegory. In these books Hoban has pushed at all kinds of boundaries.

The Mouse and His Child is widely regarded as his most challenging book, but this may be a demonstration of the principle that the less like a children's book a children's book seems, the more respectable it is. At the least, the range of reference and its reflections on the nature of existence may well simply place it outside the comprehension of relatively inexperienced readers. It may be that *The Mouse and His Child* explores areas rarely if ever approached in children's fiction: not merely nihilism, but the whole question of experience – questions that are embodied in the obsessive Manny Rat: 'He was there all at once and with a look of tenure, as if he had been waiting always just beyond their field of vision, and once let in would never go away.'

The simple moral might be as the Frog says: 'I don't suppose anyone ever is completely self-winding. That's what friends are for', but the book is littered with philosophers like the muskrat and C. Serpentina the ancient snapping turtle, who would not be out of place in *Alice's Adventures in Wonderland*, were that an even darker book than it is.

But if *The Mouse and His Child* is obvious Ph.D.-fodder, there is importance and value in apparently slighter books. The joint masterwork *How Tom*

Beat Captain Najork and His Hired Sportsman (1974) has text by Hoban and illustrations by Quentin Blake (q.v.), and can be held up as an exemplar of the possibilities of the picture book. It not only explores the balance of power between adults and children, but also pokes fun at the arbitrariness of the rule-bound world of adult behaviour. Tom beats the Captain at games whose rules are totally obscure even – especially – with the 'help' of the illustrations: the pictures deliberately do *not* illustrate (thus shifting the power in the text from book to reader).

While picture books have received a good deal of attention in terms of theory, books designed for those who are learning or have just learned to read have been neglected. Hoban's work in this field, notably the Frances books, are virtuoso demonstrations of manageable elisions. Here, in *A Baby Sister for Frances* (1964), Frances makes a protest against her new sibling:

> After dinner that evening, Frances packed her little knapsack very carefully. She put in her tiny special blanket and her alligator doll. She took all the pennies out of her bank, for travel money, and she took her good luck coin for good luck. Then she took a box of prunes from the kitchen and five chocolate biscuits.
>
> 'Well,' said Frances, 'it is time to say good-bye. I'm on my way. Good-bye.'
>
> 'Where are you running away to?' said Father.
>
> 'I think that under the dining-room table is the best place,' said Frances. 'It's cosy, and the kitchen is near if I run out of biscuits.'
>
> 'That's a good place to run away to,' said Mother, 'but I'll miss you.'
>
> 'I'll miss you too,' said Father.
>
> 'Well,' said Frances, 'good-bye,' and she ran away.

The telling is so spare and understated that it may allow inexperienced readers to recognize themselves and their peers, and to see slightly more than the characters do, and it makes them work to fill in the gaps.

Hoban's other noteworthy excursions into eccentricity are a (lesser) sequel, *A Near Thing for Captain Najork* (1975), undercut, perhaps, by its shift to adults as central characters, and also with Quentin Blake, a fine tall-tale, *The Twenty-Elephant Restaurant* (1978). The kind of domestic observation found in the Frances books is extended to adolescence in the dry wit of *Dinner at Alberta's* (1975), illustrated by James Marshall (himself responsible for the laconic Fox series from 1988).

In short, Hoban is an original who demonstrates that it is a mistake to categorize texts, especially certain forms of text as 'minor': he remains a writer who operates with equal subtlety and intelligence, at and beyond the extreme reaches of 'children's literature'.

Bibliography

Allison, Alida 2000: *Russell Hoban/Forty Years: Essays on his Writings for Children.* New York: Garland.
Crips, Valerie 1993: 'Mistaken Identity: Russell Hoban's *The Mouse and His Child.*' CL 21, 92–100.
Wilkie, Christine 1989: *Through the Narrow Gate: The Mythological Consciousness of Russell Hoban.* Rutherford: Fairleigh Dickinson University Press.

Ted Hughes (1930–1998)

The curious case of Ted Hughes as poet for children is highly instructive as to the status of children's poetry in general and the problems of discussing it. Hughes, who was English Poet Laureate from 1987 until his death, achieved his pre-eminence to some degree by his preoccupation with 'elemental' and 'basic' subject matter, in sharp contrast to the solipsistic poets around him. However his poetry may be debated, there can be no question that he was a great worker towards democracy in poetry, and encouraged thousands of young writers, notably with his book *Poetry in the Making* (Hughes, 1967).

He began writing for children with the comic-verse *Meet My Folks!* (1961) and progressed through nature poems such as *Season Songs* (1975) to the more mystic *Under The North Star* (1981). His work has become part of the canon, and its author virtually canonized:

> Ted Hughes offers those young readers who can manage it poetry of power and potency, presenting a stirring and often mythic vision of the world that has echoes, perhaps, of William Blake. (Styles, 1998: 260)

> The lithe muscularity of [poems from *What is the Truth?*], their compassion, their delicate balance between stillness and movement, their stunningly compact and vivid visual imagery, are typical of the mature confidence of Hughes's work for children, both in verse and prose. (Philip, 1996: xxxiv)

> As well as being a superb writer of straight description, Hughes also has the gift of conveying those realities which, while we all feel them, cannot be rendered in straight photographic terms but must be caught by something closer to metaphor. (Wain, 1979: 66)

One assumes that what these writers are writing about are poems like 'Rooks Love Excitement' from *What is the Truth? A Farmyard Fable for the Young* (1984):

Rooks love excitement. When I walked in under the rookery
A gale churned the silvery, muscular boughs of the beeches, and the wet leaves
streamed –
It was like a big sea heaving through wreckage –

And the whole crew of rooks lifted off with a shout and floated clear
. . .

A sudden uplifting of everything, a surfing cheer.

Hughes also theorized his position:

> One can communicate with children in a simple and whole way – not because
> they're innocent, but because they're not yet defensive. Providing one moves
> affectionately.
>   So in writing for children, it seems to me there's an attractive possibility –
> of finding, in some way, on some wavelength of imagery and feeling, a lingua
> franca – a style of communication for which children are the specific audience,
> but which adults can overhear. In other words, it reaches adults – maybe –
> because assuming this is not for them, they suspend defences and listen – in
> a way secretly – as children. (Paul, 1986: 55)

Despite this, however, when he turned to writing specifically for children
Hughes produced work that an unsympathetic observer might feel was very
inferior. An important question is why there were so few unsympathetic
observers.

Hughes wrote three types of poetry: 'for' children (such as *Meet My Folks!*,
Under the North Star), adult poetry, and a fair amount that lies somewhere
in between, accessible to both adults and children. In *Meet My Folks!* he seems
to have been overcome with a fatal attack of avuncularity, producing as weak
and patronizing a collection as one could imagine, which does not even
trouble to scan, and mixing British and American usage to force the rhymes.

> Some fathers work at the office, others work at the store.
> Some operate great cranes and build up skyscrapers galore.
> Some work in canning factories counting green peas into cans.
> Some drive at night in huge and thundering removal vans.

As is so often the case, it is not what actual children think is funny, or what
the poet thinks is funny, but what the poet thinks children should think is
funny. All of that, of course, may be questionable: what is hardly questionable is that there is no obvious skill attached to these verses.

The second kind of poetry for children produced by Hughes was a 'cut-down' version of his poetry for adults. Here he was on even more dubious ground. It can be plausibly argued that the *fewer* words, the greater the gaps that the reader must fill, and hence the more difficult the poetry. Also, far more than in his adult verses, Hughes appears to fall into the trap of anthropomorphism: a question to be addressed is how far an adult, with anthropomorphic views sympathetic to the ancients, is in contact with childlike anthropomorphism. The result seems to be nothing but patronizing in the modern context. Why else should such an ostensible respecter of animals as animals, produce *Moose*:

> The goofy Moose, the walking house-frame,
>   Is lost . . .
>
> He meets another moose
> He stares, he thinks: 'It's only a mirror!'
>
> 'Where is the world?' he groans. 'O my lost world!
>   And why am I so ugly?
>   And why am I so far away from my feet?'
>
> He weeps.
>   Hopeless drops drip from his droopy lips . . .
>
> Two dopes in the deep woods.

A good test-text is Hughes's *Collected Animal Poems 1: The Iron Wolf.* Are the poems 'for children' actually distinguishable by their mediocrity: 'Lowly, slowly / A pink, wet worm / Sings in the rain: / "O see me squirm"'? What is the distance between the opening poem, 'Amulet' ('Inside the Wolf's fang, the mountain of heather') and the first poem, 'The Mermaid's Purse' ('She'd opened her purse / For an aspirin – / What a shock! / Out came a shark / With a great black fin')?

To some, an even more puzzling phenomenon is the success of Hughes's short fable, *The Iron Man* (1968). The first chapter is a *tour de force*, an ingenious and powerful enigma: the Iron Man falls over a cliff, disintegrates, rebuilds himself and strides into the sea. The remaining episodes, in which he battles a space-bat–angel–dragon virtually as big as the earth, have all the marks of bedtime expediency rather than coherent myth-making; they ignore scale and reason to drag in the mystical music of the spheres and a clunking moral. Why did the vast, cosmic, continent-crushing, galactic dragon (or bat

RUDYARD KIPLING (1865–1936) 81

or angel) want to eat the earth? 'It just came over me, listening to the battling shouts and the war-cries of the earth – I got excited, I wanted to join in.'

The sequel, *The Iron Woman* (1993), is an even more meretricious ecological parable ('They had all learned a frightening lesson . . .'), although a review in the *Guardian* called it 'A fiercely imagined, hugely challenging fantasy.'

It can be argued that Hughes's esteem as a writer for children betrays a great deal about criticism. His children's poems are generally (politely) ignored by adult literary critics and yet inordinately praised by children's literature critics. It is almost as if, with no faith in their own judgements, such critics are glad to accept the acceptance of an accepted poet. Or one might accept the judgement of Lissa Paul, that what Hughes can be remembered for is 'his passion for observation and feeling, his passion for making . . . I understand [she concludes] what John Bayley meant . . . when he called Ted Hughes a poet of "comfort and joy"' (Hunt and Paul, 1999: 74).

Bibliography

Hughes, Ted 1967: *Poetry in the Making*. London: Faber and Faber.
Hunt, Peter and Paul, Lissa 1999: 'On Ted Hughes.' *Signal*, 88, 69–72.
Paul, Lissa 1986: 'Inside the Lurking-Glass with Ted Hughes.' *Signal*, 49, 52–63.
Philip, Neil (ed.) 1996: *The New Oxford Book of Children's Verse*. Oxford: Oxford University Press.
Wain, John 1979: 'The *Signal* Poetry Award.' *Signal*, 29, 63–6.

[Joseph] Rudyard Kipling (1865–1936)

Given the ambiguous status of children's literature as a whole it is fitting, in a somewhat ironic way, that the most 'respectable' writer who can be paraded as 'great' (or at least, canonical) is one whose status in the literary world is also highly ambiguous. Kipling distinguished himself in more genres of children's literature than any other author (with the possible exception of the far less well known William Mayne) and, equally importantly, he demonstrates a wide range of attitudes to writing for children.

His reputation has suffered from generations of critics who have found his politics distasteful: he did, after all, write the now almost universally condemned poem, 'The White Man's Burden': 'Take up the White Man's Burden / Send forth the best ye breed . . . / To wait in heavy harness / On fluttered folks and wild – / Your new caught sullen peoples / Half devil and half child.' Some of his apologists have taken the view that Kipling can be admired, even addictively, for his mesmeric prose *despite* his regrettable racist and imperialist opinions; or as Angus Wilson put it, his imperialism was a reflection 'of the deep inner struggle between the anarchic, romantic, childlike force of his creative impulse and the ordered, complex, at times almost self-defeating pressure of the craft he imposed upon it' (Wilson, 1977: 276).

Kipling's children's books represent a fascinating part of this struggle. In them, he seems at the very least to have muted some of those ideas, as if he increasingly found that a specific audience of children compelled him to be *more* rather than less subtle. Equally, it may have been that he was unable directly to sustain prejudices that adults would accept in the face of what he felt to be a clear-eyed, innocent audience.

Thus the book that I regard as his masterpiece, *Puck of Pook's Hill* (1906), although it is steeped in the concerns of empire (its forging in early England and its loss in Roman England), is really about people. Although it is nationalistic, it considers positive and negative aspects of nation; far from being anti-Semitic, it is the bitter, ironic and noble Jew who brings the law (and civilization) to the barbaric gentile English.

Kipling never quite ceases to be problematic, but at his most playful and personal, as in the *Just So Stories for Little Children* (1902), he demonstrates his remarkable originality most clearly. Here he is directly addressing specific children (his own, and their cousins), and the book appears to be a remarkable transcription of actual oral performances, complete with incantations and very local jokes. As Kipling wrote in the introduction to the first story in *St Nicholas* (Christmas 1897): 'In the evening there were stories meant to put Effie to sleep, and you were not allowed to alter those by one single little word. They had to be told just so; or Effie would wake up and put back the missing sentence.'

> Once upon a time, on an uninhabited island on the shores of the Red Sea, there lived a Parsee from whose hat the rays of the sun were reflected in more-than-oriental splendour. And the Parsee lived by the Red Sea with nothing but his hat and his knife and a cooking stove of the kind that you must particularly never touch. And one day he took flour and water and currants and plums and sugar and things, and made himself one cake which was two feet across and three feet thick. It was indeed a Superior Comestible (*that's* Magic), and he put it on the stove because *he* was allowed to cook on that stove, and he baked it and he baked it till it was all done brown and smelt most sentimental. ('How the Rhinoceros got his Skin')

Just So Stories joins the select ranks of that theoretical category of 'single address' books: books that seem to exclude adults from their audience (although some of the lesser-known stories verge on the didactic ('How the Alphabet was Made', for example).

In contrast, *Stalky and Co* (1899) is writing for children as therapy for the adult. Kipling may be exorcising part of his own unhappy childhood: revenging himself (in the character of Beetle) on school bullies, while acknowledging those of whom he approved. As children, Kipling and his sister were sent home from India and suffered terribly as private boarders – as related in the adult-oriented story 'Baa Baa Black Sheep'. The school portrayed in *Stalky* was a version of the United Services College at Westward Ho! where Kipling gradually found his feet. In this book, the fundamental and simplistic (sometimes equated with childish) aspects of Kipling – revenge, local loyalty, initiation, insider–outsider relationships, and ultimately the British empire as a game (which the superior British win) – all emerge. *Stalky and Co* was in many ways a corrective to the pious school story and was not matched until Robert Cormier's (q.v.) *The Chocolate War* (1974). The story 'The Moral Reformers' in which Stalky and his friend beat up the bullies provoked H. G. Wells into a riposte. *Stalky* was, he thought, 'the key to the ugliest, most retrogressive, and finally fatal idea of modern imperialism; the idea of a *tacit conspiracy between law and illegal violence*' (quoted in Stewart, 1992: 46).

The huge and lasting popularity of the Walt Disney version of *The Jungle Book* (a classic example, in traditionalist terms, of a bad film being made out of a good book – the reverse of *Peter Pan*) may have distorted many contemporary children's encounters with Kipling's text (if ever they have one). In the Mowgli stories, no longer is Baloo, as it were, an affable streetwise (or junglewise) oaf; in the book, he is the sage, the wise interpreter of the law. Shere Khan does not depart, running from the flames: he is methodically, even professionally, killed.

But the books are not merely tougher than the film: they are infinitely more subtle. Kipling's preoccupations are to the fore – the inner circle, the law, the caste system – but this is not an exercise in colonialism. Mowgli the human dominates the animals, but he is also the independent outcast, the individualist; he derives his codes of behaviour *from* those he dominates. He must first learn the master words, as Baloo says: 'A man's cub is a man's cub, and he must learn *all* the Law of the Jungle.' He is the child's/dreaming adult's vision of independence; of power over the animals, but also of peaceful coexistence with them; of power over corrupt and ignorant adults.

His motivations for revenge (on Shere Kahn, on the villagers) may be essentially crude, but the means of revenge require skill, co-operation and the application of codes of behaviour. (One might compare the Water Rat's entry into the alien world of the Wild Wood in *The Wind in the Willows* (q.v.): you may be superior, but you still have to play by and respect *their* rules.)

Of course, all of this may be no more that saying that one respects some inferior race as worthy opponents; but equally it is a view that empathizes closely with childhood: learning to respect the opposition, the adults; learning to play their games, and ultimately to beat them at them.

But, finally, it may be Kipling's inimitable prose style that marks him out. In the development of narrative away from the hand-held book, and in a multimedia world in which prose has to compete as never before, the complex prose of a writer like Kipling can be held up as representing the world that is being lost.

Bibliography

Plotz, Judith A. (ed.) 1992: Kipling edition of *CL*, 20.
Lycett, Andrew 1999: *Rudyard Kipling*. London: Weidenfeld and Nicolson.
Stewart, D. H. 1992: '*Stalky* and the Language of Education.' *CL*, 20, 36–51.
Wilson, Angus 1977: *The Strange Ride of Rudyard Kipling*. London: Secker and Warburg.

E[laine] L[obl] Konigsburg (1930–)

The post-1945 American children's novel has, in broad terms, moved from a stable family environment epitomized by the Elizabeth Enright's (1908–68) Melendy books (from *The Saturdays*, 1955), which seem now to have an idyllic, elegiac air, through a period of alienation and despair in the 1970s and 1980s. As Anne Scott MacLeod has pointed out, writers 'adopted the alienation of [Salinger's *The Catcher in the Rye*], and the rejection of conventional values, but not the Romanticism that gilded its hero' (MacLeod, 1997: 126) A recent development, epitomized by the writing of Chris Crutcher, implies a more mature, even relationship between adults and children (or teenagers). Whereas Robert Cormier (q.v.) tends to require readers to make their own decisions, Crutcher has returned to an earlier model: 'I like adult characters to be able to make sense of things and that's what I use them for. And I use adult characters to give a different perception to something that probably a kid wouldn't come up with just because there are fewer experiences for him' (Smith, 1992: 68).

One of the key responses in adolescent fiction to the social upheavals of the 1960s and 1970s was as MacLeod (1997: 128) notes, not 'an accurate picture of the new social landscape, but . . . a highly ambivalent adult reaction to it'. In the midst of this the USA produced several authors who dealt with the changing world either more comfortingly or more obliquely. Most notable of the first type is Betsy Byars (1928–), whose books, while often featuring abandoned children (*The Midnight Fox*, 1968; *The Pinballs*, 1977), children facing crises such as bullying (*The Eighteenth Emergency*, 1973) or children coping with a second-rate adult world (*The Cartoonist*, 1978), generally arrive at some kind of upbeat resolution: characters find their inner strengths or at least negotiate a method of survival.

Byars's books subsist in a transitional area, between the thoughtful, allusive, *well-made* text and the novel of more portable ideas. The same is true of Katherine Paterson (1932–), who has won the generally conservative Newbery Medal twice, for *Bridge to Terabithia* (1977) and *Jacob Have I Loved* (1981). Paterson's books (much like Nina Bawden's in the UK) cover similar emotional areas to Byars's, but add far more complex symbolic structures and considerable intertextual reference. It is instructive to compare *The Pinballs* with Paterson's *The Great Gilly Hopkins* (1978), both moving books 'about' foster children: both end characteristically. *The Pinballs* ends with Carlie, a fostered child, deciding that 'when I go to this new school, I'm really going to try'; whereas Gilly faces the fact that her mother does not want her: as her foster-mother says:

> All that stuff about happy endings is lies. The only ending in this world is death. Now that might or might not be happy, but either way, you ain't ready to die, are you . . . there's lots of good things, baby. But you just fool yourself if you expect good things all the time. They ain't what's regular – don't nobody owe 'em to you.

Gilly's reaction is positive in the sense that Holden Caulfield's reactions are positive. Paterson's subsequent elevation to canonical status reflects the considerable urge to create an unassailable corpus and validate a certain approach to writing.

These are morally serious and highly intelligent books, and it is in this context that the erratic, witty and highly intelligent books of E. L. Konigsburg appeared. Her distinction lies not in any agglomeration of symbolism but in subtle structural touches. The key point about *Jennifer, Hecate, Macbeth, William McKinley and Me, Elizabeth* (1967) is that race is insignificant: the intricate games and fantasies of two children make it so: it is the inner life that matters. Similarly, *(George)* is predicated on a literal split personality, but the whole thrust of the book is against either a conventional or a depressing resolution. Here is Ben explaining his problem to his mother:

> Ben added . . . 'I never thought much about what other kids might think of me before this year. I was so busy listening to George. I was happy listening to him. And you, you happen to be lucky that George has always been on your side.'
>
>   'George? George who?'
>
>   'George Carr. That George who. George, the little man who lives inside of me. I told Dr Herrold about him this morning, but George wouldn't talk to him. And he probably won't talk to you either, even though he's always been on your side and has always made me take out the garbage and keep everyone in the family on time.'
>
>   'Did George ever tell you to do something that you didn't want to do?'
>
>   'Mother, it is just that kind of thinking that has me in the trouble that I'm in now. Right now.'

From the Mixed-Up Files of Mrs Basil E. Frankweiler (1967) is based around Claudia, who feels unappreciated and who, with her brother, runs away from home to live in the Metropolitan Museum of Art. As the story lies on the borders of fantasy, it encourages a metaphorical reading and has other embedded structures. Roberta Seelinger Trites has noted that 'a common pattern among feminist children's novels is the use of the "nested narrative" ': the story within a frame, where frame and story reflect each other. The relationship of Claudia and Jamie to Mrs Frankweiler depends upon the stories they tell each other, and 'in the end, Claudia and Mrs Frankweiler share a maternal relationship that resides in the shared secrets of each other's narratives' (Trites, 1997: 114).

One of Konigsburg's strengths is a skewed view of the world which nevertheless addresses common problems: in *Journey to an 800 Number* (1983) Max's father is an amiable peripatetic camel keeper, while Sabrina and her mother spend their vacations tricking their way into conference hotels. But the book is also a tract for the times: ' "My mother and father are divorced." "Aren't everybody's?" '

E. L. Konigsburg's books, then, might be said (for those who like tidy versions of history) to epitomize the postwar 'golden age' of children's books in the USA, when literacy and intelligence were being brought to bear on contemporary problems, and before they were swept away (if not from the backlists) by more urgent and violent approaches, although having said that, it should be admitted that Konigsburg's *The View from Saturday* won the 1997 Newbery Medal for the best American children's book of the year.

Bibliography

Konigsburg, E. L. 1987: 'Between a Peach and the Universe.' In Harrison and Maguire 1987: 464–76.
MacLeod, Anne Scott 1997: 'The Journey Inward: Adolescent Literature in America, 1945–1995.' In Beckett 1997: 125–9.
Smith, Louisa 1992: 'Limitations on Young Adult Fiction: An Interview with Chris Crutcher.' *LU*, 16 (1), 66–74.

Patricia MacLachlan (1938–)

Since the 1960s American writing for children has been marked, if not dominated, by women writing intelligent, combative texts, very often socially involved. Notable among them are E. L. Konigsburg (q.v.), Natalie Babbitt, Betsy Byars, Virginia Hamilton (q.v.), Katherine Paterson, Ellen Raskin and Cynthia Voight. As always, it is unsatisfactory to select one writer as an exemplar of a mode (rather than a group or movement), but Patricia MacLachlan's work is an excellent starting point.

As with other writers, MacLachlan uses themes that have otherwise been marginalized – in this case by a male-dominated (literary) culture – notably family and parenting. Like Katherine Paterson, and Jill Paton Walsh and Gillian Avery in the UK, and Margaret Mahy (q.v.) in New Zealand, MacLachlan uses intricate symbol systems, often based on location and home, sound and colour to give depth to what may appear on the surface to be quite slight tales.

MacLachlan is at the centre of that writing for children which regards modern childhood as a problematic place, where children are turned inwards: the classic example is Louise Fitzhugh's *Harriet the Spy* (q.v.). 'I think', MacLachlan has said, 'I'm writing the same book over and over again. . . . All of my books seem to concern themselves with family, and who we are as people' (Zolotow and MacLachlan, 1989: 737). Her books also assume a certain attitude to reading and fiction on the part of the readership. Thus, Maria Nikolajeva points out that MacLachlan's novels

Differ radically from 'issue' books in their narrative patterns. The ideological message is not imposed upon readers; coming to an insight demands strong empathy on the readers' part, as they follow the characters' enduring reluctance to see life for what it is. (Nikolajeva, 1997: 11)

This is also reflected in intertextual literary references.

MacLachlan's books fall into two broad categories: *Sarah, Plain and Tall* (1985, which won the Newbery Medal) *Skylark* (1994), *Baby* (1993), *Journey* (1991) and *The Facts and Fictions of Minna Pratt* (1988) are centrally about the relationships between mothers and children; *Arthur, For the Very First Time* (1980), *Cassie Binegar* (1982) and *Unclaimed Treasures* (1984) are concerned with the main characters' search for self, generally within a nurturing family. In both cases, MacLachlan's belief in the interconnectedness of generations and cyclical patterns of life is clearly demonstrated. Thus the protagonists are helped in their journeys of self-discovery by a remarkable gallery of eccentrics, such as the liberating Aunt Elda in *Arthur*; MacLachlan's principle is that both children and the old are only *apparently* powerless.

Her symbolism is complex and often revolves around seeing, such as the camera lens in *Journey* and the binoculars in *Arthur*. This motif is summed up in the story told by Aunt Elda in *Arthur* (which is later fleshed out in *Sarah, Plain and Tall*). The mail-order wife meets the homesteader's children:

And then she took the youngest one on her lap. From her handkerchief she took a piece of glass. A prism. She held it up to the light, and it sent colors everywhere in that drab room. 'You won't remember your mother,' she said, 'but you will learn that her life touches yours. All of us touch each other. Just like the colors of the prism. Don't you forget that.'

MacLachlan is a 'realist', but just as Virginia Hamilton's realism is blended into a mysticism, so there is a certain romanticism in MacLachlan's work. She differs from Voight or Konigsburg in that her times and settings are vague: the farm in *Journey* could exist almost any time in the last seventy years (in contrast, again, to the specificity of Ingalls Wilder); the island in *Baby* is nebulous. And she also differs from many of her contemporaries in her deep optimism, which goes far beyond the idea of a happy ending: children are *not* necessarily damaged for life by separation or betrayal or loss. In a period which has increasingly concentrated on the alienating effects of society, MacLachlan's aim has been to give hope, to empower children to assert themselves as individuals with rights and valid feelings.

Roberta Trites (1997: 59) has argued that several of MacLachlan's books, notably *Cassie Binegar* and *Baby*, explore the silencing of the female, literal or enforced aphasia, and the acquisition of a voice, of language 'as the only force which can both define the individual and bring people together'. Certainly, female strength is asserted in *Sarah, Plain and Tall*, which emphasizes power and partnership. As such, MacLachlan is an *affirmative* writer.

With her understated feminism, drawing it seems from the roots of female concerns, MacLachlan is one of the quintessential writers for children of the past two decades, concentrating on the key preoccupations of childhood and power, but generally distancing herself from teenage *angst*. Any writer who can make a book finish (and turn) on her female hero finding her vibrato on her cello, as in *The Facts and Fictions of Minna Pratt*, is doing something quite distinctive.

Bibliography

MacLachlan, Patricia 1986: 'Facts and Fictions.' *Horn Book Magazine*, 62 (1), 19–26.
Nikolajeva, Maria 1997: 'The Child as Self Deceiver: "Postmodern" Narrative Strategies in Katherine Paterson's and Patricia MacLachlan's Novels.' *Papers*, 7 (1), 5–15.
Trites, Roberta Seelinger 1993: 'Claiming the Treasures: Patricia MacLachlan's Organic Postmodernism.' *ChLAQ*, 18 (1), 23–8.
Trites, Roberta Seelinger 1995: 'Is Flying Extraordinary? Patricia MacLachlan's Use of Aporia.' *CL*, 23, 202–20.
Zolotow, Charlotte and MacLachlan, Patricia 1989: 'Dialogue between Charlotte Zolotow and Patricia MacLachlan.' *Horn Book Magazine*, 65 (6), 736–45.

Margaret Mahy (1936–)

If there is one author whose work belies the old critical adage that children's literature cannot sustain serious critical examination, it is New Zealand's foremost children's author, Margaret Mahy. As Anne Lawrence-Pietroni (1996: 34) put it, 'Mahy's work serves to destabilize expectations of character and genre as self-contained and complete'.

Mahy's work is characteristically self-referential and unstable; she parodies the very forms that she uses. Prolific and erratic, her writing is genuinely 'child-centred', and at all 'levels' she focalizes tightly through her child characters: theirs is the real, valid and self-justifying world. Her situation *vis-à-vis* criticism mirrors this: her writing does not seem to have the intellectual discipline of, say, a Jill Paton Walsh or an E. L. Konigsburg (q.v.), but possibly as a result, it contains highly suggestive, interwoven levels of complexity that are increasingly regarded as a challenge to serious critics.

It would be difficult to find a novel – anywhere – which makes more subtle use of the metafictive than Mahy's *The Tricksters*, in which the ideas of carnival (made explicit by three characters with the surname Carnival) and life imitating art are explored through complex family and time relationships. It can be very persuasively argued that although Mahy seems to use conventional forms, her work is resolutely postmodernist, frequently (or perhaps pervasively) feminist, and continually deals in margins and eccentricities, mirroring the conflicting expansions of adolescence.

Frequently, forms blend. *The Changeover* (1984), for example, appears to be a naturalistic psychological novel about Laura's relationship with her mother, suggestively overlaid with a supernatural premise, an incubus regenerating itself by taking over Laura's young brother. This unlikely combination is played out in unremarkable suburbia in terms of an adventure, but its constant ambiguities and questioning of what is real and what (if anything) is fantastic allow it to be read as an examination of the nature of truth and reality.

> Outside in the city, traffic lights changed colours, casting quick spells of prohibition and release. Cars . . . set off . . . through the maze of the Gardendale subdivision, a labyrinth in which one could, after all, find a firebird's feather, or a glass slipper or the footprints of the minotaur quite as readily as in fairy tales, or the infinitely dividing paths of Looking-Glass land.

For Mahy, even apparently totally realistic texts have metaphysical implications. Among the best of these is *Memory*, centring around a disturbed young man, Jonny, and an old lady suffering from Alzheimer's disease. As Heather Scutter notes, Mahy's persistent concern with women and girls 'writing the world' emerges here: 'One of Mahy's chief feminist strategies is to represent, through the perceptions of Jonny, the female world as other and then to deconstruct his understanding of that otherness' (Scutter, 1995: 10).

Lissa Paul has pointed out in a comparison of *The Changeover* with Burnett's *The Secret Garden* that Laura's *female* quest is an example of the patterns identified by Annis Pratt (1992). Not only does Mahy write at a time when 'it is possible for a woman to succeed in a man's world, and where nurturing instincts need not be devalued', but in combining the male quest and the 'female' sentimental romance readers are 'alerted to the fact that the conventions of sentimental romances are in operation in serious fiction. . . . Mahy makes her book reflect the gender-crossing and genre-crossing trends of contemporary young adult fiction – and contemporary society' (Paul, 1987: 199, 200).

Some flavour of Mahy's work can be found in this characteristic passage from *The Catalogue of the Universe* (1985): Angela watches her mother scything by moonlight. As she does continually, Mahy plays with the possibilities of indeterminate symbolism and the ambiguity of the complexities of life:

> Angela could see the entranced, semi-circular swing of her shoulders, heard the whisper of the keen steel and the sigh of long grass bowing down before her. Everything around her was drenched in a light so clear and so intense it seemed as if it must have more substance than ordinary light. It was the very light of visions and prophecies. . . . Angela could plainly sees that Dido's own eyes were so flooded with moonlight that she was radiantly blind, a fairy-tale woman who, having lost her own sight, had been given pale, shining eyes of silver. . . .
>
> Like the road, Dido had a dangerous edge and sometimes she went right out to it and danced, apparently challenging it to crumble away under her. Angela feared for such a reckless dancer, though by now she knew that she, too, had an inside road as well as an outside one, and dangerous edges of her own. . . . But whatever Dido challenged by dancing on dangerous edges was no sort of happiness Angela could recognize.

This serious playfulness is not confined to her novels for teenagers. *The Librarian and the Robbers* (1978), to take a random example, is not merely farce; it is also, perhaps, a gently feminist and anarchist parody of the adventure genre.

Something of a phenomenon in New Zealand and international publishing, an indication of Mahy's status is that in 1993 she was awarded New Zealand's highest civil honour – the Order of New Zealand – for her writing. She has won the British Carnegie Medal twice (*The Haunting*, 1982; *The Changeover*, 1984). For younger children (and, of course, discerning adults), she has developed an interesting line in apparently inconsequential picture-book texts (*The Lion in the Meadow*, 1969; *The Boy Who Was Followed Home*, 1975; *Jam*, 1985) which play with the borderlines between fantasy and reality and sometimes with that between the adult and the child (*Keeping House*, 1991). This is quite apart from the huge number of 'readers' that she has produced for the New Zealand Department of Education, and stories for *School Journal*, which almost certainly need to be liberated from their 'education' ghetto.

Bibliography

Ford, Linda 1994: 'Margaret Mahy and the Problems of Teenage Fiction.' In Neil Broadbent, et al. (eds), *Researching Children's Literature – A Coming of Age?* Southampton: LSU, 49–55.

Gose, Elliot 1991: 'Fairy Tale and Myth in Mahy's *The Changeover* and *The Tricksters*.' *ChLAQ*, 16 (1), 6–11.

Lawrence-Pietroni, Anne 1996: '*The Tricksters, The Changeover*, and the Fluidity of Adolescent Literature.' *ChLAQ*, 21 (1), 34–9.

Paul, Lissa 1987: 'Enigma Variations: What Feminist Theory Knows About Children's Literature.' *Signal*, 54, 186–202. Reprinted in Hunt 1990: 148–65.

Pratt, Annis 1992: *Archetypal Patterns in Women's Fiction*. Brighton: Harvester Press.

Scutter, Heather 1995: 'Choose Our Own Agenda: Margaret Mahy's *Memory*.' *ChLAQ*, 20 (1), 9–4.

Jan [Janet Marjorie] Mark (1943-)

Jan Mark has said that the novels of William Mayne (q.v.) initially inspired her to write, and her books share Mayne's values of integrity, intelligence and a brilliant ear for dialogue. As a result, perhaps, it is tempting to see her work as exemplifying a kind of writing that is becoming rarer, that looks to standards of complexity and allusiveness that are being lost – 'literary' standards, in fact. For example, this is a paragraph from *They Do Things Differently There* (1994), which is both a sharp satire on life (or lack of it) in a new town and a neat experiment in narrative.

> The postcards in the glass case were almost illegible. *For sale: Green lady's bycicle. Three speed. Ten pound's. Found: Ginger kitten, white feet. Apply within.*
> I was so relieved that the notice said found and not lost. I knew I should have cried again at the thought of that long-ago lost kitten, wondering if it had ever come home. I hoped that the green lady had managed to sell her bicycle.

A sceptic might wonder how many of the linguistic jokes in that passage would be recognized by anyone (let alone children), or how many would notice the 'correct' use of the word 'should'. The subtle, well-crafted text infused with thoughtful humour may have been displaced, but Jan Mark (along with Mayne) represents the best of that tradition.

In general terms, those 'literary values' which might be seen in mainstream British and American writers such as Nesbit (q.v.), Kipling (q.v.), Masefield and Ransome (q.v.) – namely allusiveness, subtlety of addressing (and hiding) themes, relatively gentle pacing, oblique characterization, and careful atmospherics – were continued in a remarkable blossoming of talent broadly between 1950 and 1970, with writers like C. S. Lewis, Philippa Pearce, Mary Norton, Lucy Boston and, quintessentially, William Mayne and Jan Mark. Their writing is quite different from the writers who flourished in the 1990s – Jean Ure, Anne Fine (q.v.), Jacqueline Wilson – both in form and content. As Adèle Geras observed in 1995, 'There does seem to be . . . a growing dread of the *slow*, the leisurely, the atmospheric, and the very detailed that strikes me as sad. It goes along with a terror of the complex, the ornate, the problematic and the ambiguous' (Geras, 1995: 19). Similarly, Aidan Chambers said in the Woodfield Lecture in 1981:

> It is fashionable just now to assume – not to argue or suggest but to assume – that what children want is books which have an immediate undifferentiated appeal, that they must be either funny or pertinent, by which is usually meant, the subject must be one that is a preoccupation of the adult concerned. Complexity, multi-layering, richness of language, the kind of book which demands that the reader match the author in an act of creation that costs thought and energy: these are out of date. (Chambers, 1985: 18)

In that these 'out-of-fashion' writers are identified with 'in-school' reading, they may paradoxically suffer from an association with literariness – with 'difficulty'.

If Jan Mark's writing seems deeply rooted in the earlier tradition, it acknowledges the necessity for change. Her first book, *Thunder and Lightnings* (1976), won the Carnegie Medal, and it has been followed by a long sequence of sharply observed contemporary stories, very rarely taking an obvious or easy line or resolution, often concerned (like *Thunder and Lightnings*) with understanding the 'other'. Mark has also produced three unusually dour and serious, but highly inventive excursions into science-fiction: *The Ennead* (1978), *Divide and Rule* (1979) and *Aquarius* (1982), although her popular successes have been naturalistic books dealing with the subtleties of relationships, such as *Handles* (1983).

Mark is, however, pre-eminent as a writer of short stories, and it would be difficult to match from any writer pieces (both from *Nothing to Be Afraid Of*, 1980) such as 'The Choice is Yours' – a desperate account of a school-girl caught between two rival school-mistresses – and 'William's Version' – in which William protests against his impending sibling by subverting Granny's telling of 'The Three Little Pigs'. (The complete story is implicit in the first sentence: 'William and Granny were left to entertain each other for an hour while William's mother went to the clinic.') Others demonstrate calculated understatement: 'Frankie's Hat' (*Frankie's Hat*, 1986), the day out for an entrapped teenage mother; or witty manipulation of a large cast: 'Time and the Hour' (from *Hairs in the Palm of the Hand*, 1981) which shows the relationships within a whole class, and almost a whole school. *Enough is Too Much Already* (1988) is a masterpiece of ironic observation and teenage argot.

Mark's primary characteristic, what Neil Philip has called 'unusual intellectual toughness' (Chevalier, 1989: 637), makes her comedy all the richer. Her later books, such as *The Sighting* (1996), have maintained her impressive output during a period in which wit (rather than humour), seriousness and subtlety are rapidly disappearing from children's books. Jan Mark represents the best of what is being eroded. As she observed in her 'Introduction' to *The Oxford Book of Children's Stories*:

> One of the most evident developments in modern fiction for children has been, especially in the sophisticated form of the short story, many writers' regard for the intellectual and intuitive agility of the young reader. (*Times Educational Supplement*, 12 November, 1993)

There could hardly be a better description of Mark's own work.

Bibliography

Geras, Adèle 1995: 'What's the Rush?' *Books for Keeps*, 93, 19.

William Mayne (1928–)

> Adults can read my books if they like, it doesn't matter. I'm not interested in what they think. (Nettell, 1989: 15)

William Mayne has some claim to be the most successful individualist in the history of children's books, and the most distinctive twentieth-century children's writer. His style, oblique and subtle, is instantly recognizable: 'a form of continuous subdued recoil against the narrative shape and impetus' (Peter Hollindale, quoted in Chevalier, 1989: 651). Indeed, he has been called 'the most assured stylist of all modern children's authors' (Sarland, 1975: 217). His narrative is almost always focalized through children, with the characteristics (if not limitations) of (in)experience and (mis)understandings, but with an attendant freshness of vision of both life and language. He constantly uses elision, thus requiring the reader to supply a large amount of the background, intonation, and so on. In this respect he is at odds with a great many modern children's writers in giving the child reader the credit for being able to recognize allusions and fill in gaps. His narrative structures have become progressively more complex and innovative.

Despite his single-minded exploration of the child's view of the world, conventional children's book criticism does not regard him as an important writer: he has been called a children's writer enjoyed only by adults, but with well over 100 books to his name since 1953 (all for children) this view posits some remarkably generous publishers. As Edward Blishen remarked as long ago as 1968:

> It is . . . easy, and I think quite wrong, to claim that he is a writer for a highly literate minority; . . . I believe this view is an invention of those who see only the freshness, subtlety and obliquity of the writing, and do not observe that it is always tied to stories of considerable narrative strength, or that children everywhere have a delight in verbal ingenuity. (Blishen, 1968: 83)

This attitude to Mayne may have been taken because he very rarely gives interviews and never theorizes about his work. Here is a characteristic comment (on *A Grass Rope*, 1957):

> After the idea was there I wrote the book, a statement that, though short, is completely adequate. There is nothing particularly interesting about writing a book. In fact, it is rather a bore for everyone, and generally spoils the idea that was there in the first place. (Crouch and Ellis, 1977: 95)

In general, Mayne is not concerned with large or heroic themes, but rather the minutiae of life; of people and places and often arcane knowledge: his forte is the small-scale, local interaction, and social comedy at family level, reminiscent, perhaps, of writers like Alan Ayckbourn or Harold Pinter. This means that he apparently does not 'build into' his books themes that can be discussed in the abstract very easily: his books *are* rather than *about*, and even when he does have a strong plot, the true emphasis is on the characters within it. His dialogue is (as J. D. Salinger described the Glass family's dialogue in *Zooey*) 'a kind of esoteric, family language, a sort of semantic geometry in which the shortest distance between any two points is a fullish circle.' Here is a sample from *The Battlefield* (1967):

> 'Sugar, buttons, white cotton, butter, two dish-cloths, pound of stewing steak and kidneys for a pudding,' said Mum. 'The buttons are for Dad's shirts.'
>
> 'Go on,' said Debby, writing it all down. 'Something more romantic. A peacock, or a golden tree.'
>
> 'There should be threepence each in the change,' said Mum. 'Bring two loaves, as well.'
>
> 'I love my love with an "a",' said Lesley, reminding Debby how to spell loaves.
>
> 'I know now,' said Debby. 'It's sugar I can't spell. I know there's an "h", and I know it doesn't go with the "s", but where does it go?'
>
> 'It doesn't belong,' said Lesley. 'It's one somebody dropped.'
>
> 'Oh,' said Debby. 'Well, I can't keep it. It won't live, they never do.'
>
> 'Come on,' said Mum. 'Don't stand there. Get on down to the village.'

His texts for young children have a similar unexpectedness in their texture, as anyone who has tried to copy them out will have found. An example from *Mousewing* (1987):

> Evening and mice wake up.
>
> Youngmouse sits and watches light grow dark enough. His eyes are brown; they watch below.
>
> 'What are you thinking?' asks Mothermouse, 'so still and quiet.'
>
> 'With my eyes I see the garden fall asleep,' says Youngmouse. 'Petals fold, seeds fall. Cat's behind the window.'

His mature style for an adolescent audience relies a great deal on understatement, as in this example of the opening of *Gideon Ahoy* (1987):

> Somewhere an aeroplane.
>
> Gideon waking in the next room with a shout, his morning shout.
>
> He can't tell he does that, thought Eva, coming out of sleep herself, in the next room, opening a silent eye. Does that, she wondered, make a great noise for someone. Am I deaf to light like Gideon is deaf to sound?

Gideon getting out of bed with a thump on the floor.

Eva opened another eye. Daylight in them both, there was, and daytime too.

It's not getting in, she thought; I'm alright in here without it.

For the first twenty years after *Follow the Footprints* (1953) through what might be put forward as his masterpiece of this period, *Ravensgill* (1970), his plots often revolved around treasure hunts or the unravelling of mysteries, set in distinctive regions, notably his native Yorkshire. They are everything conventional stories with such topics are not: unspectacular, intellectual, allusive. With *Earthfasts* (1967) he widened his scope to take in fantasy, but generally speaking his plotting in his fantasy novels is their weakest point; ironically, realism allows less resolution. Since then, Mayne has ranged across genres, from satire on communist Eastern Europe in *Tiger's Railway* (1987), to the brilliant evocation of inner-city Australia, in the complex interwoven short stories of *Salt River Times* (1980), the narrative ingenuity of *Drift* (1987), in which the same 'story' is told twice, to the transformation of the teenage romance in *Midnight Fair* (1997) and the invention of a new folklore in the Hob stories (1984, and *Hob and the Goblins*, 1993). His Chorister Quartet set in Canterbury Cathedral Choir School (beginning with *A Swarm in May*, 1955) provided an individualistic counterpoint to the conventional school story.

Over the years Mayne's work has reflected broad literary trends. His work before the mid-1970s adopted a narrative stance which, as John Stephens points out,

is part of Mayne's use of the strategies of modernist fiction. . . . In the early eighties, Mayne began to emphasize further the process of analysis (and thereby to reflect an increasing use of postmodernist modes) by including in his books substantial metafictional episodes that simultaneously advance the story and act as models for interpreting the narrative techniques that inform it. (Stephens, 1993: 101)

It has been said that children are not trained to read writers like Mayne. His single-minded devotion to writing for children and his capacity to ignore (avowedly) adult critics suggests that he is closer to the real readers among real children and their perceptions than virtually any other writer. That this closeness excludes adults and puts in question their literary judgements is hardly surprising.

Bibliography

Blishen, Edward 1977: 'William Mayne.' In Dennis Butts (ed.), *Good Writers for Young Readers*. London: Hart-Davis Educational, 79–85.
Crouch, Marcus, and Ellis, Alec 1977: *Chosen for Children*, 3rd edn. London: Library Association.
Lurie, Alison 1989: 'William Mayne.' In Avery and Briggs 1989: 369–80.
Lurie, Alison 1990: *Don't Tell the Grown-Ups: Subversive Children's Literature*. London: Bloomsbury.
Nettell, Stephanie 1989: 'Authorgraph: William Mayne.' *Books for Keeps*, 58, 19–20.
Sarland, Charles 1975: 'Chorister Quartet.' *Signal*, 18, 107–13.
Stephens, John 1992: 'Modernism to Postmodernism, or the Line from Insk to Onsk: William Mayne's *Tiger's Railway*.' *Papers*, 3 (2), 51–9.
Stephens, John 1993: 'Metafiction and Interpretation: William Mayne's *Salt River Times, Winter Quarters, Drift*.' *CL*, 21, 101–17.

A[lan] A[lexander] Milne (1882–1956)

It is as well to remember when reading some of the most successful children's books of all time – *Winnie-the-Pooh* (1926), *The House at Pooh Corner* (1928), *When We Were Very Young* (1924) and *Now We Are Six* (1927) – that for much of his life, A. A. Milne was deeply ambivalent about them. In a letter of 1952 he wrote: 'There was an intermediate period when any reference to [Pooh] was infuriating; but now such a "nice comfortable feeling" envelops him that I can almost regard him impersonally as the creation of one of my own favourite authors' (Thwaite, 1990: 479). Like Sir Harry Dawe in Kipling's *Rewards and Fairies*, Milne has been immortalized – in his view – for the Wrong Thing. For children's literature studies, he is perhaps the best exemplar of a writer discovering, on the page, a way of writing for children, and who for at least some of the time was writing for a 'double' audience; that is, for adults and children separately on the same page.

Milne, it must be made clear, was a professional; that is, he regarded himself as a skilled craftsman who could (and did) turn his hand to almost any genre. Thus, in the 1920s and into the 1930s he was one of the most successful dramatists and novelists in Britain and the USA: he wrote twenty-eight plays, seven novels, three books of verse, and several volumes of essays, political argument and autobiography. He was for a time assistant editor of the magazine *Punch* and a prolific writer of light verse. He even produced an excellent detective story, *The Red House Mystery*, described by Julian Symons (1972: 115) as 'probably the most entertaining book of [its] kind written during the Twenties' (although it was fiercely attacked by Raymond Chandler for its technical carelessness).

His professional approach to writing for children was summed up in his autobiography, *It's Too Late Now*:

> *When We Were Very Young* is not the work of a poet becoming playful, nor of a lover of children expressing his love, nor of a prose-writer knocking together a few jingles for the little ones; it is the work of a light-verse writer taking his job seriously even though he is taking it into the nursery. (Milne, 1939: 239)

He was not, then, of that breed of children's writers who write for children because that is what they *must* do, or who write for a specific child. Famous as his son Christopher Robin became, he had little to do *directly* with the creation of the stories.

The reputation that A. A. Milne acquired from the books – Dorothy Parker, the acerbic *New Yorker* columnist, famously (or infamously) called him 'Mr. A. A. ("Whimsy-the-Pooh") Milne' – cast a shadow over his other writing. Milne commented on Parker's attacks: 'No writer of children's books says gaily to his publisher, "Don't bother about the children, Mrs Parker will love it"'. He went on: 'but there is no artistic reward for a book written for children other than the knowledge that they enjoy it. For once, and how one hates to think it, *vox populi, vox Dei*' (Milne, 1939: 238). The phrase 'and how one hates to think it' points up Milne's ambivalence.

This can be seen in the first of the books, *When We Were Very Young*, which contains the famous 'Vespers':

> Little boy kneels at the foot of the bed,
> Droops on the little hands little gold head,
> Hush! hush! Whisper who dares!
> Christopher Robin is saying his prayers.

This poem is something of a test case. Along with 'Hoppity' it has been mercilessly parodied by writers from 'Beachcomber' ('Now We Are Sick') to P. G. Wodehouse (in *Nothing Serious*, 1950) and Richmal Crompton (q.v.) (in *William the Pirate*, 1932). The poem has been seen as grossly sentimental; *When We Were Very Young* was, after all, written at a period when the 'beautiful child' cult of the 1890s had blended with a profound desire to believe in childhood innocence. There was a high incidence of what might be called the 'oojie-woogie-boo' factor in a great deal of writing about childhood, not least in *Punch*. Milne, however, ably defended the poem on the grounds that it actually showed the amorality of childhood ('God bless Daddy / I know that's right . . .').

When We Were Very Young and the second collection, *Now We Are Six*, far from being highly original works are very similar to many other collections by writers such as E. V. Lucas and Rose Fyleman (some also illustrated by E. H. Shepard, or in a similar style). They also bear a much closer resemblance to R. L. Stevenson's (q.v.) *A Child's Garden of Verses* than is generally acknowledged. There is much the same mixture of poems about childhood from an adult point of view ('Buttercup Days', 'Sand in the Toes'), nostalgic–mystic poems ('The Invaders', 'Journey's End') and, very successfully, poems that have a gentle irony, and can be shared by adults and children ('Rice Pudding', 'The Good Little Girl'). How far there are any poems truly *of* childhood ('Market Square', 'Down by the Pond' or 'A Thought' are candidates) returns us to the general debate about whether 'pure' children's poetry can exist. To many readers, however (and this might be proven by their status as 'family' poems), Milne is at his best when he abandons a stance and produces straightforwardly *fun* poems, notably 'Bad Sir Brian Botany', 'The King's Breakfast' and 'The Knight Whose Armour Didn't Squeak':

> Of all the knights in Appledore
>   The wisest was Sir Thomas Tom.
> He multiplied as far as four,
>   And knew what nine was taken from
> To make eleven. He could write
> A letter to another knight. (*Now We Are Six*)

Milne's need to abandon any conscious attitude to his texts and his audience in order to succeed seems to me to apply to the two Pooh books, which are probably unrivalled in worldwide sales and marketing success of *any* books of the twentieth century. The Introduction and the first chapter of *Winnie-the-Pooh*, 'In Which We Are Introduced . . .', and the 'Contradiction' and final chapter of *The House at Pooh Corner* are remarkable demonstrations of a writer trying unsuccessfully to position himself *vis-à-vis* his material. 'In Which We Are Introduced' attempts a transcript of a story-telling situation, in which the addressee, the 'you', is a Christopher Robin embedded both in the story and the telling. Milne's ambivalence over where the jokes are aimed is also evident.

> Once upon a time, a very long time ago now, about last Friday, Winnie-the-Pooh lived in a forest all by himself under the name of Sanders.
>
> *('What does "under the name" mean?' asked Christopher Robin.*
>
> *'It means he had the name over the door in gold letters and lived under it.'*
>
> *'Winnie-the-Pooh wasn't quite sure,' said Christopher Robin.*
>
> *'Now I am,' said a growly voice.*
>
> *'Then I will go on,' said I.)*

Perhaps fortunately, however, for much of the rest of the stories the narrative voice absorbs itself in the telling, in the self-sufficient, enclosed world of the '100 aker wood', and in a confident, well-heeled, 1920s childhood.

Within the text there is an interesting tension between characters who are essentially 'adult-like' – Owl, Rabbit and Eeyore – and those who are essentially childlike – Pooh, Piglet, Tigger and Roo. The first group are pretentious, untruthful, devious, corrupt, corrupting and depressive – and if that seems a little extreme, consider Rabbit's suspicion of what Pooh regards as the harmless forest, Owl's pretence of reading, Rabbit's plans to get rid of Roo and Tigger, and Eeyore's entirely adult nihilism. The second group, each representing a facet of childhood, are mystically calm, dependent, timid, unquenchably enthusiastic and, in Roo's case, a self-aware five-year-old. (This is, of course, a male world, and Kanga is a highly ambiguous figure. As with the female characters in *The Wind in the Willows* (q.v.) she is approached with a mixture of suspicion, respect and fear by the other characters.)

Some of the best moments – at least for this adult reader – are generated by the contrast between adult solipsism and childhood innocence, as when Pooh comes across Eeyore on his birthday. Eeyore is bounded by the heavy speech tags and Capital Letters: Pooh drifts off into the cheerfully irrelevant.

> 'Good morning, Eeyore,' said Pooh.
>
> 'Good morning, Pooh Bear,' said Eeyore gloomily. 'If it *is* a good morning,' he said. 'Which I doubt,' said he.
>
> 'Why, what's the matter?'
>
> 'Nothing, Pooh Bear, nothing. We can't all, and some of us don't. That's all there is to it.'
>
> 'Can't all *what*?' said Pooh, rubbing his nose.
>
> 'Gaiety. Song-and-dance. Here we go round the mulberry bush.'

'Oh!' said Pooh. He thought for a long time, and then asked, 'What mulberry bush is that?'

'Bon-hommy,' went on Eeyore gloomily. 'French word meaning bonhommy,' he explained. 'I'm not complaining, but There It Is.'

Pooh sat down on a large stone, and tried to think this out. It sounded to him like a riddle, and he was never very much good at riddles, being a Bear of Very Little Brain. So he sang *Cottleston Pie* instead. (*Winnie-the-Pooh*)

The division between the characters can also be seen in terms of sexual politics, with the childlike characters espousing such traits as intuition, nurturing, valuing the family, negotiation, and so on, as against the adult-like characters' egoism, confrontation, assertion and evasion – sets of characteristics which might be seen as broadly female and male respectively.

Milne's success may be associated with the secret vice of owning and loving a teddy bear, or to the initial, essentially retreatist impulse that produced the books in the wake of the First World War, and which has since been sustained by essentially middle-class nostalgia and astute marketing. But it is clear that the double appeal of the books – to children, and to adults attempting to recapture or whimsically relapse into a lost golden world of childhood – has had a part in sustaining them. Hence, perhaps, the translations into Latin, notably *Winnie Ille Pu*, and Benjamin Hoff's explanations of Taoism, *The Tao of Pooh* (1982) and *The Te of Piglet* (1992), a good many small spin-offs (for example, *Pooh's Little Book of Calm*, 1999), and most importantly for anyone trying to talk about Milne's children's books, Frederick C. Crews's *The Pooh Perplex* (1964).

Crews's now almost legendary book is a satire on the 'student casebook' and on literary criticism as practised in the 1960s (F. R. Leavis, for example, is lampooned as Simon Lacerous, who writes an essay entitled 'Another Book to Cross off Your List'). It is a little unfortunate that Crews took *Winnie-the-Pooh* as his base material (one can only assume that a similar satire on contemporary criticism and theory has not appeared because satire is dumb before it). Crews romps around psychological, cultural and Marxist criticism (and much more) to such effect that it is quite difficult to negotiate a space to consider the books seriously (and many students – and even some critics – have mistaken Crews's work for the real thing).

Milne and Pooh have been magnificently served by two books which are models of their kind, both by Ann Thwaite: a biography, *A. A. Milne, His Life*, and a literary and sociological compendium, *The Brilliant Career of*

Winnie-the-Pooh. We wait upon a volume of criticism that can rise to these heights.

Bibliography

Crews, Frederick C. 1964: *The Pooh Perplex*. London: Arthur Barker.
Lurie, Alison 1990: *Don't Tell the Grown-Ups: Subversive Children's Literature*. London: Bloomsbury.
Milne, A. A. 1939: *It's Too Late Now*: London: Methuen.
Symons, Julian 1972: *Bloody Murder*. London: Faber and Faber.
Thwaite, Ann 1990: *A. A. Milne, His Life*. London: Faber and Faber.
Thwaite, Ann 1992. *The Brilliant Career of Winnie-the-Pooh, the Story of A. A. Milne and his Writing for Children*. London: Methuen.

E[dith] Nesbit (1858–1924)

Edith Nesbit has a formidable position in the history of children's literature, not merely for her 'domestic fantasies' such as *Five Children and It* (1902), in which magic intrudes into the natural world, or 'family' stories such as *The Treasure Seekers* (1899) which have remained in print. The American fantasist Lloyd Alexander wrote that 'Today's writers owe her a debt. We are modern thanks largely to her. As much as anyone . . . she helped us to find our twentieth-century voices' (Alexander, 1985: 355). Barbara Wall has summed up critical opinion:

> Nesbit created a narrative personality for her narrator unlike any which had come before, and allowed that narrator to communicate freely and frequently with a narratee, not merely overtly, but outside the story being told. . . . Nesbit was the first professional writer for children who did not feel the need to justify her writing for children . . . by insisting on the intellectual and moral differences between herself and her readers. . . . She did this with great poise and dignity, and in doing so made it possible for a new kind of children's literature to develop. . . . It is true that her idiosyncratic dominant narrators are possible teller-surrogates, but the strong emphasis she placed on the partnership of narrator and narratee has made the child's interests rather than the adult's the real concern of the stories. (Wall, 1991: 148, 149)

Nesbit's pivotal position can be exaggerated: there were in the nineteenth century many experiments in trying to adopt a tone of voice – by

Kingsley, Carroll (q.v.) and Molesworth for example. There were domestic fantasies and domestic tales of ingenious children, and there were thousands of well-written, readable, exciting texts. But her books show the form of children's literature developing, trying to find a voice appropriate to a new kind of child (which, of course, contributed to the development of that new kind of child); and they demonstrate the development of an *awareness* of the degree of politicization appropriate to the children's book.

Nesbit took the attitude to childhood exemplified by Kenneth Grahame in his two books about childhood (rather than for children), *The Golden Age* (1895) and *Dream Days* (1899). Grahame had given his fictional children intelligence, wit and shrewdness, while maintaining their innocence *vis-à-vis* the adult world: Nesbit let this be owned by the children. She made a break from the concept of the child as actor in the adult-controlled world, a stance so characteristic of the nineteenth century, when the ministering children tend to be – for all their occasional individuality – acting out a role. Nesbit allowed children to function in a world bounded but not totally controlled by adult value systems.

Her most famous exemplar is the self-conscious and unironic Oswald Bastable, narrator of *The Treasure Seekers* and its sequels:

> There are some things I must tell you before I begin to tell about the treasure-seeking, because I have read books myself, and I know how beastly it is when a story begins: ' "Alas!" said Hildegarde with a deep sigh, "we must look our last on this ancestral home" ' – and then some one else says something – and you don't know for pages and pages where the home is, or who Hildegarde is, or anything about it. Our ancestral home is in the Lewisham Road. It is semi-detached and has a garden, not a large one. We are the Bastables. There are six of us besides father. Our mother is dead, and if you think we don't care because I don't tell you much about her you only show that you do not understand people at all.

Nesbit allowed children to satirize adults rather than the other way around, and this is engineered partly by the literary awareness of her characters: they *act* books, as later characters would do (as in Ransome's books).

Her most interesting characteristics can be found in *The Railway Children* (1906); like many of her books it was serialized (in the *Strand*) and has an episodic structure. There is an absent father, a strong mother who supports the family by her pen, who gets involved (very marginally) in revolutionary politics, but who is eventually dependent upon males (balance is restored at the end by the dramatic return of the father). All of these features reflect Nesbit's own life: she was involved with George Bernard Shaw and H. G. Wells and the Fabian movement; she regarded herself as an 'advanced' or liberated woman, who provided the income for the family, and yet she placed herself in an inferior position to her husband.

In *The Railway Children* her attempts to bridge the class divide (for example, the confrontation with Perks or the signalman) tend to depend for their resolution on sentimentalization and simplification: she sets up a potentially difficult situation and then withdraws from it. The narrative voice is, however, somewhat ambivalent. In one notable incident, the children rescue a baby from a canal narrowboat that has caught fire:

> . . . and it was Bobbie who ran like the wind across the bridge and up the long white quiet twilight road towards the 'Rose and Crown'.
>
> There was a nice old-fashioned room at the 'Rose and Crown' where Bargees and their wives sit of an evening drinking their supper beer, and toasting their supper cheese at a glowing basketful of coals that sticks out into the room under a great hooded chimney and is warmer and prettier and more comforting that any other fireplace *I* ever saw.
>
> There was a pleasant party of barge people round the fire. You might not have thought it pleasant, but they did; for they were all friends and acquaintances, and they liked the same sort of thing and talked the same sort of talk. That is the real secret of pleasant society.

However, when it comes to the reconciliation between bargee and children, Nesbit turns – very much in the manner of Kenneth Grahame in *The Wind in the Willows* (q.v.) – to abstract reportage. It is very difficult to see the most unlikely thing done. Even the resolution is ambiguous, not simply in its balance between innocence and scepticism, but in the intended audience:

> 'So you've made another lot of friends,' said Mother. . . .
>
> 'Oh, yes,' said Bobbie: 'I think everyone in the world is friends if you can only get them to see you don't want to be *un*-friends.'
>
> 'Perhaps you're right,' said Mother; and she sighed.

Nesbit's fantastic tales, which are retaining their popularity (on tape and television and in abridgements), notably *Five Children and It* and *The Phoenix and the Carpet* (1904), rest largely on the simple premise of an eccentric magic intermediary – the Psammead, the Phoenix – with a literalist approach to wishes. It is largely to these books that we might apply Humphrey Carpenter's sardonic comment: 'She is an author whose methods are comparatively easy to copy, and many have done so, although whether to the ultimate benefit of children's literature seems questionable' (Carpenter, 1985: 137). Julia Briggs, in her exemplary biography, summarized Nesbit's position rather more positively:

> Something within her clearly responded and corresponded to the position of the child in her society: second-rate citizens, then as now, they practised a quiet subversiveness, an irony at the expense of the absurd world of adults which appealed strongly to her. She experienced all the child's primitive desire to control the world around her, yet she was conscious, as the children in her books are, of being a subject in a world where the rules are laid down by full-grown men – and where women, like children, are relegated to marginal positions and occupations. (Briggs, 1989: 399)

Nesbit was a professional writer for much of her life. Her early stories from Shakespeare seem to have been written with the Lambs' *Tales from Shakespeare* (1808) open in front of her (Hunt, 1997: 105–6), and her later career was marked by a decline into further hack work. But for perhaps ten years she produced a group of books which, for many, shaped British children's literature for nearly a century.

Bibliography

Alexander, Lloyd 1985: 'A Second Look: *Five Children and It.*' *Horn Book Magazine*, 61, 354–5.

Briggs, Julia 1989: *A Woman of Passion: The Life of E. Nesbit 1858–1924.* London: Penguin Books.

Hunt, Peter 1997: 'Afterword.' In E. Nesbit, *The Best of Shakespeare.* New York: Oxford University Press (The Opie Library).

[Helen] Beatrix Potter (1866–1943)

Beatrix Potter's works have become part of British and perhaps world iconography. Her twenty-three small books, with water-colours and wry text, from *The Tale of Peter Rabbit* (1902) to *The Tale of Little Pig Robinson* (1930), have become an international industry. Margaret Mackey has traced over ninety *categories* of merchandising of the books, and over sixty versions of *Peter Rabbit* alone (not counting videotapes and CD-ROMs) (Mackey, 1998:

197–206). Potter's work has been taken seriously by scholars of biology and graphic art, as well as literature and education (see, for example, Linder, 1971). The Beatrix Potter Society is a model of enthusiasm and high-quality scholarship, avoiding the eccentricity sometimes surrounding such organizations; it publishes the Beatrix Potter Studies series (1985–) and organizes the Linder Memorial Lectures. In one of these, Peter Hollindale summarized one aspect of her appeal:

> She moves with ease . . . between the biological reality of the animal and the social behaviour of the human. By taking her seriously as both a naturalist and a satirist, and reading the books as conversations through the medium of fantasy between these two selves, these two Beatrix Potters, we can appreciate the originality of her achievement. (Hollindale, 1999: 18)

Potter demonstrates the blend of precise language and hard-headed, largely unsentimental pragmatism that characterizes some of the most effective children's writers (but not, unfortunately, all of Potter's adapters).

Brought up in a repressive atmosphere, keeping an extensive journal in code for many years, Potter became a highly proficient natural-history artist. *The Tale of Peter Rabbit* originated in a picture-letter and went through several detailed revisions and a privately printed edition (1900) before publication by Warne in 1902. From then on, Potter kept firm control of the design and marketing of her 'little books', which were designed quite deliberately and consciously for 'small hands'.

The fine water-colour illustrations (which were re-reproduced from 1987) are accompanied by deceptively complex texts. Almost all the tales of 'naughty' children, such as *Peter Rabbit*, *Squirrel Nutkin* (1903) and *Benjamin Bunny* (1904), have dark undertones. Others are sharp social comedy, such as *The Pie and the Patty-Pan* (1905), or nightmares with disreputable characters such as *The Roly-Poly Pudding* (1908; as *The Tale of Samuel Whiskers*, 1926) and *The Tale of Mr Tod* (1912). Not only can the vocabulary be sophisticated, but Potter constantly treats her audience with great respect, making extensive use of two devices which conventional wisdom holds to be outside the range of 'small children': elision and irony. A classic example is *The Tale of Jemima Puddle-Duck* (1908), in which Jemima meets the fox:

> She was startled to find an elegantly dressed gentleman reading a newspaper.
> He had black prick ears and sandy coloured whiskers.

'Quack?' said Jemima Puddle-duck, with her head and her bonnet on one side – 'Quack?'

The gentleman raised his eyes above his newspaper and looked curiously at Jemima –

'Madam, have you lost your way?' said he. He had a long bushy tail which he was sitting upon, as the stump was rather damp.

Jemima thought him mighty civil and handsome.

Almost every text makes assumptions of understanding and highly-skilled use is made, for example, of the page-turn as a significant gap. In *Peter Rabbit*, for example, Peter's expedition to Mr McGregor's garden reads thus:

First he ate some lettuces and some French beans; and then he ate some radishes. [Page turn] And then, feeling rather sick, he went to look for some parsley.

The gaps here might not seem obvious, but they might be compared (see Hunt, 1991: 26–32; Mackey, 1998: 38–42) with the revised text by David Hately for the 1987 Ladybird edition ('based on the original and authorized story') which assumes a much less astute readership:

There were lots of vegetables in Mr McGregor's garden. Peter Rabbit loved vegetables. He began to eat them. First he tried the lettuces. Next he tried the beans. Then he ate some radishes. [Page turn]. Peter ate too much, because he was greedy. He began to feel sick. I must find some parsley to nibble,' he said to himself. 'That will make me feel better.'

The implications of such adaptations, and a very early version by Canon Rawnsley – 'And rabbits like children / who run very quick / After eating too largely / are sure to feel sick' – have been discussed by Brian Alderson. He suggests that Potter would have 'had no truck with the reductive procedure' of educationalists who regard the child as the 'measure of children's literature and that it is the duty of those who publish for him to make straight his pathway to literacy' (Alderson, 1993: 18) – and, presumably, morality.

After her marriage in 1913, Potter (now, very emphatically, Mrs Heelis) virtually gave up writing and became a successful farmer and breeder of Herdwick sheep, buying many farms. She gave or left thousands of acres of land in the Lake District to the National Trust.

It would be a mistake, as John Goldthwaite (1996: 289–92) has pointed out, to suppose that Potter was free of sentimentalism or whimsy. He cites

Benjamin Bunny as 'less a book addressed to children than a book about children, illegitimately addressed to adults with a taste for the sweet and sentimental'. But it is the Potter of *The Tale of Mr Tod* and *Peter Rabbit*, 'that stoical naturalist who cuts against the popular grain: dry-eyed, earth-wise, a little uncanny', who 'counts in the end' (ibid.: 291).

Perhaps one of the key paradoxes of Potter is her blend of apparent simplicity and a deep-seated subversion. Humphrey Carpenter sees *Peter Rabbit* as 'a parody. . . . The leg of the moral tale is being gently but quite definitely pulled' (Carpenter, 1989: 287–8); the morals of her stories, if they exist, are very ambiguous. As Hollindale observes: 'Post-fabulist can be a helpful term for Potter. She recognizes Aesop . . . but he is truly "in the shadows", while she is an imaginative artist in the daylight of a scientific age. . . . This means that Potter the moralist is a slippery customer' (Hollindale, 1999: 118).

She is, in fact, a slippery customer on many levels, and her subtlety and intelligence far outweigh that of her many impersonators and adapters. Perhaps more than anything she stands for a world that is rapidly being lost. A comparison between the original version of *Peter Rabbit* and the highly controversial adaptation (illustrated with photographs of stuffed animals) by David Hately, noted above, reveals more than changes in assumptions about child readers. The new version speaks volumes about the changed relationships between parent and children, of the image of the parent (as 'old' or not), of children's supposed responses to death, and the general freedom of children in the world. First, Potter; her four rabbits

> lived with their Mother in a sand-bank, underneath the root of a very big fir-tree.
> 'Now, my dears,' said Old Mrs Rabbit one morning, 'you may go into the fields or down the lane, but don't go into Mr McGregor's garden: your Father had an accident there; he was put in a pie by Mrs McGregor.'

Second, Hately, in a world that is at once less benign and more protective:

> They lived in a burrow under the root of a big tree. One day they were allowed to play outside. 'Stay near home,' said their mother. 'Please don't go to Mr McGregor's garden.'
> 'Why not?' asked Peter.
> 'Because he doesn't like rabbits,' answered Mrs Rabbit. 'He will try to catch you.'

Beatrix Potter, one feels, would have enjoyed the ironies, especially the irony that she has come to stand as an exemplar for many of the critical and sociological difficulties that surround children's literature.

Bibliography

Alderson, Brian 1993: 'The Case of Peter Rabbit (and Others): Some Reflections on "the Impossibility of Children's Fiction".' In Enid Bassom, Rowena Knox and Irene Whalley (eds), *Beatrix Potter's Little Books: Beatrix Potter Studies V*. Ambleside: The Beatrix Potter Society, 9–18.

Carpenter, Humphrey 1989: 'Excessively Impertinent Bunnies: The Subversive Element in Beatrix Potter.' In Avery and Briggs 1989: 271–88.

Hollindale, Peter 1999: 'Aesop in the Shadows.' The Annual Linder Memorial Lecture. *Signal*, 89, 115–32.

Lane, Margaret 1985: *The Tale of Beatrix Potter*. Revd edn. London: Penguin Books.

Linder, Leslie 1971: *A History of the Writings of Beatrix Potter*. London: Frederick Warne.

Mackey, Margaret 1998: *The Case of Peter Rabbit: Changing Conditions of Literature for Children*. New York: Garland.

Taylor, Judy 1996: *Beatrix Potter: Artist, Storyteller and Countrywoman*. London: Frederick Warne.

Taylor, Judy, Whalley, Joyce Irene, Hobbs, Anne Stevenson, and Battrick, Elizabeth M. 1987: *Beatrix Potter 1866–1943: The Artist and Her World*. London: Frederick Warne with the National Trust.

Terry Pratchett (1948–)

Terry Pratchett is a satirist and a moralist and has some distinguished pre-decessors in using fantasy. He seems to have a rather more benign attitude to humanity than, for example, Jonathan Swift, with whom he shares an ironic and eccentric imagination. I do not know how Pratchett is regarded in the community of fantasy writers, but I imagine that he is roundly feared: the man is a literary vacuum-cleaner, hoovering up whole genres and sub-genres of fantasy and remaking them with a humour which is by turns scathing and ironic, but fundamentally optimistic. And as the man whose Discworld novels created Unseen University, a comprehensive parody and demolition of academic pretentiousness, he is someone whom academics might approach somewhat circumspectly.

Pratchett respects his audience, particularly the readers of his children's books. By using as his focalizers people who have an innocent, fresh view of the universe, he is able to rethink – and direct his readers towards rethinking – morality, logic, society, life in general. Johnny Maxwell is the best of these:

> Normal people just ignored almost everything that was going on around them, so that they could concentrate on important things like, well, getting up, going to the lavatory, and getting on with their lives. Whereas Johnny just opened his eyes in the morning and the whole universe hit him in the face. (*Johnny and the Dead*)

Just as the Discworld books overflow with fantastic scenes and characters, so the three Johnny Maxwell books overflow with ideas. *Only You Can Save Mankind* (1992) takes a pugnacious stand against thoughtlessness – and against computer games, high-rise housing, racial stereotyping, Australian television soaps, bad parenting . . . and the Gulf War. It rests on the simple premise that the aliens in a computer game, tired of being wantonly attacked, actually surrender. Johnny, used to zapping and killing impersonally, is forced to realize (in a very complex way) that the enemy is not simply faceless and killing is not a game. Some critics have suggested that the close parallel with the real war is a trifle heavy handed, but it is fuelled by a very obvious disgust.

Only You Can Save Mankind is an excellent example of Pratchett's continuous questioning of any easy answer and his continuous intellectual pursuit of the contingent. *Johnny and the Dead*, therefore, seems on the surface to be a parable about developers destroying communities, and it is strident enough:

> 'You dug up the High Street. It had a lot of small shops. People lived there. Now it's all walkways and plastic signs and people are afraid of it at night. Afraid of the town where they live! I'd be ashamed of that, if I was you.'

But, Pratchett almost says, it was ever thus, and the book explores very painfully such genuine horrors as the Pals' Regiments of the First World War, which resulted in the men of whole communities being wiped out at a stroke.

Both of these books are eclipsed by the ingenuity of *Johnny and the Bomb* (1996), which is a very complex exploration of the implications of time travel. If our critical mind balks at that (forgetting, perhaps, Laputa), it is as well to remember that Pratchett is speculating on parallel universes and the consequence of *any* action. Also, in Terry Pratchett's books *everyone* is knowing: the author, the characters and, necessarily, the readers. Here, Johnny and his friends are, as it were, transported:

> Johnny opened his eyes. The ground sloped up all around him. There were low bushes at the top.
> 'If I asked what happened,' said Yo-less, from somewhere under Bigmac, 'what'd you say?'
> 'I *think* we may have travelled in time,' said Johnny. . . .
> 'Which way did we go?' said Yo-less, still talking in his deliberate voice. 'Are we talking dinosaurs, or mutant robots? I want to know this before I open my eyes.'
> Kirsty groaned.
> 'Oh dear, it's going to be *that* kind of adventure after all,' she hissed, sitting up. 'It's just the sort of thing I didn't want to happen. Me, and four token boys. Oh, dear. Oh, dear. It's only a mercy we haven't got a dog.' She sat up and brushed some grass off her coat. 'Anyone got the least idea where we are?'

The only real question is, how much do they know? Book blurbs have quoted Pratchett as saying that he writes for anyone who can understand. Thus the trilogy of *The Bromeliad*, comprising *Truckers* (1989), *Diggers* (1990) and *Wings* (1990), is an ingenious account of the adventures of a race of Nomes, initially living beneath the floor of a department store – a version of the device of 'small people compared to humans' of Swift, Mary Norton and many others. But the trilogy's overriding metaphor is of the bromeliad itself, a flower 'that grows on the top of very tall trees in wet forests a long way away, and little frogs spend their whole lives in it. Your whole life in one flower. Imagine that' (*Diggers*).

Pratchett's relationship with 'conventional' science-fiction can be seen in *The Carpet People*, a book remarkable for the fact that it was written when Pratchett was seventeen, published in 1971, and rewritten in 1992. Here, the serious concerns of the morality of empire which (it seems) replaced the original rollicking adventure, produce a somewhat more ambiguous ambiguity than elsewhere.

Pratchett has firm views on fantasy:

> So let's not be frightened when children read fantasy. It is compost for a healthy mind. It stimulates the inquisitive nodes. . . . Like the fairy tales that were its forebears, fantasy needs no excuses. (Pratchett, 1995: 7)

One of the reasons for reading Pratchett is his constant linguistic awareness and his war on the stereotype. One of Johnny's friends, Yo-less (so called because he is not stereotypical), is the agent of continuous and often bitterly ironic anti-racist jokes, as in *Johnny and the Dead.*

> 'I've got a question, too,' said Yo-less, standing up.
> The chairman, who had her mouth open, hesitated. Yo-less was beaming at her, defying her to tell *him* to sit down.
> 'We'll take the question from the other young man, the one in the shirt – not, not you, the – ' she began.
> 'The black one,' said Yo-less helpfully.

The distinction between Pratchett's 'children's' books and the Discworld series has been blurred by critics, largely because Discworld seems to mislead the prejudiced by its very form. It seems to me unquestionable that the Discworld books are meant for intelligent adults: they are deeply allusive and frequently deadly serious. The books provide a complete course in narratology; academics who have laboriously catalogued and pondered on narrative devices, ways of telling and authorial stance might look upon them and despair. Of course, given that children are so often (and most curiously) directed to fantasy, that does not mean that inexperienced readers cannot enjoy the books as far as they may. The question of what you need to know in order to recognize these amazing displays of erudition as jokes is central to the whole distinction between children's books and adults' books.

Bibliography

Manlove, Colin 1999: *The Fantasy Literature of England.* London: Macmillan.
Pratchett, Terry 1995: 'Let There Be Dragons.' *Books for Keeps,* 83, 6–7.

Philip Pullman (1946–)

Of the writers of the final decades of the twentieth century, Philip Pullman stands out as an intelligent and inventive voice, and some may find it encouraging that he was voted by readers of the British children's book magazine *Books for Keeps* (November 1999) as their favourite twentieth-century author. This judgement was based on two seriously bestselling books, *Northern Lights* (entitled in the USA *The Golden Compass*) (1995) and *The Subtle Knife* (1997).

These are the first two volumes of a trilogy, *His Dark Materials*, which have been widely described as masterpieces, heralding the return of both the epic novel and the philosophical novel to children's literature. Pullman has had the unenviable task of finishing the third book, *The Amber Spyglass*, under critical scrutiny.

In many ways, he writes in the tradition of the 'well-made-book'. His Sally Lockhart trilogy, beginning with *The Tiger in the Well* (1991), although deeply infused with the spirit of the penny dreadful and the melodrama, and carried through with obvious relish, is preoccupied with serious themes. Pullman's choice of a strong female hero shows his political agenda – and Sally Lockhart is inclined to voice it on occasion:

> 'I was telling you about evil,' she said, 'now that I know what it is. . . . It's what takes an old couple who've got nothing left but each other and splits them up to go in the workhouse so they each die alone. It's what takes rent of tenements and slums and refuses the responsibility of mending the drains so that children have to wade knee-deep through filth to get into their houses. . . . But I did it. . . . So I'm guilty, me and all the other shareholders and speculators and capitalists. . . . You know where *evil* is? . . . It's in . . . [*sic*] Pretending not to know things when once you've seen them.'

Pullman has also produced several highly ingenious (if occasionally overpraised) books which combine text and graphics, such as *Spring-Heeled Jack: a story of Bravery and Evil* (1989), using a technique borrowed from Shirley Hughes's *Chips and Jessie* (1985). *Clockwork* (1996), a near-Moebius strip of a book, raises for quite a young audience matters springing out of the folk-tale, of narrative shapes and techniques. Pullman uses the device of a parallel authorial commentary, rather in the manner of Kipling in *Just So Stories*.

Pullman has said that 'what I find most irritating in my contemporaries among writers [is] lack of ambition. They are not trying big things. They are doing little things and doing them well' (Parsons and Nicholson, 1999: 117). *His Dark Materials* does not lack ambition: it is nothing less than a version of *Paradise Lost*, but with the idea that grace can be regained and that it is a necessary part of maturing. As Pullman puts it:

> It's in contrast to C. S. Lewis's idea, for example, the Christian idea, that the Fall is a terrible thing; that we are all children of sin, and there's no hope of doing any good unless we believe in God and then only if he chooses to bless us with his grace. I think that's a pessimistic and defeatist view, and I don't like it at all. (Parsons and Nicholson, 1999: 119)

The books are set in three parallel worlds and follow Pullman's Eve-figure, Lyra, on a complex quest involving a remarkable range of settings and concepts: in *Northern Lights* the scenes range from what seems to be nineteenth-century Oxford to Dickensian London Docks, to an experimental research station in the Arctic – a world populated by armoured fighting bears, flying witches and an American balloonist. Initially, the most striking feature is that in the first world each human has a visible alter ego, a *dæmon* which alters shape when the person is a child and later becomes fixed. (Pullman had foreshadowed this idea with the 'little malevolent shadow', the monkey who sits on the evil Mr Lee's shoulder in *The Tiger in the Well*.) This device provides, in effect, a metaphor for the whole sequence, but Pullman has also incorporated the idea of infinite universes, infinite choices:

> I am surely not the only writer who has the distinct sense that every sentence I write is surrounded by the ghosts of the sentences I could have written at that point but didn't. (Pullman, 1998: 47)

Pullman has shown himself to be a straightforward theorist, believing in and applying such principles as 'Don't be afraid of the obvious', or the 'three very interesting laws of the Quest: *the protagonist's task must be hard to do, it must be easy to understand, and a great deal must hang on the outcome.*' His primary, central concern is to tell a good story in a simple way, but rather like Ursula Le Guin's books, his apparently simple stories only exist in the context of the 'grand narratives' and their complex offspring.

Bibliography

Fox, Geoff 1997: 'Authorgraph: Philip Pullman.' *Books for Keeps*, 102, 12–13.
Parsons, Wendy and Nicholson, Catriona 1999: 'Talking to Philip Pullman: An Interview.' *LU*, 23 (1), 116–34.
Pullman, Philip 1998: 'Let's Write it in Red: The Patrick Hardy Lecture.' *Signal*, 85, 44–62.

Arthur Ransome (1884–1967)

Writer and foreign correspondent by trade; sailor and fisherman by vocation; and children's writer more or less by accident, Arthur Ransome was probably the most influential British children's writer of the twentieth century, with his twelve Swallows and Amazons books, which epitomize what is now seen as a lost benchmark of style and attitude. He treated his readers as peers, respecting their capacities; he was unmanipulative; his style was spare; his narrative technically complex; his manner leisured; he assumed a solid intertextual knowledge on the part of his readers; he was largely realistic both about family relationships and action; and he empowered his characters (and by implication his readers). *And* he more or less invented the holiday adventure genre.

He brought to children's books two quite paradoxical characteristics: the first was a tightly honed style, the by-product of a long literary apprenticeship. As a young man, Ransome had written anything for a living, from quasi-mystical essays to *A History of Storytelling* (1909), and from *Oscar Wilde: A Critical Study* (1912) – as a result of which he was sued (unsuccessfully) for libel by Lord Alfred Douglas – to a romance in the style of Poe, *The Elixir of Life* (1915). His theoretical grasp of narrative structure was consolidated by the classic retellings, *Old Peter's Russian Tales* (1916): by adopting the voice of a Russian peasant, Ransome overcame many of the archaic-dialect characteristics of previous *rédacteurs*. But it was the dispatches that he sent from Russia to the *Daily News* and the *Observer* between 1916 and 1918 – more than 600 of them – that brought his mature style to a pitch of spareness and precision.

His second and greatest characteristic as a writer for children (and perhaps as a man) was – despite or because of his experiences – his 'innocence' and single-minded enjoyment of unworldly play. His affinity with a certain sort of childhood was no affectation. In 1937, having won the first Carnegie Medal for the best British children's book of the year with *Pigeon Post*, he wrote to the magazine *Junior Bookshelf* quoting Robert Louis Stevenson's dictum: 'You just indulge the pleasures of your heart'. He added: 'You write not *for* children but for yourself, and if, by good fortune, children enjoy what you enjoy, why then you are a writer of children's books' (Crouch and Ellis, 1977: 6).

This statement has been challenged as specious – his books are, after all, 'obviously' for children – and yet Ransome was writing for anyone who felt as he did. Just as he felt that there were 'no lower orders' in the Lake District, so he clearly did not distinguish between children and adults when they were occupied with skills such as fishing, sailing and camping. This may well account for the loyalty his books provoke in adults: his attraction is not, for them, nostalgia, but a shared enthusiasm. Nor is the criticism that he delivers a golden world no longer relevant to children particularly valid: his world was always solipsistic, and the fact that the settings he used are now grossly over-crowded in fact, is irrelevant to both the internal and external adventures of his characters.

Swallows and Amazons (1930) is set in the idyllic, scarcely populated English Lake District of 1929, and introduces the four children of the Walker family, dominated by an off-stage father-figure, nurtured by an on-stage mother (made 'other' by being Australian) and bounded by strict codes of conduct. One of these is the need to do things well, and like Jefferies and Kipling (q.v.) before him, Ransome has a great deal to imply about being insiders and outsiders. Consider this account of rigging the dinghy, *Swallow*:

> John and Susan had done plenty of sailing, but there is always something to learn about a boat that you have not sailed before. They stepped the mast the wrong way round, but that was set right in a moment.
>
> 'She doesn't seem to have a forestay,' said John. 'And there isn't a place to lead the halyard to in the bows to make it do instead.'
>
> 'Let me have a look [said Mother] . . . Is there a cleat under the thwart where the mast is stepped?'
>
> 'Two,' said John, feeling. The mast fitted in a hole in the forward thwart, the seat near the bows of the boat. It had a square foot, which rested in a slot cut to fit it in the kelson.

Ransome *half* explains his terms: we, the readers, are assumed to be insiders.

The children are trusted to behave sensibly ('BETTER DROWNED THAN DUFFERS IF NOT DUFFERS WONT DROWN' reads the telegram from their father) and they camp alone on an island on the lake: every action is meticulously described; everything is *possible*. Ransome, focalizing closely through his child characters, allows them a single-minded and serious view of a make-believe world rooted in literature, from *Robinson Crusoe* onwards. But as with the characters in Richard Jefferies' *Bevis* (1882) (q.v.) (an obvious precursor), they can survive pragmatically in two worlds simultaneously: after a day of chasing pirates, Captain John

> woke in ordinary life. Well, he thought, one could hardly expect that sort of thing to last, and it was almost a pity it had begun. After all, even if there were no pirates, the island was real enough and so was *Swallow*. He could do without pirates. It was time to fetch the milk.

The children are apparently free, but they are in a world made safe by the adults around them, as well as by their own efforts. The only real drama in the book is when John is accused of being a liar (a violation of a basic code), and his response is a physical one – to prove his own worth to himself by swimming around the island.

The structure of the world may appear to be sexist, especially with Nancy and Peggy, the Amazon Pirates, determined to behave as boys. Yet Ransome constantly validates the 'female' characteristics of negotiation, nurturing, co-operation, family and spirituality, against the 'surface' activities of confrontation, competition, exploration and conquest. The male may give permission and set the agenda, but it is the female that ensures success. This theme is developed through the series, notably in the introduction of Dick and Dorothea, two alter egos for Ransome: one, the intelligent, studious boy, the other the literary, romantic girl.

Ransome had studied both the folk-tale and the structure of narrative, and this is evident as the series progresses. Whereas *Swallows and Amazons* has a firm narrative closure, beginning and ending at the same place (the symbolic home), its sequel *Swallowdale* (1931) both begins and ends at some distance from 'home'; by the twelfth book, *Great Northern* (1937), the structure is open ended: the book begins and ends out on the Scottish minches. The only exception is what has been seen as Ransome's masterpiece, *We Didn't Mean to Go to Sea* (1937), in which the Walker children face really serious danger: they sail a small yacht, alone, across the North Sea, in storm and darkness – and such is the displacement that the book is provided with a strong, compensating return to its secure beginning. This book has a very clear folk-tale structure: in the first third, the Walker children learn how to handle a yacht, and in the rest of the book, they apply their knowledge.

As the series proceeds, the world widens. *Swallowdale*, a remarkably slow-paced, not to say bucolic book, expands on the theme of camping and demonstrates Ransome's deep affection for and knowledge of the English Lake District. *Pigeon Post* (1936) and *The Picts and the Martyrs* (1943) round out the landscape, both being virtuoso demonstrations of the art of narrative construction; indeed, if one were to offer a single chapter as an object lesson in this, the first chapter of *Pigeon Post* would be a prime candidate. Not only are all the key characters introduced, but all the key themes, and even the denouement is foreshadowed. Ransome also set two of the books on the Norfolk Broads: *Coot Club* (1934), a disarmingly slow chase-story, and a classic example of the detective novel, *The Big Six* (1940).

Ransome was writing in a period when pre-First World War books still dominated children's reading, while new writers for children, like A. A. Milne (q.v.), Hugh Lofting and John Masefield, were turning to fantasy, in Lofting's case, specifically as a reaction to the war. Ransome's books are, in a sense, retreatist, in that he provides (generally) a secure, child-friendly environment which may even then have had nostalgic elements.

Ransome's immediate imitators – Geoffrey Trease, Peter Dawlish, Aubrey de Selincourt and Marjorie Lloyd – made use of the trappings of his books (sailing, camping, family life) but failed to imitate Ransome's intricate use of narrative structure to give depth and significance to characters and landscapes.

Margery Fisher observed that 'Ransome's genius as a story-teller is not likely to be recognized until his books are read as period pieces . . . so that their social and emotional content are seen in proportion and not as awkward or incomprehensible alternatives to the world today' (Fisher, 1986b: 287). Whether this is true or not depends not on whether the readers are adults or children, but on whether they share Ransome's innocent enthusiasms, whereby *de facto* class and privilege and wealth are not a problem. Of course this argument conveniently supports the status quo, legitimizes Ransome's sexism and naturally appeals to the middle-class, nostalgic critic. But the real qualification to Fisher's argument is whether Ransome will ever again be regarded as a good storyteller because what is recognized as good storytelling will have changed beyond recognition.

Bibliography

Brogan, Hugh 1984: *The Life of Arthur Ransome*. London: Cape.

Erisman, Fred 1989: 'Arthur Ransome, Children's Play, and Cultural Literacy.' *IRCLL*, 4 (2), 107–44.

Hardyment, Christina 1984: *Arthur Ransome and Captain Flint's Trunk*. London: Cape.

Hunt, Peter 1991: *Arthur Ransome*. Boston: Twayne. Revised edition as *Approaching Arthur Ransome*. London: Cape, 1992.

Steward, Dave (ed.) 1997: '*The Swallows and the Amazons*, A transcription of an early draft of *Swallows and Amazons*.' Kendal: Amazon Publications.

Michael Rosen (1946–)

Michael Rosen is, most visibly, a poet, a performance poet, an anthologist, a stand-up comic, a serious political animal, Jewish, a broadcaster (primarily on children's books), an academic, a father and a human being, and a critic: not necessarily in that order. (All of that is quite academically incorrect: such a list is generally only acceptable in the past tense, but energy and conviction need to be met with at least an attempt at energy and conviction.) In short, Rosen has been one of the most influential shapers of the British children's book scene over the past twenty years.

This book might be expected to annotate him as primarily one of the most engaging and prolific poets for children. He was nominated in the 1999 *Books for Keeps* poll as the outstanding twentieth-century children's poet (ahead of Ted Hughes), *and* as *BfK*'s readers' favourite twentieth-century poet (ahead of Roger McGough). He has used free-verse forms to chronicle childhood jokes and traumas, and he is funny and touching about human relations (especially between adults and small children). He has considered the problems of form:

> Maybe what I write aren't poems
> maybe this isn't a poem
> the only way we can find out if this is a poem
> is to find an expert
> do we have an expert here?
> We need someone to tell us
> if this has got the right qualifications
> to be a poem.
> If it hasn't
> then it should be put in a bin marked:
> 'Bin-for-things-we-experts-
> haven't-got-a-name-for-yet-
> but-very-soon-will.'

He is anarchic about 'accepted' values:

> Welcome to the museum.
> First we'd like to show you round the Dress Collection.
> Here you can look at the clothes:
> dresses, shoes, hats, coats and so on
> worn for the last 400 years
> by rich shits.

And he is passionate about racism:

> What fun it is to be a critic
> reading poems that are anti-Semitic.

Eliot, Chesterton, Thackeray too
loved to write of the hateful Jew . . .
Cuddly Stevie Smith as well
wanted us to go to hell.
Our lives are so much the richer
For reading English Literature.

As those lines show, being a poet is not separable from his other beings. He is the kind of man who takes on governments: characteristic was this 1993 onslaught:

> But let's be clear, this government, in spite of all the rhetoric concerning literacy levels, has declared war on the reading of books. . . . The limitation of the expertise [of school librarians] has meant that teachers, hard-pressed to try and catch up with the latest whirligig of demands handed down from the junta running education, have lost the leisure, and for some, the will to gobble up the latest children's literature in their spare time. The national curriculum – changing as it does from month to month, depending on which trusty hack can be put in charge – is squeezing out reading for pleasure . . . the reading of fiction and poetry is becoming increasingly tied into serving functional and utilitarian purposes. (Rosen, 1993: 108, 109)

In an attempt to preserve some kind of innocence, not only for childhood but for the writing surrounding it, some critics might classify or dismiss Rosen as a political writer. To do so is to conveniently overlook the fact that the status quo is profoundly and insidiously political (and far more deadly), while racism is not an academic issue. Thus, although at first sight Rosen may seem to be a purveyor of 'urchin verse' – the easy, the colloquial, the accessibly funny – his poetry is a weapon on the side of both small-scale love and large-scale humanitarianism.

The poems quoted here are from *Mind the Gap* (1992), designed primarily for teenagers; a characteristic Rosen book for younger children is *Wouldn't You Like to Know?* (1977).

Bibliography

Lockwood, Michael 1999: 'Michael Rosen and Contemporary British Poetry for Children.' *LU*, 23 (1), 57–66.
Rosen, Michael 1993: 'Books and Schools: Books in Schools. The 1992 Patrick Hardy Lecture.' *Signal*, 71, 103–14.

J[oanne] K. Rowling (1965–)

Students of literature, popular culture and children's literature ignore the bestseller at their peril. Such books are of course difficult to write about in anything but socio-economic terms, and there is an inevitable analytic pull towards revealing just what their secret is, presumably so that it can be repeated. The mechanics of how J. K. Rowling earned a reputed £14.5 million from three books in three years, and is believed to be the world's highest-earning author in the year 2000 with a projected £80 million in royalties, make abstract analyses of the symbolic resonances of *Harry Potter and the Philosopher's Stone* (1997), *Harry Potter and the Chamber of Secrets* (1998), *Harry Potter and the Prisoner of Azkaban* (1999) and the record-breaking *Harry Potter and The Goblet of Fire*, with nearly 6 million copies in print on publication day, faintly absurd.

This kind of proto-criticism sees finding a model or an association as some-how revealing: it simultaneously cuts a successful author down to size if we can note derivations, and gives us a spurious sense of superior scholarship. It also suggests that books can be reduced to a formula – one of the plagues of popular publishing.

The critic's job can hardly be to point out felicities, which seem to be abundantly obvious to readers. Instead, it might be interesting to analyse the books, not – as with most literary criticism – as an end in itself, but in order to inspect the minds of their readers. What, then, is in the minds of those readers who took these four books to the top of both the adults' and children's bestseller lists in the USA and the UK? It could be argued (*pace* received wisdom in the publishing industry) that the success of a writer like Rowling might, at least initially, derive from the fact that, like Roald Dahl (q.v.) with *James and the Giant Peach*, she was *not* following a formula for what a children's book should be like: rather, she seems to have been tracing echoes. Thus the Harry Potter books are public (that is, private) school stories, with all the accoutrements of the school stories (q.v.) that have played such a noble role in British fiction for 150 years. They are not the first to deal with a school of magic: Jill Murphy's Worst Witch series (from 1974) deals with pupils at Miss Cackle's Academy for Witches (who arrive for each new term on their broomsticks).

Harry and his friends form a conventional 'buddy' group, even including a token (highly intelligent) female, Hermione. Harry is an archetypal anti-hero, an insouciant, inadvertent rebel reminiscent of Anthony Buckeridge's

Jennings, and a figure easy for some of us to identify with: the modest outsider actually marked for greatness (one of these days). Many features of the plotting are reminiscent of Terry Pratchett, as are jokes such as the three-headed dog (Fluffy) that Hagrid owns ('bought him off some Greek chappie I met in the pub las' year'), or the name of the school caretaker (Argus Filch). Wendy Doniger (2000: 26) observed that 'Rowling is a wizard herself at the magic art of *bricolage*: new stories crafted out of recycled pieces of old stories' such as T. H. White, *Mary Poppins*, *Peter Pan* and Snow White. But that is only to say that Rowling is an individual, making skilful use of both her allusions and intricate plotting (Sirius Black, a character mentioned once, in passing, in the first chapter of the first book, becomes a major character in the third – and the significance of that first mention only then becomes dreadfully clear). And, of course, there are moments of grotesquerie and doggerel that echo Roald Dahl, a writer who, quite unfairly to Rowling, has been evoked as a comparison largely, one suspects, because reviewers have heard only of Roald Dahl.

But then, Dahl's *Charlie and the Chocolate Factory* is little more than an extended *Struwwelpeter* with Belloc rhymes; and Blyton's fantasies are pot-pourris of late-nineteenth-century versions of fairy- and folk-tales; and Grahame's *Wind in the Willows* is merely a compilation of fashionable Thames river stories and echoes of music hall sketches. To say that the Harry Potter books are built from the furniture of a mind that has absorbed a good cross-section of children's reading (for the purpose of being a child, rather than the writing of children's books) is not to say that the books are derivative (or, fashionably, intertextually rich). Rather (and it would be insulting the obvious intelligence of Rowling to suggest that this is accidental), she has produced an eccentric blend of the comfortably predictable and the unsettlingly unexpected. Individually, the incidents and characters – the quiddich games, the mysterious messages, the suspicious behaviour of the masters, the gang of bullies – have, in other guises, served many a well-selling author; combined with twenty-first century preoccupations, such as surveillance and the ambiguity of evil, they become new again.

The conditions of publishing in the late 1990s meant, as Rowling observed, that children looking forward to the next volume are anticipating events in the context of their media knowledge: 'They've watched so many movies where the hero's best friend gets killed' (Gray, 1999: 88). The books, planned as a seven-volume epic, have already included a wealth of addictive incident and detail that tends towards a feeling of community: the readers, like the characters, become *insiders*. Rowling herself has become part of the fantasy, with background anecdotes (single destitute parent, writing the book while spinning out cups of coffee in sympathetic cafés), however grossly distorted, adding to the larger myth.

After the unedifying spectacle of the Potter books being derided (with no visible arguments) as 'inferior' to Seamus Heaney's version of *Beowulf* in the debate over the 2000 Whitbread literary awards, the most unlikely people have weighed in on the Potter side: Auberon Waugh (among others) suggested that the books 'may have saved a generation from total illiteracy'. Equally, the Potter books had the dubious distinction of being the most 'challenged' (that is to say, censored) books in the USA in 1999, on the grounds that they advocate or describe witchcraft.

But, there is no need to apologize for Rowling, who must in any case find the pronouncements of some critics whimsical in the extreme. At one point in *Harry Potter and the Chamber of Secrets* Harry and his friend Ron, both of them with a year of magic tuition behind them, have borrowed Ron's father's magical Mk 2 Ford Anglia (a 105E, for *aficionados*). As they fly above the clouds on their way to the school of wizardry, the narrator comments: 'It was as though they had been plunged into a fabulous dream.' Quite.

Bibliography

Doniger, Wendy 2000: 'Can You Spot the Source?' *London Review of Books*, 17 February.
Gray, Paul 1999: 'Wild About Harry.' *Time*, 154 (14), 79–88.
Horn, Caroline 1999: 'The Harry Potter Phenomenon.' *Books for Keeps*, 117, 6–7.

Maurice [Bernard] Sendak (1928–)

Probably the most famous of twentieth-century illustrators/picture-book writers, Sendak had a long career as illustrator (notably Ruth Krauss's *A Hole is to Dig*, 1952) before producing one of the most successful picture books of the century, *Where the Wild Things Are* (1963), described by its publisher as 'the first American picture book for children to recognize that children have *powerful* emotions' (Hentoff, 1980: 341).

Although the book is a victim of over-praise, there is no doubt that Sendak's use of the form is masterly. In *Where the Wild Things Are* the mischievous Max is sent to his room, visits the fantasy land of the wild things, conquers them and returns home for his supper. As his imagination grows, so the size of the pictures grow, until they bleed off the page and eventually cover the whole opening. The images, the design and the words all reinforce each other.

The book has come in for a good deal of analysis and has been read as a sublimation of Max's anger, through which he is able to become independent, relate to his mother, come to terms with his ego, and so on. Sendak sees the book in terms of the games that children play,

> to combat an awful fact of childhood: the fact of their vulnerability to fear, anger, hate, frustration – all the emotions that are an ordinary part of their lives and that they can perceive only as ungovernable and dangerous forces. To master these forces, children turn to fantasy: the imagined world where disturbing emotional situations are solved to their satisfaction. Through fantasy, Max . . . discharges his anger against his mother, and returns to the real world sleepy, hungry, and at peace with himself. . . . [It] is through fantasy that children achieve catharsis. It is the best means they have for taming Wild Things. (Sendak, 1988: 151)

Although the low-key, closely hatched drawings are undoubtedly powerful, it seems that the symbolism was sufficiently effective for the book to be widely criticized as frightening.

The second book of Sendak's 'trilogy', *In the Night Kitchen* (1970), is a more cartoon-like treatment of a somewhat more sensual fantasy and was directly censored. Again, although this was ostensibly because it depicted a young boy's genitals (Sendak observed: 'It is hard to understand these people because their state of mind is so irrational': West, 1988: 88), it is probable that the visual metaphors touched on powerful and emotive psychological areas.

The symbolism of *Outside Over There* (1981) is more complex (or obscure), the illustrations highly allusive, and the compositions extremely subtle (see Doonan, 1986). It seems clear that Sendak's major analogue is the work of Arthur Hughes for George Macdonald's books, but beyond that, *Outside Over There* has been regarded as a book about violation, loss, transfiguration, the id, responsibility and nightmare (although the story, in which Ida's baby sister is kidnapped by goblins who turn out to be babies themselves, might creak a little under the weight of these interpretations).

Sendak has also worked in opera and is regarded as a major mainstream artist. What status his picture books are actually accorded in the world of high culture remains questionable, although his *We Are All in the Dumps with Jack and Guy* (1994), a blending of two old nursery rhymes and with deeply religious symbolism, moves the picture book into new (or perhaps old) territory. As Jane Doonan observed, it might seem that

> only adults with a religious background, and with knowledge of the Holocaust, would be able to make anything of *Dumps* and that Sendak has produced a picture book for them rather than for children. It would be truer to say that he has created something that does not conform to generic expectations about picture books as children's literature only. *Dumps* shares with certain other modern picture books a quality that was formerly the preserve of folk and fairy tales: an open address. (Doonan, 1994: 166)

It is possible to argue that Sendak is both directly and indirectly responsible for the remarkable development of the picture book since the 1960s and the serious critical attention that it has been given.

Bibliography

deLuca, Geraldine 1984: 'Exploring the Levels of Childhood: The Allegorical Sensibility of Maurice Sendak.' *CL*, 12, 3–24.

Doonan, Jane 1986: *Outside Over There: A Journey in Style*. *Signal*, 50, 92–103; 51, 172–87.

Doonan, Jane 1994: 'Into the Dangerous World: *We Are All in the Dumps with Jack and Guy* by Maurice Sendak.' *Signal*, 75, 155–71.

Hentoff, Nat 1980: 'Among the Wild Things.' In Egoff, Stubbs and Ashley 1980: 323–46.

Lanes, Selma G. 1980: *The Art of Maurice Sendak*. New York: Abrams.

Sendak, Maurice 1988: *Caldecott and Co. Notes on Books and Pictures*. New York: Noonday Press/Farrar, Straus and Giroux.

Steig, Michael 1985: 'Reading *Outside Over There*.' *CL*, 13, 139–53.

Mary Martha [Butt] Sherwood (1775–1851)

Those evangelical writers (to use a convenient general description) who dominated children's literature in the English-speaking world from the 1780s until the 1840s epitomize one of the central dichotomies of the study of children's literature. Their books are highly unlikely to be read by any but a very few living children, and then under somewhat unlikely circumstances. That is not to say that they could not be read and appreciated, for despite their reputation for hellfire and retribution, very many of the books remain highly readable.

Equally, to bracket together all writers with religious conviction, as if they were an undifferentiated mass, is clearly untenable. It is also quite easy for a generally non-religious generation at the beginning of the twenty-first century to dismiss such writing as bordering on the fanatical and sadistic. These highly prolific writers (usually women) were driven by firm religious convictions, but they were pragmatic and humane, and many of them were very skilled storytellers. In the limited space available, Mary Martha Sherwood ('Mrs Sherwood') may be allowed to stand for a movement which, in all psychological probability, left its mark on a whole empire for well over a century.

Mrs Sherwood was the heir of nearly a hundred and fifty years of evangelical writing, from James Janeway's *A Token for Children* (1672), John Bunyan's *A Book for Boys and Girls* (1686), through Isaac Watts's *Divine Songs* (1715) (q.v.), Anna Laetitia Barbauld's *Lessons for Children* (1778 onwards), Sarah Trimmer's *Fabulous Histories* (1786) and *The Guardian of Education* (1802–6), to Maria Edgeworth's *Early Lessons* (1801). These are merely high points in the vast output of writers who felt (of course, in many different ways) that children's books were the vehicle for the saving of unregenerate souls.

Mrs Sherwood was also characteristic of the often bewildering industry of these writers. While living in India, she founded schools for children of the army and wrote her first bestseller, *Little Henry and His Bearer* (1814), in which the orphan Henry dies at the age of eight, after many attempts to convert his native servant, Boosy. This tale, together with its sociological and religious implications, echoed down the century. Thereafter Sherwood produced over 400 books, often described (with not always deserved arid connotations) as tracts.

Her most famous book, *The History of the Fairchild Family, or, the Child's Manual: being a Collection of Stories Calculated to Shew the Importance and Effects of a Religious Education* (1818, with sequels in 1842, 1847), is sometimes taken as an extreme expression of repressive evangelical and Victorian attitudes. Each story makes a strong moral or ethical point and is rounded off by a prayer.

As an example, in the 'Story on the Absence of God' young Henry refuses to learn his Latin grammar; his father flogs him well ('with a small horse whip') and he is left with bread and water to consider his sins. When he is still recalcitrant, Mr Fairchild addresses him:

'I stand in the place of God to you, whilst you are a child; and as long as I do not ask you to do anything wrong, you must obey me: therefore, if you cast aside my authority, and will not obey my commands, I shall not treat you as I do my other children. From this time forward, Henry, I have nothing to do with you: I shall speak to you no more, neither will your mamma, or sisters, or John, or Betty. Betty will be allowed to give you bread to eat, and water to drink; and I shall not hinder you from going to your own bed to sleep at night; but I will have nothing more to do with you: so go out of my sight.'

But, as M. Nancy Cutt observes,

The omniscient Victorian parent was not the creation of Mrs Sherwood, but of the Victorians themselves; nevertheless, by presenting the parent as God's vicar in the family, she had planted and fostered the idea. (Cutt, 1974: 98)

It is interesting to compare a similar incident in an American example of domestic life and discipline: Catharine Maria Sedgwick's *Home* (1835), when Wallace drowns his sister's kitten in a fit of anger:

'Go to your own room, Wallace,' said his father. 'You have forfeited your right to a place among us. Creatures who are slaves of their passions, are, like beasts of prey, fit only for solitude.' . . .
    The days passed on. Wallace went to school as usual, and returned to his solitude, without speaking or being spoken to. His meals were sent to his room, and whatever the family ate, he ate. For the Barclays took care not to make rewards and punishments out of eating and drinking, and thus associate the duties and pleasures of a moral being with a mere animal gratification.

It is only when Wallace has proved to *himself* that he can restrain his anger that he can come to his father and say: 'I feel as if I had a right now to ask you to forgive me, and take me back into the family.'

Two scenes in *The Fairchild Family* have become notorious in literary history. In one, Mr Fairchild takes his quarrelling children to a gibbet and forces them to look upon the decayed corpse while he reads them a moral lesson; in another, the spoiled Miss Augusta ('brought . . . up in great pride, without fear of God or knowledge of religion') is burned to death, playing with forbidden candles. The burning incident was very common in evangelical literature, so much so that it can be seen as a marker of changing attitudes. In Catherine Sinclair's *Holiday House* in 1839, a similar (but not fatal) incident is treated more or less as a joke; in 1845, Heinrich Hoffmann parodied it in *Struwwelpeter*, and as late as 1907, Hilaire Belloc finally demolished it in 'Matilda' in his *Cautionary Tales*.

Across the Atlantic, and through the century, then, attitudes shifted and (it might be said) softened, but Mrs Sherwood had set, or had contributed to the setting of, a very stiff agenda. And yet . . . ? Modern parents may (or may not) be horrified by the strictness of the Fairchilds' regime, but, as Cutt points out,

> The little Fairchilds were neither left to the care of servants nor handed over to the outside agencies of school, camp, or cinema. They had at all times their parents' undivided attention. Mr and Mrs Fairchild, though strict, are not unpredictable; they explain the reasons for prohibitions and punishments; they invite questions; they are loving and demonstrative. . . . Most episodes end [with the children] kissed and reassured . . . tucked into bed by a mother who always had time for them, the little Fairchilds felt thoroughly secure. (Cutt, 1974: 67–8)

The same is true of many families in nineteenth-century fiction, which followed in Mrs Sherwood's footsteps. Maria Louisa Charlesworth's *Ministering Children* (1854) encapsulated a fashion for Christian virtue to be expressed in action, although it was not until writers like 'Hesba Stretton' (Sarah Smith) with *Jessica's First Prayer* (1867) that attention genuinely shifted to the plight of the poor, rather than concentrating on the charitable impulses of the middle classes.

Mrs Sherwood's convictions are the foundations of her book, and reading them at nearly two centuries' distance might seem to require a distinctive mindset and critical vocabulary. On the other hand, the number of moralists in the field of children's literature, writing what are essentially tracts, but for modern times – Cynthia Voight, Anne Fine (q.v.), Robert Swindells – has, in some ways, hardly declined.

Bibliography

Avery, Gillian 1975: *Childhood's Pattern: A Study of the Heroes and Heroines of Children's Fiction 1770–1950*. London: Hodder and Stoughton.

Avery, Gillian 1994: *Behold the Child: American Children and their Books 1612–1922*. London: Bodley Head.

Cutt, M. Nancy 1974: *Mrs Sherwood and her Books for Children*. Oxford: Oxford University Press.

Cutt, Margaret Nancy 1979: *Ministering Angels: A Study of Nineteenth-century Evangelical Writing for Children*. Wormley: Five Owls Press.
Pickering, Samuel F., Jr 1993: *Moral Instruction and Fiction for Children, 1749–1820*. Athens, Ga.: University of Georgia Press.

Robert Louis Stevenson (1850–1894)

Stevenson thought that he would be remembered for 'no more than a handful of stories for boys', and apart from *The Strange Case of Dr Jekyll and Mr Hyde* (1886), *Treasure Island* (1883) (q.v.) and to a lesser extent *Kidnapped* (1886) are the most visible remains of his once outstanding popular and critical reputation.

However, the most influential book that he wrote may have been what he called in a letter to Edmund Gosse, *The Complete Proof of Mr R. L. Stevenson's Incapability to Write Verse*, otherwise known as *A Child's Garden of Verses* (1885). Critical opinion differs over the book, but it is generally held that up till then, as F. J. Harvey Darton, the doyen of children's literature historians, put it, 'Ninety per cent of all verse written for children . . . was poetry-substitute, manufactured in good faith, but in a deliberate purposeful way. It was not perceived that children were their own spontaneous poets' (Darton, 1982: 314). Stevenson's book was hugely popular and can be seen as the founder of a genre; rather than didacticism, poetry for children could now explore the 'small' concerns of childhood ('The stone, with white and yellow and grey / We discovered I cannot tell *how* far away'); its fears ('All around the house is the jet-black night; / It stares through the window pane; / It crawls into the corners, hiding from the light, / And it moves with the moving flame.'); and (to the adult) its mystic insights ('The world is so full of a number of things / I'm sure we should all be as happy as kings'). In short, as Darton put it, this is poetry 'written as a child, given word-skill, might have written it' (ibid.: 315).

Morag Styles supports this view, arguing that 'Stevenson captured, as faithfully as it is possible for an adult to do, what it feels like to be a child' (Styles, 1998: 171). This is, of course, the nub of a very complex argument (see 'Poetry', p. 292): is it possible for an adult to write, as it were, out of childhood, rather than as an observer, nostalgically and sentimentally distorting the child's (inarticulate) view, or introducing ironies from the adult perspective ('Little Indian, Sioux or Crow, / Little frosty Eskimo, / Little Turk or Japanee, / O! don't you wish that you were me?').

However, in his day Stevenson was certainly thought to have achieved this distinctive voice, to the extent that a vast amount of poetry has followed much the same pattern. It seems probable that *A Child's Garden of Verses* contributed to the 'beautiful child' cult, which continued well into the 1920s. Much of the verse of A. A. Milne (q.v.), Rose Fyleman and even Enid Blyton (q.v.) is scarcely distinguishable from Stevenson's, although it might be argued that Stevenson is less sentimental: 'When I am grown to man's estate / I shall be very proud and great, / And tell the other girls and boys / Not to meddle with my toys.'

There is, however, another view, trenchantly expressed by Goldthwaite; this is that Stevenson was writing, not a view *from* childhood, but a view *of* childhood, and particularly a sentimentalized view of his own childhood:

> Where Greenaway was giving innocence a look, Stevenson was giving it a voice and things to do and think and hum to oneself while being childlike. No one had ever lied up a stereotype so sweetly or at this artistic level before, and a genteel reading public doted on Stevenson's image of itself '[s]itting safe in nursery nooks, / Reading picture story-books.' (Goldthwaite, 1996: 28–9)

In one sense, *A Child's Garden of Verses* deserves its place as a landmark because it absorbed many features of nursery rhyme, refined them and moved the form onwards, although there is clearly a division of opinion as to whether the direction was valuable.

Stevenson's masterpiece, *Treasure Island* (q.v.), similarly absorbed the past, but has been almost universally seen as emphasizing (if not introducing) moral ambiguities. Similar ambiguities, and a similarly major character, emerge in the figure of Alan Breck Stewart, the anti-hero of *Kidnapped*. The relationship between Stewart, the mercurial Roman Catholic Highlander, and David Balfour, the sober, inexperienced Protestant lowlander, gives depth to a breathless and highly competent thriller. As Margery Fisher has suggested, Stevenson may also be 'taking a shrewd look at the emotional and nostalgic aspects of Jacobitism as he felt them in himself' (Fisher, 1986b: 114). Stevenson was also, perhaps inevitably, writing in the tradition of Sir Walter Scott: he played down that writer's gothic elements, but shared his knowledge of the subtleties of clan loyalties. The difference may well be that 'there is a prevailing, pointed, mischievous humour which is vastly different from the harsh, dangerous sense of comedy in *Waverley*' (Fisher, 1986b: 114).

The romance, it might be said, is the half-way house between realism and fantasy, and in his best books Stevenson combined enough subtlety of character to convince, and enough improbability to excite. He also proved that 'mere adventure' can be an oxymoron.

Stevenson led a life appropriate to a writer of romances, and there have been several biographies; a representative sample is listed in the bibliography.

Bibliography

Aldington, Richard 1957: *Portrait of a Rebel: The Life and Work of Robert Louis Stevenson*. London: Evans.
Davies, Hunter 1994: *The Teller of Tales: In Search of Robert Louis Stevenson*. London: Sinclair-Stevenson.
McLynn, Frank 1993: *Robert Louis Stevenson: A Biography*. London: Hutchinson.

Rosemary Sutcliff (1920–1992)

The 'historical novel' might well epitomize some of the central issues of children's literature: whatever else it is doing, it must *inform* and *interpret*; it must tell a story, but it must provide the setting and the rationale; it must aim at truth, but manage horror and complexity. It must also choose a language which is accessible to the contemporary reader but which in some way suggests the dialogue of the past. Geoffrey Trease, whose *Bows Against the Barons* (1934) and *Cue For Treason* (1940) have some claim to be the precursors of the modern form, felt that 'the revolution in diction has probably contributed more than any other single factor to overcoming children's prejudice against the historical tale' (Trease, 1964: 97) In his pioneering critical book *Tales Out of School*, he gives some examples of such diction:

> ' "Yonder sight is enough to make a man eschew lance and sword forever, and take to hot-cockles and cherry pit" (popular games), explained the Earl of Pembroke, adding an oath which the sacred character of the building did not in the least restrain.' . . . In more recent books by much better writers we find remarks such as 'I joy me' and 'Wot you what?' . . . and making the worst of both worlds – Carola Oman's 'I'm not in a great hurry, if you truly desire aught, but I think I ought to be turning home now.' (Ibid.: 96)

Whether the historical novel can properly or usefully be considered as a genre could be debated, for although relatively unfashionable in recent years, it has had a striking presence in children's literature, and it exists in many modes. There is the romantic, of which Sir Walter Scott is generally seen as the precursor, and the realistic, originating in Captain Marryat and *The Children of the New Forest* (1847). There is the overtly political, with Geoffrey Trease's communist Robin Hood in *Bows Against the Barons*, books that blend history with fantasy, such as Alison Uttley's *A Traveller in Time* (1939) and Kipling's *Puck of Pook's Hill* (1906); and those that use it as a vehicle for propaganda, as with G. A. Henty. There is comedy, such as Randolph Stow's Australian farrago, *Midnite* (1967); and those who play with history, such as Joan Aiken's novels of a Jacobean nineteenth century or Leon Garfield's foggy eighteenth century. In the USA there has been a similar range: the civil war has been treated in notable books such as Harold Keith's *Rifles for Watie* (1957) and Irene Hunt's *Across Five Aprils* (1964); Elizabeth George Speare's *The Witch of Blackbird Pond* (1959) is set in New England in 1687. Paula Fox's *The Slave Dancer* (1974) and Mildred D. Taylor's 1930s trilogy beginning with *Roll of Thunder, Hear My Cry* (1976) have set a standard for documentary-style writing that avoids the obvious pitfalls of didacticism.

However, historical fiction reached a peak (as shown by many of the dates listed above) in the 'second golden age' after the Second World War, presaged by books like Esther Forbes's *Johnny Tremain* (1943).

Among a distinguished, serious company, Rosemary Sutcliff stands out:

> From the Fosseway westward to Isca Dumnoniorum the road was simply a British trackway, broadened and roughly metalled, strengthened by corduroys of logs in the softest places, but otherwise unchanged from its old estate, as it wound among the hills, thrusting further and further into the wilderness.
>
> It was a busy road and saw many travellers: traders with bronze weapons and raw yellow amber in their ponies' packs; country folk driving shaggy cattle or lean pigs from village to village; sometimes a band of tawny-haired tribesmen from farther west; strolling harpers and quack-oculists, too, or a light-stepping hunter with huge wolf-hounds at his heel; and from time to time a commissariat wagon going up and down to supply the Roman frontier post. The road saw them all, and the cohorts of the Eagles for whom all other travellers must make way.

Thus the opening of *The Eagle of the Ninth* (1954), the first of a sequence about Roman Britain, illustrating the twin concerns of the historical novelist – to provide information as well as a story – and also giving a flavour of the incantatory prose to which novelists are often drawn. Sutcliff was greatly influenced by Kipling's style, but also by his major theme of reconciliation between the peoples who came to make up Britain. Consequently, as Margery Fisher has pointed out, 'the enemy of today becomes the ally of the future and this is Rosemary Sutcliff's answer to that question "Who is the enemy?" which is forced upon the writer tackling the problem of war. The sense of continuity transcends the pattern of invasion and conquest' (Fisher, 1986b: 374).

It is this acceptance of the ambiguities and complexities of human behaviour that has moved matters on from the days when teachers saw 'far more historical stories deadened by ill-digested facts than distorted by falsehood' (Trease, 1964: 99). Nonetheless, as Margery Hourihan suggests, it may be that 'relatively simple, heroic societies [that] are themselves at an adolescent stage of development' are the ideal settings for 'stories which dramatize the primary concern of adolescents – the development of the ego . . . and the achievement of an integrated personality' (Hourihan, 1987: 169).

Sutcliff is characteristic of postwar children's writers in Britain in that she confronts change while attempting to celebrate the past. Her landscapes are inevitably somewhat romantic, having to be reconstructed from corrupted places; consequently there is a sense of inevitable loss and nostalgia. To some degree this extends to a regret at the loss of simple (right-wing) virtues such as valour and obedience and discipline, and the nostalgic acceptance of 'traditional' (right-wing) values.

In recent years the historical novel has tended to turn away from big battles – men's preoccupations – to more intimate, inward incidents, which may be a reflection of the emergence of the feminine voice. Characteristic – and characteristically female – have been Joan W. Blos's gentle account of life in New England in the 1830s, *A Gathering of Days* (1980), Jill Paton Walsh's story of the consequences of Grace Darling's heroic rescue, *Grace* (1991), or the English civil war seen from the point of view of a dog, Henrietta Branford's *Fire, Bed and Bone* (1997). Not only an exemplar of problems, the historical novel also tracks the gender patterns of children's literature remarkably accurately.

Bibliography

Fisher, Janet 1994: *An Index of Historical Fiction for Children and Young People.* Aldershot: Scolar.

Hourihan, Margery 1987: 'Versions of the Past: The Historical Novel in Children's Literature.' In Saxby and Winch 1987: 163–74.

Trease, Geoffrey 1964: *Tales Out of School.* London: Heinemann.

Patricia Wrightson (1921-)

Australian children's literature has had to negotiate its relationship with the old world of Europe and the even older world of Australia itself. The work of Ethel Turner and Mary Grant Bruce (q.v.), for example, show the tensions involved.

To some extent, Australian fiction has followed (and sometimes improved upon) general fashions and developments: it has been Australian, but not essentially or distinctively Australian. For example, E. B. Kennedy's *Blacks and Bushrangers* (1889) is set in Australia, and we do meet the native people, but with its shipwreck and kidnapping and romance, and the easy superiority of the upright young heroes, we could easily be in any nineteenth-century empire-building novel. Louise Mack's *Teens: A Story of Australian School Girls* (1890) reflects worldwide urbanization; Ivan Southall's nine Simon Black books feature a character of sterling uprightness and stiff-upper-lip valour. Contemporary writers include world-class performers such as Gillian Rubenstein (*Beyond the Labyrinth*, 1988), Nadia Wheatley (*The Blooding*, 1987), Robin Klein (*Hating Alison Ashley*, 1984) and Maurice Gleitzman (*Two Weeks With the Queen*, 1989), all of whom could hold their ground in any company (and sustain an entry in a guide to children's literature), but they too are concerned with themes and ideas explored elsewhere.

A more difficult theme, perhaps, has been the relationship to the land and an older culture. Several, now classic, texts have portrayed what the rest of the world has assumed to be essentially Australian features, such as independence of mind, and distinctive flora and fauna: thus Norman Lindsay's *The Magic Pudding* (1918), May Gibbs's *Snugglepot and Cuddlepie* (1918) and Dorothy Wall's *Blinky Bill* (1933). But even with these comedies, the question of how far this is exploitative colonization is unclear. In the 1960s and 1970s Ivan Southall used the background of the bush for a group of very superior thrillers (for example, *Hill's End*, 1963), in which the land progressively became more than merely a challenge to the white population, so that the novels developed a subtle ecological stance.

What seems to an outsider to be an early attempt to relate the incoming culture with the existing one is Ethel C. Pedley's *Dot and the Kangaroo* (London, 1899; Sydney, 1906). This explores the Australian love–hate relationship with the outback and is rife with local colour, although we are still very close in spirit to an animal fable like Richard Jefferies' *Wood Magic* (1881). Thus the very modern-sounding conservationism is mixed with rather blunt satire: when Dot, lost in the bush, is tried by the birds 'for the wrongs we Bush creatures have suffered from the cruelties of white Humans', the Welcome Swallow explains how human juries work:

> Their business is to do just what they like with you when all the talking is done, and whether they find you guilty or not, will depend on if they are tired, or hungry, or feel cross; or if the trial only lasts a short time. . . . If this is human law . . . it isn't funny at all.

Patricia Wrightson's distinctive contribution has been to approach aboriginal thinking with respect; not to borrow or retell, but to empathize with the mode of thought, relate it to western thinking, and thus produce a 'new' mythology which is accessible to western readers. In a note appended to *An Older Kind of Magic* (1972), Wrightson discusses the principles involved:

> Magic must be real in place, as well as in kind, for men were never stupidly gullible. The spirits they saw at the edge of their vision were shaped by something real: by the swirling of the snow, the darkness of a pool, or the terror of a mountain.
>
> Those of us who were bred in the old lands and live in the new have found this out. We have tried to plant here the magic that our people knew, and it will not grow. It is time we stopped trying to see elves and dragons and unicorns in Australia. They have never belonged here, and no ingenuity can make them real. We need to look for another kind of magic, a kind that must have been shaped by the land itself at the edge of Australian vision.

These ideas were explored in *An Older Kind of Magic* and *The Nargun and the Stars* (1973), which contain a vision of eternally powerful relentless forces. As a character says in *The Ice is Coming* (1977), the first book in her major trilogy that includes *The Dark Bright Water* (1978) and *Journey Behind the Wind* (1981), 'What does a man know about size? Bigger than you is big and smaller than you is small; you know no more than that.' Similarly, the books are concerned with ownership: the land tolerates human presence, and no more. Thus, *An Older Kind of Magic* is founded on a simple premise of a car-park being built on part of Sydney's botanical gardens and the reactions of the spirits of the place; *A Little Fear* (1983) draws an empathetic parallel between a tough old lady incomer and a tough old spirit of the land.

Wrightson's achievement has been to be aware of the Otherness of the Australian land and people: 'I can't be an Aborigine, but one thing I share with them is the land itself. So take a step behind the Aborigine to the land and get the feel of the spirits from that' (Nieuwenhuizen, 1991: 316). This attitude is fundamental to the ways in which children's books are now developing in Australia, and can be seen in such remarkable metafictions as Gary Crew's *Strange Objects* (1990). Such an attitude may be fundamental in many other ways and it represents the kind of nature-mysticism that has surfaced quite rarely in western writing, but which can be found (perhaps for romantic reasons) in children's books. Certainly this may represent an Australian mindset: 'We live in this country, but we do not belong to the country, it is not part of us . . . we do not, newcomers or old hands, call Australia home. Not really' (Max Harris, quoted in Nimon, 1994: 50). Nor should we assume that the literary gesture can rectify anything. Melissa Lucashenko, referring to the way in which the Aborigine culture has been systematically and brutally destroyed, concluded:

> Your history, our history, is not pretty. And so the cry goes up from white academics and white authors, oh, these stories must be told. And yes, they do need to be told, but what non-indigenous people don't understand is that you cannot heal yourself through *more* theft and *more* appropriation. . . . That's not to say that the shame must linger – it can end. Healing can and will occur. But the way to overcome our tragic history isn't by your stealing our indigenous voices. (Lucashenko, 1998: 90)

Where a written culture meets an oral culture, and where there has been colonization and oppression of that kind, we might reflect on the position that authors such as Patricia Wrightson occupy, and the role that they play.

Bibliography

Evans, Emrys 1989: 'Series as Epic: Patricia Wrightson's *The Book of Wirrun.*' *ChLAQ*, 14 (3), 165–70.
Lucashenko, Melissa 1998: 'Whose Dreaming, Whose Story? The Aboriginal Writer.' In Sieta van der Hoeven (ed.), *Time Will Tell: Children's Literature into the 21st Century.* Adelaide: Children's Book Council of Australia.
McVitty, Walter 1981: *Innocence and Experience: Essays on Contemporary Australian Children's Writers.* Melbourne: Nelson.
Nieuwenhuizen, Agnes (ed.) 1991: *No Kidding: Top Writers for Young People Talk About Their Work.* Sydney: Pan Macmillan.
Nimon, Maureen 1994: 'Australia: Literary Landscapes and Identity.' In Wendy Parsons and Robert Goodwin (eds), *Landscape and Identity: Perspectives from Australia.* Adelaide: Auslib Press, 43–51.
Saxby, Maurice 1990: *The Proof of the Puddin': Australian Children's Literature 1970–90.* Sydney: Ashton Scholastic.
Scutter, Heather 1999: *Displaced Fictions: Contemporary Australian Fiction for Teenagers and Young Adults.* Carlton South: Melbourne University Press.

Key Texts

L[ucy] M[aud] Montgomery (1874–1942), Anne of Green Gables (1908)

L. M. Montgomery's Anne of Green Gables novels, one of the select group of international bestsellers that have come to be icons of a national way of life (such as *The Magic Pudding* (q.v.), *Winnie-the-Pooh* (q.v.) or *The Adventures of Tom Sawyer* (q.v.)), stand squarely within two traditions. One is literary: the romantic, child-centred, triumphant fairy-tale of the lost, deprived child finding happiness and changing the lives of the staid adults around her; and the other, the tale of the pragmatic author extending a good idea for a children's book until it becomes something else – at best a series to grow with, at worst a matter of extemporizing. (When Montgomery sold the copyright to the first book in 1918, she noted that it had earned her $22,119.38; Rubio, 1985: 174.)

The loquacious orphan Anne Shirley arrives at Green Gables (based closely on a real house on Prince Edward Island) by a mistake. She gradually wins over her guardians, Matthew and Marilla, shines at school, and when Matthew dies suddenly, gives up her college career to teach school nearby. The seeds of a romance are sown in her rivalry with Gilbert Blythe, whom she marries several books later.

The first book, *Anne of Green Gables*, is by far the most successful of the series, having a clear narrative drive. Chasing derivations and influences is a fairly arid academic game, but it is impossible not to note the resemblance of its opening chapter to the opening of Kate Douglas Wiggins's *Rebecca of Sunnybrook Farm* (1903), or its highly satisfying confrontations with those in many other books, notably *Pollyanna* (1913) (q.v.). Anne's genius for confrontation is balanced by Marilla's acerbic irony and Matthew's transparent honesty: the child-as-sage caters for a lot of sublimated frustrations, and the narrator adds a level of ironic comment, largely (but not exclusively) directed at adults.

The incident in which Anne meets the formidable Mrs Rachel Lynde can stand for a whole genre.

> 'Well, they didn't pick you for your looks, that's sure and certain,' was Mrs Rachel Lynde's emphatic comment. Mrs Rachel was one of those delightful and popular people who pride themselves on speaking their mind without fear or favour. 'She's terribly skinny and homey, Marilla. Come here, let me look at you. Lawful heart, did anyone ever see such freckles? And hair as red as carrots! Come here, child, I say.'
>   Anne 'came there', but not exactly as Mrs Rachel expected. . . .
>   'I hate you,' she cried in a choked voice, stamping her foot on the floor. 'I hate you – I hate you – I hate you –' a louder stamp with each assertion of hatred. 'How dare you call me skinny and ugly? How dare you say I'm freckled and red-headed? You are a rude, impolite, unfeeling woman!'

Like *Little Women* (q.v.) and *The Secret Garden* (q.v.), *Anne of Green Gables* presents an illuminating view of the position of women and the possibly ironic, possibly ambivalent position of the authors. Thus, in discussing female survival tactics and women's necessary use of deviousness or 'fraud', Lissa Paul points out that it

> is not so successfully deployed in times and places where women are supposed to like being trapped. In the nineteenth century, for instance, girls might start out using guile, but growing up was regarded as a process of civilizing guile out. So Anne in *Anne of Green Gables* is an engaging child, whose imagination allows her to escape from the banality of everyday existence, but in growing up, she actively chooses to stay at home (at Green Gables, on Prince Edward Island) rather than go off to university. She chooses to be trapped. Jo, in *Little Women*, undergoes much the same repressing process. She is also an engaging, even naughty, girl, but as she grows up and learns to stifle her anger, she becomes much less interesting. For both Anne and Jo, this process is seen (overtly anyway) as a positive one. But I would be willing to bet that one of the reasons that *Anne of Green Gables* and *Little Women* remain such favourites is that readers intuitively understand the tension between the vital girl and the repressed woman. Even if guile gets civilized out, its traces remain. (Paul, 1987: 192)

Anne of Green Gables, then, combines defiance and domestication, with intricate, small-town, small-life doings; other books in the sequence (as happened with the Little Women and Pollyanna books) lose something of the original charm (if not actually becoming pot-boilers). Some of their sentimentality is questionable, and by the end of the series, with *Anne of Ingleside* (1939), we are deep into family saga territory. Anne, now mother of five, surveys the sleeping nursery in a way which seems to be directed at an audience quite some emotional distance from the readers of *Anne of Green Gables*, but which may strike chords with both.

> They were all growing so fast. In just a few short years they would all be young men and women . . . youth tiptoe . . . expectant . . . astir with its sweet, wild dreams . . . little ships sailing out of safe harbour to unknown parts. The boys would go away to their life work, and the girls . . . ah, the mist-veiled forms of beautiful brides might be seen coming down the old stairs at Ingleside. But they would be still hers for a few years yet . . . hers to love and guide . . . to sing the songs that so many mothers had sung.

Bibliography

Drain, Susan 1996: 'Telling and Retelling: L. M. Montgomery's Storied Lives and Living Stories.' *CCL*, 81, 7–18.

Epperly, Elizabeth R. 1992: *The Fragrance of Sweet Grass: L. M. Montgomery's Heroines and the Pursuit of Romance*. Toronto: Toronto University Press.

Paul, Lissa 1987: 'Enigma Variations: What Feminist Theory Knows About Children's Literature.' *Signal*, 54, 186–202. Reprinted in Hunt 1990: 148–65.

Rubio, Mary 1985: 'L. M. Montgomery's *Anne of Green Gables*: The Architect of Adolescence.' In Nodelman 1985: 173–87.

Solt, Marilyn 1985: 'The Uses of Setting in *Anne of Green Gables*.' *ChLAQ*, 9 (4), 181–3.

Wiggins, Genevieve 1992: *L. M. Montgomery*. New York: Twayne.

[John] Richard Jefferies (1848–1887), Bevis (1882)

The conventional construction of literary history nominates 'landmark' or highly influential books as a way of making comprehensible the indescribable complexity of literature. *Bevis, The Story of a Boy* by the naturalist and nature mystic Richard Jefferies falls into this category; it is almost an object-lesson in how a book finds its true audience and its 'minor classic' status almost by accident and against the odds.

In *Bevis*, written at the height of Victorian conventionality in children's books, when boys were manly boys, when the lower classes were treated sentimentally or patronizingly by the middle classes, and the cult of the 'beautiful child' was beginning, Jefferies presented a picture of an anarchic childhood, with amoral (if manly) boys spending a summer virtually free of adult influence. While it is far from breaking away from its culture (there is an underlying machismo directly linked to conquest, exploration and empire), it was new and liberating, and can be argued to have had an extensive influence.

Although it was not a purposed children's book, rather a book *about* children, it was by a writer who, partly for romantic–mystic reasons and partly for pragmatic reasons, could engage totally with childhood. Jefferies was an offbeat character, in many ways neither a natural nor a skilled writer. His output includes some very weak novels in the manner of Thomas Hardy (such as *Restless Human Hearts*, 1875), an apocalyptic novel well ahead of its time (*After London*, 1885) and one of the very few English mystic books (*The Story of My Heart*, 1883), which was (and is) regarded as highly eccentric. But his real genius lay in writing about the countryside, and in a long series of articles and books (*The Gamekeeper at Home*, 1878, is the most famous, and was much read by children) he demonstrated a detailed and authoritative knowledge of country matters. He also wrote *Bevis* and one children's book, *Wood Magic*.

Wood Magic, which was back in print in the late 1990s, is a peculiar mixture of animal fable and melodrama, and it would be a singular child or adult today who could wade through its treacly beautiful–mystic-child dialogue or its nihilistic excesses ('although a man very soon gets tired of swimming, the water never gets tired of waiting, but is always ready to drown him'). 'Sir' Bevis is introduced as a child who, at first metaphorically but then literally, understands the birds and animals and soon becomes involved in a complex political intrigue amongst the birds. Despite this unconvincing (not to say tedious) plot, the book succeeded in portraying a genuinely amoral child, especially in the final chapter. At first Bevis rides on the straw waggon:

> When Bevis saw the horses brought out of the stable . . . nothing would do but he must go with them. As his papa and the Bailiff were on this particular occasion to accompany the waggon, Bevis had his own way as usual. . . . Bevis insisted upon building the load, that is putting the straw in its place when it was thrown up; but in three minutes he said he hated it, it was so hot and scratchy, so out he jumped.

This naturalistic portrait is perfected in the first two chapters of *Bevis*, a picture of a young boy at play which has produced an empathetic response in children and adults. As Humphrey Carpenter observed:

> If Jefferies had concluded *Bevis* there, he would have produced a masterpiece. Scarcely anywhere in literature is there quite such a vivid, sympathetic, uncondescending account of a boy's intense absorption in a task he has set himself – and at the same time his fitful attitude to the whole thing. (Carpenter, 1985: 113–14)

However, empathy and nostalgia together elide irrelevancies, and the rest of the book condenses a whole childhood into a single summer. Bevis and his friend Mark make a raft and learn to swim and sail; they stage a full-scale 'Roman' battle with local boys; they build a working gun; they spend three weeks alone on a lake island, where they build a hut and shoot their own game. And it is all done with a self-absorption which takes everything seriously and is in many ways mesmeric.

Despite purple passages, digressions into novella-land and some blatant padding, *Bevis* retains an awareness of a certain part of childhood, a kind of innocence which allows the boys to move effortlessly between their literature-dominated imaginations and reality. Jefferies is not concerned with moral upbringing, but with skills; not with romantic ideas of the countryside, but with a mystic empathy between humans and nature which allows his boys to slaughter wildlife at random: 'This is the jolliest day we've had. . . . All shooting and killing and real hunting.'

Bevis was originally published as a three-decker novel for adults, but it very soon became adopted as a book *for* boys. It was very popular for perhaps seventy-five years after its publication, largely in abridged editions. It is now slipping rapidly into the limbo of the 'classic'; indeed, it is a classic 'adult's children's book': male-orientated, rural, and about 'masculine' preoccupations such as conquest, independence and initiation. It is also thoroughly sexist.

But despite all that, here are *real* boys at play, with *real* freedom. And despite Jefferies' waywardness of narrative stance and his air of always wanting to be writing something else, *Bevis* recreates and validates childhood from, as it were, the inside. Arthur Ransome, possibly the most influential twentieth-century children's writer, wrote consciously or unconsciously in the Jefferies mould, and passed on many of his characteristics almost to the end of the twentieth century.

Bibliography

Keith, W. J. 1965: *Richard Jefferies: A Critical Study*. Toronto: University of Toronto Press; London: Oxford University Press.

Anna Sewell (1820–1878), Black Beauty, his Grooms and Companions; the Autobiography of a Horse. Translated from the Original Equine *(1877)*

There are some books, such as Harriet Beecher Stowe's *Uncle Tom's Cabin* (1851–2), which would be worth including in a literary canon (whether children's or adults') for their social consequences alone, but *Black Beauty* (whose structure bears some resemblance to *Uncle Tom's Cabin*) is an extraordinary achievement in its own right. Written, as the author said, 'to induce kindness, sympathy, and an understanding treatment of horses', it achieved its aim, especially with regard to the fashionable cruelty of the bearing-rein, but almost every episode is vivid, intense and self-contained: it is a classic case of art concealing art.

The device of the animal narrator is akin to that of the innocent, as in Voltaire's *L'Ingenu* and its successors in the eighteenth century, and allows an extensive – perhaps childlike – critique of human behaviour. But it was, as Margaret Blount has noted, 'not quite as original a work as it appears to be' (Blount, 1974: 249–50), at least as far as the literary historian is concerned. Writers had used the first-person animal narrator in the service of the moral tale: notable examples were Dorothy Kilner's *Life and Perambulations of a Mouse* (1783) and *The Rambles of A Rat* (1857) by A. L. O. E. (A Lady of England), the pseudonym of Charlotte Maria Tucker (1821–93). The focus in that book is not on the plight of the rats, but on the conditions of the human poor, and the message is hammered home:

> Let not my readers suppose that in writing *The Rambles of a Rat* I have simply been blowing bubbles of fancy for their amusement, to divert them

during an idle hour. Like the hollow glass balls which children delight in, my bubbles of fancy have something solid within them – facts are enclosed in my fiction.

At one point Furry, 'an old, blind rat, who in his day has travelled far and seen much of the world', explains to his companions the effects of opium on Man, 'whom I believed to be as much wiser as they are stronger than the race of Mus, to which I belong.' The conclusion of the narrator, Ratto, is 'Ugh . . . leave opium to man; it is a great deal too bad for rats.'

Black Beauty is in this tradition of slightly sentimental social criticism, but the viewpoint of the animal rather than of an evangelically minded narrator adds particular force to its criticism of the thoughtless rich. It is a far more single-minded and enthusiastic narrative than *The Rambles of a Rat*, in which the 'rattishness' of the narrator is almost incidental. In *Black Beauty* the coincidences and the relatively happy ending are quite conventional, but much of the rest has an individual clarity: the pictures of rich and poor, both honest and degenerate, are, if anything, understated – although occasionally the anger of the social reformer comes through. Here is York, the coachman, forced by his mistress to deal with horses maddened by the bearing-rein:

'Confound these bearing-reins!' he said to himself; 'I thought we should have some mischief soon – master will be sorely vexed; but there – if a woman's husband can't rule her, of course a servant can't; so I wash my hands of it, and if she can't get to the Duchess' garden party, I can't help it.'

Or again, when the honest coachman is kept waiting in the snow for a card party:

At a quarter past one the door opened, and the two gentlemen came out; they got into the cab without a word, and told Jerry where to drive, that was nearly two miles. My legs were numb with cold, and I thought I should have stumbled. When the men got out, they never said they were sorry to have kept us waiting so long, but were angry at the charge: however, as Jerry never charged more than was his due, so he never took less, and they had to pay for the two hours and a quarter waiting; but it was hard-earned money to Jerry.

The limited viewpoint of the horse-narrator is particularly effective in the melodramatic episodes, for example when Black Beauty refuses to cross the flood-weakened bridge, or the wild ride after Lady Anne and her runaway horse; here the excitement is muted by the calm, detached tone of the narrator.

Whether or not the book was initially intended for children, the viewpoint has the effect of empowering a relatively inexperienced reader who can, nevertheless, understand more than the narrator. It is also the perfect introduction to the nineteenth-century moral tale and, especially, to the narrative skill very often found there.

The subtlety of *Black Beauty* can be demonstrated by comparing it with one of its most direct descendants, *Beautiful Joe* (1894), the Canadian autobiography of a dog by [Margaret] Marshall Saunders (1861–1947). That book begins with a brutal account of the killing of Joe's siblings and his mutilation, and ends with a resounding, nineteenth-century moral: 'My last words are, "Boys and girls, be kind to dumb animals, not only because you will lose nothing by it, but because you ought to; for they were placed on the earth by the same Kind Hand that made all living creatures."'

The first-person animal narrator remains a staple of popular children's books and is occasionally used in the 'pony story'. It is widely considered that the most effective attempt to mirror an animal's actual mental processes is Kipling's *Thy Servant, a Dog* (1930), despite its affectations of spelling and dialect: 'We rolled before Feets, asking not to be pushed into Empty places. I did a Beseech.'

In the twentieth century, the most effective animal stories have tended to be those that portray wild animals 'from the inside', without any anthropomorphism, notably Jack London's *White Fang* (1906), Henry Williamson's *Tarka the Otter* (1927) and the work of Ernest Thompson Seton. The fact that they are 'about animals' has tended to leave such books in a limbo between the adults' and children's markets.

The use of animal characters in children's books may have its roots in folk-tale, or the supposition that the developing reader is in some way closer to animals, or that they believe that animals are closer to them. Certainly animals in one form or another (from real to stuffed) have been a staple of children's fantasy, generally caricaturing both human and animal features. But from Dorothy Kilner's mouse, through *Black Beauty* to the hugely successful Animal Ark series of the 1990s (by 'Lucy Daniels'), they have provided writers with the opportunity to make serious points about human responsibility in a palatable form.

Bibliography

Blount, Margaret 1974: *Animal Land: The Creatures of Children's Fiction*. London: Hutchinson.

Chitty, Susan 1971: *The Woman Who Wrote Black Beauty*. London: Hodder and Stoughton.

Stibbs, Andrew 1991: *Reading Narrative as Literature: Signs of Life*. Milton Keynes: Open University Press.

Mary Norton (1903–1992), The Borrowers (1952), The Borrowers Afield (1955), The Borrowers Afloat (1959), The Borrowers Aloft (1961), The Borrowers Avenged (1982)

The ingenuities of scale which drove the children's versions of that many-layered satire, but from T. H. White's eccentric *Mistress Masham's Repose* (1947) through to Terry Pratchett's exuberant *The Bromeliad* (1989–90) and *The Carpet People* (1992), managing the miniature *seriously* leads almost inevitably to serious concerns.

British fantasy in the 1950s and 1960s is very commonly struggling with change, with a new and fractured world which is replacing the old certainties, the old 'grand narratives'. The books show a tension between nostalgia for the days of settled truths and an awareness that the future belongs to their readers. (The same tension, with much the same causes, can be seen in *The Wind in the Willows* (q.v.) and *The House at Pooh* corner.) The tension is shown in the embattled old house in Lucy M. Boston's Green Knowe series (from *The Children of Green Knowe*, 1954), Pearce's *Tom's Midnight Garden* (q.v.), in the work of Alan Garner (q.v.) and even in the assumptions about empire that infuse the Paddington Bear books (1958 onwards).

The Borrowers might be described as the quintessence of the 'second golden age' of British children's literature. The ingenious and diverting device of small people living off (and under and beside) the world of humans is described with appropriate attention to scale and detail; but the books very rapidly develop a darker side, becoming not only a chronicle of pursuit and persecution but also, in the case of the teenage Arrietty (even her name is borrowed), an account of loneliness and inhibition:

> 'Oh, I know papa is a wonderful borrower. I know we've managed to stay when all the others have gone. But what has it done for us, in the end? I don't think it's so clever to live on alone, for ever and ever, in a great, big, half-empty house; under the floor, with no one to talk to, no one to play with, nothing to see but dust and passages, no light but candlelight and firelight and what comes through the cracks.' (*The Borrowers*)

Throughout the series, traditional values, the 'organic' community, the rural, are set against the urban and the acquisitive, most notably represented by Mr Platter:

> Mr Platter was a builder and undertaker. . . . Mr Platter had amassed a good deal of money. But people weren't dying as they used to; and when the brick factory closed down there were fewer new inhabitants. This was because Mr Platter, building gimcrack villas for the workers, had spoiled the look of the countryside. . . . He had a tight kind of face and a pair of rimless glasses which caught the light so that you could not see his eyes. He had, however, a very polite and gentle manner; so you took the eyes on trust. (*The Borrowers Aloft*)

The books have a slow, reflective pace and at some points the first three are almost sunk for some readers by the complexity of their narrative frames, which marginalize the importance of the stories. However, the difficulty, as it were, of coming to grips with the story is a parallel to the difficulty of coming to grips with a Borrower, and it can be argued that the frame narrative and the 'inner' narrative 'are linked thematically. Who sees the Borrowers and how they react to them determines much of the meaning of the story' (Stott, 1996: 203). Equally, 'the gradual withdrawal of human narration from their story may well symbolize freeing the Borrowers from god-like human intervention' (Kuznets, 1985: 78).

In the 1980s and 1990s the books were adapted for television in a form faithful to their spirit and plot, and for film in a form radically modernized, with a new plot and a good many witty anachronisms. The fact that the latter caused hardly any fuss might suggest either that the books are now so little known (or loved) as to make them invisible, or that they have they passed into folklore, thus making them infinitely adaptable.

The Borrower books, then, are about growing up, and family, and the human condition: if not purposed allegories, certainly readable as such, down to the last detail. In *The Borrowers Afield*, for example, the Clock family contemplate living in a boot, but it is a 'gentleman's boot':

> 'Why, Mother,' asked Arrietty, irritated, 'what's wrong with a working man's boot? Papa's a working man, isn't he?'
>
> Homily smiled and shook her head in a pitying way. 'It's a question,' she said, 'of quality.'

The books also have a serious, even solemn, undercurrent to them. As Pod reflects on the way humans 'break out':

> 'They don't mean it,' he explained, 'they just does it. It isn't their fault. In that they're pretty much like the rest of us: none of us means harm – we just does it.'

Bibliography

Hall, Linda 1998: 'The Pattern of Dead and Living: Lucy Boston and the Necessity of Continuity.' *CLE*, 29 (4), 223–36.

Hopkins, Chris 2000: 'Arietty, Homily, Pod: Home, Size, Gender, and Relativity in *The Borrowers*.' *ChLAQ*, 25(1), 21–9.

Kuznets, Lois 1985: 'Permutations of Frame in Mary Norton's 'Borrowers' Series.' *Studies in the Literary Imagination*, 18 (2), 65–78.

Stott, Jon C. 1996: 'Mary Norton.' In Hettinga and Schmidt 1996: 197–206.

E[lwyn] B[rooks] White (1899–1985), Charlotte's Web (1952)

Reputed to be the most-read children's book in the USA, by virtue of being a school textbook (read, I have been told bitterly by American friends, several times in a school career), *Charlotte's Web* must be a strong contender for the book with the most striking opening sentence in all of literature:

> 'Where's Papa going with that ax?' said Fern to her mother as they were setting the table for breakfast.

It is perhaps unsurprising that, as an institution as much as a book, *Charlotte's Web* has received a good deal of critical attention, with articles such as 'The Miracle of the Web: Community, Desire, and Narrativity in *Charlotte's Web*' (Rushdy, 1991); 'The Reproduction of Mothering in *Charlotte's Web*' (Rollin, 1990); and 'Lacan with Runt Pigs' (Coats, 1999). At another point in the critical universe, as it were, we can read that it is 'unquestionably the most beloved animal fantasy of our time . . . the story has humor, pathos, wisdom, and beauty' (Huck, Hepler and Hickman, 1987: 347–8).

To the impartial observer, *Charlotte's Web* is a curious performance. It strays cheerfully between a kind of realism, when Fern saves the runt piglet Wilbur and brings him up, to an animal fable focalized through the innocent Wilbur and his more worldly friends, Templeton the rat and Charlotte the spider, who between them get Wilbur a bronze medal and a long life. Of course, the book pivots on the moment when Charlotte weaves the words 'SOME PIG' into the web above Wilbur's head. Farmer Zuckerman says to his wife:

> 'There can be no mistake about it. A miracle has happened and a sign has occurred here on earth, right on our farm, and we have no ordinary pig.'

'Well,' said Mrs Zuckerman, 'it seems to me you're a little off. It seems to me we have no ordinary *spider*.'

'Oh, no,' said Zuckerman. 'It's the pig that's unusual. It says so, right there in the middle of the web.'

'Maybe so,' said Mrs Zuckerman. 'Just the same, I intend to have a look at that spider.'

Silencing of the female voice? The power of the word? Ironic nonsense?

The structure of the novel has received a good deal of attention. Perry Nodelman (1985) points out that the first two chapters, while apparently quite out of key with the tone of the rest of the book, in fact act as an idyllic summary. (In this, *Charlotte's Web* resembles books as disparate as *Anne of Green Gables* (q.v.), *Treasure Island* (q.v.), *Harriet the Spy* (q.v.), and Ransome's (q.v.) *We Didn't Mean to Go to Sea*.)

Whether Wilbur can be considered 'a figure of the romantic great refusal' implicitly critiquing 'the gender roles designated for men' (Zipes, 1990: 142, 143); or whether 'part of the fascination of *Charlotte's Web* comes from its insertion of a male into the chain of mothering among the book's females' (Rollin, 1990: 42); or whether the book is 'an explanation for the perennial war that exists between housewives intent on spotlessness and spiders intent on creating cobwebs' (Alberghene, 1985: 39) – or all of these and more – can be left safely to the reader.

What is fairly certain is that White would have been highly amused (or possibly appalled) at some of Charlotte's critical offspring. This is the man who devoted a good deal of his time to advocating clarity, elegance and simplicity of language, and revised William Strunk Jr's *The Elements of Style* (1959) so that 'Strunk and White' became, and remains, probably the most influential of all writing manuals. James Thurber illustrated White's first book, *Is Sex Necessary?* (1929) with his first published drawings. What, I wonder, would the man of whom Thurber once wrote 'No one can write a sentence like White's or successfully imitate it' have made of this view of farmer Zuckerman?

> Zuckerman is here represented as actively representing the possibility of a performative subjectivity, as well as the role of the Other in that performance. Considering his role as the Name-of-the-Father, this move on his part is uniquely appropriate in that it is part of his function to delimit the possibilities of being. A performative subjectivity implies endless possibilities, constrained only by the unpredictable desire of the mother, who channels the desire of the subject in the first place. (Coats, 1999: 123)

As it were.

White's two other books for children, which have become minor classics, both have somewhat odd premises: the title of *The Trumpet of the Swan* is to be taken literally, while *Stuart Little* begins – to the consternation and distaste of many readers – thus:

> When Mrs Frederick C. Little's second son was born, everyone noticed that he was not much bigger than a mouse. The truth of the matter was, the baby looked very much like a mouse in every way. He was only about two inches high; and he had a mouse's tail, a mouse's whiskers, and the pleasant, shy manner of a mouse.

(The 2000 film of *Stuart Little* soothes sensibilities by having the little family *adopt* Stuart.) Whether or not White's ironic conclusion to *Charlotte's Web* – 'It is not often that someone comes along who is a true friend and a good writer' – means more than it seems to say, the book has indisputably brought to several generations the idea that children's books can be complex as well as charming.

Bibliography

Alberghene, Janice 1985: 'Writing in *Charlotte's Web*.' *CLE*, 16 (1), 32–44.

Coats, Karen 1999: 'Lacan with Runt Pigs.' *CL*, 27, 105–28.

Huck, Charlotte S., Hepler, Susan, and Hickman, Janet 1987: *Children's Literature in the Elementary School*. 4th edn. New York: Holt, Rinehart and Winston.

Neumeyer, Peter F. 1982: 'The Creation of *Charlotte's Web*: From Drafts to Book.' *The Horn Book Magazine*, 58, 489–97, 617–25.

Nodelman, Perry 1985: 'Text as Teacher: The Beginning of *Charlotte's Web*.' *CL*, 13, 109–27.

Rollin, Lucy 1990: 'The Reproduction of Mothering in *Charlotte's Web*.' *CL*, 18, 42–52.

Rushdy, Ashraf H. A. 1991: 'The Miracle of the Web: Community, Desire, and Narrativity in *Charlotte's Web*.' *LU*, 15, 35–60.

Zipes, Jack 1990: 'Negating History and Male Fantasies Through Psychoanalytic Criticism.' *CL*, 18, 141–43.

Susan [Mary] Cooper (1935–), The Dark is Rising sequence: Over Sea, Under Stone (1965), The Dark is Rising (1973), Greenwitch (1974), The Grey King (1975), Silver on the Tree (1977)

If there is a single book that epitomizes the 'second golden age' of children's books in Britain (the period from the mid-1950s to the mid-1970s), Susan Cooper's *Over Sea, Under Stone* might well qualify. (Other candidates are Penelope Lively's *The Ghost of Thomas Kempe*, 1973; Philippa Pearce's *Tom's Midnight Garden*, 1958 (q.v.); and Penelope Farmer's *Charlotte Sometimes*, 1969, all of which are fantasies written by women.) Cooper's book is one of a brief but powerful fashion for books that linked contemporary children with legend (often Arthurian or Celtic). Apart from the work of Alan Garner (q.v.), who produced the most complex of these in *The Owl Service* (1967), there were notable contributions from Penelope Lively (*The Whispering Knights*, 1971, and *The Wild Hunt of Hagworthy*, 1971) and Nancy Bond (*A String in the Harp*, 1977).

Literate, articulate, middle class, *Over Sea, Under Stone* is a holiday story, with three children searching for the legendary grail in the context of a cosmic fight between light and darkness. Quite apart from the mismatch in significance between action and theme, its stereotyping of characters, menacing villains, underground adventures and 'stupid children, tampering with things you don't understand' dialogue, it might easily be mistaken for very superior Enid Blyton.

But with the second book, *The Dark is Rising*, and the introduction of Will Stanton, the twelve-year-old boy who is the last of the Old Ones, the guardians of the light, we are in altogether more portentous and more intense literary territory. In the weather-ridden first chapter, Will encounters a farmer who mutters, gnomically, 'The Walker is abroad. . . . And this night will be bad, and tomorrow will be beyond imagining.' *The Dark is Rising* does its best both to develop a complex symbolism and to maintain the dramatic pace. Cooper demonstrates considerable skill with the latter, notably in the evocation of fear. Will is having trouble getting to sleep:

> He switched off the light again, and instantly everything was even worse than before. The fear jumped out at him for the third time like a great animal that had been waiting to spring. . . . Outside, the wind moaned, paused, rose to a sudden howl, and there was a noise, a muffled scraping thump, against the skylight in the ceiling of his room. And then in a dreadful furious moment, horror seized him like a nightmare made real; there came a wrenching crash, with the howling of the wind suddenly much louder and closer, and a great blast of cold; and the Feeling came hurtling against him with such force and dread that it flung him cowering away.

And that is only the first chapter. With Cooper's books, one is reminded of the dictum variously attributed to Sam Goldwyn and Cecil B. de Mille, that a good film should start with an earthquake and build up to a climax. Thereafter, *The Dark is Rising* is built around the idea of the Old Ones who repeatedly battle the dark, and sets up the search for the mystic symbols of light, the grail (again) in *Greenwitch*, a golden harp in *The Grey King*, and a crystal sword in *Silver on the Tree*.

Like Alan Garner's first two novels, *The Weirdstone of Brisingamen* (1960) and *The Moon of Gomrath* (1963), Cooper's books can be accused of being no more than skilful (and often erudite) weavings together of whatever scraps of myth and legend have come to hand, appropriate or not. C. W. Sullivan, for example, observes that Merriman (Great Uncle Merry/Merlin), 'like Arthur, Guinevere and the Grail, has very little of the Celtic about him,' and Arthur and Guinevere 'are as much products of the French romancers as they are of the Celtic bards' (Sullivan, 1989: 67). Cooper's borrowing from 'The Tale of Taliesin' in *Silver on the Tree* changes story, settings and characters. Elsewhere, in *The Dark is Rising* and *Silver on the Tree*, Cooper invokes Herne the Hunter and the wild hunt, but appropriates them to the side of the 'good'.

Nonetheless, a persuasive case can be made that her blending of ancient and modern does produce a powerful cohesion of themes. In *Greenwitch*, for example, an ancient ritual is used to relate 'wild' magic to old evil, contemporary evil, and the redemptive power of love, with both religious and folk-tale resonances. Equally, as Sullivan points out, Cooper's use of festive or significant days throughout the sequence provides cohesion, and her parallels of mythic patterns and individual rites of passage is particularly adept.

Certainly, Cooper seems to have felt called upon to explain her cosmography. In *Silver on the Tree* Will tells his brother that he, Will, is the last of the Old Ones, who are 'a great circle . . . all over the world and beyond the world, from all places and from all corners of time', and explains the relationships not only of good and evil, but also of the cosmic arrangements under which they operate. It is a reasonable if slightly mechanistic summary of the cosmos of many hundreds of fantasies of this type: homocentric, cyclical, essentially pagan and heroic:

> This where we live is a world of men, ordinary men, and although in it there is the Old Magic of the earth, and the Wild Magic of living things, it is men who control what the world shall be like. . . . But beyond the world is the universe, bound by the law of the High Magic, as every universe must be. And beneath the High Magic are two . . . poles . . . that we call the Dark and the Light. No other power orders them. They merely exist. The Dark seeks by its dark nature to influence men so that in the end, through them, it may control the earth. The Light has the task of stopping that from happening.

The difference, then, between the traditional 'children's book' exemplified in *Over Sea, Under Stone* and the more ambitious *Silver on the Tree* is the level of cosmic commitment. In *Over Sea, Under Stone* Great Uncle Merry also talks about the struggle between good and evil:

> 'The struggle goes on all round us all the time, like two armies fighting. And sometimes one of them seems to be winning and sometimes the other, but neither has ever triumphed altogether. Nor ever will,' he added softly to himself, 'for there is something of each in every man.'

This is much the same sentiment as expressed by the wizard Cadellin in Garner's *The Weirdstone of Brisingamen*: that when the evil Nastrond arises from Ragnarok, 'there would be none pure enough to withstand him since, by that time, he would have put a little of himself into the heart of all men'. In contrast, in *Silver on the Tree* the stakes have become much higher. Will says of the Dark that

> now very soon it will rise for the last and most perilous time. It has been gathering strength for that rising, and it is almost ready. And therefore, for the last time, until the end of Time, we must drive it back so that the world of men may be free.

Cooper herself traces the sequence back to John Masefield's *The Midnight Folk* (1927) and *The Box of Delights* (1935) (Harrison and Maguire, 1987: 199), two other books where borrowings from the 'myth kitty' are eclectic, not to say chaotic. More generally, in a tradition that runs back at least as far as Kipling (q.v.), she is intensely aware of place, and perhaps derives the underlying coherence of her books from her sense of place. Kipling regarded his Sussex as a place where layer upon layer of history was waiting to be unearthed (physically and metaphorically); Cooper felt the same about Wales:

> [Britain has had] people living in it for God knows how many hundreds or thousands of years, especially in Wales. You walk those mountains and the awareness of the past is all around you. And I intend to write from that kind of awareness. The magic, if you like, is all around. There is no moment at which one slips down the rabbit hole. (Harrison and Maguire, 1987: 202)

The complete sequence, then, for all its theoretical weaknesses, is a *tour de force* of its kind. There is an alarming tendency for conservative critics to assume that the naming or reworking of ancient myths and stories somehow validates or deepens in some way a modern text (by osmosis, one assumes: see 'Folk-tale, Fairy-tale, Myth, Legend', p. 273). At the other extreme are critics who dismiss a book for its inaccuracies. Given that myth is, by its very nature, developing and flexible, rather than a fixed phenomenon, any treatment of it, however apparently cavalier, seems to be quite legitimate. As Ursula K. Le Guin (1993: 22) put it, 'The mythopoeticists err, I think, in using the archetype as a rigid, filled mold. If we see it only as a vital potentiality, it becomes a guide into mystery'. It is, for example, cheering that Cooper admitted making up the ritual in *Greenwitch* (Cooper, 1979: 27).

Cooper has provided an ironic gloss on her earlier work (paralleled in a more serious vein by Le Guin's *Tehanu*) with *The Boggart* (1993), in which a traditional and powerful figure is taken to the new world and collides (literally) with computer technology.

Bibliography

Cooper, Susan 1979: 'In Defense of the Artist.' *Proceedings of the Fifth Annual Conference of the Children's Literature Association*. Villanova, Penn.: Villanova University for the Association, 20–8.

Drout, Michael D. 1997: 'Reading the Signs of Light: Anglo-Saxonism, Education, and Obedience in Susan Cooper's *The Dark is Rising*.' *LU*, 21 (2), 215–29.

Le Guin, Ursula K. 1993: *Earthsea Revisioned*. Cambridge: Green Bay.

Scott, Carole 1997: 'High and Wild Magic, the Moral Universe, and the Electronic Superhighway: Reflections of Change in Susan Cooper's Fantasy Literature.' In Beckett 1997: 91–7.

Schlobin, Roger C. 1982: *The Aesthetics of Fantasy Literature and Art*. Notre Dame, Ind.: University of Notre Dame Press; Brighton: Harvester.

Sullivan III, C. W. 1989: *Welsh Celtic Myth in Modern Fantasy*. Westport, Conn.: Greenwood Press.

Isaac Watts (1674–1748), Divine Songs Attempted in Easy Language for the Use of Young Children (1715)

The earliest books in English designed primarily to entertain children date from the mid-eighteenth century (see John Newbery, *A Little Pretty Pocket Book*, p. 186), but a good deal was produced for children before then, notably in the way of schoolbooks. As Gillian Avery remarked, 'Historians of children's literature commonly brush these aside, but this is to jettison much of what formed the literate adult, and is particularly obtuse when applied to the pre-eighteenth-century period, when children had little else' (Avery, 1995: 2) The simplest form of such books were hornbooks, commonly with the alphabet and the Lord's Prayer printed on wood, or on paper protected by a thin sheet of horn. Primers added verses and prayers, the Creed, the Commandments, a Catechism, and so on. The most prominent of these was probably *The New England Primer* (first edition *c.* 1690) compiled by Benjamin Harris. It is some indication of the importance of such books that *The New England Primer* was, well into the mid-nineteenth century, the USA's most popular book after the Bible, with its last (known) edition being published in 1886.

The earliest example of the puritan tradition of writing for children, based on the premise that children needed to be saved from their state of sin, is possibly Thomas White's *A Little Book for Little Children* (*c.* 1671), which drew on a tradition of adult religious writing, notably John Foxe's vivid, not to say gruesome, *Actes and Monuments of These Latter Perilous Times Touching Matters of the Church* (1563), otherwise known as the *Book of Martyrs*. This essentially anti-Roman Catholic tract was immensely influential, and anti-Catholic feeling can be found well into the nineteenth century in writers such as Mary Martha Sherwood (q.v.) and Charlotte Elizabeth Tonna (1790–1846). Puritan writing is famously encapsulated in James Janeway's (1636?–74) *A Token for Children: Being an Exact Account of the Conversion, Holy and Exemplary Lives, and Joyful Deaths of Several Young Children* (1671–2).

Although it is sometimes suggested that 'the late-seventeenth-century child could have found few books really to entertain him, and even fewer that contained pictures likely to interest the young' (Quayle, 1983: 27), it is no easy thing to imagine ourselves in the mind of such a reader. Certainly there were many books available to children who could read, from John Bunyan's verses in *A Book for Boys and Girls* (1686) to Comenius's *Orbis Sensualium Pictus* (1658; translated into English by Charles Hoole in 1659), sometimes regarded as the first picture book for children, emblem books, chapbooks and so on. Clearly, the early history of children's books is a highly complex specialist field, still relatively neglected in academic terms, and presenting a major opportunity for the scholar–historian.

However, the feature of almost all these books is the explicit control exercised by the writers: there is no question that the child is anything but subordinate, nor that the doctrine is anything but divine.

Despite this, with *Divine Songs* Isaac Watts produced 'an early and outstanding attempt to write verses for children which should give them pleasure but at the same time point and urge to the paths of virtue', and it was hugely successful. Around twenty editions were published during Watts's life, and it is estimated that the last edition, of 1896, was at least the 650th, and that eight million copies had been printed (Pafford, 1971: 1, 2). Certainly, Watts's verses were written on principles which still survive, and it is worth quoting at some length from his 'Preface To all that are concerned in the Education of CHILDREN':

> My Friends,
> It is an awful and important charge that is committed to you. The Wisdom and Welfare of the succeeding Generation are intrusted with you beforehand, and depend much on your Conduct. . . .
> Verse was at first design'd for the Service of God, tho' it hath been wretchedly abused since . . . but . . . there are these four advantages in it.
> 1. There is a greater Delight in the very learning of Truths and Duties this way. There is something so amusing and entertaining in Rhymes and Metre, that will incline Children to make this part of their Business a Diversion. . . .
> 2. What is learnt in Verse is longer retaine'd in memory, and sooner recollected. . . . And it may often happen that, the End of a Song running in

the Mind may be an effectual means to keep off some Temptation, or to incline to some Duty, when a Word of Scripture is not upon the Thoughts.

    3. This will be a constant Furniture for the Minds of Children. . . .

    4. These Divine Songs may be a pleasant and proper Matter for their daily or weekly Worship.

Some of the verses are now best known by their parodies. Song XX, *Against Idleness and Mischief*, which begins 'How dothe the little busy Bee / Improve each shining hour', was lampooned by Lewis Carroll (q.v.), which is a good indication of the longevity of *Divine Songs* and, perhaps, of its old-fashionedness by the 1860s.

    Other of Watts's verses have become almost proverbial:

> Let Dogs delight to bark and bite,
> For God has made them so;
> Let Bears and Lyons growl and fight,
> For 'tis their Nature too.
>
> But, children, you should never let
> Such Angry Quarrels rise;
> Your little Hands were never made
> To tear each others Eyes.
> *(Song XVI.* Against Quarrelling and Fighting*)*

As far as interpretation of these poems is concerned, Pafford places the book in its context:

> There is . . . a widespread belief in 'depth' in literary study and that if you can only drill deeply enough almost anywhere you are bound to strike something important. However true, or untrue, that may be in general, it is certainly not true here. Watts was writing in what has been called the age of reason . . . an age when enthusiasm, romanticism, the free play of the imagination were . . . condemned. Hobbes took it for granted that imagination was most commonly found in children, lunatics, and the uneducated. Watts's contemporaries in the literary world did not write for or about children. For Dryden, Pope, and Swift, since children had not acquired reason it was unreasonable to write for or about them. (Pafford, 1971: 48)

In later editions other poems were added, notably, towards the end of the eighteenth century, 'The Beggar's Petition', actually written by one Thomas Moss:

> Pity the sorrows of a poor old man,
> Whose trembling limbs have borne him to your door,
> Whose days are dwindled in the shortest span,
> Oh! give relief, and heaven will bless your store.

Such a pragmatic attitude to charity would find an echo in those 'ministering children' who populate many nineteenth-century children's books.

Thus, in 1715, Isaac Watts signalled something of a change in attitude and wrote so persuasively that his influence was pervasive for over a hundred and fifty years. It is only with writers like Robert Louis Stevenson who replaced, it could be argued, adult domination by religion with adult domination by sentiment, that poetry for children took a new direction.

Bibliography

Avery, Gillian 1989: 'The Puritans and their Heirs.' In Avery and Briggs 1989: 95–118.

Avery, Gillian 1995: 'The Beginnings of Children's Reading to *c.* 1700.' In Hunt 1995: 1–25.

Demers, Patricia 1993: *Heaven upon Earth: The Form of Moral and Religious Children's Literature, to 1850.* Knoxville: University of Tennessee Press.

Jackson, Mary V. 1989: *Engines of Instruction, Mischief and Magic: Children's Literature in England from it Beginnings to 1839.* Lincoln: University of Nebraska Press.

Lewis, Jayne Elizabeth 1996: *Aesop and Literary Culture 1651–1740.* Cambridge: Cambridge University Press.

Macdonald, Ruth K. 1989: *Christian's Children: The Influence of John Bunyan's The Pilgrim's Progress on American Children's Literature.* New York: Peter Lang.

MacLeod, Anne Scott 1993: 'Reappraising the Puritan Past.' *CL,* 21, 179–84.

Pafford, J. H. P. (ed.) 1971: Isaac Watts, *Divine Songs.* Oxford: Oxford University Press.

Quayle, Eric 1983: *Early Children's Books: A Collector's Guide.* Newton Abbot: David and Charles; Totowa: Barnes and Noble.

Ursula K[roeber] Le Guin (1929–), *The Earthsea Quartet:* A Wizard of Earthsea *(1968)*, The Tombs of Atuan *(1972)*, The Farthest Shore *(1973)*, Tehanu *(1990)*

'Fantasy,' Ursula Le Guin has written, 'is the natural, the appropriate language for the recounting of the spiritual journey and the struggle of good and evil in the soul' (Le Guin, 1992: 64). It is this essential seriousness of purpose that marks Le Guin's novels for children, widely regarded as classics of the genre.

Given that science-fiction and fantasy (q.v.) are, or have been, very low on the status-ladder of literature, anyone who works seriously in both must needs have a robust approach. Le Guin is a very forceful apologist: her essay, 'Why Are Americans Afraid of Dragons?' took the stance that 'a great many Americans are not only antifantasy, but altogether antifiction' (Le Guin, 1992: 35). She is equally direct about writing for children. Often, she says, she encounters 'the adult chauvinist piggery . . . "I love your books – the real ones, I mean, I haven't read the ones for children, of course! . . . It must be relaxing to write *simple* things for a change." Sure it's simple, writing for kids. Just as simple as bringing them up' (ibid.: 49).

With a very sharp intelligence infusing the books, it is scarcely surprising that the Earthsea novels have a rather more reflective tone than most, even if, as Le Guin later acknowledged, the first three books were essentially hero-tales. *A Wizard of Earthsea* scarcely features women; indeed, the wizards' university on the island of Roke rigidly excludes them, and the main quest is a 'buddy' tale. The central idea of balance, mystic enough in itself, actually reduces the use of magic:

But you must not change one thing, one pebble, one grain of sand, until you know what good and evil will follow on the act. The world is in balance, in equilibrium. A wizard's power . . . can shake the balance of the world. It is dangerous, that power. . . . It must follow knowledge, and serve need. To light a candle is to cast a shadow.

Given this unpromising stasis at the centre of a quest novel, it is the concept of evil as the other side of a coin whose visible face is goodness which provides the thrust of the narrative. Ged, the hero, releases his dark spirit and spends much of the book in pursuit of it. The climax is as much an acceptance as a confrontation, for, like Philip Pullman (q.v.), Le Guin takes the view that the Fall is necessary to development: human weakness and the inevitability of evil within humans must be accepted.

If *A Wizard of Earthsea* has its bleak side, *The Tombs of Atuan* is even bleaker, and symbolically comparatively crude. Tenar is the virgin keeper of empty catacombs in a female community in an arid desert; she is only 'saved' from this existence by the wizard, Ged, and his magic staff. The implication seems to be that without men, women's nature is distorted. In *The Farthest Shore* the sickness of the whole world is caused by a renegade wizard's refusal to die, thus upsetting the natural order of things. The world can only be cured by Ged's sacrificial venture into the land of death – although the complex and subtle symbolism is rather undercut by the mechanical explanation of opening a hole in the time-space continuum (rather as Peter Dickinson's influential British fantasy novel *The Weathermonger*, 1968, founders on the massive national changes being explained by Merlin's drug addiction).

There is a tension in these books between form, with its conventions of action, quest, confrontation and mutual support, and its considerable inventiveness, and philosophical intentions. However, for the most part, the structures of the books are conventional indeed; Colin Manlove (1983) entitled his account of them 'Conservatism in Fantasy', which in view of subsequent developments proved to be either highly ironic or deeply perceptive.

Earthsea, as a trilogy, was a solid achievement, bringing an unusual depth of ideas to the genre, but seventeen years after *The Farthest Shore* Le Guin added a remarkable fourth volume, *Tehanu*. In an explanatory essay, *Earthsea Revisioned*, she explored the tenets of her own stories: how she thought that previously she had written 'as a male', with male assumptions: 'The deepest foundation of the order of oppression is gendering, which names the male normal, dominant, active, and the female other, subject, passive' (Le Guin, 1993: 22), and she concluded:

> Certainly, if we discard the axiom *what's important is done by men*, with its
> corollary *what women do isn't important*, then we've knocked a hole in the
> hero-tale, and a good deal may leak out. (Ibid.: 13)

Consequently, that which was 'female' was silenced or marginalized. In *Tehanu*,
as Lissa Paul has pointed out,

> The problem with a 'typical' archetypal quest . . . (as outlined by the typically
> male cartographers, Joseph Campbell, or C. G. Jung, or Northrop Frye, for
> example) is that it is about turning boys into men, not girls into women,
> or children into people. When the quest ends, the hero gets his rewards, his
> property, his integrity and, often, a princess thrown in among the other goods
> and chattels.
>   A female quest doesn't look quite like that, and a story that simply
> exchanges a female protagonist for a male one usually ends up making the
> heroine look like a hero in drag. (Paul, 1987: 199)

What is fascinating about *Tehanu* is the working out of its premise that
whatever happens must be different from or opposite to what happens in a
male-dominated text. This makes for a good deal of tension, as the female
'hero' resolutely does *not* do conventionally heroic things: in male terms,
Le Guin's female characters are victims. (Annis Pratt, 1982, argues that female-
identity quest-patterns are quite different from those of the male.) This
strategy goes much further than Le Guin's attempts to portray 'otherness'
in the earlier books (Ged is actually black, although that is easily overlooked).
Women are different: men may know the language of dragons, but only
women can truly communicate with them. And they are different in terms
of power. As Old Moss the witch says:

> Ours is only a little power, seems like, next to theirs. But it goes down deep.
> It's all roots. It's like an old blackberry thicket. And a wizard's power is like
> a fir tree, maybe, great and tall and grand, but it'll blow right down in a storm.
> Nothing kills a blackberry bramble.

There has been some debate (e.g. Hatfield, 1993; Nodelman, 1995) as
to whether the ideas made explicit in *Tehanu* were implicit or inherent in
the first three books, which in turn questions our readings of archetypal
patterns. *Tehanu* was a fascinating experiment, and opinion is naturally enough
divided as to Le Guin's success. Whether the book is the turning point that
it deserves to have been remains to be seen.

Earthsea has had no obvious successors thematically, although many of its elements have been satirized – although not necessarily directly – by Terry Pratchett (q.v.), notably in the behaviour of the celibate wizards in his Unseen University on the Discworld. Pratchett has, however, devoted at least one novel, *Equal Rites* (1987), to exactly those male–female issues that Le Guin addresses, with a far more optimistic (if no less philosophical) result.

Bibliography

Hatfield, Len 1993: 'From Master to Brother: Shifting the Balance of Authority in Ursula K. Le Guin's *Farthest Shore* and *Tehanu*.' *CL*, 21, 43–65.

Jenkins, Sue 1985: 'Growing Up in Earthsea.' *CLE*, 16 (1), 21–31.

Le Guin, Ursula K. 1992: *The Language of the Night: Essays on Fantasy and Science Fiction*. Revd edn. New York: HarperCollins.

Le Guin, Ursula K. 1993: *Earthsea Revisioned*. Cambridge: Green Bay Publications.

Manlove, Colin 1983: *The Impulse of Fantasy Literature*. London: Macmillan.

Nodelman, Perry 1995: 'Reinventing the Past: Gender in Ursula K. Le Guin's *Tehanu* and the Earthsea "Trilogy".' *CL*, 23, 179–201.

Paul, Lissa 1987: 'Enigma Variations: What Feminist Theory Knows About Children's Literature.' *Signal*, 54, 186–202. Reprinted in Hunt 1990: 148–65.

Pratt, Annis 1982: *Archetypal Patterns in Women's Fiction*. Brighton: Harvester.

Louise Fitzhugh (1928–1974), Harriet the Spy (1964)

Harriet the Spy has been marketed as a comedy (the cover of the 1982 Dell edition declares, perhaps with an air of desperation, 'The Zany Adventures of a Young Spy'), which says a great deal about marketing and children's books. Ann Fine's (q.v.) *Madame Doubtfire* suffered – if that is the word for a bestseller – a similar fate. *Harriet the Spy*, for all its sometimes breathless appearance of comedy, actually walks along the edge of tragedy for most of the time. It is a remarkable account of an isolated, highly strung child and a scathing portrait of the American rich, focalized, with absolutely no visible authorial intervention, through an eleven-year-old.

Harriet writes compulsively in her notebook, spies on the neighbourhood (and generally sees rather sad things), and only relates to her idiosyncratic nurse, Ole Golly. When Ole Golly leaves to get married and Harriet's friends read her notebook, her isolation becomes complete. Her mother, neurotic herself, only then begins to take notice:

> Her mother hugged her and kissed her a lot. The more she hugged her the better Harriet felt. She was still being hugged when her father came home. He hugged her too, even though he didn't know what it was all about. After that they all had dinner and Harriet went up to bed.
>   Before going to sleep she wrote in her notebook:

THAT WAS ALL VERY NICE BUT IT HAS NOTHING TO DO WITH MY NOTEBOOK. ONLY OLE GOLLY UNDERSTANDS ABOUT MY NOTEBOOK. I WILL ALWAYS HAVE A NOTEBOOK. I THINK I WILL WRITE DOWN EVERYTHING, EVERY SINGLE SOLITARY THING THAT HAPPENS TO ME.

> She went peacefully to sleep. The next morning the first thing she did when she woke up was to reach for her notebook and scribble furiously:

WHEN I WAKE UP IN THE MORNING I WISH I WERE DEAD.

Having disposed of that, she got up, put on the same clothes she had had on the day before . . .

As Bosmajian (1985: 73) suggests, the book 'meshes two modes of fiction – satire and psychological realism [and] both modes are ironic'. There is, for example, profound irony in Harriet (the writer) being dependent upon Old Golly (the reader): that is, Ole Golly continually quotes but the quotations mean nothing. It is only when Ole Golly says something real and (like Mary Poppins, q.v.) tough, that Harriet responds. When Harriet has in effect a breakdown, Ole Golly is persuaded to write to her the kind of letter that might have appeared in a J. D. Salinger novella, for we are in Salinger territory here. Specifically, it is the territory of *Zooey* and *Raise High the Roofbeam, Carpenters*, in a way that the thousands of novels that merely imitated the language of *The Catcher in the Rye* are not.

Another thing. If you're missing me I want you to know I'm not missing you. Gone is gone. I never miss anything or anyone because it all becomes a lovely memory. I guard my memories and love them, but I don't get in them and lie down.

There is enough ambiguity here and throughout *Harriet the Spy* to set the book apart from most books that purport to psychological realism. The resolution, such as it is, when Harriet is accepted by her friends ('three little oysters' as Bosmajian, 1985: 82, puts it), is as delicate as Harriet's parents' attempts to apply therapy are crude. This is childhood seen by a clever child, and while critics have tended to see Ole Golly's quotation from Dostoievsky ('If you love everything, you will perceive the divine mystery of things') as central, it may well be that the performance by Harriet and Ole Golly of a stanza from *The Walrus and the Carpenter* is more important. Harriet's view of the world is exactly like Alice's – the intelligent child confronting the madness of the adult world – only here, a hundred years on from Carroll, the incipient madness of the child is kept at bay by an acceptance *by the child* of the irony of it all.

The sequel, *The Long Secret* (1965), explores the same ground, centring on the repressed anger of another poor little rich girl, Beth Ellen. Nothing here is quite so subtle as *Harriet the Spy*, but the book seems to be driven by (and perhaps implodes because of) anger. Beth Ellen has been loved and nurtured by her grandmother (a common theme of the period) and rejected by her mother, Zeeney. Katherine Paterson's *The Great Gilly Hopkins*

(1978) shares many of the motifs of *The Long Secret*, although the ex-hippy mother is less developed as a character and the grandmother is ineffectual.

Fitzhugh's *Nobody's Family is Going to Change* (1974) is an even more sombre performance, in which family concern (as a substitute for love) becomes positive (or negative) hatred. Children have to survive in a hostile world, even within the family.

These books, along with those of E. L. Konigsberg (q.v.), Natalie Babbitt, Katherine Paterson and Patricia MacLachlan (q.v.), are the benchmarks for the post Second World War 'golden age' in the USA. They share a fundamental intelligence, humour and awareness of complexities and ambiguities – the psychological brutality of urban affluence, rather than the physical brutality that was soon to engulf teenage literature.

This is a universe far removed from the reassuring world of writers like Eleanor Estes (*The Moffats*, 1941 and sequels), Elizabeth Enright (the Melendy family books, beginning with *The Saturdays*, 1941) and Maud Hart Lovelace (with the Betsy-Tacy series from 1940), who celebrated a protected childhood after the threats of the interwar years. The urban reality is a long way from the rural or suburban American dream; the actualities of children's lives – even the rich and privileged – exist in the context of a paradoxical liberty of thought and action for children.

The term 'masterpiece' should be kept tightly locked up, but on almost any criteria *Harriet the Spy* would qualify for the title. Almost on a par with it, and almost as deceptive in its form, is *The Westing Game* (1979), by another writer/artist and contemporary of Fitzhugh, Ellen Raskin (1928–84). Raskin's predilection for writing 'puzzle' books, most notably *The Mysterious Disappearance of Leon (I Mean Noel)* (1971) and *The Tattooed Potato and Other Clues* (1975), leaves criticism at a loss. *The Westing Game* is so intricately structured as intellectual detective work that it is easy to overlook the careful progress of the young female hero, Turtle Wexler, an Alice in a chess-game that Carroll would have approved of.

With Fitzhugh and Raskin American children's books reached a peak of a kind of excellence which, one fears, is unlikely to be repeated.

Bibliography

Bosmajian, Hamida 1985: 'Louise Fitzhugh's *Harriet the Spy*: Nonsense and Sense.' In Nodelman 1985: 71–83.
Paul, Lissa 1989: 'The Feminist Writer as Heroine in *Harriet the Spy*.' *LU*, 13 (1), 67–73.
Wolf, Virginia L. 1976: '*Harriet the Spy*: Milestone, Masterpiece?' *CL*, 4, 120–6.

J[ohn] R[onald] R[euel] Tolkien (1892–1973), The Hobbit, or There and Back Again (1937)

'In a hole in the ground there lived a hobbit. Not a nasty, dirty, wet hole . . . it was a hobbit hole, and that means comfort.' One of the most famous openings in children's literature begins a book which, although set in an 'alternative', other world and in an indeterminate era, seems to be very clearly of the 1930s. The First World War casts its shadow over it, as it does over many books of the period: *The Hobbit* looks back to a lost world, both in its sense of place and in its innocent heroics. Quite how these elements gel into a children's book of such longevity is unclear.

This adventure is rooted in a bucolic, peaceful, little England. Hobbiton and the Shire are at the same time a non-industrialized idyll, the Arcadia that is always just a generation or two ago, and an adult's nostalgic view of childhood. Their inhabitants represent children, in that they are empowered within their own world and are actually superior to the grown-up world outside, by virtue of a romantic purity of heart and a certain native cunning.

They are also, of course, adults, with adult habits, indulgences and freedoms. All in all, *The Hobbit* encapsulates the 'adults' children's book': male, rural, with a circular narrative and a secure ending. This apparently adult focus causes some problems: it is, after all, a children's book. The pleasures of Hobbits are those of middle-aged Englishmen: large meals, pipes, beer, the occasional stroll. (This is also a major problem for those who think that *The Wind in the Willows* (q.v.) must be a children's book.) And, of course, the Hobbit world (the heroic, male-order world) is non-heterosexual: females scarcely exist; the orcs may burn and pillage, but they don't rape. Violence is male and adult, and curiously thereby made unreal and *safe*. Consequently, children, too, are scarcely mentioned and are certainly excluded from violent situations. In *The Lord of the Rings*, the progression from, rather than sequel to, *The Hobbit*, the Hobbits cease even to have much to do symbolically with the state of childhood: they are simply small English*men*. (A current books-in-print catalogue of a major bookseller includes an audio-tape of *The Hobbit* subtitled *Children's Version*.)

The book epitomizes *modern* fantasy in general: a heroic adventure supposedly appealing to children because it does not appeal to adults. What is missing from the heroic world is what is supposed to be missing from a particular construction of childhood: subtlety, moral ambiguity, sexuality, lack of plot resolution, lack of closure. This is, again supposedly, compensated for by a certain resonance imparted by the use of the trappings of ancient legend; you are not expected to ask awkward questions about human rights, love, or the wages of invisible servants.

The difficulty with that view of fantasy is – what if there is a passionate sub-text, which in this case seems to be strongly adult? Childhood becomes only a mask for the needs of the adult, and the worst suspicions of those who see children's literature as an inevitable violation of the innocence of childhood (Rose, 1984; Lesnik-Oberstein, 1994) are confirmed.

If *The Hobbit* contains a classic adult quest structure, it also contains some straightforward action, some cumbersome characterization and some uncertainty about the seriousness of it all. Bilbo is launched on his adventure by Gandalf, a wizard who is sometimes a comic caricature and sometimes a gnomic mystic. His companions the Dwarves are caught between being comic, heroic and being ironically viewed. In comparison with *The Lord of the Rings*, *The Hobbit* reads as the apprentice piece that it is.

In literary terms it was ahead of its time, despite its strong links with the folk- and fairy-tale 'fashion' of the late nineteenth century – children of Tolkien's generation were brought up on Andrew Lang's Colour Fairy Books. The mode of *The Hobbit* remained a rarity until the worldwide popularity of *The Lord of the Rings* (1954–5) rehabilitated fantasy in general and other-world fantasy in particular. As Tolkien observed in 1938:

> Fairy stories offer . . . Fantasy, Recovery, Escape, Consolation, all things of which children have, as a rule, less need than older people. Most of them are nowadays very commonly considered to be bad for anybody. (Tolkien, 1964: 43)

Twenty-five years later, little had changed. In her 1974 article, 'Why Are Americans Afraid of Dragons?', Ursula Le Guin reported a friend as saying: 'Ten years ago, I went to the children's room of the library of such-and-such a city, and asked for *The Hobbit*; and the librarian told me, "Oh, we keep that only in the adult collection; we don't feel that escapism is good for children"' (Le Guin, 1992: 34).

The element of dedicated or obsessive play, of intricate world-building in Tolkien's books has been emulated many times and is ideally suited to both the postmodernist turn of mind and the new media. An alternative world can be constructed for its own sake, and any adventures that happen in it are more or less incidental. The 'back story', often crossing media and so well demonstrated in George Lucas's Star Wars project, has rarely been done with such scholarly weight as by Tolkien, but its addictive appeal is quite clear. 'A lot of it', Tolkien said, 'is just straight teen-age stuff. I didn't mean it to be, but it's perfect for them. I think they're attracted by things that give verisimilitude' (quoted in Manlove, 1975: 156). J. K. Rowling's (q.v.) Harry Potter sequence seems likely to generate a similar virtual world.

It is perhaps curious that *The Lord of the Rings* contains a more convincingly childlike character – or, at least, a character for children to identify with – than does *The Hobbit*. Sam Gamgee, the stoic serving-man, self-consciously excluding himself from the councils of the great, is the one whose quest ends in family, fulfilment and closure; whose dreams are human, rather than presumptuously or pretentiously divine. He is of course rather like the figure of the Mole, Grahame's child-representative, who has been taught to know his place and whose simple, regressive, domestic place is set up as admirable.

Whatever its limitations, *The Hobbit* remains the forerunner of a great release of fantasy, and its descendants and derivatives remain a powerful force in literature as much for adults as for children.

Bibliography

Green, William H. 1998: '"Where's Mama?" The Construction of the Feminine in *The Hobbit*.' *LU*, 22 (2), 188–95.

Harvey, David 1985: *The Song of Middle-Earth: J. R. R. Tolkien's Themes, Symbols, and Myths*. London: Allen and Unwin.

Le Guin, Ursula K. 1992: *The Language of the Night: Essays on Fantasy and Science Fiction*. New York: HarperCollins.

MacIntyre, Jean 1988: '"Time Shall Run Back": Tolkien's *The Hobbit*.' *ChLAQ*, 13 (1), 12–17.

Manlove, C. N. 1975: *Modern Fantasy: Five Studies*. Cambridge: Cambridge University Press.

Shippey, Tom 1983: *The Road to Middle Earth*. Boston, Mass.: Houghton Mifflin.

Tolkien, J. R. R. 1964: 'On Fairy Stories.' In *Tree and Leaf*, 11–70. London: Allen and Unwin.

Imported Classics

However famous, influential and well-translated, *Madam Bovary* and *War and Peace* never become classics of English literature, but there are certain children's books whose 'foreign' ancestry has been virtually forgotten: they have been absorbed into the culture and are included, generally without comment, in reference works and essay collections on 'children's literature'.

There is obviously a considerable organizational danger in such wanton polyglotism, but as we have seen, children's literature does not fit neatly into any particular territory, and many themes seem applicable to all childhood. Felix Salten's *Bambi: Eine Lebensgeschichte aus den Walde* (1923, translated 1928) gives an accurate and often brutal picture of the life of the deer (although for some critics it is undermined by the dialogue). Astrid Lindgren's Pippi Longstocking (from 1945) represents 'an irrepressible life-force, fusing the dream of freedom with the desire to rebel and seize power and turning these adult concepts back upon the adult world. Basically she is questioning society and its values' (Westin, 1991: 23). Tove Jansson's Moomin books (1945–70) are far from the whimsical eccentricities that they appear to be, for the series discusses questions of personal and family identity, and over many of the books there hangs a feeling of postwar insecurity.

Five of the most important imports into English are discussed here.

The Swiss Family Robinson

Like *Peter Pan*, *The Swiss Family Robinson* is an 'unstable' text. The German original by Johann David Wyss (1743–1818), *Der schweizerische Robinson* (1812–13) passed through a French version into English in 1814, acquiring additions and changes along the way. It is perhaps unsurprising that it continues through so many versions: from its origins in *Robinson Crusoe*, the idea seems to be a universal one. Not only can we see humans triumphing over nature, but we can escape into a golden world in which we can indulge our imaginations and control our environment: just as Wyss populated his island with what Margery Fisher (1986a: 50) called 'riotously inaccurate natural history', so contemporary computer games allow 'readers' to play at populating anything from hospitals to civilizations.

The Swiss Family Robinson is particularly important in the history of English-language children's literature in that it provoked rather than inspired Captain Marryat. Marryat found Wyss's work neither 'probable nor possible. . . . Fiction, when written for young people should, at all events, be *based* on truth.' On this principle he wrote the first of his many children's books, *Masterman Ready, or, the Wreck of the Pacific* (1841–2), and he was instrumental in establishing the adventure-story genre in Britain.

Struwwelpeter

Generally regarded as the antidote to the 'awful warning' school of evangelical literature, *Struwwelpeter* was first published as *Lustige Geschichten und drollige Bilder – für Kinder von 3–6 Jahren* in 1845 and translated into English in 1848. It was called by Maurice Sendak 'graphically the most beautiful book in the world' and it 'must hold the world record as the most widely disseminated text to have been consistently accompanied by versions of its author's original illustrations' (Alderson, 1999: 32). It is only touches like the two cats whose tears form a little lake over the ashes of the little girl who played with matches that gives away the satire: many little girls (as for example in Mrs Sherwood's (q.v.) *The History of the Fairchild Family*) were burned in earnest. Equally, one might assume that the 'long, red-legged scissor-man' who chops the thumbs off 'naughty little suck-a-thumb', or the little boy who would not eat his soup and so dies, are figures of farce. Not necessarily so: as Jack Zipes noted, a socialist critique of the book might run as follows:

> *Struwwelpeter* . . . has indeed stamped the consciousness of German children for generations. To a great extent, it reflects a peculiar hostility to children (what Germans call *Kinderfeindlichkeit*) which has been a disturbing element in the history of German civilization. *Struwwelpeter* glorifies obedience to arbitrary authority, and in each example the children are summarily punished by the adult world. (Zipes, 1976: 165)

While this might make us reconsider our assumptions about reading, there is no doubt that *Struwwelpeter*'s savage humour treads the boundaries of nightmare and bad taste – both of which have perennial appeal.

Heidi

Heidis Lehr- und Wanderjahre (1880) and *Heidi kann brauchen, was es gel-ernt hat* (1881) by the Swiss author Johanna Spyri came into English as *Heidi's Early Experiences and Heidi's Further Experiences* (1884) and has proved to have a robust constitution. It shares many of the elements that made books such as *What Katy Did* (1872), *Anne of Green Gables* (q.v.), *The Secret Garden* (q.v.) and *Pollyanna* (q.v.) so successful. Heidi wins over her dour grand-father, the Alm-Uncle, and later restores his faith. Malcolm Usrey (1985) believes that of all the sour adults converted by cheerful children, from George Eliot's *Silas Marner* (1861) to Aunt Miranda Sawyer in Kate Douglas Wiggins's *Rebecca of Sunnybrook Farm* (1902) and beyond, the Alm-Uncle comes closest to being the true Byronic hero. Heidi is virtually abducted by her cousin and suffers agonies of loneliness during her stay in Frankfurt, only to be saved by the wise doctor:

> This is not an illness that can be cured with pills and powders. The child's not robust, but if you send her back to the mountains at once she'll soon be herself again. If not . . . you might find you have to send her back ill, incur-able, or even not at all. (Trans. Eileen Hall, Penguin Books, 1956)

Finally, Heidi and her friend Peter (despite his jealousy) are responsible for the invalid Clara being able to walk again. The message, like that of *The Secret Garden*, is clear: children hold the key, through their purity, to spir-itual and physical health. The only thing lacking for *Heidi* were sequels, and these were supplied by Charles Tritten: *Heidi Grows Up* (1939) and *Heidi's Children* (1950). Christina Hardyment has commented on Heidi's total lack of interest in 'the pursuit of traditional female accomplishments':

> I don't know if *Heidi* has ever been officially canonized by the women's move-ment but it is no bad reader for today's feminist young idea. Joanna Spyri was . . . part of a circle of liberated Zürich intellectuals . . . [and] would certainly have been no party to Heidi marrying the gormless Peter [in Tritten's sequel]. (Hardyment, 1988: 195–6)

Pinocchio

> Once upon a time there was . . .
> 'A king!' my little readers will say straight away. No, children, you are mistaken. Once upon a time, there was a piece of wood.

One of the most translated books in the world (Lawson Lucas, 1996: viii), *Le Avventure di Pinocchio: Storia di un Burattino* (1883, translated into English 1892), like *Bambi*, is probably best known in its Walt Disney version, although *Bambi* fared a little better in terms of authenticity.

Pinocchio is the quintessential naughty boy, and his adventures, which very often topple into nightmare, are an energetic and at times expedient conglomeration of vivid episodes. The story originally ended at chapter 15, where Pinocchio, hung from a tree by two murderers, is left for dead. Author 'Carlo Collodi' was persuaded to continue and, as John Goldthwaite put it,

> The result is an epic comedy of errors in celebration of life even while, like Aesop or Kingsley, it warns us to have a care. Collodi has swept up all of folklore in the telling: characters wander in from puppet theater, from the commedia dell'arte, from the beast fable, from fairy lore and saints' tales, from real life. (Goldthwaite, 1996: 181)

It is slightly surprising to find that the ending has the soundest of moral tones, even if as Fisher (1996a: 12) suggests, 'few doses of moral medicine have been administered in such a richly flavoured spoonful of jam'. In a dream, the good Fairy, before turning him into a real boy, says

> Well done, Pinocchio! On account of your kind heart, I forgive you all the pranks that you have played before now. Children who lovingly help their parents in their hardship and their infirmity always deserve great praise and great affection, even if they cannot be cited as models of obedience and good behaviour.

His father, Old Joe [Geppetto], says that 'These unexpected changes in our house are all thanks to you. . . . Because when naughty children become good, they have the power to bring about a happy transformation at home for all their family.'

Or, 'The kid, in short, has screwed up everything, as most children do, and still come out of it a hero' (Goldthwaite, 1996: 181).

Emil and the Detectives

It is curious that the detective story is such a late arrival in mainstream children's literature, as opposed, that is, to the popular/pulp-fiction scene. There, in the UK, Sexton Blake had appeared in the *Marvel* in 1893 and later in *Union Jack*; in the USA Old Sleuth and Old Cap Collier were at work in Munro's Dime Novels. Nelson Lee even joined the staff of St Frank's school at one point, thereby combining two popular genres (Turner, 1976: 127–80).

However, they were adults and their world was fantasy. The book which brought detection to children – and real children at that – was Erich Kästner's cheerful *Emil and the Detectives* (1929, translated 1931). It also lies behind vast numbers of far less distinguished 'gang' books (notably by Enid Blyton), which picked up the refreshing ideas of freedom and group activity, but not the realistic ingenuity displayed by the children of Berlin and the insouciant Emil. There is not a great deal of plot: Emil Tischbein has his money stolen on a train; he pursues the thief and is helped by a gang made up largely of boys. Some of the book's atmosphere comes from the lightly sketched streets of Berlin, but for the modern reader it arises more from the innocence of its world. Emil is impressed that Berlin parents allow their sons to stay out late:

> 'Oh, on the whole they're pretty reasonable,' returned the Professor. 'Most of them know that as long as they trust us we aren't likely to deceive them. I promised my father never to do anything mean or dangerous and, as long as I abide by that, I can do pretty well as I like.'

But *Emil* could not be written today. Even twenty-five years or so later, another successfully translated book, Paul Berna's *La Cheval Sans Tête* (1955, as *A Hundred Million Francs*, 1957), inhabits a rather tougher landscape. The treatment of the reporters – benign in Kästner, savage in Berna – might be an ironic comment on the change in the world.

Kästner was also indirectly responsible for the film *The Parent Trap* (1961, 1998), which was based on his book *Lottie and Lisa* (translated 1950).

The list of distinguished imports might be extended to include Jean de Brunhoff's six Babar books (1933–41), although they seem to have kept their Gallic flavour; Hergé's Tintin books; and individual books such as André Maurois's *Patapoufs et Filifers* (1930, as *Fattipuffs and Thinifers*, 1941) and

Anne Holm's *David* (1963; translated from the Danish as *I Am David*, 1965). The traffic in translation is notoriously one-way, but the books that are translated *into* English have had an influence out of all proportion to their number.

Bibliography

Alderson, Brian 1999: 'Classics in Short: *Struwwelpeter*.' *Books for Keeps*, 119.
Hardyment, Christina 1988: *Heidi's Alp: One Family's Search for Storybook Europe*. New York: Atlantic Monthly Press. Published in the UK in 1987 as *The Canary-Coloured Cart*. London: Heinemann.
Koppes, Phyllis Bixler 1979: 'Spyri's Mountain Miracles: *Exemplum* and Romance in *Heidi*.' *LU*, 3, 62–73.
Lawson Lucas, Ann (trans.) 1996: Carlo Collodi, *The Adventures of Pinocchio*. Oxford: Oxford University Press.
May, Jill P. and Mork, Gordon R. 1987: 'Felix Salten.' In Bingham 1987: 497–501.
Turner, E. S. 1976: *Boys Will Be Boys*. Harmondsworth: Penguin Books.
Usrey, Malcolm: 'Johanna Spyri's *Heidi*: The Conversion of a Byronic Hero.' In Nodelman 1985: 232–42.
Westin, Boel 1991: *Children's Literature in Sweden*. Stockholm: Swedish Institute.
Zipes, Jack 1976: 'Down with Heidi, Down With Struwwelpeter, Three Cheers for the Revolution: Towards a New Socialist Children's Literature in West Germany.' *CL*, 5, 162–80.

Laura Ingalls Wilder (1867–1957), the Little House series: Little House in the Big Woods *(USA 1932/UK 1956)*, Farmer Boy *(1933/1965)*, Little House on the Prairie *(1935/1957)*, On the Banks of Plum Creek *(1937/1958)*, By the Shores of Silver Lake *(1939/1961)*, The Long Winter *(1940/1962)*, These Happy Golden Years *(1943/1964)*, The First Four Years *(1971/1973)*

'We as a society', observed the American critic Elizabeth Segal,

> must . . . tell ourselves the truth about our past if we are not to be trapped in it. . . . Wilder was able in her books to implicitly criticize as well as honour and love those complex and imperfect women and men who settled the American West. . . . She believed that the complexity and the tragedy were not beyond the comprehension of young children. (Segal, 1977: 70)

For the outsider, the Little House books might seem to be an ideal introduction to twentieth-century American attitudes to history. The books appear to be authentic, exciting and intrinsically interesting portraits of pioneer life; they are, in fact, an edited and tidied-up version of the Ingalls family travels from Wisconsin to Kansas, Minnesota and North Dakota between 1871 and 1889, written with the encouragement and extensive collaboration of Wilder's journalist daughter, Rose. As an examination of the author's original notebooks has shown (Moore, 1975), the changes were of three kinds: shaping incidents to make a more exciting narrative; romanticizing Pa Ingalls; and politicizing the texts.

The books do not follow the real-life journeys exactly, for the Ingalls family left Wisconsin in 1868 and travelled into Kansas and settled just inside Indian Territory. The complexity of the situation is shown (in the 'fiction') by young Laura's romantic (if sometimes terrified) view of the Indians, and Pa's tacit acknowledgement of their rights. Pa is far from being a supporter of the doctrine of Manifest Destiny, and when he and his family are forced to move he turns his anger onto the government:

> I'll not stay here to be taken away by the soldiers like an outlaw! If some blasted politicians in Washington hadn't sent out word it would be all right to settle here, I'd never have been three miles over the line into Indian Territory.' (*Little House on the Prairie*)

This version of events seems partly to criticize governmental interference, written as it was in the context of Roosevelt's interventionist New Deal policies of the 1930s, and partly to gloss over the 'real' Charles Ingalls's shortcomings as a pioneer father.

Pa's presence dominates the first three books quite profoundly: he is a symbol of security, comfort and power. It has been suggested (Romaines, 1995) that the authors' view of him is an implicit acceptance of the subservient role of the female, both in pioneer society and in the rural society of the 1930s.

However, with *The Long Winter* the tone of the books shifts towards a more maturely realized portrait of both Laura and Pa; the book has a multiple focus, which moves away from the young Laura's idealizing eye. It is also in *The Long Winter* that the fictionalized Laura encounters her future husband, and although one can assume that the real-life Almanzo appears in the books in a somewhat improved form from the reality, the same ambivalence – of truth-telling through a sub-text – is evident. As Virginia Wolf put it, '*The Long Winter* . . . marks the transition from adventure story to psychological realism, family story to adolescent novel, childhood to adulthood, experience to understanding' (Wolf, 1985: 169). It also marks the same shift in the implied readership: Wilder's technique of allowing quite complex issues to be made accessible to an audience with limited experience operates on an obvious surface level, but also as a matter of deduction. In the following extract there is a revealing contrast between the explicit para-phrase of emotion and the implied: behind it all is an ambiguous morality on the part of Almanzo.

In the depths of the winter, when the trains cannot get through and the townspeople (in actual life, of de Smet, North Dakota in 1881) are on the verge of starving, Almanzo Wilder and his friend Cap make a dangerous trip to buy seed wheat from a homesteader. The account of their almost suicidal journey across the literally featureless frozen prairie is a masterpiece of under-stated fear and unacknowledged heroics. The young men sell the corn to the local storekeeper at cost: which is all very noble until you consider that Almanzo has his own stock of seed wheat, which *he* refuses to sell, hidden behind a false wall in his house. Loftus, the storekeeper, tries to profiteer, attempting to sell the wheat that he bought at $1.25 a bushel for $3, thus producing a hostile reaction among the towns*men*. Laura's father is the most reasonable.

'Alright, I'll take the lead,' Mr Ingalls agreed. 'The rest of you boys come along and we'll see what Loftus has to say.'

They all tramped along after him single file over the snowdrifts. They crowded into the store where Loftus, when they began coming in, went behind his counter. There was no wheat in sight. Loftus had moved the sacks into his back room.

Mr Ingalls told him they thought he was charging too much for the wheat.

'That's my business,' said Loftus. 'It's my wheat, isn't it? I paid good money for it. . . . You fellows as much as touch my property and I'll have the law on you! . . . I've a right to charge any price I want to for it.'

'That's so, Loftus, you have,' Mr Ingalls agreed with him. 'This is a free country and every man's got a right to do as he pleases with his own property.' He said to the crowd, 'You know that's a fact, boys,' and he went on, 'don't forget every one of us is free and independent, Loftus. This winter won't last forever and maybe you want to go on doing business after it's over.'

'Threatening me, are you?' Mr Loftus demanded.

'We don't need to,' Mr Ingalls replied. 'It's a plain fact. If you've got a right to do as you please, we've got a right to do as we please.'

This could be almost a credo for the books, but as Suzanne Rhan has pointed out, it is the explicit individuality versus the implicit formation of com-munities that underlies and provides a tension for the books: 'These cracks of self-contradiction running through the plaster of a series that has become an icon of conservative political and family values in America . . . the cracks hint at subsurface strains' (Rhan, 1996: 125). One might speculate whether this characteristically American attitude accounts for the books' delayed publication in the UK, although there are many universal and traditional elements.

Like the Little Women (q.v.), Anne of Green Gables (q.v.) and Pollyanna (q.v.) sequences, the Little House books follow their main character from childhood to marriage and, not surprisingly, the sequence has been embellished. Roger Lea McBride, Wilder's executor, published *The First Four Years*, an unrevised last work by Wilder which demonstrates the extent of Rose's editing. *On the Way Home* (1962) is Laura's diary of her trip from South Dakota to Missouri in 1894; *West From Home* (1974) her letters written on a trip to San Francisco in 1915. McBride has also written three fictionalized accounts of Rose's childhood in the manner of Wilder, beginning with *Little House on Rocky Ridge* (1993). The distance between the original books and the latest attempt to exploit them, the *Little House in Brookfield* series (Maria D. Wilkes, 1996 onwards), about the childhood of Laura's mother, would make a fascinating study in popular culture.

The Little House books are profoundly American, at once fatalistic and romantic, serious contributions to social history, as well as carefully modulated texts for developing readers.

Bibliography

Fellman, Anita Clair 1990: 'Laura Ingalls Wilder and Rose Wilder Lane: The Politics of a Mother–Daughter Relationship.' *Signs*, 15 (3), 535–61.

Moore, Rosa Ann 1975: 'Laura Ingalls Wilder's Orange Notebooks and the Art of the Little House Books.' *CL*, 4, 105–19.

Moore, Rosa Ann 1978: 'The Little House Books: Rose-Colored Classics.' *CL*, 7, 7–16.

Rhan, Suzanne 1996: 'What Really Happens in the Little Town on the Prairie.' *CL*, 24, 117–26.

Romaines, Ann 1995: 'Preempting the Patriarch: The Problem of Pa's Stories in *Little House in the Big Woods*.' *ChLAQ*, 20 (1), 15–18.

Segal, Elizabeth 1977: 'Laura Ingalls Wilder's America: An Unflinching Assessment.' *CLE*, 8, 63–70.

Wolf, Virginia 1985: 'The Magic Circle of Laura Ingalls Wilder.' *ChLAQ*, 9 (4), 168–70.

John Newbery (1713–1767), A Little Pretty Pocket Book (1744)

Two books have a claim to be the earliest significant 'commercial' books for children, both of which date (or survive) from 1744. Out of the complex matrix of the chapbook with its rhymes and fables, the ABCs, the puritan tradition, the rational education of John Locke, and the mushrooming publishing industry, came Mary Cooper's (d. 1761) *Tommy Thumb's Pretty Song Book Voll. II* (see Nursery and Playground Rhymes, Storytelling, p. 000) and John Newbery's *A Little Pretty Pocket Book*.

Newbery was already a successful publisher and dealer in what would later be called patent medicines, having in his stable of writers such notables as Smollett, Goldsmith, Christopher Smart and Dr Johnson, who amiably satirized him in number nineteen of *The Idler* as: 'the great philosopher, Jack Whirler, whose business keeps him in perpetual motion. . . . Jack's trade is extensive and he has many dealers; his conversation is sprightly and he has many companions; his disposition is kind, and he has many friends.'

The reputation of *A Little Pretty Pocket Book* has not survived unscathed. Geoffrey Summerfield regarded its 'continuing *succès d'estime*' as a mystery: 'Whatever the archæological interests [sic] of this and other Newbery volumes – and they are clearly considerable for some bibliographers – the philistinism of the *Pocket Book*, the smell of the shopkeeper that pervades the volume, has received remarkably little attention . . . it is a sneaky piece of work' (Summerfield, 1984: 86).

One might argue, on the contrary, that it is a refreshingly honest piece of work: the title-page establishes exactly the commercial, educational and multimedia preoccupations of the children's book that can be found in any bookshop today (or, come to that, in many television programmes and films for children). Apart from the progress of technology, little seems to have changed – from the sexist marketing to the intertextual references – which may say a great deal for the acuity of Newbery, or for the eternal verities of the children's book trade:

> A Little Pretty Pocket Book, intended for the Instruction and Amusement of little Master Tommy and Pretty Miss Polly, with an agreeable Letter to read from Jack the Giant Killer, as also a Ball and a Pincushion, the use of which will infallibly make Tommy a good Boy, and Polly a good Girl.

The first edition also made a distinction in the price of the 'spin-offs': 'Price of the Book alone, 6d., with a Ball or Pincushion, 8d.' The Pocket Book had a long life and was issued in many variants: a 1767 edition included 'A Little Song-Book, being A New Attempt to teach Children the Use of the English Alphabet, by Way of Diversion.' A glance at Isaac Watts's preface to *Divine Songs* (q.v.) demonstrates how very similar words could carry a remarkable shift of emphasis.

Newbery's subsequent output included as Townsend (1994: 15) put it, 'books . . . more notable for their titles than their texts'. Among them were *The Little Lottery Book for Children: Containing, a new Method of playing them into a Knowledge of the Letters, Figures &c* (1756); *The Newtonian System of Philosophy Adapted to the Capacities of young Gentlemen and Ladies . . . by Tom Telescope, A. M.* (1761), and most famously, *The History of Little Goody Two-Shoes* (1765), whose title page suggested that the reader 'See the Original Manuscript in the Vatican at Rome, and the Cuts by Michael Angelo.'

Newbery and his successors stand, as it were, somewhere between the chapbook merchants and the puritan and evangelical writers such as Anna Laetitia Barbauld (1743–1825), Lady Eleanor Fenn (1743–1813) and Dorothy Kilner (1755–1836). These writers, whom Eric Quale called rather libelously 'this heavy brigade of formidable matrons [who] seemed determined to root out any tendency on the part of the young to read solely for their own entertainment and amusement' (Quale, 1983: 60), were highly influential and remain grossly under-researched. The most interesting of them was perhaps Sarah Trimmer (1741–1810), whose *Fabulous Histories Designed for the Instruction of Children Respecting their Treatment of Animals* (1786; title later changed to *The History of the Robins*) remains deeply conservative and rationalist despite its apparently whimsical premise – the parallel lives of the Benson children and the young robins. Resolutely moralist and set in a rural, stable society, it is 'in line with the tenets of the Age of Reason'; as Wilfried Keutsch remarks, 'disturbances that occur (for didactic purposes only), are nothing but temporary errors within a perfect system' (Keutsch, 1994: 46).

With their very different attitudes to life and to the children's book, Newbery and Trimmer encapsulate the two forces in children's literature that were to do battle through the nineteenth century.

Bibliography

Keutsch, Wilfried 1994: 'Teaching the Poor: Sarah Trimmer, God's Own Handmaid.' *Bulletin of the John Rylands University Library of Manchester*, 76 (3), 43–57.

Quayle, Eric 1983: *Early Children's Books: A Collector's Guide*. Newton Abbot: David and Charles; Totowa: Barnes and Noble.

Summerfield, Geoffrey 1984: *Fantasy and Reason: Children's Literature in the Eighteenth Century*. London: Methuen.

Townsend, John Rowe 1994: *Trade & Plumb-Cake for Ever, Huzza! The Life and Work of John Newbery 1713–1767*. Cambridge: Colt Books.

Louisa May Alcott (1832–1888), Little Women (1868)

If one had to compile a list of the top five children's books that have been influential, original and which are still widely read and appreciated by children, *Little Women* would be an undisputed candidate. There can be little question that the book challenged a sentimentalized and – it might be said – degenerate genre, and many critics would argue that since its publication no children's novel with a domestic setting or ambience has been free of its influence. It has also been an epicentre for contemporary criticism, which has transformed what was long assumed to be a comfortable paean to middle-class American values to at best the site of considerable cultural and gender ambiguity, and at worst to one of grotesque and violent betrayal of ideals.

Conventional readings of this domestic tale – a year in the lives of Jo, Meg, Amy and Beth March and their mother, 'Marmee', while their father is away at the civil war – might focus on the twin virtues of its conscious parallels with *The Pilgrim's Progress* and its accurate and affectionate portrayal of a real family. Equally, it can be argued that the strength of *Little Women* lies precisely in the fact that Louisa Alcott (it would appear) did not particularly want to write it, and was not happy with it until she saw the proofs. 'I don't enjoy this sort of thing', she wrote. 'Never liked girls or knew many except my sisters, but our queer plays and experiences may prove interesting, though I doubt it.' She was, in effect, balancing the generic necessities of the form with 'genuine' material. The result is a book which subtly satirizes the most popular formula elements of the nineteenth-century 'girls' book', while making use of them for its own popular success.

Little Women blends the genres of the family story with the genre of evangelical benevolence, in its various forms. The ideal of the independent

family (often living in a rural home) which survived into the twentieth century in Laura Ingalls Wilder's Little House books and beyond, can be seen
in an influential novel by Catharine Maria Sedgwick (1789–1867), *Home*
(1835). With its firm ideas on democracy and self-help, that book was
part of a series of novels with the overall title of 'Scenes and Characters
Illustrating Christian Truth' which might well have been a sub-title for Alcott's
book (if somewhat ironically). *Home* contrasts 'the family – that hive, where
every little busy bee did its appointed task' with the corrupt world of society, just as Alcott does. It is also characteristic of the evangelical writing
of its time in that the lingering death of Charles, the eldest son, stresses
a joyous Christian acceptance of death. Sedgwick's *A New-England Tale*
(1822) – she herself lived in Massachusetts – which praised humility, was
also highly successful.

The evangelical or perhaps 'post-evangelical' elements of *Little Women*
can be traced to immensely popular books such as Mary Louisa Charlesworth's (1819–80) *Ministering Children* (1854); indeed, the title of that
book became a by-word for middle-class philanthropy. Charlesworth wrote
that there was 'no child upon earth who may not be a ministering child:
because the Holy Spirit of God, even the blessed Comforter Himself, will
come to every-one who asks for Him.' The book is a sequence of pious deaths:
in the very first chapter, one of the poor and hungry female heroes, Ruth,
sings a hymn over a dying child:

> Ruth sang it two or three times, and then she stopped; and the poor child
> had shut her eyes and seemed asleep, but she soon opened them again, and
> said, 'Oh, do sing about "Jesus, let me to Thy bosom fly!"', and while Ruth
> sang, and the mother stood weeping by, the little child fell asleep, and died.
> . . . And so Ruth became a ministering child to the poor, childless widow.

The attitudes inherent in this book were deeply ingrained in readers
on both sides of the Atlantic, and the mixture of benevolence and piety (as
well as a tacit reinforcement of the social status quo) is seen in very many
writers, notably 'Hesba Stretton' (Sarah Smith, 1832–1911), whose *Jessica's
First Prayer* (1876) – again, hugely successful – moved the emphasis of
philanthropy away from its benefits to the givers and towards the plight of
the receivers. Hesba Stretton's imitators, such as Mrs O. F. Walton and
'Brenda' (Mrs Castle Smith), mixed religion and pathos in various measures.
Major producers of such books were the Religious Tract Society (from 1799)
in Britain, and the New York (later American) Tract Society (from 1812).

In the USA the approach was much less class-bound than in the UK, and the American ideals of upward mobility through self-help provided a different tone (notably in the work of Horatio Alger).

By the time that Alcott was writing *Little Women* the family story was a 'mature' genre: perhaps its most important landmark was Charlotte M[ary] Yonge's (1823–1901) *The Daisy Chain, or Aspirations* (1856), a rambling tale that begins with the tragic death of the mother. Yonge described it as 'an overgrown book of a nondescript class, neither the "tale" for the young, nor the novel for their elders, but a mixture of both', and some historians regard it as the direct model for *Little Women*. The book, with its view that imagination must be bounded by worldly responsibility, just as the freedom of childhood must be bounded by adult values, certainly has clear resonances in *Little Women* and other family stories (although with even more explicit reactions to it), such as Turner's *Seven Little Australians* (1894) (q.v.) and Nesbit's (q.v.) *The Story of the Treasure Seekers* (1899).

One feature of the family story that was to become increasingly popular (and to produce its own genre) was the forceful, independent female hero. The highly sentimental story of Ellen Montgomery in *The Wide Wide World* (1850) by 'Elizabeth Wetherell' (Susan Bogert Warner, 1819–85) made the book among the most popular of the century. Similarly, the eponymous female hero of Martha Farquharson Finley's (1828–1909) *Elsie Dinsmore* (1867) and its twenty-seven sequels ending with *Grandmother Elsie* (1905), demonstrated an interesting balance between independence and conformity. Some critics have seen in these books a link between religion and repressed sexuality, an inadvertent invention of the 'adolescent' novel with all its inherent ambiguities.

Little Women draws on this literary background and transforms it into something even more complex. There are obvious morals drawn from pride ('Meg Goes to Vanity Fair') and benevolence; there is the death of a baby (in Beth's arms); and a long and fairly lachrymose sick-bed scene. However, it is easy to read the contents page as a mild joke at the expense of any reader soaked in the conventions of the genre, with the successive chapter titles 'Dark Days' and 'Amy's Will.'

Thus, although Mr March – despite his absence – is the dominant force in the household, there are nevertheless many hints to suggest that the book subtly opposes the subservience of women to the patriarchal model. It shows the growth and development of independent girls, even if they revert to type and marry respectably and become 'good wives'. Jo resists this for as long as the novelist could hold out against pressure from her publisher and readers; Amy manages Laurie quite firmly; and even Meg, the most conventional of them, takes a strongly independent line against Aunt March on her choice of partner.

The result was particularly successful in Britain, where there was a clear contrast between the apparent freedom of the March girls (notably in association with the boy next door) and the real-life restrictions on teenage behaviour.

The delicate balance between providing what her audience was accustomed to, and moving her books towards some form of ironic realism, might be demonstrated by Alcott's account of Beth's death in *Good Wives*, and its aftermath:

> Seldom, except in books, do the dying utter memorable words, see visions, or depart with beatified countenances. . . . As Beth had hoped, the 'tide went out easily'; and in the dark hour before the dawn, on the bosom where she had drawn her first breath, she quietly drew her last, with no farewell but one loving look, one little sigh.

Jo's reaction is portrayed with self-conscious authorial irony:

> Now, if she had been the heroine of a moral story-book, she ought at this period of her life to have become quite saintly, renounced the world, and gone about doing good in a mortified bonnet, with tracts in her pocket. But, you see, Jo wasn't a heroine; she was only a struggling human girl, like hundreds of others, and she just acted out her nature, being sad, cross, listless, or energetic as the mood suggested.

Recent critics such as Lissa Paul (1998), have pointed out just how deeply female subservience was embedded in nineteenth-century culture, and that despite her personal convictions, Alcott was unable to introduce too radical ideas into her books. Their interest, then, might be seen to lie in how far she can be considered a 'foremother' of feminist fiction; how well she negotiated with the male hegemony. Questions have been raised as to whether the all-female family image is one of powerful matriarchy, or whether Alcott is herself ambivalent: as Foster and Simons put it: '*Little Women* . . . maintains an uneasy equilibrium between the fantasies of rebellion it dramatizes and the moral message it claims to promote' (Foster and Simons, 1995: 99).

While many traditionalist critics have suggested that even Jo finds fulfilment, and that Alcott provides a natural and satisfying resolution to her ambitions and development, others have seen a profound betrayal of the female in the text. Estes and Lant (1989), as an extreme example, find a sub-text

– the savage disempowerment of Jo – to be every bit as sadistic and perverted as the action in Alcott's gothic novels. For example, Alcott initially refused the imprecations of her public to marry Jo March to the obvious candidate, Laurie, but eventually yielded. 'Jo should have remained a literary spinster', she wrote. Eventually, though, the pressure became too much: 'I didn't dare to refuse & out of perversity went & made a funny match for her' (quoted by Estes and Lant, 1989: 104). Thus (in Estes and Lant's reading) the rebellious, individualistic Jo becomes little more than a walking corpse after the death of Beth and her marriage to a man who continually derides the profession of writing. Indeed, the position of the female writer can be seen to be inscribed in the books, for good or ill.

Little Women is undoubtedly a deeply self-aware book and richly rewards an intertextual approach. It also raises questions about the validity of literary psychoanalysis and of uncontextualized judgements.

Bibliography

Alberghene, Janice M. and Clark, Beverly Lyon (eds) 1988: *Little Women and the Feminist Imagination*. New York: Garland.

Estes, Angela M. and Lant, Kathleen Margaret 1989: 'Dismembering the Text: The Horror of Louisa May Alcott's *Little Women*.' *CL*, 17, 98–123.

Keyser, Elizabeth Lennox 1989: ' "The Most Beautiful Things in All the World"?: Families in *Little Women*.' In Butts 1992: 50–64.

Norman Lindsay (1879–1969), The Magic Pudding (1918)

The Magic Pudding, which its author referred to as a 'little piece of piffle', falls into the select category of books which have come to represent a national identity.

Norman Lindsay was quite clear about his intention to base a book on the fundamental wishes of children: 'humour and adventure. Sentimental tenderness and prettiness are strictly repudiated'. And, of course, food: the central character is a perpetually renewed pudding of great and dubious character. Its owners, Sam Sawnoff the Penguin and Bill Barnacle, helped by the koala Bunyip Bluegum, spend most of the book thwarting Puddin' Thieves. As a sample of the level of humour, at one point the villainous Wombat hides the pudding under his hat, but he is forced to reveal it when the others strike up the National Anthem.

The humour reaches very robust and surreal levels. For instance, the three puddin' owners, in pursuit of the Possum who has stolen the pudding, encounter a Bandicoot carrying a watermelon:

> Conceiving that his hour had come, the Bandicoot gave a shrill squeak of terror and fell on his knees.
>
> 'Take me watermelon,' he gasped, 'but spare me life.'
>
> 'Stuff an' nonsense,' said Bill. 'We don't want your life. What we want is some information. Have you seen a singed possum about this morning?'
>
> 'Singed possums, sir, yes sir, certainly sir,' gasped the Bandicoot, trembling violently.
>
> 'What!' exclaimed Bill, 'Do yer mean to say you have seen a singed possum?'
>
> 'Singed possums, sir, yes sir,' gulped the Bandicoot. 'Very plentiful, sir, this time of the year, sir, owing to the bush fires, sir.'
>
> 'Rubbish,' roared Bill. 'I don't believe he's seen a singed possum at all.'

'No, sir,' quavered the bandicoot. 'Certainly not, sir. Wouldn't think of seeing singed possums if there was any objection, sir.'

'You're a poltroon,' shouted Bill. 'You're a slaverin', quaverin', melon-carryin' nincompoop. . . . As far as I can see . . . if we can't find somethin' better than stone-deaf hedgehogs, peevish parrots and funkin' bandicoots we may as well give way to despair.' (Second Slice)

This farrago, spiritedly illustrated by Lindsay himself, contains a very high proportion of verse, is conducted with, as it were, a strong Australian accent, and concludes with an Australian idyll. The final illustration shows Bunyip and Sam and Bill in their tree house, while Ben the market-gardener tends his garden and the Puddin' sulks in his private paddock; in the distance, on the horizon, is the outline of a city. A way of life, symbolized by *The Magic Pudding*'s free-ranging energy, is under threat, for Australia was fast becoming an urban society and its children's literature was becoming urbanized too.

In some symbolic ways *The Magic Pudding* bridges the gap between two conditions of Australian society. Along with another eccentric Australian classic, the first volume of May Gibbs's *Snugglepot and Cuddlepie* (1918), it established a tradition of fantasy. The inherent toughness and independence shown in *The Magic Pudding* was emulated in later fantasies, such as Dorothy Wall's Blinky Bill series (from 1933) and S. A. Wakefield's *Bottersnikes and Gumbles* (1967 and sequels).

Bibliography

Hetherington, John 1973: *Norman Lindsay: The Embattled Olympian.* Melbourne: Oxford University Press.

P[amela] L[yndon] Travers (1906–1996), Mary Poppins (1934)

In the latter years of Victoria's reign, those writers choosing the real world as a setting for their miracles increasingly began to favour secular mimics of the muse to preside over their fancies. . . . Animated by the national and ethnic mythologies then being assembled, children's authors were catching up at last with the literary paganism that had been a mainstay of adult letters for centuries. Thus the growing profusion of pantheistic deities, *fin-de-siècle* fairies, and colourful demonologies in children's books from the 1880s onwards, and the appearance of everyday divines like the flying nanny of P. L. Travers's *Mary Poppins*. (Goldthwaite, 1996: 206)

Goldthwaite's might seem a somewhat inflated view of a fictional character, especially if we approach her, as a majority must, from a knowledge of the 1964 Disney film rather than the book. This is doubly ironic, as Travers attacked Disney in 1938 for the anthropomorphism of his films in which she detected 'a corresponding deflation of all human values [and] a profound cynicism at the root'; she found the film of *Mary Poppins* 'so externalized, so oversimplified, so generalized' (Demers, 1996: 275, 277). The seemingly endless popularity of the film, despite or because of its wooden direction, indifferent special effects (even by the standards of 1964), and Dick van Dyke's accent, was achieved without touching on the elements of the mystic that increasingly suffused the books, nor the troublesome fact that Mary Poppins is apparently quite charmless.

She paused outside the Chemist's shop at the corner so that she could see herself reflected in the three gigantic bottles in the window . . . and smiled a pleased and satisfied smile. She spent some time changing the hand-bag from her right hand to her left, trying it in every possible position to see how it looked best. Then she decided that, after all, it was most effective when tucked under her arm. So she left it there.

Jane and Michael stood beside her, not daring to say anything but glancing across at each other and sighing inside themselves. And from two points of her parrot-handled umbrella the rain trickled uncomfortably down the backs of their necks.

'Now then – don't keep me waiting!' said Mary Poppins crossly, turning away from the green, blue and red reflections of herself. (*Mary Poppins Comes Back*, 1935)

The magical nanny who can dance with the sun, talks to animals and who finds random magic in everyday places – and who bonds with her charges without actually being nice to them – is not merely a vehicle for flights of the imagination (which can be rather pedestrian). She is the exemplar of Travers's philosophy of the unity of all things: the Hamadryad in *Mary Poppins* reflects

After all . . . it may be that to eat and be eaten are the same thing in the end. . . . We are all made of the same stuff, remember, we of the Jungle, you of the City. The same substance composes us – the tree overhead, the stone beneath us, the bird, the beast, the star – we are all one, all moving to the same end.

And forty-eight years later, *Mary Poppins in Cherry Tree Lane* ends with this cosmic idea: 'Earth and sky, like neighbours chatting over a fence, had exchanged the one same word. Nothing was far. All was near.'

The secret of Mary Poppins might simply be the utter randomness of the magic, the disregard for scale (Mary Poppins can change the seasons and care for individuals) and the eccentric, self-satisfied remoteness of Mary herself: she is a still point in a world where the boundaries of reality and the imagination blur. However, that is to take Travers at her own estimation. Perry Nodelman, in justifying why *Mary Poppins* was *not* regarded as a 'touchstone' novel, and excluded from the Children's Literature Association's tentative 'canon', takes issue not only with what he sees as the lack of action and excitement in the books, but in Travers's portentous attitudes.

Travers' device of having Mary refuse to explain her actions or display her feelings is clearly meant to make her more mysterious, but it backfires by quickly becoming wearying. . . . Travers *insists* that we focus on Mary. *Mary Poppins* sometimes reads less like a novel than like a public-relations release for its star performer; we are even told that, in comparison with other human beings,

Mary Poppins is 'the Great Exception' – the capitals are Travers'. *Mary Poppins* is not so much a fantasy as it is propaganda for fantasy, fantasy at one remove and made to be an example of its own significance. (Nodelman, 1989: 8–9)

Nodelman compares the book with Barrie's *Peter Pan*: 'all that is lacking is Barrie's sadism' (ibid.: 8), although it finds, in my view, closer company in the two extravagant imaginative excursions by John Masefield, *The Midnight Folk* (1927) and *The Box of Delights* (1935). In both of these books there is an energetic disregard for consistency of genre – characters from melodrama rub shoulders with characters from legend – and the character of Cole Hawlings is as mysterious and cosmic (if not as smug) as Mary.

In a period that produced so many figures of fantasy – some apparently immortal, like the Hobbits and Superman, some more ephemeral, such as Katharine Tozer's engaging Mumfie (from *The Wanderings of Mumfie*, 1935) – Mary Poppins occupies a curious position. In a talk given in 1974, Travers explored what she saw as the indefinable boundaries between writing for adults and for children, and quoted a sixteen-year-old's comment to her: 'I've just been reading *Mary Poppins* again and I have come to the conclusion that it could only have been written by a lunatic.' She took this as a compliment, for a writer 'needs to be moonstruck, which is to say absorbed in, lost in, and in love with his [*sic*] own material' (Travers, 1975: 17).

Bibliography

Burness, Edwina and Griswold, Jerry 1982: 'The Art of Fiction LXXIII: P. L. Travers.' *Paris Review*, 86, 210–29.
Demers, Patricia 1991: *P. L. Travers*. Boston: Twayne.
Demers, Patricia 1996: 'P. L. Travers.' In Hettinga and Schmidt 1996: 272–80.
Travers, P. L. 1975: 'On Not Writing for Children.' *CL*, 4, 15–22.

C[live] S[taples] Lewis (1898–1963), the Narnia series: The Lion, the Witch and the Wardrobe (1950), Prince Caspian (1951), The Voyage of the 'Dawn Treader' (1952), The Silver Chair (1953), The Horse and his Boy (1954), The Magician's Nephew (1955) and The Last Battle (1956)

If there is a single, central example of the divergence of popular and critical taste, then the seven books concerning the mythical land of Narnia written by the Oxford academic and popular Christian apologist, C. S. Lewis, must qualify. They have been perennial steady sellers and they played a major part in the post-1945 revival of children's literature, especially the legitimization of fantasy. Undoubtedly well-paced, with colourful borrowings from a variety of traditions, and underpinned by an apparently respectable Christian theology, they have achieved the rare double of commercial success and social respectability.

The first and last novels are the most obviously symbolic (rather than allegorical). *The Lion, the Witch and the Wardrobe* ends with a loose reworking of Christ's passion (and was once banned in parts of the USA for blasphemy as a result), while *The Last Battle* is an exercise in eschatology. In between, there are mystic quests, stirring battles and adventures in a very eclectic landscape (in *The Lion, the Witch and the Wardrobe*, witches, ogres and talking animals rub shoulders with Father Christmas), while Aslan the lion–Christ figure moves through Narnia winnowing the chosen from the rest.

At least part of the books' respectability (although probably not their popularity) may stem from their pedigree. Despite a good deal of criticism, but aided by the sympathetic dramatized version of his life, *Shadowlands*, C. S. Lewis continues to enjoy a solid reputation as a Christian apologist. His association in the public mind, as well as in real life, with J. R. R. Tolkien, may also have served him well. His criticism, notably the essay 'On Three Ways of Writing for Children', has been influential and contains one of the best defences of reading children's literature: 'When I became a man I put away childish things, including the fear of childishness and the desire to be very grown up' (Lewis, 1966: 25). It also contains one of the worst critical dicta: 'I am almost inclined to set it up as a canon that a children's story which is enjoyed only by children is a bad children's story' (ibid.: 24).

Something of the ambivalence of his approach to writing for children emerges in that second quotation: the books are apparently about freedom, but are actually about control; not far beneath the genial surface of the books lie some very sexist, racist and violent attitudes.

The most famous critique of Lewis was by David Holbrook, who suggested that the Christ-figure Aslan in effect took away all free-will from the characters, thus removing the very point of the adventures, such as they are:

> In a sense, nothing happens in the Narnia books except the build-up and confrontation with paranoically conceived menaces, from an aggressive posture of hate, leading towards conflict. And in this there is often an intense self-righteousness, which must surely communicate itself to children. . . . I doubt whether the hate, fear and sadism in them is relieved by humanizing benignity. (Holbrook, 1976: 117, 124)

It is certainly not difficult to find passages to illustrate this thesis, but a far more fundamental criticism was developed by John Goldthwaite (1996). Leaving aside Goldthwaite's casual character assassination ('Lewis's career as misanthrope, misogynist, xenophobe, and classroom bully has been well and depressingly documented'; ibid.: 223), his case is that the books represent Lewis's personal distortion of Christianity. The creation of an alternative world is a rejection of the present one, in which Christianity subsists: 'it allowed Lewis to leave out everything about the world that he disliked or to summon up what he disliked in such a way that he could knock it about however he wished' (ibid.: 224). Goldthwaite therefore finds a deeply sinister motivation behind the parades of Lewis's personal prejudices (non-smokers, non-drinkers and vegetarians among them: see *The Voyage of the 'Dawn Treader'* to cite the least generally offensive) and the continual denigration of women. 'Once you have granted yourself license to say the snide thing, you are only a smirk away from the wicked one' (Goldthwaite, 1996: 228), and so in *Prince Caspian* the 'dumpy, prim little girls with fat legs', and in *The Last Battle* (ex-Queen) Susan ('interested in nothing nowadays except nylons and lipstick and invitations') are excluded not merely from happiness, but *from heaven itself.*

Having drawn attention to these critics, it would also be possible to read for a long time through commentaries on Lewis without once being aware that it was possible to criticize him. There is a preoccupation with the range of his imaginative synthesizing and the potency of his symbols, plus a tendency to discipleship rather than analysis. Marion Lochhead, for example, views the apocalypse of *The Last Battle* as an occasion for 'total redemption for all creatures with any good in them and with any will towards Aslan' (Lochhead, 1977: 100), which, even if it were true, might give some readers pause. Consequently, with the possible exception of Roald Dahl (q.v.), C. S. Lewis remains the writer most likely to provoke strong loyalties. The critic who has the temerity to question the pleasure given to children by this series is very likely to be met with incredulity.

Bibliography

Holbrook, David 1976: 'The Problem of C. S. Lewis.' *Writers, Critics and Children*. New York: Agathon; London: Heinemann.
Lochhead, Marion 1977: *The Renaissance of Wonder in Children's Literature*. Edinburgh: Canongate.
Quinn, Dennis B. 1984: 'The Narnia Books of C. S. Lewis: Fantastic or Wonderful?' *CL*, 12, 105–12.
Swinfen, Ann 1984: *In Defense of Fantasy*. London: Routledge and Kegan Paul.

J[ames] M[atthew] Barrie (1860–1937), 'Peter Pan' (1904)

J. M. Barrie's *Peter Pan* was retold before he had written it, and then rewritten after he had told it. By 1911, *Peter Pan* had become such a universally acclaimed cultural phenomenon that Barrie himself could only intervene back into its history from outside. The paradox is that Barrie's attempt to reclaim *Peter Pan* . . . failed. *Peter Pan* went on without him. I would go further and suggest that *Peter Pan* could *only* go on without him, because it had come to signify an innocence, or simplicity, which every line of Barrie's 1911 text belies. (Rose, 1984: 67)

Jacqueline Rose sums up two issues concerning *Peter Pan*: that it is an unstable text – when we talk about it, which version are we talking about? – and that its sub-text is particularly curious. To the impartial reader it must surely be top of the league of thoroughly peculiar books that have become famous children's books: this is the 'beautiful child' cult become very dubious.

It is not really necessary to turn to biographical criticism (which comes into its own with writers like Barrie, Kingsley, Carroll (q.v.) and Grahame) to note the uncomfortable paradoxes of the book. Harvey Darton, in a seminal history of children's books, thought that the 'fullest, most careless exhibition' of the new freedom of children's books at the end of the nineteenth century was *Peter Pan*, 'which for all its dramatic form has influenced the spirit of children's books, and the grown-up view of them, more powerfully than any other work except the *Alices* and Andersen's *Fairy Tales*. . . . What matters historically is that Barrie made all but shrivelled pedagogues see the value of [the all-conquering reality of fairyland]' (Darton, 1982: 309, 310). This may well be true, but as Margery Fisher retorted,

If so, the influence has had to be paid for in a long period when children's stories by prescription trivialized and distorted experience, isolating the young from the adult world, turning away from the substantial spheres of behaviour described by Mrs Ewing and others. Peter Pan is still a classic, if only for the terrifyingly true, bleak definition of a type always with us. As a story to offer to children it should be approached with caution, for there is much to dislike in its curiously twisted, self-conscious, indulgent humour. (Fisher, 1986: 8)

To put it even less encouragingly, 'Why did the private, half-mad dream of such a strange individual have such huge appeal to playgoers and readers?' (Carpenter, 1985: 176).

What kind of book can have produced such criticism in the face of such popularity? Peter Pan first appeared in Barrie's novel *The Little White Bird* (1902) and the play *Peter Pan, or The Boy Who Wouldn't Grow Up* was first performed in 1904. It resulted in many 'unauthorized' prose versions. Barrie then wrote the book of the play, *Peter and Wendy* (1911), and authorized an abridged version, *Peter Pan and Wendy* (1915), since when there has been a large number of adaptations and retellings: as with the fairy-tale, Peter Pan has become – and became very quickly – the common property of the culture. The best-known version is probably the 1953 Walt Disney film, which may be Disney's finest hour: his version smooths out many of the oddities of the play and the book. Its treatment of the violent play of the lost boys with the pirates and the Indians is made safe by cartooning (unlike the unpleasant massacre in the book), and while Disney has often been criticized in his other adaptations for sentimentalizing, he was not in the same league as Barrie.

At the centre of the play is the idea of the boy who never grows up, but the dream of eternal childhood is not a child-dream. As Tolkein said, 'Children are meant to grow up, and not become Peter Pans. Not to lose innocence and wonder, but to proceed on the appointed journey: that journey upon which it is certainly not better to travel hopefully than to arrive, though we must travel hopefully if we are to arrive' (Tolkien, 1964: 42). Peter Pan's is a sterile existence: at the end of the book, when Wendy, Michael and Peter return home, Pan is left outside. 'He had ecstasies innumerable that other children can never know; but he was looking through the window at the one joy from which he must be for ever barred.'

Pan's notorious line, 'To die will be an awfully big adventure' (actually a quotation from Barrie's child-friend George Llewellyn Davies) has been seen as a violation of the very idea of childhood and the tip of an iceberg of ambivalence. Barrie's mode of address in *Peter and Wendy* constantly moves between that of the knowing but sympathetic adult and the bitter and cynical adult, and both voices address adults and children. And so it is not simply that very many of the jokes (such as Hook's preoccupation with 'good form') do not seem to be the province of children; it is that Barrie has no sense of balance. Tinkerbell, for example, is not simply jealous of Wendy ('Tink hated her with the fierce hatred of a very woman'), but part of a triangle between an apparently sexually mature fairy, a boy who denies all sexuality, and a little girl playing at being a mother. This leads us into fairly murky waters.

It may well be that what works on stage does not work on the page; it is the narrator who brings with him the serpent into the simple Eden of wish-fulfilment. The same difficulty that certain writers had in working out their own position with regard to childhood can be seen in Charles Kingsley's *The Water Babies* (q.v.) and even in A. A. Milne's *Winnie-the-Pooh*. Thus, the central discomfort of the play is compounded by the character of the narrator, who by turns loves and hates, empathizes with and despises the childhood created in the book. The exuberance of the theatrical/film experience did, as Fisher observed, leave a legacy of children's stories which have apparently ignored the adult–child relationship, but in doing so they have ignored the intricate and disturbing negotiation between adult and child which is so evident in Barrie's work, and have replaced it with simple, invisible, autocratic control.

Bibliography

Hollindale, Peter 1993: 'Peter Pan: The Text and the Myth.' *CLE*, 24 (1), 19–30.
Tolkien, J. R. R. 1964: *Tree and Leaf.* London: Allen and Unwin.

Eleanor H[odgman] Porter (1868–1920), Pollyanna (1913)

If the 'bad boy' story was an influential strand of American children's literature, the 'glad girl' was certainly another. Not many book titles have entered the language, even though the meaning of 'Pollyanna' might well have slipped over the last century from 'indomitable optimist' to 'a foolishly or blindly optimistic person' (Griswold, 1992: 216). *Pollyanna* was a phenomenal bestseller with forty-seven printings by 1920, a successful film and a series of twelve sequels by other hands: in short, it became a byword for cheerfulness.

Pollyanna, an orphan, comes to stay with her proud and sour Aunt Polly, and by a somewhat relentless application of her 'glad' game – finding something to be glad about in every circumstance – transforms the lives of virtually everyone she meets. She is knocked over by a car and temporarily paralysed – which also temporarily dents her gladness – but she recovers and reflects: 'Why, I'm glad now I lost my legs for a while, for you never, never know how perfectly lovely legs are till you haven't got them – that go, I mean.'

Perhaps not surprisingly, by the mid-century and in more cynical times the book's popularity had declined sharply, especially in the USA, and Pollyanna had acquired a reputation for being 'the most exasperating heroine in fiction . . . the epitome of everything that is priggish and sentimental in the fiction [of the period]' (Fisher, 1975: 287).

Pollyanna was the latest in a long line of books that used a repertoire of similar devices (the brave orphan girl, innocence confronting experience, protracted sick/death-bed scenes) and is at once sentimental and assertive. Its most powerful element may be the idea that purity and simplicity can, in satisfyingly dramatic style, change the ways of the worldly and the unpleasant. It is almost an ideal image of children's literature itself; it was a prominent theme in the USA and can also be seen in *Heidi* (see 'Imported Classics') and *Anne of Green Gables* (q.v.).

An early example of the type – and one which has been described as founding the 'adolescent novel' – is *Elsie Dinsmore* (1867) by Martha Farquharson Finley (1828–1909), in which the lively but essentially conventional Elsie wins over her disapproving father (if not her immediate relatives). *Little Women* (1868) (q.v.) promotes optimism and healthy truthfulness, and the shy Beth melts the heart of the stern Mr Laurence, although – as *Little Women* is nothing if not pragmatic – Aunt March proves a tougher nut to crack. *What Katy Did* by 'Susan Coolidge' (Sarah Chauncy Woolsey, 1845–1905) has a model of cheerful stoicism in Cousin Helen (despite the fact that she may seem somewhat sanctimonious to the modern reader), who persuades the bedridden Katy to be 'the heart of the house'. This book is, as it were, a step on the way towards *Pollyanna* for, as Foster and Simons suggest (1995: 107–26), Katy's disablement is an extended punishment for her disobedience – in effect for her temerity in pushing back the boundaries of acceptable female behaviour. There was also, of course, an epidemic of back injuries in children's books of the period.

Rebecca of Sunnybrook Farm by Kate Douglas Wiggin (1856–1923) is altogether more pragmatic and moves away from the inherent evangelism of *What Katy Did*. Rebecca does not perform miracles, but her intelligent good nature changes the world around her. The book even satirizes the sick-bed: Rebecca's mother lying in bed after an accident remarks: 'If a woman of my age and the mother of a family hasn't got sense enough not to slip off haymows, she'd ought to suffer.'

Another element in these stories which is particularly evident in *Rebecca of Sunnybrook Farm* and another important example, *Daddy Long-Legs* (1912) by Jean Webster (1876–1916), is incipient sexuality. Jerry Griswold has observed that 'The Spinster Aunt, the Sugar Daddy, the Child-Woman – these are stock characters in American girls' books. They constitute a kind of desexualized oedipal triangle' (Griswold, 1992: 87), although quite how desexualized is a matter for some debate, given the contemporary critical tendency to see writing for children as an area of manipulation and violation of childhood. (Alice Mills (1999: 100) sees Porter's two books as an 'oedipal farrago'.) While this problem is circumvented in *Anne of Green Gables* – perhaps the most dramatically satisfying of the genre – by a protracted romance lasting over several volumes, or somewhat fudged in Jo's story in *Little Women* and *Good Wives*, its treatment in *Pollyanna* and especially *Pollyanna Grows Up* (1915) demonstrates how far Pollyanna is a character of fantasy.

She could very easily be a character created by the most skilled exponent of the genre, Frances Hodgson Burnett. *Pollyanna* has some close detailed similarities to *The Secret Garden*, while Cedric Errol, the eponymous hero of *Little Lord Fauntleroy*, quite innocently uses Pollyanna's persuasive devices on his grandfather.

It can be argued that Pollyanna is not quite as naive as she appears to be: she is 'not a simple-minded waif. In the way she manipulates Mrs Snow [tricking her into liking the food she is brought], wins herself a better room in the mansion, and defuses her aunt's punishments, it is clear that she uses optimism as a tool' (Griswold, 1992: 221). Yet the way in which Porter manipulates her cast of stock characters, from Jimmy Bean to the Byronic Mr Pendleton, suggests a much more straightforward attitude. The great difference in *Pollyanna* from its predecessors in the nineteenth century is that it is taking on the religiously self-righteous – Aunt Polly and the Ladies Aid Society are established Christianity – rather than colluding with them. This is a secular innocence, not simply a general critique of adult pessimism.

If, as suggested by Griswold (1992: 5–9, 223–5), not only *Pollyanna* and the other orphan/glad girl/challenge-the-adults books, but also other books of the period, such as Mark Twain's *The Adventures of Huckleberry Finn* (1885) and *Toby Tyler* (1881) by James Otis [Kaler] (1848–1912) have the same underlying pattern, *Pollyanna* told the story with the most extravagance.

Bibliography

Fisher, Margery 1975: *Who's Who in Children's Books*. London: Weidenfeld and Nicolson.
Mills, Alice 1999: 'Pollyanna and the Not So Glad Game.' *Children's Literature*, 27, 87–104.

[Joseph] Rudyard Kipling (1865–1936), Puck of Pook's Hill (1906)

Puck of Pook's Hill is possibly Kipling's masterwork for children, but it raises many issues: it is a deeply political text, an example of an adult attempting to influence children though a medium (a history lesson) acceptable to adults. How can a book that is fundamentally nationalistic history (and which assumes a good deal of knowledge in the child reader which can probably now *not* be safely assumed) survive changes in political outlook? 'The Children's Song' which ends *Puck* contains very unfashionable elements:

> Land of our Birth, our faith, our pride,
> For whose dear sake our fathers died;
> O Motherland, we pledge to thee,
> Head, heart, and hand through the years to be!

The book is concerned with empire and fairies, and it is sexist (although arguably not racist). Does it survive because it is the classic example of the 'adult's children's book', which is canonical precisely because it does *not* address contemporary childhood? Here is Kipling's beloved Sussex:

> Then they walked through the grass to the knoll where Little Lindens stands. The old farmhouse, weather-tiled to the ground, took almost the colour of a blood-ruby in the afternoon light. The pigeons pecked at the mortar in the chimney-stacks; the bees that had lived under its tiles since it was built filled the hot August air with their booming; and the smell of the box-tree by the dairy-window mixed with the smell of earth after rain, bread after baking, and a tickle of wood-smoke. ('Hal o' the Draft')

In its defence, I would argue that nothing in Kipling is quite what it seems.

Dan and Una, the children, accidentally conjure from the Sussex countryside Puck, the oldest spirit in England, who brings them storytellers from
the past. Kipling, notably in his autobiography *Something of Myself* (1937),
describes in some detail the genesis of the book, which is set around his
home, Bateman's, and draws upon the layers of history and legend of the
surrounding countryside.

The book has two main strands: first, the idea of the growth of England.
A sword is given by a heathen god, Weland, to a young Saxon, Hugh, as
a result of a kind deed, and it betrays him in his first fight – the Battle of
Hastings. Under the eye of the wise Norman Knight, De Aquila, Hugh and
his Norman friend, Sir Richard, unify Saxons and Normans at their manor.
Later, they voyage to Africa and bring home a fortune in gold, which they
hide in Pevensey Castle. In the last story, that same gold, sought out and
sunk into the sea by Kadmiel the even wiser Jew, is indirectly responsible
for the signing of the Magna Carta ('I saw well that if the evil thing remained,
or if even the hope of finding it remained, the King would not sign the
New Laws, and the land would perish.'). In the end, justice is brought by
the marginalized and despised, who are shown to be more noble and more
wise than their persecutors.

> 'Well', said Puck, calmly, 'what do you think of it? Weland gave the Sword!
> The Sword gave the Treasure, and the Treasure gave the Law. It's as natural
> as an oak growing.'

Here are Kipling's recurrent themes: of initiation, of what might now
be called 'buddy-ism', of the elder statesman passing on wisdom, of the
marginalization of women (who are virtually non-existent in the book). The
premise behind all this, that Englishness is a superior state, seems only to
be marginally important and is perhaps as invisible as it can be to readers
in what is a very different culture.

Similarly, the series of stories about the Roman Wall, in which two
young British Romans hold out against the invading Norsemen, are at root
a warning or a lament for the loss of empire. But this is a *children's* book
and it centres on the friendship of Parnesius and his friend Pertinax – and
for all the great events circling the characters, what is clear is that the 'adults'
– Allo the Pict, Maximus the Emperor, even Parnesius's father – are fallible.

The other stories in the book, set in Sussex, similarly centre on place, friendship and growth, with the additional overlay of tradition and respect for craft;
in all of them, one is left with the idea that hope lies in the young and (a

further irony) that they must make the future for themselves: the listeners to the stories *forget* each story as soon as it is finished.

It may seem to be naive to attempt to rehabilitate Kipling through his writing for children, yet ironically, readers a hundred years on from the appearance of these books may well interpret the ideas of empire as being no more than the most childish impulses writ large; Kipling seems, almost, to be looking through children's eyes and seeing the nonsense that passes for adult logic.

Kipling's world is seductive and, for some, suspect: a Sussex without motorways, a prose that is endlessly subtle, are symbols of worlds we have lost, and we are in danger of being drawn into a deeply reactionary psyche. But children's books are not *safe*. Certainly, the sequel to *Puck of Pook's Hill*, *Rewards and Fairies* (1910), tales which, as Kipling wrote in *Something of Myself*, 'had to be read by children, before people realized that they were meant for grown-ups' (Kipling, 1977: 142), moves into even more complex (and unsafe) areas.

In *Puck of Pook's Hill*, especially, we have an example of the children's book as it was; writers from Edith Nesbit (q.v.) to Philippa Pearce, or from Louisa Alcott to Katherine Paterson and Patricia MacLachlan (q.v.) are in the same tradition of thoughtful, intricate writing, that acknowledges the complexity of the world and of ways of seeing it.

Bibliography

There are excellent introductions to *Puck of Pook's Hill* and *Rewards and Fairies* in the edition by Donald Mackenzie (Oxford University Press, 1993), and to *Puck* in the edition by Sarah Wintle (Penguin Books, 1987).

Kipling, Rudyard 1977: *Something of Myself*. Harmondsworth: Penguin Books.

McCutchan, Corinne 1992: 'Puck and Co. Reading *Puck of Pook's Hill* and *Rewards and Fairies* as a Romance.' *CL*, 20, 69–89.

Frances Hodgson Burnett,
The Secret Garden *(1911)*

Although for the first fifty years after its publication *The Secret Garden* was never as popular as *Little Lord Fauntleroy* or *A Little Princess*, recently it has become the centre of a minor critical industry. Christine Wilkie summarized the general drift of this criticism as follows:

> These . . . critical readings have played up the nurturing, pastoral qualities of Romanticism, emphasizing *Bildungsroman* characteristics of growth and change much favoured by children's literature criticism, to establish *The Secret Garden* as a paradigmatic text in the canon of children's literature's unceasing evocation of the Romantic child. (Wilkie, 1997: 73)

The story of *The Secret Garden* seems at first to be another working of (anti)imperialist and folk-tale themes. The unpleasant, orphaned Mary Lennox (whose character has, by implication, been ruined by the empire) is sent back to England from India. It is an unromantic beginning:

> When Mary Lennox was sent to Misselthwaite Manor to live with her uncle everybody said she was the most disagreeable-looking child ever seen. She had a little thin face and a little thin body, thin light hair and a sour expression. Her hair was yellow, and her face was yellow because she had been born in India and had always been ill in one way or another.

Under the influence of a local Yorkshire boy, Dickon (who has 'cheeks as red as poppies . . . a wide, red, curving mouth and his smile spread all over his face'), she transforms both an abandoned garden and the life of her sickly cousin, Colin. In the process she is herself transformed: she loses her pride and temper, and becomes strong and healthy.

There are plenty of romantic–gothic elements; for example, Mary walks into the forbidden wing of the old manor house where she finds the hysterical Colin – the equivalent, perhaps, of the mad woman in the attic. Archibald Craven, the tragic father, is a romantic Mr Rochester, who dreams that he is being called home. Mrs Medlock is the sinister servant, Ben Weatherstaff the gnomic gardener. Some of these elements – especially the wuthering scenery and the local characters, notably the earth-mother Susan Sowerby – have an engagingly proto-early-Hollywood artificiality about them. As in her other books, Burnett has embraced the conventions and clichés of a whole genre with professional enthusiasm, and apart from two pages at the beginning of the last chapter in which she laboriously explains her view of the book's meaning (with ideas which may have been influenced by Mary Baker Eddy and the Christian Scientists), she lets the symbolism grow as riotously as the garden.

Discussion of the book has centred around a number of themes, the most common being gender and growth. In relation to gender, how far is Burnett a feminist or a failed proto-feminist? Is Mary empowered by her actions and then disempowered by the male hegemony at the end of the book, when her central, focalizing role is replaced by the actions of Archibald Craven, and her physical centrality replaced by Colin? Knowles and Malmkjær (1996: 77–80) produce stylistic–linguistic evidence to support readers' intuition of Mary's displacement. The book can be read in terms of the contrast between the feminine elements of pragmatism, nurture, family and growth (which include Susan Sowerby and Dickon), and corrupt analytical and romantic masculine isolationism.

There is no shortage of symbolic readings, many of them with sexual overtones: the Robin, locks and keys, flowers opening, Dickon as Pan, Colin as Rajah, Mary as the Virgin and the garden as Eden. Not unnaturally, the garden has richly rewarded symbolists, being seen variously as a protected area; as a link between the house (itself a symbol of masculine repression) and country (the wild, rich, untamed), an intermediate stage between repression and freedom; a place where sexual awareness begins; a place where life grows out of death; and in general as a place empowering the children.

All of which is merely a beginning; after all, as Christine Wilkie observes, 'We might be forgiven for overlooking indicators of erotic Dionysianism in *The Secret Garden* because they have been shrouded in Christian mysticism' (Wilkie, 1997: 80). As with *A Little Princess*, *The Secret Garden* has also become popular with cultural critics as an exemplar of changes between the book and other media.

Of all this critical activity, most of it very illuminating, perhaps the most straightforwardly entertaining article has been Judith Plotz's perfectly serious and perfectly convincing 'Secret Garden II: or *Lady Chatterley's Lover* as Palimpsest,' the title of which speaks for itself – and for a whole world of academia.

Bibliography

Keyser, Elizabeth Lennox 1983: ' "Quite Contrary": Frances Hodgson Burnett's *The Secret Garden*. *CL*, 11, 1–15.

Knowles, Murray and Malmkjær, Kirsten 1996: *Language and Control in Children's Literature*. London and New York: Routledge.

Mackey, Margaret 1996: 'Strip Mines in the Garden: Old Stories, New Formats, and the Challenge of Change.' *CLE*, 27 (1), 3–22.

Plotz, Judith 1994: 'Secret Garden II: or *Lady Chatterley's Lover* as Palimpsest.' *ChLAQ*, 19 (1), 15–19.

Stephens, John and McCallum, Robyn 1996: 'Ideological Re-shapings: Pruning *The Secret Garden* in 1990s Film.' *Paradoxa*, 2, 3–4, 357–68.

Wilkie, Christine 1997: 'Digging Up *The Secret Garden*: Noble Innocents or Little Savages?' *CLE*, 28 (2), 73–83.

Ethel S[ybil] Turner (1872–1958), Seven Little Australians (1894)

Ethel Turner's Woolcot family stories seem to have been written to some extent as a reaction to Victorian sentimentality in the family story, with the result that they were partly parody (of books like Charlotte Yonge's *The Daisy Chain*) and partly something quite fresh, and as such were echoed in writers like Edith Nesbit (q.v.).

Thus, while Turner has been called the Australian Louisa Alcott, *Seven Little Australians* reads like a corrective to the romanticism and religiosity of *Little Women* (q.v.). There are some obvious similarities: apart from the family name, both books feature a Meg who suffers for her vanity; both show a loving and supportive family of children. But the differences are also obvious. The saintly (absent) Mr March becomes the aloof and unpleasant Mr Woolcot, a father with a horse-whip and an irascible temper; the efficient Marmee is replaced by a fairly ineffectual stepmother. And although the children form a loving and supportive group, life is a good deal harder: Jo March may be rebellious, but she does not walk much of the 77 miles home after running away from school, nor does she end up with inflamed lungs, as does her counterpart, Judy Woolcot. (In any case, this is Australia, and 'Not one of the seven is really good, for the very excellent reason that Australian children never are.')

The greatest difference is the lack of religion: in contrast to the insistent piety of a thousand fictional deaths throughout the nineteenth century, and even in contrast to the piety of the death of Beth in *Good Wives* (even though Jo March is shown as rebelling against it, or at least being human in the face of it), Judy's death is shocking in its desperation.

Judy's brow grew damp, her eyes dilated, her lip trembled.

'Meg!' she said in a whisper that cut the air. 'Oh, Meg, I'm frightened! *Meg*, I'm so frightened!'

'God!' said Meg's heart.

'Meg, say something. Meg, help me! Look at the dark, Meg. *Meg*, I can't die! Oh, why don't they be quick?'

Nellie flew to the fence again – then to say, 'Make her better, God – oh, please, God!

'Meg, I can't think of anything to say. Can't you say something, Meg? Aren't there prayers about dying in the Prayer book? I forget. . . .'

Meg's lips moved, but her tongue uttered no word.

'Meg, I'm so frightened! I can't think of anything but "For what we are about to receive" and that's grace, isn't it? And there's nothing in Our Father that would do either. Meg, I wish we'd gone to Sunday school and learnt things. Look at the dark, Meg! Oh, Meg, hold my hands!'

'Heaven won't – be – dark,' Meg's lips said.

Even when speech came, it was only a halting, stereotyped phrase that fell from them.

'If it's all gold and diamonds, I don't want to go!' the child was crying now. 'Oh, Meg, I want to be alive! How'd you like to die, Meg, when you're only thirteen? Think how lonely I'll be without you all. . . .'

Seven Little Australians, therefore, is not only or merely one of the first books to make use of an authentic Australian setting in children's fiction and to infuse a whole genre with realism. It is almost a statement of national intent, although as Maureen Nimon has pointed out, Australia was still bound to Britain:

> For essentially, *Seven Little Australians* was innovative for asserting the validity of an Australian viewpoint alongside that of the British. In Turner's books, the measure of all things was still what was English. What she argued was that the Australia she knew was worthy of attention because, in its own way, it met English standards. . . . Thus for Turner, Australia was at once both 'home' and 'not home'. The home where she lived was Australia, but all her values and culture made sense only in terms of the home left behind. (Nimon, 1987: 48)

Of Ethel Turner's twenty-seven books, three others were about the Woolcots: *The Family at Misrule* (1895), an immediate sequel, was a success; *Little Mother Meg* (1902) and *Judy and Punch* (1902) which were produced, with some reluctance, at the request of Turner's publishers, are shadows of the original.

Bibliography

Niall, Brenda 1982: *Seven Little Billabongs: The World of Ethel Turner and Mary Grant Bruce*. Ringwood, Victoria: Penguin Books.

Nimon, Maureen 1987: 'Ethel Turner. A Reassessment of Some Aspects of Her Work.' *Orana*, 23 (1), 17–22.

Nimon, Maureen 1994: 'Australia: Literary Landscapes and Identity.' In Wendy Parsons and Robert Goodwin (eds), *Landscape and Identity: Perspectives from Australia*. Adelaide: Auslib Press, 43–51.

Prain, Vaughan 1993: 'The Australian Family Story and "The Universal Child."' In Stone 1993: 27–37.

Alan Garner (1934–), the Stone Book Quartet: The Stone Book (1976), Granny Reardun (1977), The Aimer Gate (1978), Tom Fobble's Day (1977)

Alan Garner once said that he 'wrote onions' – books that could be 'unpeeled' as far as the reader was able to do so. (Kipling wrote of weaving material together in 'overlaid tints, which might or might not reveal themselves according to the shifting light of sex, youth, and experience'.) The question is, whether this posits a superior, ultimate reading which is essentially 'adult', while incomplete (or selective) perceptions are thus necessarily inferior. The temptation to elevate these books to classic status may well be because they seem to be discussable in traditional academic terms (indeed, they may have been constructed in much the same way).

Alan Garner sees himself as a craftsman, and the Stone Book Quartet is about craft: about tradition and initiation and, perhaps, the failure of craft in the modern world. In its intricate and allusive prose style, conservative politics, sexism, and even self-satisfaction, it is reminiscent of Kipling's work, and may be popular with adults for much the same reasons. The books can be read as depressive, nostalgic texts that accept the young and new only as dependent upon the past and as inferior to it. They describe four crucial days in the lives of four children in different generations. These days may for a while seem liberating, but in the long run are seen to be merely dreams of escape. Ironically, they may illustrate the view of Jacqueline Rose and other critics that children's books are necessarily instruments of entrapment.

The books rest on lacunae, what is *not* said, and tend to fail when too much is said (as when Joseph berates Robert's ignorance in *The Aimer*

Gate, or when the generations are tied together at the end of *Tom Fobble's Day*).

The Stone Book, with its spectacular (not to say Freudian) set pieces of the child Mary climbing the church steeple with her father's 'baggin' (lunch), or finding the prehistoric marks which are her father's masonic signs deep under the earth, seems to be about liberation. Mary's father, the stone-mason, wishes to initiate her, but as she cannot follow him into the craft (she is a female, after all) he makes a book for her.

> He took the one pebble and worked quickly with candle and firelight, turning, tapping, knapping, shaping, twisting, rubbing and making, quickly, as though the stone would set hard if he stopped. He had to take the picture from his eye to his hand before it left him.
> 'There,' said Father. 'That'll do.'
> He gave Mary a prayer book bound in blue-black calfskin, tooled, stitched and decorated. It was only by the weight that she could tell it was stone and not leather.
> 'It's better than a book you can open,' said Father. 'A book has only one story . . .'
> Mary turned the stone over. Father had split it so that the back showed two fronds of a plant, like the silk in skeins, like the silk on the water under the hill. . . . And Mary sat by the fire and read the stone book that had in it all the stories of the world and the flowers of the flood.

Yet the stone book, for all its mystic possibilities, in effect condemns Mary to illiteracy and uneducated drudgery. There are plenty of political implications here, too: Mary's father despises the masters (church, squire) who buy his craftsmanship, but most of all there is the implication in Mary, and later in her illegitimate son Joseph, that the world and the craft are in inevitable decline.

All of which does not fit neatly into the optimistic paradigms constructed for children's literature. In *Granny Reardun* Joseph rejects his grandfather, the master mason reduced to lamenting both the poor stone he has to work on and his grandson's poor technique, and decides to 'get aback' of him by becoming a smith. Again, this seems to be affirming, but in effect he joins and strengthens the sterile, all-male community. By the time of *The Aimer Gate*, set during the First World War, he is middle-aged, fearful of losing his skills, an obsessive time-keeper locked into his craft. In comparison, his son Robert is portrayed as shiftless and craftless. This book, with its intense, oblique view of the war, its reflections on the nature of time, and its poetry of country life, is a requiem: but is such a requiem any business of children?

> The men stood in line at the field edge, facing the hill, Ozzie on the out-side, and began their swing. It was a slow swing, scythes and men like a big clock, back and to, back and to, against the hill they walked. They walked and swung, hips forward, letting the weight cut. It was as if they were walking in a yellow water before them. Each blade came up in time with each blade, at Ozzie's march, for if they ever got out of time the blades would cut flesh and bone.
>   Behind each man the corn swarf lay like silk in the light of poppies.

The climactic revelation that the craft of Uncle Charlie is the craft of killing – he is a sniper – seems to spell the end of a tradition, the final corruption.

Garner, then, is writing *about* childhood, but it is essentially a dark view that childhood can have only momentary epiphanies, inevitably linked to the past. In *Tom Fobble's Day* the trivialization of the modern, as in *Red Shift* and *The Owl Service* (see 'Alan Garner', p. 66), continues: William's ability to sledge fast seems to be a vacuous skill compared to the lifetime of craft of his grandfather. This is made worse by the fact that the sledge that his grandfather makes for him, as a last act of craftsmanship, is all that is left of several lives. Even his grandparents' marriage-horseshoes (lovingly polished each week for a lifetime) become no more than scrap-iron in a pocketful of shrapnel. And all this play goes on underneath a bomber's moon.

The Stone Book is an immaculately crafted book; Garner's language is strongly flavoured by West Mercian and he chose the words 'because I wanted them to taste as I remembered their taste from childhood' (Chambers, 1980: 314). On the surface the Stone Book Quartet is (apart from *The Aimer Gate*) a series of assertions of the validity of childhood, both to react against and to live with adults, but the deeper the reading, the more total the experience, then the more reactionary and depressive the message. Is children's literature no more than the protection of innocence through the deprivation of knowledge? Child readers, through books like these, may read themselves out of childhood.

Bibliography

Chambers, Aidan 1980: 'An Interview with Alan Garner.' In Chambers 1980: 276–328.
Philip, Neil 1981: *A Fine Anger: A Critical Introduction to the Work of Alan Garner*. London: Collins.

Elizabeth Enright (1909–1968), The Thimble Summer (1938)

At the end of *The Thimble Summer* there is a key image. Garnet Linden, the nine-year-old Wisconsin farm girl, is so happy with life

> She could hold it in no longer. The time had come to make a noise, and whooping at the top of her lungs, she leapt out of the shadowy willow grove.
>
> Griselda, the finest of the Jersey cows, raised mild, reproachful eyes and stared for a long time at Garnet turning handspring after handspring down the pasture.

Here is all the innocence, nostalgia and apparently simple delight of one of the most characteristically American genres of children's literature, the family story which celebrates the ideal of rural or small-town life. It has its roots deep in the American psyche, and books like Dorothy Canfield Fisher's *Understood Betsy* (1917), about the city girl learning a new life in rural Vermont, emphasize the superiority of the old ideals of independence and toughness very clearly.

In the 1920s and 1930s especially, when British children's writers were retreating into fantasy (with *Winnie-the-Pooh*) or rural quietism (*Swallows and Amazons*), writers in the USA, in the face of depression and dustbowls, drew their inspiration from conservative values. The need to celebrate independence produced books like Laura Ingalls Wilder's *Little House in the Big Woods* (1932); the need to provide or return to an idealized childhood, safe in the heart of the USA, led to books like *The Thimble Summer*.

This is the timeless world of Frank Capra's *It's A Wonderful Life* (1947): nostalgic, pragmatic and sometimes sentimental. Set in the early 1930s, *The Thimble Summer* nods at drought and hardship (with the story of the orphan Eric working his way around the country) but focuses on the optimistic, the local, the things significant to a child. Thus the generally undramatic, small adventures of Garnet – a chicken crate falling off a truck, being locked in the town library for a few hours, winning a prize for her pig – are described in an episodic, low-key manner. The clear implication is that the work ethic and the rural constitute the good life, the life of (relative) plenty:

> And canning! Oh those weeks of harvesting and peeling and preparing apples, peaches, tomatoes, cucumbers, plums and beans. All day the kitchen smelled like heaven and was filled with steam. The stove was covered with kettles and vats, and upside down on the window-sill stood processions of mason jars full of bright color and hot to the touch.
> Then in the middle of it all came the time for threshing.

The same values are found in Enright's Melendy books which, except for the first, *The Saturdays* (1941), show an inventive, co-dependent family at play in a rural setting well away from the war. The same images of relatively abundant food and the purity of nature surrounding the children recur in *Then There Were Five* (1944) and the idyll has its nostalgia built in. Randy considers the summer as it draws to a close:

> I'm going to appreciate it. I'm going to walk in the woods noticing every-thing, and ride my bike on all the roads I never explored. I'm going to fill a pillow with ladies' tobacco so I can smell it in January and remember about August. I'm going to dry a big bunch of pennyroyal so I can break pieces off all winter and think of summer. I'm going to look at everything and smell everything, and listen to everything.

Eleanor [Ruth] Estes (1906–88) created a similar atmosphere with the family at its centre in the episodic *The Moffats* (1941), set around 1914, and its sequels; the town may be bigger, but it is a world away from both world wars. Even more removed into Eden were the ten Betsy-Tacy books (1940–55) by Maud Hart [Palmer] Lovelace (1892–1980), set in a small Minnesota town (Mankato), around the beginning of the twentieth century. The girls of Deep Valley grow up largely untroubled by the world, into strong, successful women. Here is a characteristic vision of purity from *Betsy-Tacy Go Downtown* (1943):

> Snow loaded the bare arms of the maples; it lodged in the green crevices of firs; it threw sparkling shawls over the bare brown bushes shivering on Hill Street lawns.

The lawns themselves were billowing drifts, and so were the terraces, and so were the sidewalks. Men and boys came out with shovels to make Indian trails that children might follow to school. Along with the scraping of shovels came the frosty tinkle of sleighbells, as runners replaced wheels on the baker's wagon, cutters replaced carriages and buggies, and farm wagons creaked into town on runners. To steal a ride on those broad runners, or to hitch a sled thereto, was a delightful practice, shocking to parents.

This is a world where family values are taken for granted, where adults may be vulnerable but are generally reliable. The settings and the gentle tone of all these books may seem to epitomize the kind of children's book that represents a retreatist adult ideal. But not only do the children in them develop towards the wider world; the books also empower their characters by finding significance in the large things of large lives (as far as the characters are concerned) which are labelled small and insignificant by a culture concerned with the 'male-order' version of significance. Their very 'inconsequentiality', their fidelity to a vision of childhood, may well overcome their nostalgia: in *The Thimble Summer* one character innocently wonders what the word 'insidious' means: ideologically and emotionally, it means the work of Elizabeth Enright and her peers.

Bibliography

Smeadman, M. Sarah 1988: 'Elizabeth Enright (1909–1968).' In Bingham 1988: 215–20.
Smith, Louisa 1985: 'Eleanor Estes' *The Moffats:* Through Colored Glass.' In Nodelman 1985: 64–70.

Thomas Hughes (1822–1896), Tom Brown's Schooldays, by an Old Boy (1857)

Thomas Hughes set out consciously to write a book for boys (specifically for his eight-year-old son, about to go to boarding school) that was not didactic; he succeeded, in effect, in founding a genre. In *Tom Brown's Schooldays* Hughes invented or more probably drew together from earlier sources many of the ingredients later copied, exaggerated and parodied in the school story: the initiation into strange school rites; bullying and the defeat of the bully; the hero who is nearly led astray, but who is saved by a good friend; the God-like headmaster; the local inhabitants (in this case nicknamed 'louts'), and the codes of honour. As Michael Taylor (1997) has demonstrated, elements of the book can be found notably in women writers of the previous sixty years: Maria Edgeworth, Mary Martha Sherwood (q.v.), Esther Copley and Harriet Martineau (see 'School Stories', p. 298).

The revelation of *Tom Brown's Schooldays*, at least for this modern reader, is the avuncular narrative tone of the first two-thirds of the book, which is far closer to Kingsley's button-holing style than it is to many of Hughes's evangelical contemporaries. The narrator becomes almost a major character in the book, indulging in many social and political asides. Just as Robinson Crusoe takes a surprisingly long time to get to his island, so Tom does not arrive at Rugby school until chapter 5; before that the narrative meanders ostensibly through Tom's boyhood, but actually through a bucolic vision of rural England contrasted with 'these racing railroad times'. The account of Tom's stage-coach journey in chapter 4 is a classic of social observation in itself.

There are a good many social and political asides: Hughes was a Liberal MP from 1865–71 and a Christian Socialist, under the influence of

F. D. Maurice. Hughes's brand of muscular Christianity infuses the book. After Tom acquits himself well in a fight with Slogger Williams (who is two inches taller and 'peels well'), the narrator interposes:

> And now, boys all, three words before we quit the subject. I have put in this chapter on fighting of malice prepense, partly because I want to give you a true picture of what everyday school life was in my time, and not a kid-glove and go-to-meeting-coat picture; and partly because of the cant and twaddle that's talked of boxing and fighting with fists now-a-days. Even Thackeray has given in to it; and only a few weeks ago there was some rampant stuff in *The Times* on the subject, in an article on field sports.
>
> Boys will quarrel, and when they quarrel will sometimes fight. Fighting with fists is the natural and English way for English boys to settle their quarrels. What substitute for it is there, amongst any nation under the sun? What would you like to see take its place?

The story is itself simple. Tom's father muses at Tom's departure:

> Shall I send him to mind his work, and say he's sent to school to make himself a good scholar? Well, but he isn't sent to school for that – at any rate, not for that mainly. . . . If he'll only turn out a brave, helpful, truth-telling Englishman, and a gentleman, and a Christian, that's all I want.

And so Tom is precipitated into a world dominated by intense, local codes, rituals and characters who were soon to become stock features of popular literature. He makes friends with 'Scud' East ('frank, hearty and good natured'), is bullied by the archetypal bully, Flashman, whom he helps to beat; he is befriended by an older boy, Diggs, who ensures fair play. He joins in huge football matches and ends the book as captain of the cricket team. His interim moral decline is relatively short-lived: he is caught poaching, gambles, and is flogged for going to the local fair, but he is redeemed by being teamed with the pious Arthur.

The nearest that the book gets to the conventional sentimental–evangelical tale is in Arthur's illness, and the final third of the book is noticeably more sober in tone. (Biographical critics may point out that this is a result of the death of Hughes's daughter, Evie, while he was writing it.) But it nowhere approaches the melodramatic moralizing of its successors, notably Frederick Farrar's *Eric, or Little By Little* (1858), despite the fact that Hughes was given to sermonizing. In a preface to the sixth edition he wrote:

I can't see that a man has any business to write at all unless he has something which he thoroughly believes and wants to preach about. . . . [L]et him by all means put it in the shape in which it is most likely to get a hearing; but let him never be so carried away as to forget that preaching is his object.

But he does get carried away, to the extent that when the book came out it was condemned by the *Christian Observer* as likely to produce 'sensual, careless, book-hating men – low in morals, lower in religion' (quoted by Quigly, 1984: 65). It was not until Kipling's *Stalky and Co* (1899) that the public school was portrayed quite so sharply again. Kipling's characters were famously dismissed by H. G. Wells as 'Mucky little sadists'.

Ideologically, *Tom Brown's Schooldays* is infused with a state of mind engendered by a confident, powerful empire: life at school is a preparation; boys must be tough, honourable, and understand the codes of correct behaviour; playing up and playing the game is the central metaphor. As Brooke, the departing 'head of the eleven, the head of big-side football' says:

First, there's a deal of bullying going on. . . . It's very little kindness for the sixth to meddle generally – you youngsters, mind that. You'll be all the better football players for learning to stand it, and to take your own parts, and fight it through. . . . Bullies are cowards, and one coward makes many; so good-bye to the School-house match if bullying gets ahead here. . . . Then there's fuddling about in the public house and drinking bad spirits, and punch, and such rot-gut stuff. That won't make good drop-kicks or chargers of you, take my word for it. You get plenty of good beer here, and that's enough for you; and drinking isn't fine or manly, whatever some of you may think of it.

Tom Brown's Schooldays is sometimes cited as being interesting historically for its oblique and perhaps sentimentalized view of Thomas Arnold, a seminal figure in the development of the English public school system. As it happened Hughes, through this book, became a seminal figure himself, both for the public school and the empire, for both of which he provided a credo:

Quit yourselves like men then; speak up, and strike out if necessary for whatever is true, and manly, and lovely, and of good report; never try to be popular, but only to do your duty and help others to do theirs, and you may leave the tone of feeling in the school higher than you found it, and so be doing good which no living soul can measure to generations of your countrymen unborn.

Bibliography

Quigly, Isabel 1984: *The Heirs of Tom Brown: The English School Story*. Oxford: Oxford University Press.

Richards, Jeffrey (1988): *Happiest Days: The Public Schools in English Fiction*. Manchester: Manchester University Press.

Taylor, Michael 1997: 'Women Writers, Gender and Tom Brown's Schooldays.' *Children's Books History Society Newsletter*, 57, 4–13.

Philippa Pearce (1920–), Tom's Midnight Garden (1958)

Tom's Midnight Garden was for many years regarded as the best British postwar children's novel, epitomizing the 'literary' and the 'modernist' – humanist, romantic, believing in individualism, self-realization, truth and reality. However, like Mary Norton's *The Borrowers* (q.v.), it reflects tensions between tradition and change, between the settled past, violently ruptured by war, and the unsettled, revolutionary present. This was, after all, the 'angry decade' when writers such as John Osborne, Kingsley Amis and Colin Wilson were disrupting the British literary establishment.

Children's literature was naturally more conservative, and it is easy to read *Tom's Midnight Garden* as characteristically nostalgic, dealing with large themes (time, personal growth, change, loss, the inevitability of death), highly allusive, and mesmerically low-key; indeed, Pearce intended it to have 'a minimum of plot. . . . At least it has more of a theme than a plot' (Townsend, 1971: 170). Although the premise seems simple (at midnight the garden of an old mansion goes back in time fifty or sixty years) the book has a carefully constructed form, and plotting and symbolism are both intricate. At the centre is the symbolic garden, of which Pearce was well aware: 'The garden provided a powerful image of childhood. The walled garden – the old *hortus conclusus* – represents the sheltered security of early childhood' (Crouch and Ellis, 1977: 98).

The garden into which Tom escapes at night (eternally in his pyjamas) and meets Hatty as she progresses, in her own time, from child to adult, is a place of dream: it is, 'in fact', dreamed by Hatty as an old woman. It is, in a sense, 'women's time', cyclical and subtle and peaceful and mystic, in direct contrast to the theories of time inarticulately and angrily propounded by Tom's Uncle Alan. The only people who can see Tom in the garden are those who are in some way closest to nature – Hatty, the gardener Abel, and the animals – and as Hatty grows older, so Tom fades. Thus it seems that childhood is validated, as is the past, which is symbolized by the purity of the river. Tom sees it, in the past, from the garden wall:

> Tom saw beyond the garden and the house to a lane, down which a horse and cart were plodding. Beyond the lane was a meadow, and then a meandering line he knew must be the river. The river flowed past the meadow, and reached the village, and passed that. It reached a white handrailed bridge and slipped under it; and then away, towards what pools and watermills and locks and ferries that Hatty and Tom knew nothing of?

This seems to be assured writing, carrying its symbols confidently. In comparison, here is the heavy-handed picture of the river as it is in Tom's present time:

> 'Here's your river, Tom!' said Aunt Gwen, triumphantly.
> It *must* be the same river [but] this river no longer flowed beside meadows: it had back-garden strips on one side and an asphalt path on the other . . . a notice . . . said: 'WARNING. The Council takes no responsibility for persons bathing, wading or paddling. These waters have been certified as unsuitable for such purposes, owing to pollution.'
> 'What is pollution?' Tom asked.

If at points like this the subtlety of the book falters it may be an indicator of change, for if we compare *Tom's Midnight Garden* with books written around forty years later, such as Gillian Cross's *Wolf* (1990) or Melvin Burgess's *Junk* (1996), the contrast is startling. These later books illustrate at least some broad aspects of postmodernism: they are about disintegration, fragmentation, loss of identity; secure, loving (if stifling) homes are replaced by squalid squats; the excesses of solid, conventional food are replaced by junk takeaways; an awareness of the past is replaced by a desperate presentism; the idea that large issues such as time, although discussable, are still absolute, is replaced by a loss of faith in the 'grand narratives'.

Yet much of this is presaged in *Tom's Midnight Garden*. Tom is ultimately helpless in the face of the arbitrary workings of time: he is cast out of Eden and barred from it by the symbolic angel on the clock. Adults are themselves trapped: Aunt Gwen and Uncle Alan, in their way, are as dismally lost figures as Cassy's mother in *Wolf* or the addicts in *Junk*. Nor, despite the apparent coherence of the symbolism and the attempt at resolution, is the book free of postmodern ambiguities and mismatches between dream and reality.

No critical–theoretical distinctions can be absolute. *Tom's Midnight Garden*, although it seems to be a classic in the mode that had dominated twentieth-century writing, contains many elements that look forward to another mode, although one might wonder whether the postmodern is, after all, the natural condition of childhood.

Tom's Midnight Garden remains a *tour de force* of its kind, not least for its manipulation of time. At one point Tom persuades Hatty to hide her skates in the house for him to find in his own time; then he returns to her time, having found the skates:

> now Hatty and Tom were ready for the ice: two skaters on one pair of skates, which seemed to Tom both the eeriest and the most natural thing in the world.

Tom's view summarizes many critics' responses to *Tom's Midnight Garden* itself.

Bibliography

Townsend, John Rowe 1971: *A Sense of Story*. Harmondsworth: Longman Young.

'Mark Twain' (Samuel Langhorne Clemens) (1835–1910), The Adventures of Tom Sawyer (1876)

It is *not* a boy's book, at all. It will only be read by adults. It is only written for adults.

Mrs Clemens decides with you [William Dean Howells] that the book should issue as a book for boys, pure and simple – and so do I. It is surely the correct idea.

Mark Twain's indecision or pragmatism about the nature of *Tom Sawyer* was reflected in its ambiguous narrative stance: at times this is an absorbed account of childhood, at other times a wry observation of it. Such ambiguity, which has itself given the book an ambiguous status in literature, is further compounded by Twain's ambivalence about his childhood.

Tom Sawyer can be seen as a parallel to Richard Jefferies' *Bevis*; a whole childhood is encapsulated in an idyllic world. In *Tom Sawyer* it is the American nostalgic world of the small-town mid-west, bathed in sunshine and full of salty adult characters, but there is the same freedom, the same image of the anarchic, amoral child, living half in a world created out of literary romance. The famous opening scene in which Tom persuades his friends to paint the fence for him may have commercial undertones, but it has become an icon of a lost world – of society as well as childhood. Any doubts about *Tom Sawyer* being a children's book might be dispelled by the relish shown in the descriptions of the boys' exploits, notably when Tom, Huck and Joe attend their own funeral.

But *Tom Sawyer* is also a much more complex book which comments on many aspects of American society, parodies evangelical pictures of boyhood, and combines the romantic with the ironic. There is darkness to balance the sunshine, and this side of the book is provided not only by the horrors of the murder, or Injun Joe's death: there is a sub-text of bitterness.

'As to the past', Twain wrote to a friend, 'there is but one good thing about it, and that is that it *is* past.' Thus, as Michael Patrick Hearne has noted, *Tom Sawyer* can be read as a subversive and cynical book, 'perhaps the first in American literature to consider the eternal battle between the generations' (Hearne, 1988: 575). Seen in this way, there are no admirable adults in the book, for they are all tyrants, fools or hypocrites, and Tom is the only person with any real moral fibre. The narrator's voice is constantly interjecting quite complex ambiguous comments. For example, when the drunken grave-robber Muff Potter is exonerated of the (grave-robbing) Doctor's murder, by Tom's evidence,

> Tom was a glittering hero once more – the pet of the old, the envy of the young. His name even went into immortal print, for the village paper magnified him. There were some that believed he would be President yet, if he escaped hanging.
>
> As usual, the fickle, unreasoning world took Muff Potter to its bosom, and fondled him as lavishly as it had abused him before. But that sort of conduct is to the world's credit; therefore it is not well to find fault with it.

Historically, Twain's book is a major contributor to the male counterpart to the 'glad girl' of American children's literature, the 'bad boy' story. Twain was writing directly in reaction to the evangelical tradition of good, ministering children and was aware of what is usually regarded as the founding book of the genre, *The Story of a Bad Boy* (1869) by Thomas Bailey Aldrich (1836–1907). Aldrich was not portraying 'the impossible boy in a story-book':

> I call my story the story of a bad boy, partly to distinguish myself from those faultless young gentlemen who generally figure in narratives of this kind, and partly because I really was *not* a cherub. I may truthfully say I was an amiable, impulsive lad, blessed with fine digestive powers, and no hypocrite.

His description of the adventures of the Centipede club at the school at Rivermouth (Portsmouth, New Hampshire), which include things as extreme as blowing up the battery and as traditional as an epic snowball fight, leans very much towards an adult's point of view. 'There is', he wrote 'a special Providence that watches over idiots, drunken men, and boys', a sentence which suggests that boys are not his primary focus, and this ambivalence is reflected in Twain. His preface to *Tom Sawyer* claims that 'part of my plan has been to try to pleasantly remind adults of what they once were themselves.'

Tom Sawyer's successors include the robust satirical comedy of George Wilbur Peck (1840–1916), 'Peck's Bad Boy', which ran as a Saturday column in *Peck's Sun* published in Milwaukee (and advertised as 'The Funniest Paper in America!'). *Peck's Bad Boy and his Pa* was published in 1883. Comedy, however, has defused much of the subversiveness, and even the drunken father has become part of the joke.

Ironically, as Peck was writing for the popular press, he incorporates the characteristics of another well-selling genre, the 'rags to riches' novel, which had been exemplified by the work of Horatio Alger Jr (1832–99). Books like *Ragged Dick; or, Street Life in New York with the Boot Blacks* (1868) were a combination of the 'street urchin' stories, also very popular in Britain, with the addition of the American ingredient of self-help. Good luck was the reward of hard work, provided that the characters were really good in the first place. Peck wrote in a prefatory 'A Card from the Author',

> The 'Bad Boy' is not a 'myth', though there may be some stretches of the imagination in the articles. The counterpart of this boy is located in every city, village and country hamlet throughout the land . . . his coat-tail is oftener touched with a boot than his heart is by kindness. But he shuffles through life until the time comes for him to make a mark on the world, and then he buckles on the harness . . . and becomes successful.

The dual audience at which Twain aimed – the growing boy and the nostalgic adult – is also found in Booth Tarkington's *Penrod* (1914) and sequels; although Tarkington has shaken off the moralizing and moved his books towards farce, his stance is still that of the adult contemplating a lost golden world. It is widely assumed that Richmal Crompton's (q.v.) William books, which continue the development of the genre into the area of pure comedy–farce, owe much to *Penrod* (despite Crompton's denial (see p. 56)). However, while there are many similarities of character and incident, the whole thrust and tone is much more in the tradition of wry, un-nostalgic, adult observation of childhood.

For many critics the line between children's and adults' books falls quite firmly between *Tom Sawyer* and its sequel, *The Adventures of Huckleberry*

Finn (1884). And so, although it would be pleasant for children's book scholars who are tired of being at the bottom of the literary heap to feel that 'the great American novel' might actually be a children's book, it is, at best, only partially so. Margery Fisher suggests that 'read as an allegory of questing man, [*Huckleberry Finn*] is not a children's book: read as a funny, touching, rambling, shrewd and honest story of boyhood, it is' (Fisher, 1975: 361).

Bibliography

Cadogan, Mary 1993: *The Woman Behind William: A Life of Richmal Crompton.* London: Macmillan.

Hearne, Michael Patrick 1988: 'Mark Twain.' In Bingham 1988: 573–82.

Stone, Albert E., Jr 1961: *The Innocent Eye: Childhood in Mark Twain's Imagination.* New Haven, Conn.: Yale University Press.

Towers, Tom H. 1976: '"I Never Thought We Might Want to Come Back": Strategies of Transcendence in *Tom Sawyer.*' *Modern Fiction Studies*, 21, 509–20.

Robert Louis Stevenson (1850–1894), Treasure Island (1883)

By the time Stevenson came to write *Treasure Island* – one of the handful of modern stories which have become part of popular culture and have (more or less) crossed the adult–child divide – tales involving pirates, exploration, desert islands and seafaring in any combination were common, especially in boys' books and in the underbrush of literature, the penny dreadfuls.

Stevenson readily admitted that this 'landmark' book, which synthesizes a genre and marks a move towards (ironically) greater psychological serious-ness in the children's novel, grew from the compost of nineteenth-century 'bloods'. He wrote in 'My First Book':

> No doubt the parrot once belonged to Robinson Crusoe. No doubt the skeleton is conveyed from Poe. I think little of these, they are trifles and details; and no man can hope to have a monopoly of skeletons or make a corner in talking birds. The stockade, I am told is from *Masterman Ready*. . . . It is my debt to Washington Irving that exercises my conscience, and justly so, for I believe plagiarism was rarely carried farther. I chanced to pick up the *Tales of a Traveller* some years ago . . . and the book flew up and struck me; Billy Bones, his chest, the company in the parlour, the whole inner spirit, and a good deal of the material detail of my first chapters – all were there. (Stevenson, 1976: 415)

All of these books may plausibly enough be traced back to Defoe and Smollett (an echo, perhaps, in the captain of the *Hispaniola*), but only in the useful sense that several generations owed their light or surreptitious reading to imitators and innovators of the seagoing, island-visiting, empire-conquering, villainous-crews-in-Cornish-harbour-villages, buried-treasure genre.

The difference (and it is a surprisingly subtle one) is that while Stevenson thought he was being a hack, he was being an enthusiast. Of *Treasure Island* he wrote: 'It seems as though a full-grown experienced man of letters might engage to turn out *Treasure Island* at so many pages a day and keep his pipe alight' (Stevenson, 1976: 416). As it happened, inspiration failed him, so that he was still writing the last chapters when the first were appearing in serial form in *Young Folks*.

The novel emerged as far more than an exercise in professionalism. The moral ambiguity which Stevenson explored in *The Strange Case of Dr Jekyll and Mr Hyde* (1886), and which made *The Black Arrow* (1888) so unsatisfactory, is epitomized in the apparent villain, Long John Silver, 'that smooth and formidable adventurer', as Stevenson called him. It is Silver, despite being a vicious murderer, who has engaged readers most strongly – a point that did not escape his creator. In a short fable 'The Persons of the Tale' he imagines that 'after the 32nd chapter of *Treasure Island*, two of the puppets [Smollett and Silver] strolled out to have a pipe before business should begin again.' What follows is a fascinating reflection on fiction and the narrator as God, as well as a sly satire on catechistical writing:

> 'Were you never taught your catechism?' said the Captain. 'Don't you know there's such a thing as an Author?'
>
> 'Such a thing as an Author?' returned John, derisively. 'And who better'n me? An the p'int is, if the Author made you, he made Long John, and he made Hands, and Pew, and George Merry – not that George is up to much, for he's little more'n a name; and he made Flint, what there is of him; and he made this here mutiny you keep such a work about; and he had Tom Redruth shot; and – well, if that's an Author, give me Pew.'
>
> 'Don't you believe in a future state?' said Smollett. 'Do you think there's nothing but the present storypaper?'
>
> 'I don't rightly know for that,' said Silver. . . . 'What I do know is this: if there's sich a thing as a Author, I'm his favourite chara'ter. He does me fathoms better'n he does you – fathoms, he does. And he likes doing me. He keeps me on deck mostly all the time, crutch and all. . . . If there is a Author, by thunder, but he's on my side, and you may lay to it!'

Stevenson was on Silver's side to the extent that at the end of the book he allowed him to escape. He escaped into at least three other books, notably Robert Leeson's *Silver's Revenge* (1979). The other revolutionary stroke was not to make Jim Hawkins, the narrator, the pure and hearty true-British hero of the *Coral Island* type, but a rather uncertain, struggling character.

Stevenson contrives this ambiguity both in the face of the conventions of the genre (which he uses enthusiastically) and in the face of his sometimes maligned technique of identifying characters emblematically. Examples are Long John Silver – against whom the gold is measured – and the grotesquely disabled Blind Pugh.

Treasure Island hovers on the borders of the 'adult' canon largely *because* it is an adventure story, and thus is automatically excluded from the realms of art. In a debate with Henry James (who was surprisingly sympathetic), Stevenson emphasized that simplicity was of the essence in this kind of writing:

> The characters need to be presented with but one class of qualities. . . . To add more traits, to be too clever, to start the hare of moral or intellectual interest while we are running the fox of material interest, is not to enrich but to stultify your tale.

His preoccupation with ambiguity also allowed *Treasure Island* to navigate the space between the adults' and the children's novel (Raich, 1996). It has been suggested that the revisions made between serial and book publication realigned the implied audience from children towards adults (Angus, 1990). It is obvious that Stevenson overcame any self-imposed genre restrictions, and reinterpretations of *Treasure Island* as novel rather than adventure story have become quite frequent. Among them is the idea that the novel is about money (Wood, 1998), 'pagan aestheticism' (Perrot, 1992) and so on, although an earlier generation of critics argued that the book is ultimately *genuinely* escapist (Kiely, 1964).

One of *Treasure Island*'s direct successors was John Meade Falkner's (1858–1932) *Moonfleet* (1898), which had similar elements of pastiche of the genre. It is set in an eighteenth-century Dorset which possibly only existed in penny-dreadfuls (and contemporary tourist brochures); the book relies rather more on atmosphere and some dramatic set-pieces (such as an escape up an impossibly narrow cliff-path) than it does on its plot. *Moonfleet* also shares with *Treasure Island* the blurring or reversal of customary moral values: at its centre is a flawed narrator, the young John Trenchard, while its real hero is the chief smuggler, the giant Elzevir Block, and the villain the local magistrate.

If *Treasure Island* did not lead anywhere specific, it enabled the popular to acknowledge the profound within itself.

Bibliography

Angus, David, 1990: 'Youth on the Prow: The First Publication of *Treasure Island*.' *Studies in Scottish Literature*, 25, 83–99.

Kiely, Robert 1964: *Robert Louis Stevenson and the Fiction of Adventure*. Cambridge, Mass.: Harvard University Press.

Perrot, Jean 1992: 'Pan and *Puer Aeternus*: Aestheticism and the Spirit of the Age.' *Poetics Today*, 13, 155–67.

Raich, Ian 1996: '*Treasure Island* and Tim.' *CLE*, 27 (3), 181–93.

Stevenson, Robert Louis 1976: 'My First Book.' In Lance Salway (ed.) *A Peculiar Gift: Nineteenth-Century Writing on Books for Children*. Harmondsworth: Kestrel/Penguin Books, 412–19.

Wood, Naomi J. 1998: 'Gold Standards and Silver Subversions: *Treasure Island* and the Romance of Money.' *CL*, 26, 61–86.

Natalie Babbitt (1932–), Tuck Everlasting (1975)

Natalie Babbitt is an individualistic writer even among her peers, that group of American writers whose work in the 1960s and 1970s – E. L. Konigsberg (q.v.), Katherine Paterson, Cynthia Voight, Betsy Byars, Patricia MacLachlan (q.v.) – parallels the writers of the 'second golden age' in Britain – Nina Bawden, Penelope Lively, Jill Paton Walsh.

Babbitt claimed that she was motivated by a fascination with the different ways in which different people view or create the 'same' reality. Her books are fantasies of a subtle kind, exploring the threshold between fantasy and reality (the importance of which she has found validated in Joseph Campbell's *Hero With a Thousand Faces;* Babbitt, 1987: 202). They discuss major philosophical questions, none more so than *Tuck Everlasting,* which is ironically about order and chaos, because, as she has said, 'the main characters in all my stories are not people, but ideas' (Babbitt, 1987: 204).

In *Tuck Everlasting* the Tuck family find the spring of immortality in a mid-western wood in 1793; having drunk from it unwittingly, they are condemned to wander forever, unchanged. In 1880 Winnie, a ten-year-old, discovers the spring and their secret, and has to decide whether to choose immortality. Angus Tuck tries to explain to her that existence is like a wheel: 'Dying's part of the wheel, right next to being born. . . . Being part of the whole thing, that's the blessing. But it's passing us by, us Tucks. Living's heavy work, but off to one side, the way we are, it's useless, too. . . . If I knowed how to climb back on the wheel, I'd do it in a minute.' Jesse Tuck, eternally seventeen, gives Winnie a bottle of the water to drink when *she* reaches seventeen, so they can be together forever.

The secondary plot concerns the nameless Man in the Yellow Suit, who also discovers the secret and wishes to exploit it. The moral questions raised by his murder by Mae Tuck provide another layer of ambiguity, and the incident points up neatly questions of response. Babbitt has noted that letters she gets from children always concern questions of immortality (or the fascinating Jesse Tuck) and never the killing. 'I suppose they feel that the man in the yellow suit, like the Wicked Witch of the West, needed killing, and so it's all right. The killing has bothered some grownups, but the children don't seem to turn a hair over it' (Babbitt, 1996: 36).

The Tucks leave Winnie and the village and return in 1950, to find the wood and the spring bulldozed beneath a gas station. In the graveyard, they find Winnie's gravestone ('Dear Wife, Dear Mother'):

> Mae said softly, without looking at him, 'She's gone?'
>
> Tuck nodded. 'She's gone,' he answered.
>
> There was a long moment of silence between them, and then Mae said, 'Poor Jesse.'
>
> 'He knowed it, though,' said Tuck. 'At least, he knowed she wasn't coming. We all knowed that, long time ago.'
>
> 'Just the same,' said Mae. She sighed. And then she sat up a little straighter. 'Well, where to now, Tuck? No need to come back here no more.'

The best of Babbitt's other books are probably *The Search for Delicious* (1969) and *The Eyes of the Amaryllis* (1978), which also set out to pose intellectual problems.

Bibliography

Babbitt, Natalie 1987: 'The Perilous Realms.' In Harrison and Maguire 1987: 195–209.
Babbitt, Natalie 1996: 'Protecting Children's Literature.' In Egoff, Stubbs, Ashley and Sutton 1996: 32–8.

Charles Kingsley (1819–1875), The Water Babies. A Fairy Tale for a Land-Baby (1863)

The Water Babies, often regarded as a landmark text which opened the 'first golden age' of British children's literature (although that claim is obviously an over-simplification), is at that phase in its history when it is hovering in the limbo between books that are well known and books that are actually read; between a book that *is* for children and a book that *was* for children; between being a children's classic and simply a classic.

This rambling, eccentric, opinionated and often apparently extempore book has become embedded in cultural folklore, partly because of its basic premise and partly for its powerful opening chapters. Tom the chimney sweep is portrayed more or less realistically, but with a wry, ironic narrator's voice.

> He cried half his time and laughed the other half. He cried when he had to climb the dark flues, rubbing his poor knees and elbows raw . . . and when his master beat him, which he did every day in the week; and when he had not enough to eat, which happened every day in the week likewise. And he laughed the other half of the day . . . and thought of the fine times coming when he would be a man, and a master sweep. . . . And he would have apprentices, one, two, three if he could. How he would bully them, and knock them about . . . and when his master let him have a pull at the leavings of his beer, Tom was the jolliest boy in the whole town.

Written at a time when children's writers were searching for a tone appropriate to a changing relationship between adults and children, *The Water Babies* is a very good example of a double-address book, in which the narrator often speaks 'over the heads' of his supposed audience to an adult audience; this is complicated by the fact that the address to the child audience is by turns affectionate and patronizing. The result is that the narrator becomes in effect a major character, continually interpolating digressions which Brian Alderson (1995: xxi) describes as 'celebratory pauses – wayside pulpits where the author can rejoice in his own perceptions' and in which he harangues his audience on his hobby-horses.

The nature of these hobby-horses, from the sexual to the philosophical, can provide the adult historian with a cross-section of mid-Victorian thought, although, as Colin Manlove (1975: 13) put it, Kingsley's 'views [were] subject to flux, his interests manifold to the point of incoherence'. *The Water Babies*, then, is the unsystematic, unbuttoned universe-view of a man who was (among other things), chaplain to Queen Victoria, Christian Socialist, Fellow of the Geological Society and friend of Darwin, Regius Professor of Modern History at Cambridge, Professor of English Literature at Queen's College, London, Canon of Westminster Abbey, poet, novelist, and the man who provoked (although the matter is exceedingly complex) John Henry Newman to write his *Apologia Pro Vita Sua* (1864) – quite apart from being a parish priest throughout all this.

There is no doubt that the book has powerful elements. At the beginning Tom, slave-driven by the drunken Mr Grimes, loses himself in the chimneys of a great house and emerges into the pure white room of the pure white little girl, Ellie, where 'for the first time in his life, he found out that he was dirty'. Pursued, he falls into a stream and drowns, turning himself into a water baby and the book into a quite different book. From here on we read (at least, in one reading) a purgatorial/redemption allegory with a good deal of heavy-handed symbolism which ranges from the stridently personal to the obscure or confused, celebrating the endless wonder of nature, couched in (as one wishes) a rambling or complex structure and featuring Rabelaisian mannerisms.

But that is not, of course, all. For example, it has been suggested that in *The Water Babies* Kingsley

> offers his most attractive, deceptively simple presentation of the argument that all purely scientific explanations of reality would benefit by being placed in the larger context of Christian revelation.
> The underlying message in little Tom's evolutionary adventure is that science must be especially careful not to trample on the realms of imagination and religion. (Hawley, 1989: 20)

One might think that this is a charitably coherent version of what is going on among the attacks on Cousin Cramchild (i.e. Peter Parley) or the violent revenges of Mrs Bedonebyasyoudid, or the satirical swipes at the lachry-mose novels of Elizabeth Wetherell and her ilk: 'but Tom thought he would sooner have a jolly good fairy tale, about Jack the Giant-killer or Beauty and the Beast, which taught him something that he didn't know already' – and a Swiftean parade of dunces. What is certainly going on in one of the sub-texts is something intensely personal to Kingsley. Humphrey Carpenter observed that he was 'the first writer in England, perhaps the first in the world with the exception of Hans Andersen, to discover that a children's book can be the perfect vehicle for an adult's most personal and private concerns' (Carpenter, 1985: 37). Given the nature of some of Kingsley's private concerns (Chitty, 1974: 79–86), it is perhaps a mercy that the sexuality in the book is more or less confined to the sensual treatment of naked (especially female) children.

The Water Babies parallels *Peter Pan* (q.v.) in its uncertainty as to its audience, its tone, and to some extent its purpose: on one level it seems to be a disguised Christian allegory, but Kingsley's universalism and extravagant symbolism lead the book into far more ambiguous waters. Like *Peter Pan* it raises serious questions about children's books and their audience: how much of this book could have been or could be understood or appreciated, and at what level?

Kingsley's books for (or adopted by) children, which were very popular in their day, are largely forgotten: *Westward Ho!* (1855) and *Hereward the Wake* (1865) are particularly marked by his (shifting) political views; his version of the Greek myths, *The Heroes* (1856), written in reaction to Nathaniel Hawthorne's *A Wonder Book* (1856) – which he thought 'distressingly vulgar' – lingers on.

A similar mix of social and religious concerns can be found in the work of George MacDonald (1824–1905), like Kingsley a friend of the Christian Socialist F. D. Maurice. His blend of the folk-tale with religion, notably in *The Princess and the Goblin* (1871) and *The Princess and Curdie* (1882), was distinctive, but the books share Kingsley's predilection for portentous symbolism, although they are rather more disciplined. Similarly, *At The Back of the North Wind* (1871), with its quasi-allegorical fantasy grounded on social realism of a rather sentimental kind, and its images of purgatory, has echoes of *The Water Babies*.

Bibliography

Alderson, Brian 1995: 'Introduction.' In Charles Kingsley, *The Water Babies*. Oxford: Oxford University Press, ix–xxix.

Chitty, Susan 1974: *The Beast and the Monk: A Life of Charles Kingsley*. London: Hodder and Stoughton.

Cunningham, Valentine 1985: 'Soiled Fairy: *The Water Babies* in its Time.' *Essays in Criticism*, 35 (2), 121–48.

Fasick, Laura 1993: 'The Failure of Fatherhood: Maleness and its Discontents in Charles Kingsley.' *ChLAQ*, 18 (3), 100–5.

Hawley, John C. 1989: '*The Water Babies* as Catechetical Paradigm.' *ChLAQ*, 14 (1), 19–21.

Manlove, Colin 1975: *Modern Fantasy: Five Studies*. Cambridge: Cambridge University Press.

Wood, Naomi 1995: 'A (Sea) Green Victorian: Charles Kingsley and *The Water Babies*.' *LU*, 19 (2), 223–31.

Kenneth Grahame (1859–1932), The Wind in the Willows (1908)

'Children's literature' is a fairly elastic category, but there are certain books that a small amount of thought should surely exclude, notably (and notoriously) William Golding's *The Lord of the Flies*, routinely taught in British schools, and other borderline cases such as Russell Hoban's *The Mouse and His Child*, or Roald Dahl's *Boy*. However, it might seem a little quixotic to attempt to exclude *The Wind in the Willows*, which almost since its publication has been a fixture of children's book publishing and of child-culture: one of the few generally undisputed classics for children. The fact that it is accepted as such, when it can equally be seen as a book fundamentally about adult male repression, is very instructive as to the condition of criticism of children's books.

The logic seems to have run thus: this book was written for a particular child; it is about furry animals; therefore it must be a children's book. What else can it be? This argument does not bear much examination.

That a book's story was told originally to a child does not make it a children's book, even when the circumstances of the telling are a little less suspect than this. The account of Grahame telling the first part of the story to his son Alastair is arguably a piece of myth-making by Elspeth Grahame, Grahame's wife (Grahame, 1944: 2–3). The manuscript letters containing the first version of Toad's adventures, addressed to Alastair Grahame ('Mouse'), were written by a father who did not choose to travel for forty minutes from London to Reading to see his son at weekends; also, after the first few, they contain no salutation. They were subsequently heavily revised, and at least half the book seems to have had no contact with an actual child.

What about the animals? An early review in *The Times* observed (notoriously, but accurately): 'As a contribution to natural history, the work is negligible' (quoted in Chalmers, 1933: 127). As Margaret Meek wryly put it, to meet these 'animals' is 'to encounter the same person, the author, variously disguised as a Rat, a Mole, a Badger, and a Toad, all equally egocentric and self-regarding' (Meek, 1991: 25). For all their superficial fur, Mole, initially closest to a kind of childlike inexperience, is a householder, well-respected in his neighbourhood; Rat is a gentleman of leisure; Badger an ageing squire; and Toad, for all his anarchy, is a substantial landowner. This is an adult world, with very adult preoccupations.

The Golden Age (1895) and *Dream Days* (1898), which had made Grahame's name, were wry, ironic and sophisticated adult views *of* childhood *for* adults, though they did influence Edith Nesbit (q.v.). Although *The Wind in the Willows* was initially described as 'a book for youth', the novelist Arnold Bennett reviewed it as 'an urbane exercise in irony at the expense of the English character', and Arthur Ransome noted that Grahame was 'quite unable to resist that appeal from dreamland to a knowledge of the world that makes the charm of his books, and separates them from children's literature' (Hunt, 1994: 16, 17).

Other evidence that *The Wind in the Willows* is not a children's book might be that the sequels by William Horton, beginning with *Willows in Winter* (1993), were not directly marketed for children, while Jan Needle's deconstructive anti-reading, *Wild Wood* (1981), was so marketed, but very arguably should not have been. A sequel exploring Toad's post-Willows psychological state, *Counselling for Toads* by Robert de Board (1997), is a serious (if witty) and practical explanation of psychotherapy. A. A. Milne's stage adaptation, *Toad of Toad Hall* (1929), fillets out the mystical and repressive elements, leaving the cheerful farcical elements to be enjoyed by children: as Milne said, perhaps a little ambiguously, 'there are both beauty and comedy in the book, but the beauty must be left to blossom there' (Milne, 1929: vi).

The characters have been used for advertising everything from banks to cars to the English Tourist Board, the appeal resting on adult perceptions of lost values of purity and innocence.

Obviously the book has been enjoyed by generations of children; it has, after all, been marketed to them and several elements of the book do chime with actual childhoods. Mole's story, for example, represents the themes of insiderism, outsiderism and belonging common to many children's books. (Ironically, however, after Mole is initiated and comes to belong to the 'inner circle' – although he is forced to acknowledge his limitations – he ends up as a represser of both Rat and Toad.) The book is studded with small-scale fears and comforts, and Toad's repression (as much as his anarchy) may strike chords with the powerless child; but again, the book is emphatically *not* about successful escape or rebellion; it is not, as one might expect of a children's book, about growth, development or personal victory.

Since the exemplary biography of Grahame by Peter Green, the ways in which the book reflects Grahame's life (to an uncomfortable degree) are difficult to ignore. In a sentence: Grahame was left parentless at an early age, but had a relatively happy childhood beside the Thames; forced to join the Bank of England – rather than going to Oxford University – he found his escape in weekend pursuits in male company; he wrote witty and quasi-mystic essays (*Pagan Papers*, 1893) and books *about* childhood (*The Golden Age, Dream Days*); he made an unhappy marriage, had one son who almost certainly committed suicide; after the success of *The Wind in the Willows* he wrote virtually nothing else, and divided the rest of his life between the Thames and southern Europe.

And so *The Wind in the Willows* book, most obviously, may be about repression and fear of change. First Mole, then Toad, and then Rat are frustrated in their attempts to change their lives. They cannot break out of their safe environment: at their first meeting, Rat forbids Mole, who thinks he has taken the first step to liberation, to mention the 'wide world' again, which is hardly the stuff for expanding childish horizons. And if any of them try to break out, they are punished (Mole is terrorized in the Wild Wood), or regarded as mad (when Rat is nearly seduced to the soft south by the Sea Rat), or bad (Toad is locked away by his friends, as well as by the law).

The fear of change that permeates the book reflects the momentous shifts away from the stable Victorian world in which Grahame had been brought up. There are the threatening working-class radicals from the Wild Wood; the devilish, noisy, *fast* motor-car encroaching on the countryside and destroying traditional ways of life; and the growing power of women. Toad Hall is regained (against the odds) by the forces of conservatism: only the deviant Toad enjoys the monsters that pollute the roads – and he is frowned upon and converted; while women are more or less excluded from the book. Any references to them are surrounded by fear, condescension, derision, and/or loathing. Sexuality has been sublimated into food orgies, a feature sometimes taken to indicate that the book is therefore suitable for children. It is, perhaps, better suited to adults who deny their own sexuality and try to find escape in the rustic, retreatist, male, middle-class idyll.

The ambivalence of all this can be seen clearly in the language, which fluctuates (evasively, it might be said) from the straightforward to the parodic and to the overblown quasi-mystic.

It was a bright morning in the early part of summer. . . . The Mole and the Water Rat had been up since dawn, very busy on matters connected with boats and the boating season; painting and varnishing, mending paddles, repairing cushions, hunting for missing boat-hooks, and so on . . .

'Oddsbodikins!' said the sergeant of police, taking off his helmet and wiping his forehead. 'Rouse thee, old loon, and take over from us this vile Toad, a criminal of deepest guilt and matchless artfulness and resource. Watch and ward him with all thy skill; and mark thee well, old grey-beard, should aught untoward befall, thy old head shall answer for his – and a murrain on both of them!'

Breathless and transfixed the Mole stopped rowing as the liquid run of that glad piping broke on him like a wave, caught him up, and possessed him utterly. For a space they hung there, brushed by the purple loosestrife that fringed the bank; then the clear imperious summons that marched hand-in-hand with the intoxicating melody imposed its will on Mole.

It is a virtuoso performance, in its way. At one point, Grahame contrives to have Toad change from a country gentleman (impersonating a washerwoman on a canal narrowboat) to small animal to middle-sized animal in the space of two paragraphs.

Toad's temper, which had been simmering viciously for some time, now fairly boiled over, and he lost all control of himself.

'You common, low, *fat* barge-woman!' he shouted; 'don't you dare talk to your betters like that! Washerwoman indeed! I would have you know that I am a Toad, a very well-known, respected, distinguished Toad! I may be under a bit of a cloud at present, but I will *not* be laughed at by a barge-woman!'

The woman moved nearer to him and peered under his bonnet keenly and closely. 'Why, so you are!' she cried. 'Well, I never! a horrid, nasty, crawly Toad! And on my nice clean barge, too! Now that is a thing that I will *not* have.'

She relinquished the tiller for a moment. One big mottled arm shot out and caught Toad by a fore-leg, while the other gripped him fast by a hind-leg.

The Wind in the Willows can be revealingly read by adults as a dark companion-piece to Jerome K. Jerome's comic masterpiece *Three Men in a Boat* (1889). Both books are in the same genre of the Victorian–Edwardian Thames holiday story; the difference is that Jerome's book is positive: its young men always look ironically outwards and onwards. *The Wind in the Willows* is its mirror image. For example, the three men find Quarry Wood at Cookham Dene (alias the Wild Wood) full of smiling faces among the leaves, rather than threatening faces among the bare boughs found in it by Mole.

In one of the earliest academic critical essays on *The Wind in the Willows*, W. W. Robson concluded that *The Wind in the Willows* was not a children's book 'unless you mean by children's literature one of those books which are ineffective unless the child in the reader responds to the child in the author' (Robson, 1982: 143). The complexity of *The Wind in the Willows* implied in this quotation has been mirrored in the extensive critical industry that has sprung up around it, legitimized by its inclusion in the adult literary canon.

Bibliography

Chalmers, Patrick R. 1933: *Kenneth Grahame: Life, Letters and Unpublished Work*. London: Methuen.

Gilead, Sarah 1988: 'The Undoing of Idyll in *The Wind in the Willows*.' *CL*, 16, 145–58.

Graham, Kathryn V. 1999: 'Of School and River: *The Wind in the Willows* and its Immediate Audience.' *ChLAQ*, 23 (4), 181–6.

Grahame, Elspeth (ed.) 1944: *First Whisper of 'The Wind in the Willows'*. London: Methuen.

Green, Peter 1959: *Kenneth Grahame, 1859–1932: A Study of his Life, Work and Times*. London: John Murray.

Hunt, Peter 1994: *The Wind in the Willows: A Fragmented Arcadia*. New York: Twayne.

Kuznets, Lois 1987: *Kenneth Grahame*. Boston: Twayne.

Marshall, Cynthia 1994: 'Bodies and Pleasures in *The Wind in the Willows*.' *CL*, 22, 58–69.

Meek, Margaret 1991: 'The Limits of Delight.' *Books for Keeps*, 68, 24–5. Reprinted in Chris Powling (ed.) *The Best of Books for Keeps*. London: Bodley Head, 1994, 27–31.

Milne, A. A. 1929: *Toad of Toad Hall*. London: Methuen.

Robson, W. W. 1982: *The Definition of Literature*. Cambridge: Cambridge University Press.

Steig, Michael 1981: 'At the Back of *The Wind in the Willows*: An Experiment in Biographical and Autobiographical Interpretation.' *Victorian Studies*, 24, 303–23.

Watkins, Tony 1984: 'Making a Break for the Real England: The River-Bankers Revisited.' *ChLAQ*, 9 (1), 34–5.

L. Frank Baum (1856–1919), The [Wonderful] Wizard of Oz (1900)

Baum intended *The Wizard of Oz* to be a modern 'wonder tale' which would replace what he regarded as the outdated nineteenth-century (European) fairy-tales. He wanted to write a book in which 'the wonderment and joy are retained and the heartache and nightmares left out', but *The Wizard of Oz* is notable for the 'intriguing tension that develops in it between delightful fantasies that are clearly meant to give readers pleasure, and a healthy, very practical, and very American cynicism about the usefulness of such meaningless frippery' (Nodelman, 1989: 11).

Although *The Wizard* is sometimes regarded as a pioneer in a form that did not flourish in the USA, Baum was far from the first writer to wrestle with the transplantation of the folk- and fairy-tale. As Mark West has noted, 'the fact that most of the fantasy literature published for children during the nineteenth century never made it into the history books raises some interesting questions about the historiography of children's literature' (West, 1989: 1). The middle years of the nineteenth century in children's books in the USA were dominated by the educational non-fiction of Samuel Griswold Goodrich (1793–1860), who produced over a hundred Peter Parley books, beginning with *The Tales of Peter Parley About America* (1827). But even Peter Parley, who ostensibly disapproved of fairy-tales with a fervour that matched that of the British evangelical writers, published a book of fables (albeit with moral purpose) in 1836.

The first, sceptical hands to be laid on the European tale appear to be those of James Kirke Paulding (1778–1860), whose *A Christmas Gift from Fairyland* (1838) was based on the idea that the European tales were not suited to the democratic new world. One of the stories, 'The Fairy Experiment', describes a community of fairies who 'had sought refuge from the persecutions of science and philosophy, two deadly foes to these playful fantasies, and airy inventions of the imagination' in the new world. However, they bring with them undesirable elements of the old world; as the narrator notes, 'despotism cannot exist in our new world'. The king and queen return home, Puck finds a new life among the native Americans, and the fairies form a republic. Fantasy does not necessarily equal escapism.

The 'romantics' of New England, notably Nathaniel Hawthorne (*A Wonder Book*, 1851) and Louisa M. Alcott (q.v.) (her first book was *Flower Fables*, 1855), produced fantasies of various kinds; one of the most interesting was *The Last of the Huggermuggers, a Giant Story* (1855, dated 1856) by Christopher Pearse Cranch (1813–92). This book consciously borrows from *Gulliver's Travels* and 'Jack and the Beanstalk', but the central character, Jacky Cable – 'Little Jacket' – is a forerunner of an important type of character in American children's fiction, the 'bad boy': 'though small in size he was big in wit, being an uncommonly smart lad, though he did play truant sometimes, and seldom knew well his school-lessons.' And the plot hinges on the activities of a showman who tries to exploit the gentle giants.

Where *The Wizard of Oz* did something new, it was in the breadth of Baum's imagination. 'The astonishing world Baum describes has no overriding law or principle except variety', wrote Perry Nodelman (1989: 10) in the course of justifying the exclusion of *The Wizard of Oz* from the canon proposed by the Children's Literature Association. Variety is not enough to gain respectability, and curiously the book has never achieved any great literary stature in the USA, despite its popularity. This may be due partly to its prose, which is at best utilitarian, and partly to the pragmatic–magical paradox at the heart of the book: one theme of the book (as an *American* book) seems to be self-reliance and self-confidence – the lion is actually brave, the tin woodman already has a heart, the scarecrow is clever – but they actually succeed by magical luck. And, after all, at the centre of this whole magical land is not a Merlin or a Gandalf, but a confidence trickster. Perhaps as a result, it is not uncommon for the illustrator, W. W. Denslow, to be given the credit for the book's initial success.

More recently, *The Wizard of Oz* has been recognized as having central cultural significance. Critics have seen Oz as a utopian dream (in contrast to 'the great grey prairie' of Kansas), or as a satirical map of the USA or California. Alternatively, as Jerry Griswold puts it,

> *The Wizard of Oz* . . . like other American childhood classics needs to be understood in a doubled, psychohistorical fashion. The Land of Oz is the Kingdom

without: an imaginative and extravagant version of America. But it is also and simultaneously the Kingdom within: Dorothy's own circumstances reimagined at large, an extrapolation of her own oedipal or family problems, her personal problems. (Griswold, 1992: 41)

The twin American themes of pragmatism and home are clear: however brightly coloured Oz may be, it is to sour Aunt Em and dismal Kansas that Dorothy spends the whole book trying to return.

The Wizard of Oz, famously named after a drawer in Baum's filing cabinet, produced at least fourteen sequels by Baum, and many readers think that, for all the episodic chaos of many of them, they show his immensely fertile imagination at its best, without the dilemma of disclaiming fantasy while in the act of writing it. There were a large number of 'Oz' books by other writers, and of course MGM's 1939 Mervyn LeRoy–Victor Fleming film (said to be among the most popular films of all time) has fixed the story (if not the book) in the mind of popular culture. The adaptation for the screen – in contrast to the equally successful film adaptation of *Mary Poppins* – introduced more complex motifs than appeared in the book, notably with the correspondence between characters in the grey world of Kansas and the colourful world of Oz. In one respect, however, the film was retrogressive: Dorothy is given a far more conservative gender-role than she has in the book, with the result that 'the script writers' portrayal of Dorothy seems outdated and sexist by contemporary standards while Baum's Dorothy comes across as a heroine whose time has nearly arrived' (West, 1992: 131).

The Wizard of Oz is an interesting example of the triumph of popular culture. Baum, one feels, might have been very pleased by the judgement of a modern critic, John Goldthwaite:

> Baum was essentially a pulp writer who drew at need from every passing fashion, sometimes to the benefit of the story, sometimes not. . . . [But he] was the Edison of narrative fantasy, finding ways of lighting it up and making it talk that no one had ever thought of before. (Goldthwaite, 1996: 212, 211)

Bibliography

Gilman, Todd S. 1996: '"Aunt Em: Hate You! Hate Kansas! Taking the Dog. Dorothy": Conscious and Unconscious Desire in *The Wizard of Oz*.' *ChLAQ*, 20 (4), 161–7.
Hearne, Michael Patrick 1973: *The Annotated Wizard of Oz*. New York: Potter.
Hearne, Michael Patrick (ed.) 1983: *The Wizard of Oz (The Critical Heritage)*. New York: Schocken Books.

Nodelman, Perry 1989: 'Introduction: On Words and Pictures, Neglected Noteworthies, and Touchstones in Training.' In Nodelman 1989: 1–13.

West, Mark I. (ed.) 1989: *Before Oz: Juvenile Fantasy Stories from Nineteenth-Century America*. Hamden: Archon.

West, Mark I. 1992: 'The Dorothys of Oz: A Heroine's Unmaking.' In Butts 1992: 125–31.

Topics

Censorship

People censor children's books, it has been said, because they can. As children's books are an expression of a power-relationship, are mediated through adults, and are unprotected by any supposed literary status, adults commonly feel free to put their judgements into practice and control the books just as they control their children. Ironically, these unprotected materials for the least powerful of audiences are taken very seriously by adults, from evangelical groups such as the Moral Majority in the USA, to totalitarian powers such as the *Gleichschaltung* in Nazi Germany and the *Literaturentwicklungsprozess* in the former East Germany.

There are examples of children's books being of practical political importance, such as the Norwegian Fridtjof Sælens' *Snorre Sel* (1941). Equally, some books were so popular as to *escape* censorship: Erich Kästner's *Emil and the Detectives* (1929) is reported to have survived when his other books had been burned by the Nazis.

Some indication of the lingering status of *the book* is that children's books are usually awarded more censorial attention than videos or other media. Censorship in parts of the USA of writers like Judy Blume (q.v.), Robert Cormier (q.v.), or even J. D. Salinger and Shakespeare exists alongside the widespread availability of violent and sexually degrading images.

Censorship in the USA, at least since Anthony Comstock's *Traps for the Young* in 1883, has tended to be more direct and active than elsewhere. A list of books banned as a result of organizations such as Mel and Norma Gabler's Texas-based Educational Research Analysts includes *The Diary of Anne Frank* and *The Wizard of Oz* (q.v.) and books that portray 'disgusting and degrading' actions, such as Beatrice Sparks's *Go Ask Alice* (1973). There have been considerable swings of opinion: in 1964 *Harriet the Spy*

(q.v.) caused an uproar because Ole Golly advises Harriet that 'little lies
. . . are not bad'; by the 1970s 'teenage sexuality, including homosexuality
had become a commonplace topic' (MacLeod, 1994: 182); in 2000, books of
that kind were once more under fire. The latest targets of censoring organizations are books that mention topics such as AIDS or homosexuality, on the
principle (in direct opposition to broadly liberal thinking) that what children don't know about can't hurt them. (See also Matters of History, pp.
15–18.) The *Newsletter on Intellectual Freedom* of the American Library
Association records such examples; the National Council for the Teachers
of English has a Committee Against Censorship; and the International Reading
Association has an Intellectual Freedom Committee. In 1999 J. K. Rowling's
Harry Potter books were among the most complained-about, on the grounds
that they make witchcraft seem admirable, in contrast to the witches who
objected to Roald Dahl's negative portrayal of them on the grounds that
'We're not such bad people' (West, 1988: 73).

However, across the world, such is the interrelationship between mediat-
ing audience (parents, teachers, media, pressure-groups) and publishers and
authors, that authors commonly and necessarily censor themselves. How
far this can be seen as protecting rather than depriving is central to the debate:
even though the 'horror' comics banned by the Children and Young Persons
(Harmful Publications Act) in the UK in 1955 might seem to be 'obvious'
targets. (Frederick Wertham's *Seduction of the Innocent*, 1954, is still worth
seeking out, as it demonstrates the tastelessness, if not perversion of the material, as well as the dedicated manicness of the censor – just what *was* the
relationship between Batman and Robin?)

The question remains, what is an obvious case for censorship? What, indeed,
is tastelessness? What needs to be restricted depends upon interpretations
of childhood and 'affect' – both notoriously slippery concepts – except,
perhaps, for those with absolute faith.

Childhood is of course commonly seen as a potentially subversive state.
Some authors, such as Roald Dahl and Enid Blyton, collude or appear to
collude with it; ironically, however, they tend to be criticized or censored
on classist or sexist or racist grounds. Other writers who exploit childhood
commercially (as in series depicting horror) tend to escape; those who attempt
basic social engineering (as in 'readers' for the very young) may be censored
for political–ideological reasons. Overall, fear and mistrust of childhood
seem as strong as the desire to protect a certain supposed, remembered or
wished-for innocence.

Matters are complicated by the shelf-life of children's books. The books
of Blyton (with bad Gollywogs called Nigger) and Lofting (with his black

Jollijinkies), for example, were marked by racist attitudes characteristic of their time. Books like Helen Bannerman's *Little Black Sambo* (1899) and Joel Chandler Harris's *Uncle Remus: His Songs and Sayings* (1880) have been retrospectively condemned and rewritten. Roald Dahl's black pygmy slaves in *Charlie and the Chocolate Factory* (1964) might well have escaped notice even ten years before. (Interestingly, it is hard to find a 'classic' of a hundred years ago which is not blatantly sexist or racist, although such texts have been protected, until very recently, by their status.)

In the UK where, as Dahl observed, censorship tends to emanate from the Left of politics as much as the Right (West, 1988: 73), in what has been labelled 'political correctness', control of writers or of access to their books has generally been covert. Attempts by publishers to change what authors have written, from Beatrix Potter – naked kittens in *The Tale of Tom Kitten* (1907) – to Alan Garner – night sledging in *Tom Fobble's Day* (1979) – have been resisted: others, reported by the novelist Jean Ure – expurgation of swearing (see Powling, 1989: 19) – or the artist Jan Ormerod – covering part of a picture of a five-year-old in *Sunshine* (1981) – have been acceded to. Generally, the dominance of a few bookselling chains with 'pragmatic' book-buying policies are highly effective in determining what may or may not be read. It has been estimated that fewer than 6 per cent of children's books published each year appear on the shelves of Britain's major retailers, a fact that discourages radical writing or 'taboo' subjects: it is, for example, still extremely difficult to find a book for younger children which treats of the death of a sibling.

Thus the history of children's literature worldwide is characterized by the struggle to control it: from criticism of folk- and fairy-tales in the eighteenth and nineteenth centuries, to debates about the dumbing-down effects of the Tellytubbies in the 1990s. Liberalization (or tolerance, or corruption, depending on your viewpoint) has trickled down to children's books to the point at which an excremental book like *The Story of Little Mole Who Knew it was None of His Business* (Werner Holzwarth and Wolf Erlbruch, 1989; trans. UK 1994) is received with amusement rather than disgust, and Babette Cole's *Mummy Laid an Egg* (1993), with its witty and explicit approach to sex education, is accepted, on the whole, tolerantly – but only in certain places.

In short, there is no simple answer to questions of censorship, especially as actions in cultures other than our own (whoever *we* are) can seem bewildering or ludicrous: Maurice Sendak's (q.v.) *In the Night Kitchen* (1970) was widely 'modified' by librarians to cover a little boy's genitals, and Julie Vivas's *The Nativity* (1986) was objected to on the grounds that her pictures of the angel Gabriel, Mary and Joseph were blasphemous (because, presumably, they were inaccurate). Typical of the simplistic thinking very often attached to censorship was the case of Gillian Rubenstein's *Beyond the Labyrinth*, which won the Australian Children's Book Council Book of the Year for Older Readers in 1989. Because of a few taboo words the book became a *cause célèbre*, to the point at which a Melbourne magistrate refused to convict a young man who swore at the police because the same kind of language was found in a prize-winning book: '[He] said that if that was the quality of literature that children in the community were encouraged to read then he found himself hard-pressed to punish young people for using it' (Kroll, 1996: 337).

Children's books have been and will continue to be about control, and attempts at control will continue to be an accurate reflection of the intellectual acuity of the censors and the sensibilities of societies.

Bibliography

Burress, Lee 1989: *Battle of the Books: Literary Censorship in Public Schools*. Metuchen, NJ: Scarecrow Press.

Hunt, Peter 1997: 'Censorship and Children's Literature in Britain Now, or, The Return of Abigail.' *CLE*, 28 (2), 95–104.

Jenkinson, Edward B. 1979: *Censors in the Classroom*. Carbondale: Southern Illinois University Press.

Kroll, Jeri 1996: 'Gillian Rubenstein's *Beyond the Labyrinth*: A Court Case and its Aftermath.' In Alleen Pace Nilson (ed.) Censorship in Children's Literature; Special Issue of *Paradoxa. Studies in World Literary Genres*, 2 (3–4), 323–45.

Powling, Chris (ed.) 1989: Issue on Censorship, *Books For Keeps*, 58.

Colonialism, Postcolonialism, Multiculturalism

'Children's literature' is forced into a direct engagement with matters that may be only theoretically important in other literary fields for two reasons: the internationalism inherent in the concept of 'children's literature' and an awareness of the *consequences* of children's books. Thus the study of colonialism and postcolonialism, which gives attention to previously neglected or invisible cultures (that is, neglected by and invisible to the 'central', Anglo-American colonizing culture), is closely related to the effects of texts that promote certain ways of thinking, especially in the classroom. Ironically, children's literature has itself remained largely invisible in revisionist thinking about colonialism; indeed, children's literature has been treated by the literary establishment in much the same way as colonial literatures were (and are).

If we accept children's literature as a worldwide form, then the short history of children's literature in Africa is a paradigm. Even after two hundred years, the literacy imposed by colonialists (and with it, social status) has not been accepted culturally; the oral still has precedence over the written, and non-fiction over fiction; European children's books still dominate over local writers. Given this, the emergence of a genuinely African children's literature might be a logical impossibility, or it may produce something quite new, requiring different modes of criticism.

Australian critics have been particularly conscious of this element within their own country: how far literature is a weapon of 'assimilation' and how far the 'dominant' culture can speak of, or to, others; whether cultural awareness amounts to cultural violation (Bradford, 2000).

Even more fundamentally, the way in which the history of children's literature has been constructed is a result of colonialist thinking – the very language of comparison and value (for example, the structures of archetypes) is often invisibly colonial. Considering the huge numbers of British books dealing with empire and its decline, and American children's books which carry cultural imperialism across the world, critical neglect is difficult to justify, although a recent *Encyclopedia of Post-Colonial Literatures in English* (Benson and Conolly, 1994) contains eleven articles on children's literature from Australia, Singapore and South and West Africa.

In nineteenth-century Britain, imperialism infused all children's literature, and children's literature was (and is) a potent transmitter of cultural values. Thus the progress of imperialism can be traced very clearly – not to say rawly – in children's books. From Captain Marryat, still deeply embedded in a puritan (but not necessarily empire-building) ethic, through W. H. G. Kingston's 'visionary' empire-building, to the full-blooded confidence of Charles Kingsley and G. A. Henty, and on into the doubt and decline shown in Kipling's *Puck of Pook's Hill*, the conscious and unconscious desires and fears of the nation are demonstrated.

Implicit in all these texts is the racial superiority of the British and the superiority of the male, which is a problem, of course, for those liberals who wish to preserve the 'classics'. The virus of imperialism infected English public schools, was to some extent their driving force and that of the school story (q.v.), the Boy Scouts and the Girl Guides, and centred on gender role-models which influenced girls' stories and even fairy-tales. Books as diverse as *The Wind in the Willows* (q.v.), Rider Haggard's *King Solomon's Mines* (1885) and *The Secret Garden* (q.v.) chart aspects of the decline of empire (instability, resistance and corruption, respectively) without necessarily damaging the central ideas of white male supremacy.

In the twentieth century, although the British empire disappeared, its influence has remained in literature. This is clear enough in comic books, but equally as strong in post-1945 fantasy. Michael Bond's very popular Paddington Bear books, for example, and the bestselling *Watership Down* (1972) are predicated on British/male superiority and a sometimes explicit belief in empire. Ironically, the burgeoning of fantasy in the USA since the 1960s has carried with it a strongly imperialist tinge – even George Lucas's Star Wars cycle is predicated on the assumption that one empire (albeit American and apple-pie) is superior to another. As Marjorie Hourihan has put it:

> In the postcolonial world the assumption of Western cultural superiority endures as is evident from the widespread acceptance of the role of the West, and especially of the United States, as international peace-keeper and moral

guardian. . . . The racism, inequality and violence which disfigure American life, the ruthless consumerism and the moral deficiencies of the economic rationalism which drives Western policies are perceived as merely external sores upon an inner purity, the pure superiority which the hero myth inscribes. (Hourihan, 1997)

If children's literature is going to be validly self-aware, then the implications of its colonialist heritage – notably racism, but equally many scarcely acknowledged attitudes and assumptions – cannot be suppressed. On the whole, conscious efforts at social engineering (the inclusion – to use another magnificently colonial expression – of 'ethnic minorities' in books) have been no more successful than in adult literature. The small number of children's books concerning 'people of color' was deplored by Nancy Larrick in a famous article 'The All-White World of Children's Books' in 1965. Since then, it is estimated that there has actually been a decline in books published in the USA dealing with African American and Hispanic life, to around 4 percent of the total in the early 1990s (Cullinan and Galda, 1998: 347–8). There still remains a formidable body of such work, most famously by writers like Virginia Hamilton (q.v.), Mildred Taylor, Julius Lester, Laurence Yep and Gary Soto in the USA, and by the Caribbean poets in the UK, but if cultural change ultimately depends on children, then there is still a great deal to be done.

Bibliography

Benson, Eugene and Conolly, L. W. (eds) 1994: *Encyclopedia of Post-Colonial Literatures in English*. London: Routledge.

Bradford, Clare 2000: 'Saved by the Word: Textuality and Colonization in Nineteenth-Century Australian Texts for Children.' In McGillis 2000: 89–110.

Cullinan, Bernice E. and Galda, Lee 1998: *Literature and the Child*. 4th edn. Fort Worth, Texas: Harcourt Brace College Publishers.

Hourihan, Marjorie 1997: *Deconstructing the Hero*. London: Routledge.

Khorana, Meena and McGillis, Roderick (eds) 1997: 'Postcolonial/Postindependence Perspective: Children's and Young Adult Literature.' Special issue of *ARIEL: A Review of International English Literature*, 28.1.

Larrick, Nancy 1965: 'The All-White World of Children's Books.' *Saturday Review*, 11 September, 63–5.

Whitehead, Winifred 1988: *Different Faces: Growing Up with Books in a Multicultural Society*. London: Pluto Press.

Criticism and Theory

In the field of children's literature there are some strong divisions as to what can be said about the subject and how it should be said.

The first is between those who believe that 'real' children are irrelevant to criticism because they are too immature and inexperienced either to make a valid judgement or articulate one if they could, and those who think that the immanence of children, actual or implied, in the text marks the fundamental difference between children's and other literatures, and therefore its criticism. The second division (which does not necessarily overlap with the first) is between those who study the subject academically (in the abstract, for the sake of study) and those who study it for a specific (generally practical) purpose. The third division is within the academic and practical groups themselves, for there are as many schools of critical theory and practice (from stylistics to deconstruction) as there are practical concerns (from translation studies to literature and the disabled).

The self-contained world of academia produces a vast number of studies, intellectually spearheaded by the Yale journal *Children's Literature*, originally founded by the American pioneer of academic children's-book studies, Francelia Butler. While many papers in this journal and others spring from genuine intellectual fervour, there is no doubt that many are solipsistic and confident of their own validity without regard to the 'outside world'. Increasingly, the academic critical study of texts has ignored both the intended and implied child-audience of the primary texts, despite the fact that the author's construction of the child must necessarily be reflected in those texts. However, as the bibliographies in this volume indicate, there is a kaleidoscopic range of criticism available.

It can be argued that the kind of fundamental textual and historical scholarship which has been applied to literature in general is lacking in children's literature, although this is gradually being remedied by books such as Lynne Vallone's *Disciplines of Virtue* (Vallone, 1995).

The best books about applying various established critical methods (Roderick McGillis's *The Nimble Reader*, 1996, and Perry Nodelman's *The Pleasures of Children's Literature*, second edition, 1996) both concentrate on defamiliarizing the reading process and ensuring that their readers go beyond the pseudo-criticism of classification and description. For them, and for writers like Aidan Chambers (*Booktalk*, 1985), children's literature is an inspirational area for a productive interaction between adult, child and book. Chambers has also explored the articulation of children's responses (*Tell Me*, 1993) and there is an increasingly fruitful interaction between educational theorists and literature: for example, Robert Protherough (1983) and Charles Sarland (1991).

Possibly because there exists a very real scepticism about the obscurantist dialect of much literary theory, children's literature is 'under-theorized'. Among the most discussed theoretical approaches are cross-writing, childist criticism and childhood studies.

Cross-writing

Knoepflemacher and Myers have developed the idea that

> a dialogic mix of older and younger voices occurs in texts too often read as univocal. Authors who write for children inevitably create a colloquy between past and present selves. Yet such conversations are neither unconscious nor necessarily riven by strife. (Knoepflemacher and Myers, 1997: vii)

Childist Criticism

This theory grew from the idea that children were under-represented in the critical process and, on an analogy with feminist criticism, suggests that children read distinctively from adults, and that this should be taken into account when interpreting texts. Its two primary implications are that children's responses are unknowable, and that conventional value judgements are inapplicable (Hunt, 1991: 189–201). The theory has been challenged by (among others) Karín Lesnik-Oberstein over difficulties with the concept of the 'real reader' (Lesnik-Oberstein, 1994: 148–58) and Maria Nikolajeva on the grounds that it is ghettoizing and anti-theoretical (Nikolajeva, 1997: 23).

Childhood Studies

Many of the conflicts in critical approaches can be productively addressed and perhaps resolved, as Richard Flynn put it, by 'a more consciously theorized and historicized inquiry into the construct "childhood"' (Flynn, 1997: 143). Notable recent contributions to this concept have been on children in culture by Lesnik-Oberstein (1998) and work on 'new historicism' by Myers (1988) and Watkins (1992). Peter Hollindale has usefully revived (it appears in *The Winter's Tale*) the word 'childness', defined as

> 'the quality of being a child' which is shared ground, although differently experienced and understood, between child and adult. . . . Childness is the distinguishing property of a text in children's literature . . . and it is also the property that a child brings to the reading of a text. . . . The childness of the text can change the childness of the child, and vice versa. (Hollindale, 1997: 47)

Other notable contributions to criticism and theory have been John Stephens (1992) on ideology, Roberta Seelinger Trites (1997) on feminism, and Barbara Wall (1991) on style and narrative voice.

However, the innate conservatism of the British and American education systems is still inclined to produce readers accustomed to (if not actively seeking) criticism based on 'absolute' judgements. There is no question that such writing produces invigorating and combative criticism, as with Fred Inglis (1981) and John Goldthwaite (1996).

Bibliography

Chambers, Aidan 1993: *Tell Me: Children, Reading and Talk*. South Woodchester, Glos.: Thimble Press.
Flynn, Richard 1997: 'The Intersection of Children's Literature and Childhood Studies.' *ChLAQ*, 22 (3), 143–5.
Hollindale, Peter 1997: *Signs of Childness in Children's Books*. South Woodchester, Glos.: Thimble Press.
Knoepflemacher, U. C. and Myers, Mitzi 1997: ' "Cross Writing" and the Reconceptualizing of Children's Literary Studies.' *CL*, 25, vii–xvii.
Myers, Mitzi 1988: 'Missed Opportunities and Critical Malpractice: New Historicism and Children's Literature.' *ChLAQ*, 13 (1), 41–3.

Nikolajeva, Maria 1997: *Introduction to the Theory of Children's Literature*. 2nd edn. Tallinn: TPÜ Kirjastus.

Protherough, Robert 1983: *Developing Response to Fiction*. Milton Keynes: Open University Press.

Sarland, Charles 1991: *Young People Reading: Culture and Response*. Milton Keynes: Open University Press.

Watkins, Tony 1992: 'Cultural Studies, New Historicism and Children's Literature.' In Hunt 1992: 173–95.

Drama, Film, Media

In any literary–educational system the drama has a somewhat ambiguous place: what is the relationship between studying a play as written text and studying it in performance? It is interesting that, despite a long and robust tradition of drama *performed* by children and written for performance by them, it is virtually unheard-of for these plays to be read as text either by children or adults. I would argue that this is all to the good: that drama, like poetry (q.v.) and storytelling, is essentially a live, person-interactive form; to read it on a page requires a very particular kind of philosophic commitment.

The earliest examples of published plays written for children were Madame de Genlis's *Théâtre a l'Usage des Jeunes* (1779–80) and Maria Edgeworth's *Little Plays* (1827). In the twentieth century, J. M. Barrie's *Peter Pan* (1904) (q.v.) and A. A. Milne's adaptation of *The Wind in the Willows* (q.v.), *Toad of Toad Hall* (1929), stand out, although the former has been most widely read in novel form and most widely seen as a film. The plays perhaps most familiar to British schoolchildren ('for study purposes') have been Maurice Maeterlinck's *The Blue Bird* (first British performance 1909), which was widely available in school editions until the 1950s, and Robert Bolt's *The Thwarting of Baron Bolligrew* (1966). Peter Terson's *Zigger Zagger* (1967) stands out as an attempt to bring contemporary issues to children.

Otherwise, children's drama has been in the hands of those involved deeply in children's theatre, such as Charlotte Chorpenning and Aurand Harris in the USA.

The primary difficulty of including film and television productions in this category is that, with rare exceptions such as the British Children's Film Foundation in the 1950s and 1960s, so little drama is produced specifically for children. 'Children's cinema' in the first half of the twentieth century was an optimistic mixture of 'low-level' adult material and low-budget children's films; but, as Terry Staples observed,

> Throughout the century there have been tensions, anxieties and contradictions surrounding children and their pastimes. Now, as the millennium approaches . . . it is unlikely . . . that children's cinema will ever again offer the anarchy, the social adventure, the solidarity, the collective participation, and the occasional physical danger. (Staples, 1997: 243)

The vast majority of contemporary films (live-action or animated) ostensibly produced for a child audience in commercial cinema are more accurately 'family' films. That is to say, children are only a part of the audience, and so a complex double address (see the Introduction, pp. 13–15) is in operation. A majority of family films favour the adult's view of childhood, as in Chris Columbus's *Mrs Doubtfire* (from Anne Fine's *Madame Doubtfire*); a small minority, such as *The Parent Trap*, favour a child's viewpoint, and the rest (virtually any Disney main feature) are not much about childhood at all. As a sceptical observer, Jack Zipes, has noted:

> What was important for Disney was *not* the immediate and personal contact of a storyteller with a particular audience to share wisdom and induce pleasure but the impact that he as creator could have on as large an audience as possible to sell a commodity and endorse ideological images that would enhance his corporate power. (Zipes, 1997: 87)

The study of children's drama, then, can range from actual creative experiences through to media studies in general, and stretches any idea of a unified academic discipline to breaking point. But in terms of theorizing, as Peter Hollindale has argued, 'drama will remain the Cinderella of children's literature, when it is arguably the most important children's art form of all, the one they are sure to live with, through the media of film and television, all their lives' (Hollindale, 1996: 219).

This argument can be extended into the electronic media. It seems probable that the very nature of narrative will be changed by the internet and what are now (disparagingly, by implication) labelled computer 'games'. The 'literature' of the twenty-first century seems likely to be interactive, to approximate more to drama and to story*telling* than to written text, and 'texts' of this kind for childhood seem likely to be at the forefront (Dresang, 1999; Hunt, 2000).

Bibliography

Chambers, Aidan 1982: *Plays for Young People to Read and Perform*. South Woodchester, Glos.: Thimble Press.

Dresang, Eliza T. 1999: *Radical Change: Books for Youth in a Digital Age*. New York: H. W. Wilson.

Hollindale, Peter 1996: 'Drama.' In Hunt 1996: 206–19.

Hunt, Peter 2000: 'Futures for Children's Literature: Evolution or Radical Break?' *Cambridge Journal of Education*, 30 (1), 111–19.

Levy, Jonathan 1992: *The Gymnasium of the Imagination: A Collection of Children's Plays in English 1780–1860*. Westport, Conn.: Greenwood Press.

Staples, Terry 1997: *All Pals Together: The Story of Children's Cinema*. Edinburgh: Edinburgh University Press.

Fantasy

Fantasy . . . is, I think, not a lower but a higher form of Art, indeed the most nearly pure form, and so (when achieved) the most potent. (Tolkien, 1964: 44)

The conventional explanation for the supposed preponderance of fantasy in children's books is a romantic one: that children are in some way closer to the unknown, the unseen and the mystical. Children are seen as equivalent to primitives, who have (it is assumed) a simple faith in animism and an inherent understanding of certain narrative patterns; or are equivalent to the 'folk' (a naive construction) who originated the folk-tale, for whom the world outside the door of the hut was full of who-knew-what wonders and terrors.

Even more patronizing is the view that for children the distinction between reality and unreality is blurred, so therefore they scarcely have to suspend disbelief. (This view is at the root of a great deal of careless and trivial writing.) As it is not clear at what developmental stage any of this is true, or ceases to be true, it could all be treated with a healthy scepticism. The romantic idea of 'childlike', meaning innocent (however 'innocence' is constructed) and mystic, has been imposed upon actuality: to the postmodern adult reader, absorption into a text while reading is unfashionable; children (and unfashionable readers) do it; therefore, it is childish to do it. Any suggestion that developing readers may be just as capable of dual readings as other readers undermines childhood as constructed.

Socio-pyschological explanations for the human need for fantasy are, of course, very common. Humans can construct alternative futures; fantasy is a form of therapy for our pasts; in Freudian or Jungian terms it allows us to explore our psyche or connect with a collective psyche. For literary apologists, there are generally two positions: one is that fantasy is psychologically healthy; the other is that it is more effective and responsible a literary form than realism. Terry Pratchett takes the first view: 'There is some evidence that a rich internal fantasy life is as good and necessary for a child as healthy soil is for a plant, for much the same reason' (Pratchett, 1995: 7). Jill Paton Walsh takes the second view: 'A work of fantasy compels a reader into a metaphorical state of mind. A work of realism, on the other hand, permits very literal-minded readings. . . . Even worse, it is possible to read a realistic book as though it were not fiction at all' (Paton Walsh, 1981: 38).

However, if fantasy is regarded as 'escapist' (whatever that may mean), should or should not children be expected to wish to escape from childhood? A certain number of key 'children's' fantasies, such as *The Wind in the Willows* (q.v.) and *Winnie-the-Pooh*, seem rather to be using fantasy for adults to escape *into* childhood.

Fantasy cannot be 'free-floating'; it has to *react*. Very early fantasy often took the form of allegory which was designed for religious ends. Today, the same applies: fantasy can be a way of exploring moral issues without complications, or it can be the basis (very often) for satire or social or political comment. Consequently, its popularity has been cyclical.

From its origins as a myth/folk form, it was gradually either absorbed by or forced underground by religion. In the nineteenth century, in the West, it resurfaced as a subversive reaction to a utilitarian attitude of mind. Writers like John Ruskin with *The King of the Golden River* (1851) and William Makepeace Thackeray with *The Rose and the Ring* (1855) developed the links to traditional tales. In the USA the followers of the Romantic movement in New England reacted against the educational realism of Samuel Goodrich ('Peter Parley'), notably, Christopher Pearse Cranch with *The Last of the Huggermuggers* (1855). Its importance in the late nineteenth century shows a new attitude to childhood, with Nesbit (q.v.) and Baum (q.v.); also, with Carroll (q.v.) and Rossetti, it demonstrated that it could be therapeutic for adults.

In the twentieth century, fantasy was dominant in the UK after the First World War (Hugh Lofting's Dr Dolittle books (USA 1920–52; UK 1922–53) are often thought of as characteristically English – ironically enough, as Lofting lived in the USA) and the Second World War. In the USA, fantasy flowered especially after the Vietnam war, all of which is highly suggestive of the relationship between children's fantasy and the national psyche.

Definitions and classifications of fantasy have amused academics and enthusiasts endlessly, but they can, on occasion, actually illuminate the texts.

For the first, all fiction could be called fantasy, as it necessarily presents a version of the world differing from pragmatic actuality; generally, though, fantasy is defined as text which portrays some obvious deviance from 'consensus reality', whatever that could possibly be – usually a change in physical laws. (Hence fantasy's reactive position: a total difference from the known world would not be writable or comprehensible.) Beyond that, there are 'other world' fantasies (Tolkien, Le Guin, George Macdonald, Philip Pullman), future fantasies (often merging into Science Fiction, such as John Christopher's 'Tripods', Peter Dickinson's 'Changes', and much of the work of Andre Norton); books in which magic intrudes into the contemporary world (Patricia Wrightson's new Australian folklore, Kipling); dreams (Carroll, Jean Ingelow, John Masefield); excursions into other, parallel worlds (Rowling's 'Harry Potter', Alan Garner's *Elidor, The Wizard of Oz*, C. S. Lewis's 'Narnia'), animal fantasies (from articulate animals – *Black Beauty* – to 'others' – such as Paddington Bear or Rey's *Curious George*). Distinctions have been made between 'high fantasy' (Lloyd Alexander's 'Prythian' series) and 'domestic' fantasy (from *Five Children and It* to *The Parent Trap*).

Given such a vast range of ingenuity, it is perhaps inevitable that fantasy has become heavily stylized. Quests, especially, seem to be accompanied by heroes and anti-heroes, 'buddies', stereotypical tough-guys and seers; they tend to be explicitly sexist and covertly racist, regardless of the sub-genre they occupy: *The Lord of the Rings* and Richard Adams's *Watership Down* (1972) and George Lucas's *Star Wars* – and even parts of *Winnie-the-Pooh* – are siblings under the skin. Only occasionally, as in Ursula K. Le Guin's *Tehanu*, and most of Terry Pratchett's work, is there serious revisionist activity – which is not surprising, for, like comedy, deconstructing fantasy can have disconcerting (and destructive) effects.

Whether or not science-fiction is a sub-genre of fantasy has not been resolved; certainly it shares many characteristics:

Science fiction commonly portrays technological societies. . . . These societies need not always be industrial, but they involve the notion of intelligent beings changing their physical environment. . . . It involves . . . finding out how things work, on the part of the protagonist, who is often quite coolly rational and impersonal . . . indeed it is its functional tone, its concern with practicality, that profoundly marks off the bulk of science fiction from fantasy. . . . The fantasist tries to re-create, the science-fiction writer to make the wholly new. . . . The genre is fundamentally exploratory in character. (Manlove, 1982: 30–1)

It may be that science-fiction's roots in the dime novel and its use by the Stratemeyer syndicate, with 'Victor Appleton's' Tom Swift books (1910–41), have cast some doubt on its status. But certainly from Robert A. Heinlein's *Rocket Ship Galileo* (1947), arguably the first modern science-fiction novel for children, through to the work of John Christopher in the UK and Gillian Rubenstein in Australia, science-fiction has produced work of striking originality. In children's literature it is rapidly proving to be – and proving very appropriately to be – what Brian McHale called 'the ontological genre *par excellence*' (quoted in James, 1994: 203).

Bibliography

Barron, Neil 1990: *Fantasy Literature: A Reader's Guide*. New York: Garland.
James, Edward 1994: *Science Fiction in the Twentieth Century*. Oxford: Oxford University Press.
Manlove, C. N. 1982: 'On the Nature of Fantasy.' In Roger C. Schlobin (ed.) *The Aesthetics of Fantasy Literature and Art*. Notre Dame, Ind.: University of Notre Dame Press; Brighton: Harvester Press, 16–35.
Manlove, C. N. 1999: *The Fantasy Literature of England*. London: Macmillan.
Paton Walsh, Jill 1981: 'The Art of Realism.' In Hearne and Kaye 1981: 35–44.
Pratchett, Terry 1995: 'Let There Be Dragons.' *Books for Keeps*, 83, 6–7.
Smith, Karen Patricia 1993: *The Fabulous Realm: A Literary–Historical Approach to British Fantasy 1780–1990*. Metuchen, NJ: Scarecrow Press.
Sullivan, C. W., III (ed.) 1993: *Science Fiction for Young Readers*. Westport, Conn.: Greenwood Press.
Sullivan, C. W., III (ed.) 1999: *Young Adult Science Fiction*. Westport, Conn.: Greenwood Press.
Tolkien, J. R. R. 1964: 'On Fairy Stories.' In *Tree and Leaf*. London: Allen and Unwin, 11–70.
West, Mark I. 1989: *Before Oz: Juvenile Fantasy Stories from Nineteenth-Century America*. Hamden, Conn.: Archon.
Westfahl, Gary 1995: 'The Genre that Evolved: On Science Fiction as Children's Literature.' *Foundation: The Review of Science Fiction*, 62, 70–5.

Folk-tale, Fairy-tale, Myth, Legend

The defence of the folk-tale, myth and legend, and especially the fairy-tale, as a part of children's literature is rarely more than the defence of the status quo, and is actually quite difficult in terms of those variable concepts, relevance, comprehensibility, suitability and approachability. That is not to say, of course, that a good many folk-tales make a relevant point simply, clearly and entertainingly, nor – if you stretch the general classification into the area of the nursery rhyme – that the genres do not blend in the cultural mind to form a fascinating and, it could be well argued, vital world. Books which work at an intertextual level, such as Janet and Allan Ahlberg's (q.v.) *The Jolly Postman* and *Each Peach Pear Plum*, make this point very well.

However, there is a very big jump between (to pick from thousands of examples) Brian Alderson and Fritz Wegner's *The Giant Turnip* (1999) and Anthony Browne's illustrated version of the Brothers Grimm's *Hansel and Gretel* (1981). One is benign, bucolic and makes a simple, understandable point – and is what folk-tales seem to be thought to be. The other is obviously brutal and problematic – and is only saved from its ultimate savagery by the selective imagery of Browne's work. If we go one step further – to the raw Grimm, as it were, or the raw Andersen, or Ransome's *Old Peter's Russian Tales*, let alone the Greek or Scandinavian myths – what are we actually telling? On the face of it, there seems to be no logical reason why a group of texts of remarkable unpleasantness and crudity, dealing with physical violence, rape, incest, cannibalism and murder, let alone withdrawal of love, betrayal, loneliness and fear and the machinations of arbitrary and frequently malicious fate, should be placed firmly in the ambit of children. Unless, of course, it is simultaneously admitted that this sort of material is interesting, useful or actually suitable for that audience. Tolkien put the case most clearly:

> Actually, the association of children and fairy-stories is an accident of our domes-
> tic history. Fairy-stories have in the modern lettered world been relegated to
> the 'nursery', as shabby or old-fashioned furniture is relegated to the play-room,
> primarily because adults do not want it, and do not mind if it is misused. It
> is not the choice of the children which decides this. Children as a class – except
> in a common lack of experience they are not one – neither like fairy-stories
> more, nor understand them better than adults do. (Tolkien, 1964: 34)

This casual relegation, however, is being replaced (at least in critical circles) by a kind of romantic primitivism. Stephen Thomson has persuasively
argued that there is a characteristic kind of criticism of children's literature
which believes that 'children's literature has . . . kept the soul of the old community, and not just the body of its story-forms'. It supports this assertion
by citing the child's putative closeness to nature 'and the ancient innocence
of mankind. . . . [Thus] the child effectively provides the possibility of continued life to an oral tradition' (Thomson, 1998: 261).

The linking of childhood and therefore children's literature to Very Old
Stories, then, has been performed despite obvious evidence that such material would be 'unsuitable' if it had any other origin, and despite obvious
evidence that the 'innocence' assumed or wished for in contemporary childhood, and the 'innocence' of the primitive and elemental, have little in
common. Nor is it clear that there can be a pure, direct, unorchestrated connection between the two states. Stories which relate as directly as possible
to these sources have been taken to be in some way 'stronger' than their
modern counterparts; hence, in the 1960s and 1970s, the rash of novels
which related contemporary children to myth and which were, automatically it seems, accorded a higher status than other books. But as Alan
Garner's (q.v.) *The Owl Service* (1967) demonstrates, to *name* a legend does
not necessarily communicate anything, and as Edward Blishen and Leon
Garfield's overblown series of retellings *The God Beneath the Sea* (1970) demonstrates, the myths do not guarantee digestible (or even comprehensible) prose.
(Both books won the British Carnegie Medal, with all that that implies.)

All of this seems to overlook the fact that the western world has spent
three hundred years trying to suppress or sophisticate or sublimate what these
tales tell. And this in turn leads to the question rooted in Jungian and
structuralist psychology: whether the perception of archetypal patterns is

inherent or acquired. Does the apparent universality of the tales (see, for example, Propp, 1975; Warner, 1994) mean as Bruno Bettelheim (1976) suggested, that they can be understood unconsciously by children and can be directly therapeutic?

That children should not know these stories seems to some in the present educational and political climate to be little short of blasphemy. That children should only know the stories in 'debased' forms such as (it is said) the Disney versions, or be unable to recognize intertextual references, is taken to be a great loss. (It also leads to a conundrum: what do readers understand if they first encounter traditional tales in satirical versions, such as those by the British illustrator Tony Ross, or in metafictional extravaganzas such as Jon Scieszka and Lane Smith's *The Stinky Cheese Man and Other Fairly Stupid Tales* (1992)? A similar argument applies to those who come to know *The Wind in the Willows* or *Winnie-the-Pooh* through film versions.)

A sceptic might observe that retellings (especially of legends) tend to appear in bookshops under 'education' rather than 'entertainment', a tacit admission that this material is *for* rather than *of* childhood.

Whatever their 'real' relationship to childhood, traditional tales have in recent years produced some fascinating scholarship. There have been some highly instructive studies which trace the progress of individual tales: Jack Zipes (1993) on 'Little Red Riding Hood' and Betsy Hearne (1989) on 'Beauty and the Beast' demonstrate how, as public property, the tales have been reworked at different periods. These are not simply accounts of how societies have absorbed and modified these texts in accordance with current or local mores. The tales are often part of 'repressive socialization'; 'Little Red Riding Hood', for example,

> reflects men's fear of women's sexuality – and of their own as well. The curbing and regulation of sexual drives is fully portrayed in the bourgeois literary fairy-tale on the basis of deprived male needs. Red Riding Hood is to blame for her own rape. The wolf is not really male but symbolizes natural urges and social nonconformity. The real hero of the tale, the hunter–gamekeeper, is male governance. If the tale has enjoyed such a widespread friendly reception in the Perrault and Grimm forms, then this can only be attributed to a general acceptance of the cultural notions of sexuality, sex roles, and domination embedded in it. (Zipes, 1993: 81)

Many of the essential stories themselves are ancient; the Indian *Panchatantra*, for example, dates from the sixth century AD. In Britain there was a robust native tradition of folklore (see, for example, *A Midsummer-*

Night's Dream or *The Faerie Queen*), but this was overlaid by fashionable French retellings in the late seventeenth century by the Comtess d'Aulnoy (*Contes des fées*, trans. 1699) and Charles Perrault (*Histories ou contes du temps passé*, trans. 1729). By the end of the eighteenth century these were appearing in editions for children.

Major contributions in the nineteenth century included the English tales of Benjamin Tabart's *Popular Stories* (1804–9), the Grimms' *German Popular Stories* (trans. 1823), Hans Christian Andersen's *Eventyr* (trans. 1846), Annie and Eliza Keary's Icelandic stories, *The Heroes of Asgard* (1857), culminating, perhaps, with Andrew Lang's encyclopedic twelve 'colour' fairy books, beginning with *The Blue Fairy Book* (1899). For much of the nineteenth century there was an ongoing debate as to how far these tales had a bad influence on children (as opposed to religiously based writing) and how far they fed the imagination.

Until the last decades of the twentieth century, then, traditional stories were very largely marketed for children. There has been both a growing appreciation of their power for adults, which has produced much striking work (see, for example, Zipes's *Don't Bet on the Prince*, 1986), and a growing reaction to (notably) their inherent sexism. None of this, however, seems to have slowed the snowball of their largely unthoughtful production for children.

Bibliography

Bettelheim, Bruno 1976: *The Uses of Enchantment: The Meaning and Importance of Fairy Tales*. New York: Knopf.

Cook, Elizabeth 1976: *The Ordinary and the Fabulous: An Introduction to Myths, Legends and Fairy Tales*. Cambridge: Cambridge University Press.

Hearne, Betsy 1989: *Beauty and the Beast: Visions and Revisions of an Old Tale*. Chicago: University of Chicago Press.

Opie, Iona and Opie, Peter 1974: *The Classic Fairy Tales*. Oxford: Oxford University Press.

Philip, Neil (ed.) 1989: *The Cinderella Story: The Origins and Variations of the Story Known as 'Cinderella'*. Harmondsworth: Penguin Books.

Propp, Vladimir 1975: *Morphology of the Folk Tale*. Trans. Laurence Scott. Austin: University of Texas Press.

Tatar, Maria 1997: *Off With Their Heads! Fairy Tales and the Culture of Childhood*. Princeton, NJ: Princeton University Press.

Thomson, Stephen 1998: 'Substitute Communities, Authentic Voices: The Organic Writing of the Child.' In Lesnik-Oberstein 1998: 248–73.

Tolkien, J. R. R. 1964: 'On Fairy Stories.' In *Tree and Leaf*. London: Allen and Unwin, 11–70.

Warner, Marina 1994: *From the Beast to the Blonde: On Fairy Tales and Their Tellers*. London: Chatto and Windus.

Zipes, Jack (ed.) 1986: *Don't Bet on the Prince: Contemporary Feminist Fairy Tales*. London: Routledge.

Zipes, Jack (ed.) 1993: *The Trials and Tribulations of Red Riding Hood*. London: Routledge.

Zipes, Jack 1999: *When Dreams Came True: Classical Fairy Tales and Their Tradition*. New York: Routledge.

For fairy-tales, two accessible collections of tales and criticism are:

Hallett, Martin and Karasek, Barbara (eds) 1996: *Folk and Fairy Tales*. 2nd edn. Peterborough, Ontario: Broadview Press.

Tatar, Maria (ed.) 1999: *The Classic Fairy Tales*. New York: Norton.

Gender

Consider these points:

- Girls read more than boys.
- Girls read *differently* from boys (Millard, 1997).
- 'Reading patterns and practices are highly gendered' (Hall and Coles, 1999: 84).
- The vast majority of editorial staff working in publishing for children are women.
- There are and have been rather more female writers than male writers for children.
- Primary-school teaching is predominantly a female profession.
- The vast majority of university students studying children's literature are female.
- The majority of lecturers and teachers of children's literature are female (although senior posts tend to be held by males).
- Most storytelling and reading to children is done by women.

Gender is clearly an issue in this field. The key questions which have not been adequately addressed include:

- Has this dominance of the female affected the books produced?
- If so, how, and if not, why not?
- Does this make any difference to the way in which we should approach the books?

If we assume that there are any recognizable or at least culturally assumed characteristics of masculine and feminine genders (as opposed to male and female sexes), then we might expect to find distinctively feminine characteristics in children's books.

Historically, any assertion of the feminine (or feminist) in children's books has been a relatively recent and sporadic phenomenon. Before Alcott's *Little Women* (q.v.) the vast majority of books were concerned quite obviously (if subconsciously) with keeping women and girls in their subservient position and inculcating passive and domestic roles. Since then there have been a good many distinctive and assertive female heroes, from Anne of Green Gables to Harriet the Spy, Dahl's (q.v.) *Matilda* and Philip Pullman's (q.v.) Sally Lockhart and his Lyra in the His Dark Materials trilogy. However, although the balance is undoubtedly shifting, such heroes are the exceptions that prove the rule, especially at the popular end of the market and in high-profile media: virtually every Walt Disney feature, for example, ultimately hinges (for all that Belle in *Beauty and the Beast* read books) on male dominance and female submission. The idea that the proper and desirable aim for any girl is a husband, which lurked within nineteenth-century books, still survives, little changed, in the mass of series books for teenagers (although it would be a rare 'mainstream' book that could begin, as did Beverley Cleary's bestseller of the 1950s and 1960s, *Fifteen* (1956): 'Today I'm going to meet a boy, Jane Purdy told herself . . .' and end: 'She was Stan's girl. That was all that really mattered').

Contemporary cultural suppositions in some, perhaps optimistic, quarters, that girls are culturally equal to boys does not prevent the heavily sexist books of Enid Blyton (q.v.), for example, from remaining huge sellers; nor others such as *The Wind in the Willows* (q.v.), *Winnie-the-Pooh*, *The Hobbit* (q.v.) and *The Stone Book Quartet* (q.v.) from dominating or, indeed, forming the core of 'the canon'. How far does the success of these books reflect an unreformed society or some kind of collusion? How far should children's books reflect (and thus possibly reinforce) the world as currently gendered, and how far should they be a force of social engineering?

Of course, 'gender' is not confined to the feminine, and children's literature has undoubtedly had a place in constituting a masculine culture, leading, perhaps, to as much repression among men as among women – not to mention carnage. However, it can be argued that since 1900, children's literature began to construct gender in a way that rejected earlier constructions, and that this change was covert (Hunt, 1996: 68–70). Equally, one might argue that the *sex* of a writer might be misleading with regard to their gender characteristics: Enid Blyton and Anne Fine might be more profitably read as masculine writers, Arthur Ransome and William Mayne as feminine.

As Ursula Le Guin (q.v.) observed, to talk about gender is sometimes seen as politicizing children's literature; *not* to talk about it seems to be a far more dangerous and far more political act of silence and silencing.

Bibliography

Briggs, Julia 1989: 'Women Writers and Writing for Children: From Sarah Fielding to E. Nesbit.' In Avery and Briggs 1989: 221–350.

Christian-Smith, Linda K. (ed.) 1993: *Texts of Desire: Essays on Fiction, Femininity and Schooling*. London: Falmer Press.

Hunt, Peter 1996: ' "What Would Daddy Have Done?" Overt and Covert Constructions of Masculinity in Twentieth-century Children's Literature.' In Christopher E. Gittings (ed.) *Imperialism and Gender: Constructions of Masculinity*. New Lambton, NSW: Dangaroo Press.

Millard, Elaine 1997: *Differently Literate: Boys, Girls and the Schooling of Literacy*. London: Falmer Press.

Nelson, Claudia 1991: *Boys Will be Girls: The Feminine Ethic and British Children's Fiction, 1857–1917*. New Brunswick, NJ: Rutgers University Press.

Nodelman, Perry 1988: 'Children's Literature as Women's Writing.' *Children's Literature Association Quarterly*, 13, 1, 31–4.

Rudd, David 1995: 'Five Have a Gender-ful Time: Blyton, Sexism, and the Infamous Five.' *Children's Literature in Education*, 26, 3, 185–96.

Literacy

The inclusion of a section on literacy in a book broadly situated within literary criticism may seem close to an admission that our subject is not (respectable) literary study at all, but a small part of (unrespectable) educational studies. In fact, literacy appears in this book for two reasons, one essentialist, one pragmatic.

First, literacy is the hidden, or missing feature of *all* discourse about literature. The assumption is generally made by critics that we are all peer readers; we have the same technical skills and much the same cultural knowledge. This is, of course, certainly unknowable and undoubtedly untrue (and in any case, if it were true, then the role of the critic might evaporate), but its consideration is left out of theories of meaning-making, to their considerable detriment. In the case of children's literature, critics and educators frequently assume that readers may be lacking in these skills; however, the next intellectual move from that – to account for the effect of the shortfall (in critical terms) or to remedy the shortfall (in literacy terms) – is far more complex and is often, from motives political or practical, somewhat crude.

The second, pragmatic reason for including literacy is that it is where children's literature is *used* in the educational system; where, in effect, many adult readers acquire the habit of literature. The logic of its use reverberates back into the cultural valuation of the texts and ultimately to the production of the texts themselves (quite apart from the critical methods employed).

There are two problems in the discussion of literacy: the first is that its definition is, at best, problematic; the second is that the mechanisms for acquiring literacy seem far from understood.

Literacy is defined, broadly, in two ways (in both of which children's literature becomes involved). The first is 'functional' literacy: how to read and write; how to decode the language. The second (now more common in educational circles) deals with far more than this: language in its contexts of use, extending out to 'literary' literacy and 'cultural' literacy. As Ed Marum puts it, 'literacy is finally a means of establishing and acting upon identity; it needs, therefore, to be seen in its sociohistorical, living context' (Marum, 1996: 52).

There are therefore several axes of practical and political disagreement here. The most obvious is that a utilitarian culture sees the ability to read and write as paramount and looks for simple methods of achieving it. (There is clearly a difference between the 'developing' and the developed world; in the first, functional literacy may be the key to survival in a society whose imperatives have been imposed colonially, regardless of their appropriateness; in the second, there is a strong political element.) The teaching methods often used for functional literacy assume a progression, eliminate the vagaries of individual teachers and, of course, also require special teaching materials – 'reading schemes'. They also eliminate fiction on the overt grounds that it is too complex, and on the covert grounds that the unrestrained imagination is not politically malleable (see Rosen, 1995).

The essence of this concept of literacy is its testability; in the 1960s in the USA, and in the late 1990s in the UK, it seemed politically expedient to adopt this limited view of literacy. (For accounts of the historical see-sawing of approaches, see Simmons, 1996; Styles, 2000.) However, children's books are not excluded from England's National Curriculum (see Marum, 1996), much criticized for its imposition of a 'required' reading list, let alone one perceived as racist and classist (Rosen, 1995). Whether this suggests that there is still the opportunity for 'imaginative' reading, or whether these books will be reduced to providing examiners with the 'right answer', remains to be seen.

Concepts of literacy also involve storytelling: the relationship between the oral and the written is complex and reciprocal (Fox, 1993); stories and the ways in which children play with them both, provide ways of bringing cultural literacy, both in terms of content and narrative structures and concepts. The complexity may be shown by a single example. Jessie Reid observes that

> certain kinds of children's fiction do contain quoted speech which calls on quite advanced understanding of possibilities in expression, and an acceptance of its remoteness from the way people ordinarily talk.

Her example, ' "I am afraid," said Grimble, "that after Christmas will be exactly too late" ' taken from a 'simple' picture book by Clement Freud, may seem unproblematic. But, she points out,

> the inversion of the subject and verb in the source marker [is] *a form never found in conversation* [my italics]. Yet this device, along with the interpolation of the source marker at an early point in the quotation, may well have originated in the oral story-telling tradition. It is effective when read aloud, where the voice can be used to carry over the syntax and sense. . . . For young readers, however, the medially placed source marker is liable to increase the load on short-term memory . . . these modes of structuring dialogue have to be learned. (Reid, 1990: 78)

Excellent explorations of theories can be found in Kimberley, Meek and Miller (1992), Kress (1997) and Meek (1993).

Literacy, then, is a matter of broad-principled guesses, political expediencies, detailed linguistic analyses and practical applications (see, for example, Bearne, 1995). Naturally, there is a huge literature on the subject, from the seminal *The Language of Primary School Children* (Rosen and Rosen, 1973), to research on gender influence (Millard, 1997), to endless volumes of practical advice and 'teacher-proof' course materials. Recently, the subject has come to be, as one series on literacy and education puts it, 'allied closely with matters of language and culture, ideology and discourse, knowledge and power' (Cherland, 1994: cover).

Decisions on how far to include 'literature' in the orbit of literacy studies have clear economic and political overtones. However, for teachers and parents convinced of the benefits of literary readings (and who have the resources to implement them), the most pragmatic guides to theory are those by Appleyard (1991) and Meek (1988), and to practice (with a more specific, Piagetian framework) Tucker (1981); excellent practical advice can be found in Chambers (1991).

What is clear, however, is that the interface between functional and 'literary' literacy confronts a good many demonstrably erroneous assumptions about the simplicity of acquiring reading skills, of children's literature and children's responses. As Margaret Meek observed:

> Our teaching will have to begin with the understanding that the complexities of literacy are linked to the patterns of social practices and social meanings. From now on there will be multiple literacies. (Meek, 1993: 96)

Bibliography

Appleyard, J. A. 1991: *Becoming a Reader: The Experience of Fiction from Childhood to Adulthood*. Cambridge: Cambridge University Press.

Bearne, Eve (ed.) 1995: *Greater Expectations: Children Reading Writing*. London: Cassell.

Chambers, Aidan 1991: *The Reading Environment: How Adults Help Children Enjoy Books*. South Woodchester, Glos.: Thimble Press.

Cherland, Meredith Rogers 1994: *Private Practices: Girls Reading Fiction and Constructing Identity*. London: Taylor and Francis.

Fox, Carol 1993: *At the Very Edge of the Forest: The Influence of Literature on Storytelling by Children*. London: Cassell.

Hilton, Mary 1996: *Potent Fictions: Children's Literacy and the Challenge of Popular Culture*. London: Routledge.

Kimberley, Keith, Meek, Margaret, and Miller, Jane (eds) 1992: *New Readings: Contributions to an Understanding of Literacy*. London: A. and C. Black.

Kress, Gunther 1997: *Before Writing: Rethinking the Paths to Literacy*. London: Routledge.

Marum, Ed (ed.) 1996: *Children and Books in the Modern World: Contemporary Perspectives on Literacy*. London: Falmer Press.

Meek, Margaret 1988: *How Texts Teach What Readers Learn*. South Woodchester, Glos.: Thimble Press.

Meek, Margaret 1993: 'What Will Literacy be Like?' In Styles and Drummond (eds) 1993: 89–99.

Meek, Margaret, et al. (eds) 1984: *Achieving Literacy*. London: Routledge and Kegan Paul.

Millard, Elaine 1997: *Differently Literate: Boys, Girls and the Schooling of Literacy*. London: Falmer Press.

Reid, Jessie 1990: 'Children's Reading.' In Robert Grieve and Martin Hughes (eds) *Understanding Children*. Oxford: Blackwell Publishers, 71–93.

Rosen, Connie and Rosen, Harold 1973: *The Language of Primary School Children*. Harmondsworth: Penguin Books.

Rosen, Michael 1995: 'Raising the Issues.' *Signal*, 76, 26–44.

Simmons, John S. 1996: 'Literacy: Its Roller-Coaster Ride through US Education.' In Ed Marum (ed.) *Children and Books in the Modern World: Contemporary Perspectives on Literacy*. London: Falmer Press, 42–54.

Sipe, Lawrence R. 1997: 'Children's Literature, Literacy, and Literary Understanding.' *Journal of Children's Literature* (NCTE), 23, 2, 6–19.

Snyder, Ilana 1998: *Page to Screen: Taking Literacy into the Electronic Era*. London: Routledge.

Styles, Morag 2000: 'Introduction: Teaching Through Texts – Contexts, Conventions and Contributors.' In Holly Anderson and Morag Styles (eds) *Teaching Through Texts: Promoting Literacy Through Popular and Literary Texts in the Primary Classroom*. London: Routledge, 1–12.

Wolf, Shelby Anne and Heath, Shirley Brice 1992: *The Braid of Literature: Children's Worlds of Reading*. Cambridge, Mass.: Harvard University Press.

Nursery and Playground Rhymes, Storytelling

Children are *told* stories and they *transmit* songs, rhymes, tales. In the West at least, they are at the fulcrum of the survival of the oral tradition: not merely of the material, but of the oral mode with its particular mindset and narrative structures. Such are attitudes to the marginalization of childhood that what might otherwise have been an anthropological (perhaps as children's culture) or sociological study has become a peripheral part of the study of children's literature: it might, in theory, be central. However, despite some extensive historical research into rhymes and games, the actual relationship between children and oral narrative and rhyme has not been well investigated or theorized.

The survival of nursery rhymes, some of which date from the seventh century, with sources as disparate as drinking songs and political satire, is usually attributed to the fact they are rhythmic and participatory; the words are nonsensical, therefore it is their sounds, not their sense that matters. This is just as well, as a good many (such as 'Goosey Goosey Gander') are nightmarishly gruesome, and others, such as 'Ring-a-ring o' roses', have developed their own folklore:

> The invariable sneezing and falling down in modern English versions has given would-be origin finders the opportunity to say that the rhyme dates back to the days of the Great Plague. A rosy rash, they allege, was a symptom of the plague, posies of herbs were carried as protection, sneezing was a final fatal symptom, and 'all fall down' was exactly what happened. It would be more delightful to recall the old belief that gifted children had the power to laugh roses. . . . The foreign and nineteenth-century versions seem to show that the fall was originally a curtsy or other bending movement of a dramatic singing game. (Opie and Opie, 1951/1973: 365)

One might suspect that the longevity of the nursery rhyme owes much to the intimacy of the telling, and that latterly the steady popularity of illustrated versions, notably those of Arthur Rackham (1923), Raymond Briggs (1966), Quentin Blake (q.v.) (1983) and Michael Foreman (1990), and in the USA by Alice and Martin Provensen (1976), to name a very few, is a rare example of the written sustaining the oral.

The earliest collection in English is *A Little Book for Little Children* (*c.* 1702–12) by 'T. W.', and the most definitive is Iona and Peter Opie's *The Oxford Dictionary of Nursery Rhymes* (1951). The Opies' work on the children's oral tradition in Britain is unequalled (for the USA see, for example, Mary and Herbert Knapp, 1976). They observed in 1951 that while collecting ballads, folk-songs, folk-plays and dialect into books to preserve them is a sure sign 'of the oral knowledge of a people being on the wane', this is not true of nursery rhymes: 'most of the old rhymes seem to be better known today than they have ever been' (Opie and Opie, 1951/1973: 42–3). Such is the dynamism of the oral tradition that written collections may preserve but do not necessarily stabilize the verses.

The same kind of random selections from the culture surrounding the children that produced the nursery rhymes can be seen in action in the playground song and rhyme. These very obviously incorporate and distort (or consume) fragments of contemporary popular culture; words from books, films, commercials and popular songs are adapted to very ancient forms. Garbled and half-understood they may be, but they represent the furniture of young readers' minds. Thus the omnivorous nature of children's culture and the ubiquity of the media means that the oral narratives of even very young children are influenced by the different narrative forms around them. This is highly significant in terms of the future texts that they will use and that will be generated for them: the sophistication of the traditional storyteller and the sophistication of the written text is being superseded by a new hybrid. As Margaret Meek points out, 'for all their apparent informality, the stories have complex formal structures. They are layered, polysemic texts, the sources of which lie in a wide range of children's literature and with the "sounded writing" of radio and television broadcasts' (Fox, 1993: vii).

The implications of this interface between the spoken and the written for the understanding – and ultimately the concept – of 'literature' cannot be underestimated. In general terms the constraints of orality make oral narrative structures quite different from written, and in the face of a wide decline in formal literacy and the growth of storytelling media that emulate, or have similarities to, oral storytelling, this becomes a pivotal point.

Thus 'live' storytelling (which, if nothing else, militates against the static interventionism of the literary critic) is on the increase, not only 'in the flesh', but in terms of shared storying across the internet. And if that were not enough to make it a major area of literary concern, it also has (and had always had) a political axis. Jack Zipes sees the storyteller in schools as a weapon to counteract the rigid standardization of the curriculum (which attempts to standardize storytelling itself) and to rebuild a sense of community. For him, 'The process of learning how to tell a story is a process of empowerment' (Zipes, 1995: 4).

The industrial revolution and the dominance of the written word severely damaged oral culture. That dominance has also been racial; for example, Joel Chandler Harris's collections of Negro folk-tales, notably *Uncle Remus, his Songs and Sayings. The Folk-Lore of the Old Plantation* (1880, dated 1881), have been characterized as a form of cultural theft: instead of preserving an oral tradition, he was stultifying it, imposing an inappropriate static form which fossilized a living mode (quite apart from the demeaning transcription of dialect: see Moore and MacCann, 1986).

Yet oral storytelling survives, increasingly meeting the needs of an isolated and alienated society. More than that, as the future of narrative seems likely to be in a mixed-media and electronic context, ironically closely aligned to traditional oral storytelling, it may be the medium of the future.

Bibliography

Colwell, Eileen 1980: *Storytelling*. South Woodchester, Glos.: Thimble Press.

Fox, Carol 1993: *At the Very Edge of the Forest: The Influence of Literature on Storytelling for Children*. London: Cassell.

Knapp, Mary and Knapp, Herbert 1976: *One Potato, Two Potato: The Folklore of American Children*. New York: Norton.

Moore, Opal and MacCann, Donnarae 1986: 'The Uncle Remus Travesty.' *ChLAQ*, 11 (2), 96–9.

Opie, Iona 1993: *The People in the Playground*. Oxford: Oxford University Press.

Opie, Iona and Opie, Peter (eds) 1951/1973: *The Oxford Dictionary of Nursery Rhymes*. Oxford: Oxford University Press.

Opie, Iona and Opie, Peter (eds) 1959: *The Language and Lore of Schoolchildren*. Oxford: Oxford University Press.

Opie, Iona and Opie, Peter (eds) 1985: *The Singing Game*. Oxford: Oxford University Press.

Zipes, Jack 1995: *Creative Storytelling*. New York: Routledge.

Picture Books

It is sometimes claimed that the picture book is the one genuinely original contribution that children's literature has made to literature in general, all its other genres being merely imitative. If this is so, the traditional literary hierarchy might then observe, this is merely proof of the essential triviality of the form: what place is there in a respectable literary system for what is usually a thirty-two page text, often with minimal words, and intended for a scarcely literate audience? Further, what place does something essentially non-verbal have in a literary system at all?

The answers are straightforward. The first is that reading a picture book is an extremely sophisticated act. The second is that, with a minority of exceptions, the word–picture interaction is vital and fundamental.

Whatever the audience, 'simple' picture books are very often not read at 'word speed' but at picture speed; each viewing of a picture is coloured by the previous viewing; an understanding of the codes of pictures is conditioned both intertextually and extratextually: pictures teach their readers how to read them (Nodelman, 1999). Similarly, the idea that the pictures in a text for children must necessarily be simpler than those for adults is as naive and obviously untenable as suggesting that the verbal text must be simpler. As Scott McCloud has pointed out in his invaluable *Understanding Comics*, the simpler the representation of an object, the further it is abstracted from reality, and so the greater the burden of interpretation upon the reader (McCloud, 1993: 46–8).

To read picture books, then, we have to adjust our *pace* and manner of reading and to relate non-linear 'reading' of the picture to linear processing of words. Do the pictures add to the ambiguity of the words (for example, Quentin Blake's (q.v.) and Russell Hoban's (q.v.) *How Tom Beat*

Captain Najork and his Hired Sportsmen); or do they fix a specific image which has not been fixed by the words (any illustration which shows a face), thus *limiting* the imagination, or the opportunity for the imagination to interpret the words? Do they *contradict* the words (Margaret Gordon's Wilberforce series uses this device), add new dimensions to the words (Anthony Browne's *Piggybook*) or a second story (Philippe Dupasquier's *Dear Daddy*), or do they apparently have virtually nothing to do with the words (David McKee's surreal *I Hate My Teddy Bear*). Do they have symbolic relationships to the words (Maurice Sendak's *Where the Wild Things Are*), exist in ironic contrast to them (Julie Vivas's *The Nativity*) or provide closure of verbal elisions (John Burningham's *Grandpa?* or Wener Holzwarth and Wolf Erlbruch's scatological *The Story of the Little Mole Who Knew it was None of his Business*). Or, to invert the relationship, do the words provide a key to the implications of the picture (Chris van Allsberg's *The Mysteries of Harris Burdock*), or are they an indicator of significance (Janet and Allan Ahlberg's *Each Peach Pear Plum*)? How far are the words necessary at all? How far are the pictures necessary at all?

Then there is the matter of design. What is the *physical* relationship between the picture and the words? Are they interwoven (Edward Ardizonne's *Little Tim and the Brave Sea Captain*) or do they have a more formal relationship (Rudyard Kipling's *Just So Stories*)?

This is only a very small, indicative list of possibilities, for the picture book as a form has attracted large numbers of skilful, experimental author–artists and can be seen as at the cutting edge of metafictional innovation (see Moss, 1992; Lewis, 1990). It is polyphonic and necessarily highly referential. Artists have as great an intertextual resource as writers: sometimes this is exploited directly by 'quotations' from other artists (Anthony Browne's *Willie Dreams, Through the Magic Mirror*, Maurice Sendak's *Outside Over There*); elsewhere artists may relate in general terms to a school or style (John Burningham's impressionist *Mr Gumpy's Outing*): like verbal style, visual style can never be 'neutral'.

Discussing pictures clearly requires a vocabulary and great strides have been made towards this. William Moebius (1986) suggested certain codes: position, size, perspective, frame, line, capillarity, colour and so on. Jane Doonan, with a similar emphasis on aesthetics in her practically oriented *Looking at Pictures in Picture Books*, considers pictures in terms of schemes of colour, light and dark, scale and intervals, shapes, order of small- and large-scale patterning, and the network of linear rhythms (Doonan, 1993: 4–15). David Lewis, noting the tendency towards the metafictional and the postmodern in contemporary picture books, has argued that the three key features of postmodern literature, '*boundary-breaking* or "slippage", *excess*, and *indeterminacy* suggest a way of describing and evaluating picture books' (Lewis, 1990: 133). The richness of such texts and the richness of children's responses to them (which can be very illuminating to critics) can be seen in the educationally oriented work of Watson and Styles (1996) and Baddeley and Eddershaw (1994).

Illustrated texts for children can be traced back to Johann Amos Comenius's *Orbis Sensualium Pictus* in 1659; the form was exploited by the first major publisher for children, John Newbery (q.v.) in the eighteenth century, and even the cheapest chapbooks were illustrated (generally with simple wood-cuts). Improvements in technology throughout the nineteenth century were reflected in notable work by illustrators such as Richard Doyle, George Cruikshank and Arthur Hughes. Joyce Whalley sees the 1860s as the 'peak period of British book illustration for adults and children alike' (Hunt, 1996: 225–6), and the work of four major illustrators – Walter Crane, Kate Greenaway, Arthur Rackham and Randolph Caldecott – established a tradition of high-quality illustration. Caldecott's series of 'toy books' (1878–86) represent 'both a culmination in the Victorian craft of picture-book making and a model for the blending of words and pictures in books for young children' (Alderson, 1986: 8). Colour printing using tinted wood blocks or lithographic 'stones' had developed from the mid-nineteenth century and, in the hands of printers like Edmund Evans, could produce work of immense subtlety and delicacy. Rackham's work reached into a completely new era: he contributed to Walt Disney's first feature cartoon, *Snow White*.

Opinion is divided over the artistic consequences of the development of offset colour lithography, but there were some remarkable achievements up to the Second World War. Manual colour separation was a laborious business, but that did not stop the production of striking picture books such as William Nicholson's *Clever Bill* (1926), Katherine Hale's Orlando the Marmalade Cat series (from 1938), Edward Ardizonne's (q.v.) *Little Tim and the Brave Sea Captain* (1936), Diana Ross's *The Little Red Engine Gets a Name* illustrated by the Polish team of Jan Lewitt and George Him (1942), and Jean de Brunhoff's Babar series (from 1931).

The modern picture book is a phenomenon of the 1960s in the UK, largely for technical reasons; before then, it is estimated that fewer than fifty books each year would have been of any interest (Graham, 1998: 62). However, in the USA the picture book developed rather earlier, sometimes carrying political or social comment and synthesizing contemporary styles in art. A shortlist of essential texts, demonstrating the range of techniques, styles and approaches, might include Wanda Gág's *Millions of Cats* (1928), Munro Leaf and Robert Lawson's pacifist *The Story of Ferdinand* (1936), Dr Seuss's (q.v.) *And to Think That I Saw it On Mulberry Street* (1937), Virginia Lee Burton's *Mike Mulligan and his Steam Shovel* (1939), Robert McClosky's *Make Way for Ducklings* (1941) and Roger Duvoisin's *Petunia* (1950).

It is generally agreed that in the UK the landmark text is John Burningham's *ABC*, published by Oxford University Press in 1962, a stunning demonstration of what could be done with photo offset litho. And the picture book has not looked back.

It has been argued that today there is overproduction; that good as the books are technically they have become part of the general publishing treadmill: new books must be produced annually, and established illustrators consequently become drained. Nevertheless, picture books remain a remarkably rich and inventive field, especially in the context of a children's novel that is becoming increasingly bland.

It is almost invidious to provide beginners in the field with a handful of recent classics: a list such as John Burningham's *Come Away from the Water, Shirley*, David McKee's *I Hate My Teddy Bear*, Pat Hutchins's *Rosie's Walk*, David Macaulay's *Black and White*, Maurice Sendak's (q.v.) *Where the Wild Things Are* and Anthony Browne's *Gorilla*, or, more broadly, the work of David Wiesner, Chris Van Allsberg, Shirley Hughes, Charles Keeping, Michael Foreman and Quentin Blake (q.v.), might rightly be challenged a hundred times over.

As Alderson has noted, since Wildsmith's *ABC*,

> picture-book art has been used for a host of purposes, from the psychological explorations engaged in by Charles Keeping to the political commentaries of Raymond Briggs and the semi-surreal didacticism of Anthony Browne. Stylistic freedom is absolute and the difficulty of formulating any summary account of such protean activity is compounded by the speed with which editions appear and disappear and reconstruct themselves in the (often different) dress of paperbacks. (Alderson, 1994: 62–3)

Of course, the field is constantly expanding to include the comic and the graphic novel, and on into multimedia and film. Once a reader puts aside the prejudices associated with 'mixed' art forms, the picture book remains one of the richest and potentially most rewarding of literary forms.

Bibliography

Alderson, Brian 1986: *Sing a Song For Sixpence: The English Picture-Book Tradition and Randolph Caldecott*. Cambridge: Cambridge University Press in association with the British Library.

Alderson, Brian 1994: 'Some Notes on Children's Book Illustration 1915–1985.' In Alan Horne, *The Dictionary of 20th Century Book Illustrators*. Woodbridge: Antique Collectors' Club, 47–63.

Baddeley, Pam and Eddershaw, Chris 1994: *Not So Simple Picture Books*. Stoke-on-Trent: Trentham.

Doonan, Jane 1993: *Looking at Pictures in Picture Books*. South Woodchester, Glos.: Thimble Press.

Graham, Judith 1998: 'Picture Books.' In Reynolds and Tucker 1998: 60–85.

Lewis, David 1990: 'The Constructedness of Text: Picture Books and the Metafictive.' *Signal*, 62, 131–46.

McCloud, Scott 1993: *Understanding Comics: The Invisible Art*. Northampton, Mass.: Tundra.

Martin, Douglas 1989: *The Telling Line: Essays on Fifteen Contemporary Book Illustrators*. London: Julia Macrae.

Moebius, William 1986: 'Introduction to Picture Book Codes.' *Word and Image*, 2 (2), 141–51, 158. Reprinted in Hunt 1990: 131–47.

Moss, Geoff 1992: 'Metafiction, Illustration, and the Poetics of Children's Literature.' In Hunt 1992: 44–66.

Nodelman, Perry 1988: *Words About Pictures: The Narrative Art of Children's Picture Books*. Athens, Ga.: University of Georgia Press.

Nodelman, Perry 1999: 'Decoding the Images: Illustration and Picture Books.' In Hunt 1999: 69–80.

Trites, Roberta Seelinger 1994: 'Manifold Narratives: Metafiction and Ideology in Picture Books.' *CLE*, 25 (4), 225–42.

Watson, Victor and Styles, Morag (eds) 1996: *Talking Pictures: Pictorial Texts and Young Readers*. London: Hodder and Stoughton.

Whalley, Joyce Irene 1988: *A History of Children's Book Illustration*. London: John Murray.

Poetry

Anyone interested in establishing literary borders can find no more fruitful area for dispute than 'poetry for children'. The idea that this might be a contradiction in terms hangs on quite tenaciously. Poetry in its romantic conception (as opposed to narrative verse) is static, reflective (not to say solipsistic), complex, concerned with language: the child reader, as constructed in this theory, is none of these things. There is nothing new in this. The prolific and influential Anna Laetitia Barbauld (1742–1825) wrote in the preface to her (just pre-romantic) *Hymns in Prose for Children* (1781): 'It may well be doubted whether poetry *ought* to be lowered to the capacities of children . . . for the very essence of poetry is an elevation in thought and style above the common standard'. The corollary of this is that nothing written expressly for an undeveloped audience can qualify as poetry, with the further (depressing) corollary that anything written expressly for children must differ in significant ways from what is otherwise known as poetry.

Of course, all of that falls down in theory because the strategies for understanding poetry are not the province of any particular form of intelligence and are, in any case, unknowable. It also falls down in practice, in that there has been a burgeoning of what is recognizably not-prose marketed for children; this is despite the survival in publishing for children of features which have been unfashionable in adult poetry – rhyme, the ballad, the narrative – and a drift towards poetry as jokes.

Nowhere do the problems of attitude and voice surface so starkly as in poetry: what should the strategy of the adult poet be: to write to, or for, or of childhood, and which childhood? Robert Louis Stevenson (q.v.), often credited with being the first to write from the child's point of view, has also been accused of merely romanticizing his adult fantasies of childhood:

So, when my nurse comes in for me
Home I return across the sea,
And go to bed with backward looks
At my dear land of Story-books.
('The Land of Story Books')

It is clear from an examination of Ted Hughes's (q.v.) poetry 'for children' that different *standards* rather than different viewpoints or techniques were unconsciously in play. The work of a much-respected British poet, Charles Causley, can drift towards a nostalgia which is quite divorced from (almost any imaginable) reading child:

Who is that child I see wandering, wandering
Down by the side of the quivering stream . . .
When I draw near him so that I may hear him,
Why does he say that his name is my own?
('Who?')

This does not emanate from and is not empathetic with a child's viewpoint, but as A. A. Milne (q.v.) found, it was natural to write 'some *for* children, some *about* children, some by, with or from children'.

If, as seems to be clear, it is virtually impossible for a writer to articulate 'childhood' for children – the very devices of language seem to militate against it – what position can the poet take?

The editor of the excellent *New Oxford Book of Children's Verse*, Neil Philip, offers a robust defence of the form:

Some would argue that the very notion of poetry for children is a nonsense. . . . There is only poetry, good or bad. . . . Yet there is a recognizable tradition of children's verse . . . that is at once separate from and intermingled with the larger poetic tradition. . . . It is, most crucially, a tradition of immediate apprehension . . . [I]mmediate sense perceptions have an overriding importance in children's poetry, quite beyond the workings of memory and reflection, or the filters of spiritual, philosophical, or political ideas. (Philip, 1996: xxv)

Elsewhere, Philip (1999: 8) defines great poetry as 'language charged to the utmost degree', although this begs the central question of charged by whom.

The chronological history of children's poetry is largely in step with developments in prose (and the reader new to the field could do worse than trace the history through the classic collections by Opie and Opie, 1973, and Philip, 1996). Initially, children's books were concerned with religious and moral education, as in John Bunyan's *A Book for Boys and Girls: or, Country Rhimes for Children* (later *Divine Emblems*) (1686):

> This pretty Bird, oh! how she flies and sings!
> But could she do so had she not Wings?
> Her Wings, bespeak my Faith, her Songs my Peace,
> When I believe and sing, my Doubtings cease.

Isaac Watts's *Divine Songs* (q.v.) (1715) continued this approach, and the most lasting of many thousands of texts in this tradition was the work of Ann and Jane Taylor, whose *Original Poems for Infant Minds* (1804, 1805) (with Adelaide O'Keeffe) contained what was probably the most popular (and certainly one of the most sentimental) poems of the century, 'My Mother':

> Who fed me from her gentle breast,
> And hushed me in her arms to rest,
> And on my cheek sweet kisses prest?
> My Mother.

However, it is obvious that actual childhood is being completely bypassed here. More characteristic of the period was O'Keeffe's 'Never Play with Fire', in which the narrator wakes to a house on fire:

> Some burn, some choke with fire and smoke:
> But ah! what was the cause?
> My heart's dismayed – last night I played
> With Thomas, lighting straws!

The moralistic poems, which very often ended with children being drowned or burned to death, were later parodied (often quite brutally) by Heinrich Hoffman in *Struwwelpeter* (trans. 1848), Lewis Carroll (q.v.), and Hilaire Belloc with *Cautionary Tales* (1907). Parodies must hover somewhere between adults' and children's verse – motives of revenge, perhaps, being replaced by more sophisticated impulses of satire.

The Taylors' *Rhymes for the Nursery* (1806) contained one of several poems that have become part of the folklore of childhood as much as of poetry, 'The Star' ('Twinkle, twinkle, little star'). Others were Clement Clarke Moore's 'A Visit from St Nicholas' (1823) ('Twas the night before Christmas, when all through the house / Not a creature was stirring, not even a mouse'), which contributed to that curious rag-bag of traditions surrounding Christmas. (Another contribution was *Rudolph the Red Nosed Reindeer*, first written for the American department store, Montgomery Ward, by one of their copywriters, Robert L. May, for a 'give-away' booklet in 1939.) Also from the USA came Mary Howitt's 'The Spider and the Fly' (*The New Year's Gift and Juvenile Souvenir*, 1829), Sarah Josepha Hale's 'Mary's Lamb' (*Poems for Our Children*, 1830) and Eliza Lee Follen's 'Three Little Kittens' (*New Nursery Songs for all Good Children*, 1843), whose moral freight has been more or less forgotten.

But all was not piety: as early as 1806, William Roscoe published the hugely successful *The Butterfly's Ball*, although the fact that it was first published in *The Gentleman's Magazine* might suggest a certain ambiguity in the audience.

> Come take up your Hats, and away let us haste
> To the *Butterfly's* Ball, and the *Grasshopper's* Feast.
> The Trumpeter, *Gad-fly*, has summon'd the Crew,
> And the Revels are now only waiting for you.

Robert Browning's 'The Pied Piper of Hamelin' (from *Dramatic Lyrics*, 1842) had a mock-moral, while Edward Lear's *A Book of Nonsense* (1846) had no moral intent at all. Despite its reputation, *A Book of Nonsense* can be seen as a very mechanical performance, while some of Lear's later works, such as 'The Dong with the Luminous Nose' from *Laughable Lyrics* (1877), seem so obviously melancholic that one is tempted to place Lear among those authors who used writing for children as a stalking-horse for their personal problems. Lear's work, whatever its underlying sadness, has been generally seen as a liberating landmark.

The one thing that neither the evangelists nor their parodyists did (there were, naturally, exceptions) was to sentimentalize the child: that was left to Stevenson in *A Child's Garden of Verses* (1885) and his *fin-de-siècle* followers, through to A. A. Milne, Rose Fyleman, and very many indistinguishable others in the 1920s. Christina Rossetti's work is an interesting exemplar for this period. *Sing-Song* (1872) is a mixture of the grossly sentimental and the residually evangelical, and has more or less passed on its way ('A baby's cradle with no baby in it / A baby's grave where autumn leaves drop sere'); again, it is not clear what childhood is being addressed. Her *Goblin Market* (1862) on the other hand, remains with us, a sensual sexual fantasy of the most explicit kind, still haunting children's anthologies (or is this just a twenty-first century misreading?):

> She cried, 'Laura,' up the garden,
> 'Did you miss me?
> Come and kiss me.
> Never mind my bruises,
> Hug me, kiss me, suck my juices
> Squeezed from goblin fruits for you . . .
> Goblin pulp and goblin dew.
> Eat me, drink me, love me . . .'

It might well seem that children's poetry lost its way at the beginning of the twentieth century. Whereas, with Nesbit (q.v.) and Kipling (q.v.), the children's novel was becoming quite distinct from the adults', with its own characteristic voice, the relationship between adulthood and childhood as expressed in poetry was suddenly realized as complex. If Walter de la Mare, with his oblique, doom-laden eccentricities, is regarded as the major children's poet of the period, my case rests. Children's poetry became, on the whole, pedestrian and very conservative and regressive, with a few exceptions such as the Americans David McCord and Rachel Field.

Since the 1970s there have been two broad movements: the first to take serious themes into more-or-less traditional forms, such as James Simmons's 'Kill the Children':

> Some say it was the UVF
> and some the IRA
> blew up that pub on principle
> and killed the kids at play.
> They didn't mean the children,
> it only was the blast;
> we call it KILL THE CHILDREN DAY
> in bitter old Belfast.

Poems like this bring us back to those troublesome distinctions of subject-matter, viewpoint and concepts of childhood which have been a central issue.

The second movement has been towards light, funny, simple poetry deriving from the playground and the popular media, and for a time critics of a certain cast worried that this 'urchin verse', as John Rowe Townsend has called it, might drive other forms from the page: rather, it would seem that it has led a remarkable burgeoning of the form. Not only have writers like Michael Rosen (q.v.) and Roger McGough effectively tackled serious themes through this medium, but a wider audience for performance poetry has developed, particularly through the work of West Indian poets such as John Agard, Benjamin Zephania and Grace Nichols.

> Mek me tell you wha me Mudder do
> wha me mudder do
> wha me mudder do
>
> Me mudder pound plantain mek fufu
> Me mudder catch crab mek calaloo stew . . .
> (Grace Nichols, 'Wha Me Mudder Do')

As a consequence, much contemporary poetry for children, rather like children's drama, can look rather thin on the page, but it could be argued that both in the context of the new media and changes in the nature of literacy, and in multiculturalism, such a development is natural and inevitable. We may, in effect, be returning to the oral roots of poetry, which did not differentiate audiences.

Morag Styles (1998) has provided the fullest account of poetry for children, and the most detailed debate on the subject can be found in the pages of the independent British magazine *Signal*, which has given a poetry award each year since 1979.

Bibliography

Opie, Iona and Opie, Peter (eds) 1973: *The Oxford Book of Children's Verse*. Oxford: Oxford University Press.

Philip, Neil (ed.) 1996: *The New Oxford Book of Children's Verse*. Oxford: Oxford University Press.

Philip, Neil 1999: 'The Shared Moment: Thoughts on Children and Poetry.' *Signal*, 88: 3–15.

Powling, Chris and Styles, Morag (eds) 1996: *A Guide to Poetry 0–13*. Reading: *Books for Keeps* and the Reading and Language Information Centre.

Styles, Morag 1998: *From the Garden to the Street*. London: Cassell.

School Stories

The school story – generally the British public (i.e. private) school story – is one of the most addictive of the genres specific to children's literature. It is conventionally traced back to two collections of short moral tales beginning with Sarah Fielding's *The Governess* (1749), which was imitated by Charles and Mary Lamb in *Mrs Leicester's School* (1809), although the schools were, in these cases, little more than a convenient framework. The genre still survived in the biggest bestsellers at the end of the twentieth century, J. K. Rowling's (q.v.) Harry Potter books, where the boarding school ethos has been enhanced by magic.

The English private school system, with its preparatory and 'public' boarding schools, was firmly established in the nineteenth century, although it had its roots much earlier. Public schools had an influence on British life quite disproportionate to their number. The experience of public school was, as Cyril Connelly put it in 1938, 'so intense as to dominate [the pupils'] lives, and to arrest their development. From these it results that the greater part of the ruling class remains adolescent, school-minded, cowardly' (quoted in Quigly, 1984: 4). The school story, which grew up symbiotically with the real schools, may well have contributed to their survival by making immensely powerful institutions palatable to the majority.

The genre has encompassed vast numbers of stories: Charles Hamilton (aka Frank Richards and many others) (1876–1961) wrote over 5,000 stories set in over 100 fictional schools, and he was only one of hundreds of writers who provided school stories for magazines like *The Gem* (1907–39) and *The Magnet* (1908–40), notably in the first decades of the twentieth century. Although the girls' public school was a later development, writers soon caught up: Angela Brazil wrote forty-seven novels for girls in forty years to 1946; Elinor Brent-Dyer fifty-eight about the Chalet School from 1929 until her death in 1969; Enid Blyton's (q.v.) Malory Towers and St Clare's books remain among her most popular; Anthony Buckeridge's twenty-five Jennings books (1950–94) are still in print (although threatened); Anne Digby's Trebizon series (from *First Term at Trebizon*, 1978) thrives.

Although there are fewer examples in the USA, there are classics of school life such as Susan Coolidge's *What Katy Did at School* (1873) about a New England boarding school, and Edward Eggleston's story of rural Indiana, *The Hoosier Schoolboy* (1883). This book has many of the key elements of the genre, such as the new boy, the bully overcome, the small boy saved from drowning. Eggleston, like many authors, regarded schooldays with mixed feelings:

> Happy boys and girls that go to school nowadays! You have to study harder than the generations before you, it is true; you miss the jolly spelling-schools, and the good old games that were not half so scientific as baseball, lawn tennis, or lacrosse, but that had ten times more fun and frolic in them; but all this is made up to you by the fact that you escape the tyrannical old master. Whatever the faults the teachers of this day may have, they do not generally lacerate the backs of their pupils, as did some of their fore-runners.

In the twentieth century, school stories ranged from the teenage romance series, such as Francine Pascal's Sweet Valley High, which runs to well over a hundred volumes, to hard-nosed 'realism'.

The theory behind the success of the genre is simple enough. All children are familiar with the rules and rites of school life – and curious and anxious about them. School stories provide an enclosed environment where children are central; relationships and initiations can be explored within an ordered and ordering framework; options are comfortably limited. There is also, in the English tradition, the added fascination, one assumes, of class. About 7 per cent of English children attend private schools (a figure which has changed little in a hundred years), yet these are the favoured settings. This suggests that the genre drifted at a quite early stage towards fantasy.

Although Thomas Hughes's *Tom Brown's Schooldays* (1857) (q.v.) is often regarded as the true beginning of the genre, there are many precursors (see Taylor, 1997). *The Crofton Boys* by Harriet Martineau (1802–76) (published as part of *The Playfellow* in 1841) contained some of its key elements: the strangeness of school, the rituals, the bullying and the codes to be learned by the new boy, Hugh. As Hugh's friend Firth explains, boys do not talk about their feelings:

But, as sure as ever a boy is full of action – if he tops the rest at play – holds his tongue, or helps others generously – or shows a manly spirit without being proud of it, the whole school is his friend. You have done well, so far, by growing more and more sociable; but you will lose ground if you boast about your lessons out of school. To prosper at Crofton, you must put off home and make yourself a Crofton boy.

The book also has what later became a regular feature, the accident – although the amputation of Hugh's foot after he is pulled down from a wall seems a little extreme. But the fact that he won't tell who pulled him ('noble fellow') is the real point.

Despite its moralizing, *The Crofton Boys* is essentially realistic, as was *Tom Brown's Schooldays*, while the other major nineteenth-century examples, such as Frederick Farrar's *Eric, or Little By Little* (1858), at least purported to be so. However, in the case of Farrar, the temptation to use the form as the vehicle for the moral tale meant that sentimentality, overt didacticism, melodrama and even a lachrymose death swamped the child-friendly aspects (although it remains compulsively readable!). Eric's slide into dishonesty, drunkenness and his expulsion from Roslyn school, the death of his friend, and Eric's brief life at sea with its terrible beatings are highly coloured – not to say described with relish – and the narrator does not shrink from exhortation:

> Now Eric, now or never! . . . Speak out, boy! . . . Ah, Eric, Eric! how little we know the moments which decide the destinies of life!

This 'moral jellyfish left behind by the tide' as it was once described, was sufficiently famous for it to feature in Rudyard Kipling's sardonic and episodic *Stalky and Co* (1899), which lightly fictionalizes Kipling's own experience at the United Services College at Westward Ho. Stalky is sent two of Farrar's books, *Eric* and *St Winifred's, or, the World of School*, both of which are an unsellable 'drug' on the market, and his friend M'Turk glances through the book: 'oh, naughty Eric! Let's get to where he goes in for drink', and Stalky says: 'Golly, what we've missed – not going to St Winifred's!' Farrar was not amused.

The man who really popularized the genre was Talbot Baines Reed, whose school stories appeared in the *Boy's Own Paper* (his was its first story, in 1897), and his most famous book was *The Fifth Form at St Dominic's* (1887). Reed kept to the overall structures as set out by Thomas Hughes. So strong was the formula that even in 1908 when 'Frank Richards' began the Greyfriars stories in *The Magnet* (soon to be dominated by Billy Bunter), the first story, 'The Making of Harry Wharton', was of the 'flawed hero' variety.

However, as P. G. Wodehouse observed, 'the worst of school life, from the point of view of a writer is that nothing happens' (quoted in Quigly, 1984: 69), and so the formula, as it was exploited in popular magazines such as *The Magnet*, expanded to include worldwide holidays, masters who were also detectives, and so on.

Girls' school stories (as with girls' public schools) came a little later, reaching their peak in the 1930s and 1940s. The first major writer, L. T. Meade, in books like *A World of Girls* (1886), owed a lot to nineteenth-century didacticism; it was Angela Brazil who began to write about individualistic and relatively emancipated girls, and exploited other elements, rivalry, jealousy and sometimes quite passionate love (Bathurst, 1994: 87). 'Frank Richards' and later other (male) writers developed 'with extraordinary inventiveness' the Cliff House girls in *School Friend* (1919 onwards) and many others, into, as Mary Cadogan put it, 'exhilarating images of adolescent girls' (Cadogan, 1989: 15). Despite dated slang ('What a blossomy idea', 'A very jinky notion') and unfamiliar names, the often spectacular output of writers such as Elsie Oxenham, Elinor Brent-Dyer and Dorita Fairlie Bruce still survives.

Similarly, despite the demise of magazines like *The Gem* and George Orwell's famous attack on them in *Horizon* in 1940 ('sodden in the worst illusions of 1910'), the rituals of schools have kept the genre afloat. As Eva Margareta Löfgren observes of Jill Murphy's Worst Witch series (from 1974):

> you need at least a basic acquaintance with the classical school story to wholly appreciate 'Mrs Cackle's Academy for Witches' and its hideous school uniform of 'black gymslips, black stockings, black hob-nailed boots, grey shirts and black-and-grey ties'. (Löfgren, 1993: 307)

The same can of course be said of the Harry Potter books, where magic is combined with stock characters and situations in much the same way.

School remains an apparently natural and frequent setting for children's books, some of which deliberately deconstruct the genre, as in Robert Cormier's (q.v.) *The Chocolate War*, or which attack the grim reality, as in Michelle Magorian's *Back Home* (1985). Some, like Phil Redmond's Grange Hill (a television series from 1978, books from 1979) and Gene Kemp's

The Turbulent Term of Tyke Tyler (1977), transmute old formulas into quite different contemporary, state-school settings, and some, like Gillian Cross's Demon Headmaster books, use the form for comedy.

Writers like Ann Fine, Jan Mark and Bernard Ashley have also shown that the school story can speak (as perhaps it always has) to practical psychological needs – to provide blueprints for survival and types of sympathetic therapy.

The other very British genre is the pony story. There are some American examples of stories about horses, notably Will James's *Smoky the Cow Horse* (1926) and the still disconcertingly passionate *My Friend Flicka* by Mary O'Hara (1943); but it was the adult novel, Enid Bagnold's *National Velvet* (1935), soon adopted by children, that was instrumental in forming this wish-fulfilment genre. Joanna Cannan's *A Pony For Jean* (1936) set the pattern – girl who can't really afford it acquires pony and wins prizes – which was developed through the millions of books sold by Cannan's daughters, the Pullein-Thompson sisters. As with the school story, pony books inhabit a narrow, specialized world, although there have been some American examples, such as the Saddle Club series of the 1990s.

Bibliography

Bathurst, David 1994: *Six of the Best!* Chichester: Romansmead.
Cadogan, Mary 1988: *Frank Richards, the Chap Behind the Chums.* London: Viking.
Cadogan, Mary 1989: *Chin Up Chest Out Jemima!* Haslemere: Bonnington Books.
Freeman, Gillian 1976: *The Schoolgirl Ethic.* London: Allen Lane.
Haymonds, Alison 1996: 'Pony Books.' In Hunt 1996: 360–7.
Löfgren, Eva Margareta 1993: *Schoolmates of the Long-Ago.* Stockholm: Symposion Graduale.
Quigly, Isobel 1984: *The Heirs of Tom Brown: The English School Story.* Oxford: Oxford University Press.
Richards, Jeffrey 1988: *Happiest Days: The Public Schools in English Fiction.* Manchester: Manchester University Press.
Taylor, Michael 1997: 'Women Writers, Gender and Tom Brown's Schooldays.' *Children's Books History Society Newsletter*, 57, 4–13.
Turner, E. S. 1976: *Boys Will Be Boys.* Harmondsworth: Penguin Books.

War

In theoretical terms, rarely was the poststructuralist/deconstructionist ploy of looking for the blindnesses or absences of a text more justified than in the treatment or lack of treatment of war in children's books. In practical terms, rarely was there a case for more historical research.

In the nineteenth century, war was a natural part of the literature of empire. The eponymous character in Mrs Ewing's (1841–85) most famous book, *Jackanapes* (1883), dies heroically rescuing a friend on a non-specific, but characteristic battlefield of the empire. G. A. Henty's boy heroes fought current as well as historical wars. W. E. Johns's flying hero Biggles (true heir of the Henty tradition) saw service in both the First and Second World Wars. But for all that the comics and the dime novels fought, refought and refight the wars, the mainstream children's novel took several generations to recover from the First World War. It is as if the horrors were too horrific, and the sense that adults were not in control, nor shown to be admirable or responsible, to be treated with any sensitivity.

The problem of making war child-sized was faced at the time by several writers. Richmal Crompton's (q.v.) William remained thirteen throughout the war, and Crompton's comedy acquired a certain edge in dealing with air-raid shelters, Spitfire funds, supposed spies, sister Ethel's lonely week-end leaves and, hair-raisingly, an unexploded bomb. The anarchic William's remarkable positioning somewhere between adult and child audiences and between realism and fantasy allowed this to succeed. There were also several oddities, such as Katherine Tozer's *Mumfie Marches On* (1942), which ends with Mumfie, the small elephant, and his friends thwarting the invasion of England and capturing (and dispatching) Hitler:

'Shut up,' said Jelly. 'We're not the Reichstag.'

He took the yellow duster from his hat, and lifting the rat-trap, crammed the rag into the Führer's open mouth.

'Shan't be able to use that again,' he said regretfully.

The only 'serious' British books (as opposed to those that fought the propaganda battle) to survive are Mary Treadgold's *We Couldn't Leave Dinah* (1941), which gave a remarkably balanced view of the German occupation of the Channel Islands, and P. L. Travers' *I Go By Sea, I Go By Land* (1941), an evacuation story.

Only in the late 1960s was the Second World War written about (for example, Dunkirk in Jill Paton Walsh's *The Dolphin Crossing*, 1967) and at least one book, Robert Westall's *The Machine Gunners* (1975), was in the forefront of the new realism movement. Both of these books plausibly involve teenagers in notable historical (and savage) events. Nina Bawden's (masterpiece?) *Carrie's War* (1973) is a much more oblique view of war from the point of view of evacuees displaced and only partly understanding their surroundings, but aware of the adult war swirling above their heads. Alan Garner's two wartime stories in the Stone Book Quartet (q.v.) have a similar effect. In the USA there are rare examples of war-related stories: Margaret Rostkowski's *After the Dancing Days* (1986), a post-First World War story, and Ken Mochizuki's *Baseball Saved Us* (1989) about interned Japanese Americans.

Curiously, some of the most successful children's books about the war have been distressingly derivative and ersatz, notably (if not notoriously) David Rees's *The Exeter Blitz* (1978), Robert Westall's *Blitzcat* (1989) and (most successful of all) Michelle Magorian's *Goodnight Mr Tom* (1981). But these are entertainments, and there are fundamental questions here about what use should be made of such materials. What should be the place of picture books that show terrible things, like Junko Morimoto's *My Hiroshima* (1990) or Toshi Maruki's *Hiroshima No Pika* (1982) or Robert Innocenti and Chrostophe Gallaz's *Rose Blanche* (1986) (see Harrison, 1987)?

What is the distinction between books that focus on child-perceptions, such as Judith Kerr's trilogy (beginning with *When Hitler Stole Pink Rabbit*, 1971) about a Jewish family moving away from Nazism across Europe, and books which are essentially adventures which edge around graphic horrors, such as Ian Serraillier's *The Silver Sword* (1956) and Anna Holm's *[I am] David* (1963/1965)?

The difference between these books and the horrific view of the Holocaust in Gudrun Pauswang's *The Final Journey* (1992, trans. 1996), Rachel Anderson's Vietnam story *The War Orphan* (1984) and even the child's-eye-view of the war in Sarajevo, Zlata Filipovic's *Zlata's Diary* (1993, trans. 1994), suggest that there has been a change in the assumptions about what childhood can bear and understand.

Bibliography

Harrison, Barbara 1987: 'Howl Like the Wolves.' *CL*, 15, 67–90.

General Bibliography and Guide to Further Reading

These are the books most generally cited in the text, with other useful books. They do not appear in the specialist bibliographies.

Avery, Gillian and Briggs, Julia (eds) 1989: *Children and their Books*. Oxford: Clarendon Press. Essays centring on books rather than children.

Beckett, Sandra L. (ed.) 1997: *Reflections of Change: Children's Literature Since 1945*. Westport, Conn.: Greenwood Press.

Bingham, Jane M. (ed.) 1988: *Writers for Children*. New York: Scribners.

Bratton, J. S. 1981: *The Impact of Victorian Children's Fiction*. London: Croom Helm. A detailed analytical history.

Butts, Dennis (ed.) 1992: *Stories and Society: Children's Literature in its Social Context*. London: Macmillan. Essays on genres – school stories, fantasy, adventure – with detailed examples.

Cadogan, Mary and Craig, Patricia 1986: *You're a Brick, Angela! The Girls' Story 1839–1985*. London: Gollancz. Outstandingly readable survey with much to say about children's literature in general.

Carpenter, Humphrey 1985: *Secret Gardens: The Golden Age of Children's Literature*. London: Allen and Unwin. Biographical and psychological analyses of major authors.

Carpenter, Humphrey and Prichard, Mari 1984: *The Oxford Companion to Children's Literature*. Oxford: Oxford University Press. Comprehensive standard reference work.

Carter, James 1999: *Talking Books*. London: Routledge. Interviews with and views of contemporary authors of fiction and non-fiction.

Chambers, Aidan 1985: *Booktalk: Occasional Writing on Literature and Children*. London: Bodley Head. Seminal, opinionated book, focusing on the child reader.

Chambers, Nancy (ed.) 1980: *The Signal Approach to Children's Books*. Harmondsworth: Kestrel/Penguin Books. Wide-ranging essays.

Chevalier, Tracy (ed.) 1989: *Twentieth Century Children's Writers.* 3rd edn. Chicago and London: St James Press. Standard reference work, with full bibliographies.

Crouch, Marcus and Ellis, Alec 1977: *Chosen for Children.* 3rd edn. London: Library Association. The Carnegie Medal Winners, 1936–75.

Darton, F. J. Harvey 1982: *Children's Books in England.* 3rd edn, revd Brian Alderson. Cambridge: Cambridge University Press. Still the most authoritative history of children's books to *c.* 1910, if a little idiosyncratically organized.

Drotner, Kirsten 1988: *English Children and their Magazines 1751–1945.* New Haven, Conn.: Yale University Press.

Egoff, Sheila and Saltzman, Judith 1990: *The New Republic of Childhood: A Critical Guide to Canadian Children's Literature in English.* Toronto: Oxford University Press.

Egoff, Sheila, Stubbs, G. T. and Ashley, L. F. (eds) 1980: *Only Connect: Readings on Children's Literature.* 2nd edn. Toronto: Oxford University Press.

Egoff, Sheila, Stubbs, Gordon, Ashley, Ralph and Sutton, Wendy (eds) 1996: *Only Connect: Readings on Children's Literature.* 3rd edn. Toronto: Oxford University Press. A completely new selection.

Fisher, Margery 1975: *Who's Who in Children's Books.* London: Weidenfeld and Nicolson. Popular format, but incisive and comprehensive.

Fisher, Margery 1986a: *Classics for Children and Young People.* South Woodchester, Glos.: Thimble Press. Exemplary brief analyses.

Fisher, Margery 1986b: *The Bright Face of Danger.* London: Hodder and Stoughton. Highly knowledgeable exploration of the adventure story.

Foster, Shirley and Simons, Judy 1995: *What Katy Read: Feminist Re-readings of 'Classic' Stories for Girls.* London: Macmillan. From Warner's *The Wide, Wide World* to Brazil's *The Madcap of the School.*

Fox, Geoff (ed.) 1995: *Celebrating Children's Literature in Education.* London: Hodder and Stoughton. Selected essays from major literary-educational journal.

Goldthwaite, John 1996: *The Natural History of Make-Believe.* New York: Oxford University Press. Idiosyncratic, deeply conservative, highly readable survey.

Griswold, Jerry 1992: *Audacious Kids: Coming of Age in America's Classic Children's Books.* New York: Oxford University Press. Major innovative readings.

Hall, Christine and Coles, Martin 1999: *Children's Reading Choices.* London and New York: Routledge.

Harrison, Barbara and Maguire, Gregory (eds) 1987: *Innocence and Experience: Essays and Conversations on Children's Literature.* New York: Lothrop, Lee and Shepard.

Hearne, Betsy and Kaye, Marilyn (eds) 1981: *Celebrating Children's Books.* New York: Lothrop, Lee and Shepard. Essays by major authors.

Hettinga, Donna R. and Schmidt, Gary D. (eds) 1996: *Dictionary of Literary Biography*. Volume 160. Detroit: Bruccoli Clark Layman/Gale Research.

Hunt, Peter (ed.) 1990: *Children's Literature: The Development of Criticism*. London: Routledge. Key essays and linking commentary.

Hunt, Peter 1991: *Criticism, Theory and Children's Literature*. Oxford: Blackwell Publishers.

Hunt, Peter (ed.) 1992: *Literature for Children: Contemporary Criticism*. London: Routledge. Key essays and linking commentary.

Hunt, Peter 1994: *An Introduction to Children's Literature*. Oxford: Oxford University Press. Outline of theory and history.

Hunt, Peter (ed.) 1995: *Children's Literature: An Illustrated History*. Oxford: Oxford University Press.

Hunt, Peter (ed.) 1996: *International Companion Encyclopedia of Children's Literature*. London: Routledge. Over ninety long essays on most subjects on and associated with children's literature.

Hunt, Peter (ed.) 1999: *Understanding Children's Literature*. London: Routledge. Key theoretical essays from Hunt (1996).

Inglis, Fred 1981: *The Promise of Happiness: Value and Meaning in Children's Fiction*. Cambridge: Cambridge University Press. Compulsively readable liberal-humanist survey–diatribe.

Kuznets, Lois Rostow 1994: *When Toys Come Alive: Narratives of Animation, Metamorphosis, and Development*. New Haven, Conn.: Yale University Press. Scholarly pioneering work.

Le Guin, Ursula K. 1993: *Earthsea Revisioned*. Cambridge: Green Bay.

Lees, Stella and Macintyre, Pam 1993: *The Oxford Companion to Australian Children's Literature*. Melbourne: Oxford University Press.

Lesnik-Oberstein, Karín 1994: *Children's Literature: Criticism and the Fictional Child*. Oxford: Clarendon Press. Controversial dismissal of the child-as-constructed in criticism.

Lesnik-Oberstein, Karín (ed.) 1998: *Children in Culture: Approaches to Childhood*. London: Macmillan. Theorizing childhood; useful chapters on death, film, criticism.

Lewis, C. S. 1966: *Of Other Worlds: Essays and Stories*. London: Bles.

McGavran, James Holt (ed.) 1999: *Literature and the Child: Romantic Continuations, Postmodern Contestations*. Iowa City: University of Iowa Press.

McGavran, James Holt, Jr (ed.) 1991: *Romanticism and Children's Literature in Nineteenth-Century England*. Athens, Ga.: University of Georgia Press.

McGillis, Roderick 1996: *The Nimble Reader: Literary Theory and Children's Literature*. New York: Twayne. Highly readable analysis of theory.

McGillis, Roderick (ed.) 2000: *Voices of the Other: Children's Literature in the Postcolonial Context*. New York: Garland.

MacLeod, Anne 1994: *American Childhood: Essays on Children's Literature of the Nineteenth and Twentieth Centuries*. Athens, Ga.: University of Georgia Press.

Meek, Margaret, Warlow, Aidan, and Barton, Griselda 1977: *The Cool Web: The Pattern of Children's Reading*. London: Bodley Head. Seminal collection of extracts and articles.

Nikolajeva, Maria (ed.) 1995: *Aspects and Issues in the History of Children's Literature*. Westport, Conn.: Greenwood Press.

Nodelman, Perry (ed.) 1985: *Touchstones: Reflections on the Best in Children's Literature, Volume One*. West Lafayette, Ind.: Children's Literature Association. Single-book essays on classic novels.

Nodelman, Perry (ed.) 1989: *Touchstones: Reflections on the Best in Children's Literature, Volume Three: Picture Books*. West Lafayette, Ind.: Children's Literature Association.

Nodelman, Perry 1996: *The Pleasures of Children's Literature*. 2nd edn. White Plains, NY: Longman. Exemplary coursebook.

Otten, Charlotte F. and Schmidt, Gary D. (eds) 1989: *The Voice of the Narrator in Children's Literature: Insights from Writers and Critics*. New York: Greenwood Press.

Paul, Lissa 1998: *Reading Otherways*. South Woodchester, Glos.: Thimble Press. Introduction to feminist reading.

Postman, Neil 1982: *The Disappearance of Childhood*. New York: Delacorte.

Reynolds, Kimberley 1990: *Girls Only? Gender and Popular Fiction in Britain, 1880–1910*. Hemel Hempstead: Harvester Wheatsheaf.

Reynolds, Kimberley 1994: *Children's Literature in the 1890s and the 1990s*. Plymouth: Northcote House and the British Council.

Reynolds, Kimberley and Tucker, Nicholas (eds) 1998: *Children's Book Publishing in Britain Since 1945*. Aldershot: Scolar.

Richards, Jeffrey 1989: *Imperialism and Juvenile Literature*. Manchester: Manchester University Press.

Rose, Jacqueline 1984: *The Case of Peter Pan or: The Impossibility of Children's Fiction*. London: Macmillan. Controversial theory of children's literature plus scholarly analysis of the Peter Pan phenomenon.

Rustin, Margaret and Rustin, Michael 1987: *Narratives of Love and Loss: Studies in Modern Children's Fiction*. London: Verso. Psychological analysis of major texts.

Saltman, Judith 1987: *Modern Canadian Children's Books*. Toronto: Oxford University Press.

Saxby, Maurice 1969, 1971: *A History of Australian Children's Literature*. Sydney: Wentworth.

Saxby, Maurice and Winch, Gordon (eds) 1987: *Give Them Wings: The Experience of Children's Literature*. South Melbourne: Macmillan. Essays, with educational bias.

Stephens, John 1992: *Language and Ideology in Children's Fiction*. London: Longman. Seminal standard work.

Stone, Michael (ed.) 1993: *Australian Children's Literature: Finding a Voice*. Wollongong: New Literatures Research Centre.

Styles, Morag 1998: *From the Garden to the Street: Three Hundred Years of Poetry for Children*. London: Cassell. First full-length survey of children's poetry.

Styles, Morag and Drummond, Mary Jane (eds) 1993: *The Politics of Reading*. Cambridge: University of Cambridge Institute of Education and Homerton College.

Styles, Morag, Bearne, Eve and Watson, Victor (eds) 1992: *After Alice: Exploring Children's Literature*. London: Cassell. Literary essays with educational leanings.

Styles, Morag, Bearne, Eve and Watson, Victor (eds) 1994: *The Prose and the Passion: Children and their Reading*. London: Cassell.

Tatar, Maria 1992: *Off With Their Heads: Fairy Tales and the Culture of Childhood*. Princeton, NJ: Princeton University Press. Comprehensive and stimulating account.

Thwaite, Mary F. 1972: *From Primer to Pleasure in Reading*. 2nd edn. London: Library Association. History of children's books to 1914, with outline of world children's books.

Trites, Roberta Seelinger 1997: *Waking Sleeping Beauty: Feminist Voices in Children's Novels*. Iowa City: University of Iowa Press.

Tucker, Nicholas 1981: *The Child and the Book: A Psychological and Literary Exploration*. Cambridge: Cambridge University Press. Analyses books appropriate to children's developmental stages.

Vallone, Lynne 1995: *Disciplines of Virtue: Girls' Culture in the Eighteenth and Nineteenth Centuries*. New Haven, Conn.: Yale University Press.

Wall, Barbara 1991: *The Narrator's Voice: The Dilemma of Children's Fiction*. London: Macmillan. Important stylistic theory and useful general historical account.

Waterston, Elizabeth 1992: *Children's Literature in Canada*. New York: Twayne.

West, Mark I. 1988: *Trust Your Children: Voices Against Censorship in Children's Literature*. New York: Neal-Schuman.

Zipes, Jack 1997: *Happy Ever After: Fairy Tales, Children, and the Culture Industry* New York: Routledge.

Index

Page references in **bold** indicate main entries